The Bedford Guide
to the Research Process

Gathering Information from Sources Outside the Library
  Conducting personal or telephone interviews
    (pp. 99–106)
  Administering a questionnaire or a survey   (pp. 106–112)
  Examining government records   (pp. 113–116)
  Other kinds of primary research   (pp. 116–117)

Developing a Thesis and a Working Outline
  Reviewing your information   (pp. 121–122)
  Writing a thesis statement   (pp. 122–123)
  Revising your list of topics in light of your research
    (pp. 123–124)
  Developing a working outline   (pp. 124–131)

Writing Your First Draft
  Focusing on your audience   (pp. 134–137)
  Writing an introduction   (pp. 137–140)
  Writing the body of your paper   (pp. 140–141)
  Integrating sources into your text   (pp. 141–151)
  Acknowledging your sources   (pp. 151–159)
  Writing a conclusion   (pp. 159–160)
  Writing a title and an abstract   (pp. 160–162)
  Designing tables and figures for your paper   (pp. 162–171)

Revising Your Paper
  Using a computer for revision, if available   (pp. 175–176)
  Focusing on the whole paper   (pp. 176–182)
  Improving the integration of sources in paragraphs
    (pp. 182–183)
  Checking the paragraphs for unity and coherence
    (pp. 183–185)
  Strengthening sentences and eliminating unnecessary words
    (pp. 185–191)
  Correcting the grammar of your sentences   (pp. 192–195)

Preparing the Final Copy
  Editing for punctuation, spelling, and mechanics
    (pp. 198–208)
  Checking the accuracy of your documentation   (p. 208)
  Typing the final copy and the list of references
    (pp. 208–214)
  Proofreading the paper   (pp. 214–215)

The Bedford Guide
to the Research Process

Jean Johnson
University of Maryland

A BEDFORD BOOK

St. Martin's Press • New York

4 3 2 1 0
j i h g f

For information, write St. Martin's Press, Inc.,
175 Fifth Avenue, New York, NY 10010
Editorial Offices: Bedford Books of St. Martin's Press,
29 Commonwealth Avenue, Boston, MA 02116

ISBN: 0-312-07114-0

Design and typography: George McLean
Cover design: Rogalski Associates, Inc.
Cover photos (clockwise from upper left): Bill Gallery/Stock Boston; Jay Freis/The Image
Bank; © John Zoiner/Peter Arnold, Inc.; Ed Buryn/Jeroboam, Inc.; Elizabeth
Crews/Stock Boston

Acknowledgments

Stephen Barrett, M.D., from "Commercial Hair Analysis: Science or Scam?" in *JAMA: The Journal of the American Medical Association* 254:8, August 23/30, 1985, pp. 1042 and 1044. Copyright 1985, American Medical Association. Reprinted by permission of *JAMA: The Journal of the American Medical Association*.

Stephen Vincent Benet, from *Western Star* copyright page. *Western Star* by Stephen Vincent Benet. Holt, Rinehart & Winston, Inc. Copyright, 1943 by Rosemary Carr Benet. Copyright renewed © 1971 by Rachel Benet Lewis, Thomas C. Benet, and Stephanie Benet Mahin. Reprinted by permission of Brandt & Brandt Literary Agents, Inc.

Bibliographic Index: A Cumulative Bibliography of Bibliographies, 1984, from Vol. 24, entry under *School integration*. *Bibliographic Index* Copyright © 1984, 1985 by The H. W. Wilson Company. Material reproduced by permission of the publisher.

Book Review Digest, August 1985, from Vol. 81, No. 5, entry under *Drinka, George Frederick*. *Book Review Digest* Copyright © 1985 by The H. W. Wilson Company. Material reproduced by permission of the publisher.

Books in Print, 1984–1985, from *Subject Guide*, Vol. 2. Published by R. R. Bowker, Division of Reed Publishing, USA. Copyright © 1984 by Reed Publishing USA, a division of Reed Holdings, Inc. All rights reserved. Reprinted by permission of R. R. Bowker.

Truman Capote, from *Writers at Work*, George Plimpton, editor. New York: Penguin, 1981.

Choice, from M. Silverman's review of *A Software Law Primer* by Frederic William Neitzke. Reprinted by permission of the American Library Association from *Choice*, January 1985, p. 171; copyright © 1985 by the ALA.

(Continued on page 367)

Preface

The love of the search seems deeply rooted in our culture. It is reflected in the great search stories of our literature such as Sir Galahad's quest for the Holy Grail and Ahab's pursuit of Moby Dick. We celebrate the great European explorers who quested for treasure, the pioneers who went west looking for land and gold, and the modern space travelers seeking new horizons. This book helps students harness that basic enthusiasm as a motivating force while doing research. It also helps them see that research is not an esoteric activity conducted only by scholars in libraries and prescribed only in schools but a necessary and constant function of everyday life. What students already know about this process can aid them in their current research project; in turn, what they learn here can be applied to the acquisition of knowledge anywhere. Students will also be able to see that the skills they have learned in other writing classes can be used and developed further in writing the research paper.

The Bedford Guide to the Research Process will serve students in two ways: first, as a step-by-step guide to the research process for a course in which a research paper is assigned and, second, as a reference for writing papers both in college and after graduation. Researchers in any subject will find what they need in this book. At each stage in the process, examples from student writing in a wide range of subjects from engineering, biology, psychology, and geology to computer science, history, music, and literature provide scholars with a sense of how others have worked in areas related to their own. Besides illustrating each stage of the process, these examples serve as a background chorus of fellow researchers—human voices in what can at times seem like a wilderness of books, periodicals, notes, and drafts.

Chapter 1 provides an introduction to the research process and explains the three main stages of that process—searching, re-searching, and revising. Chapter 2 helps students choose a topic; after following the guidelines here, few students will say that they can't think of anything to write about. Planning the research project and designing a search strategy are discussed and illustrated in Chapter 3. In the chapters that follow, I have provided not only step-by-step guidelines for using the library card catalog and sources in the reference room but directions for developing a questionnaire, conducting an interview, recording oral history, locating data in court documents, and obtaining information from current federal files. For those who want to use graphic aids, specific instructions and examples are provided. At each stage I have given helpful suggestions for users of computers and word processors.

Chapter 7 shows students how to analyze and organize the information they have collected before they begin writing. In Chapters 8, 9, and 10, I provide a detailed guide to the process of converting information into a paper designed for a particular audience. And because inexperienced researchers often focus primarily on the first draft, I show them how to give equal care to revising their papers and preparing a final draft. Four complete student papers in the last three chapters illustrate writing and documentation styles in three major disciplinary areas: two papers in the humanities (including one in literature) using the parenthetical citation format recommended by the Modern Language Association; a paper in the social sciences using the format recommended by the American Psychological Association; and a paper in the sciences using a number system. Complete instructions and illustrations for these styles precede the papers themselves. The format for using footnotes or endnotes is also explained and illustrated for those who prefer to use them.

To help students focus on the process they are using, I encourage them to record in a search log how and where they obtained their data as well as problems they have encountered and solutions they have found. Specific advice for keeping the log is given in the text and in the exercises at the end of chapters. Students can use these accounts to compare ideas and techniques with one another and to measure their own progress. Instructors will find the logs helpful in detecting student difficulties before they become problems. The search log is presented as an option. Instructors who want to teach the research process without the use of a log can easily do so.

In Appendix 1, students will find an annotated list of reference sources for over twenty-five academic subjects. General reference works, such as encyclopedias and dictionaries, appear first, followed by a list of reference works for primary disciplines (humanities, social sciences, and sciences) and then by a list of references and professional journals arranged by subject area. This annotated list helps students locate and make choices among the many reference sources available in most libraries.

Appendix 2 lists style manuals and handbooks for over twenty-five disciplines. Students who are writing for technically knowledgeable audiences or advanced students who may wish to publish their work will find this bibliography especially useful.

Acknowledgments

This text results from the efforts of many. I want to thank especially Charles Christensen, who saw the possibilities for this book and provided the encouragement necessary to realize them, and Karen Henry for her attentive editing of the manuscript and perceptive suggestions for improvement. My thanks to others at Bedford Books: to Joan Feinberg, whose experience and advice were always helpful; to Katie Blatt, who discovered errors I could not see and brought visual order to the manuscript; and to Elizabeth Schaaf and Chris Rutigliano, who patiently and carefully turned manuscript into print.

Those who reviewed the manuscript and made helpful comments for its improvement contributed significantly to this book. Among them are Donald McQuade, University of California, Berkeley, whose perceptiveness and encouragement from the beginning were especially helpful, and Shirley Morahan, Northeast Missouri State University, who was often able to see possibilities that I could not. I also want to thank Walter Minot of Gannon University, Michael Flanigan of the University of Oklahoma, and Margaret Gooch, reference librarian at Tufts University, for their useful comments on the first draft of the manuscript. I am grateful to the following advisors for sharing their knowledge about research in other disciplines: David Bloch, University of Texas at Austin; Richard Friesner, University of Texas at Austin; Melinda Kramer, Krannert School of Management at Purdue University; Kenneth Morrison; Alan Johnson; Michael Williamson, Indiana University of Pennsylvania; and Michael Gustin, University of California at Los Angeles. My thanks to Hilary Johnson for research assistance.

The help of librarians was crucial in the preparation of this text. Betty Day, reference librarian at the University of Maryland, provided the research for the annotated bibliography. Among the many librarians who answered my numerous questions, Gail Sonneman, Marge Posner, and other reference librarians at the Fenwick Library, George Mason University, deserve special thanks.

Not the least among the many contributors to this book are my students who over the years have taught me that writing a research paper can be an adventure. I thank especially the following students who allowed their work to be included (some of them requested that pseudonyms be used or their names be omitted where their writing appears in the text): Lee Atkinson, Michael Barrett, Barbara Beard, Marit Beecroft, Jordan Brilliant, Jean M. Carroll, James R. Clark, Jr., Wendy Cohen, Carroll J. Collins, Courtenay Coogan, Pat Cornell, Thomas L. Davis, Peter DeGress, Mary Simione DeOrnellas, Deidre Dixon, Tim Donohoe, Mandana Dowlatshahi, Janelle W. Edgar, Donna L.

Ellis, Carolyn Ermantrout, Sandra Lee Eyster, Farah Farhoumand, Diana Holford, Lauren Jones, Ed Kovalcik, Stuart Levchenko, Stuart Levin, Margaret Little, Victoria P. Lumpkin, Marc H. McIntosh, Florence McMullen, Rhonda Jo Martin, Kathy Matthews, Tjinta E. May, Craig Mays, Iori Miller, Michelle Morrissey, Susan Paynter, Margaret Sharp Rizzutti, Linda Thornberry Rubenstein, Jennifer Santley, Cynthia Sebring, Vaurice Starks, Michelle Stigliano, Sandra Sweitzer, Susan E. Titus, Diane O. Wood, and David Wright.

Contents

Preface   *v*

PART I   Searching   *1*

1 **Research: Searching, Re-Searching, and Writing**   *3*

Why We Do Research   *3*

How We Do Research   *6*

Searching: Finding Answers to Your Questions   *6*

Re-Searching: The Search for Meaning   *10*

Writing the Research Paper   *10*

2 **Choosing Your Topic**   *12*

Making a List of Subjects in your Search Log   *14*

Choosing Two Possible Topics   *15*

The Controlling Idea or Thesis Statement   *16*

Dealing with Special Problems   *17*

Choosing a Topic   *20*

Exercises   *22*

3 **Planning Your Search**   *23*

Creating a Search Strategy   *23*

Making a Timetable   *24*

Composing a Preliminary Outline   *26*

Adjusting the Scope of Your Subject   *26*

Listing Possible Sources of Information in Your Search Log   *27*

The Computer as a Search Tool   *28*

Putting Your Sources in Order   *29*

Assembling Your Materials   *30*

Exercises   *31*

4 Compiling Your Working Bibliography   32

Where to Start Looking   *32*

What You Can Find in the Library   *33*

Making a List of Sources   *33*

    Recording Information on Bibliography Cards   *34*

Beginning Your Library Search   *37*

Finding Information in the Reference Area   *38*

    Encyclopedias   *39*

    General Sources of Bibliographic Information   *43*

    Trade Bibliographies and Bibliographies of Books   *44*

    Biographical Indexes   *46*

    Periodical Indexes   *46*

    Dictionaries   *52*

    Pamphlets   *54*

    Indexes to Government Documents   *55*

    Computer Databases   *56*

    Sources Obtained Through Interlibrary Loan   *58*

Finding Information in the Card Catalog   *58*

    Dewey Decimal System   *59*

    Library of Congress System   *60*

Taking Stock   *63*

    Widening or Narrowing?   *63*

    Focusing a Topic   *63*

    Keeping a Search Log: Student Examples   *65*

Exercises   *68*

5 Recording Information from Library Sources   69

Locating Books and Periodicals   *69*

Evaluating Your Sources   *70*

    Copyright Date   *71*

    Author   *72*

    Professional Journals   *72*

    Recommendations and Reviews   *73*

    Content   *75*

    Source Evaluation: Student Examples   *79*

Reading   *82*

    Scanning a Book   *82*

Scanning an Article   *83*

Close Reading   *85*

Taking Notes   *86*

Recording Your Information   *88*

Paraphrase   *88*

Summary   *90*

Quotation   *92*

Personal Comments   *94*

Avoiding Plagiarism   *96*

Exercises   *98*

6 **Gathering Information from Other Sources**   **99**

Interviewing   *99*

Personal Interviews   *100*

Telephone and Mail Interviews   *105*

Tape-Recorded Interviews   *111*

Reading Diaries, Letters, and Other Personal Papers   *112*

Examining Government Records   *113*

State and County Records   *113*

Federal Records   *113*

Observing, Exploring, and Experimenting   *116*

Exercises   *117*

PART II   Researching and Writing   *119*

7 **Re-searching and Outlining**   **121**

Reviewing Your Information   *121*

Writing a Summary Sentence or Thesis Statement   *122*

Making an Outline   *123*

The Purpose of an Outline   *124*

The Logic of an Outline   *125*

The Form of an Outline   *128*

Types of Outlines   *129*

The Arrangement of Your Cards According to Your Outline   *131*

Exercises   *131*

8 **Writing Your First Draft**   *132*

Preparing to Write   *132*

Preliminary Planning   *132*

Focusing on Your Audience   *134*

Establishing Your Own Style and Tone   *135*

Writing Your Introduction   *137*

Beginning with an Anecdote   *138*

Beginning with Background   *138*

Beginning with a Definition   *139*

Beinning with a Summary   *139*

Beginning with a Review of the Literature   *139*

Getting Started without a Plan   *140*

Writing the Body of Your Paper   *140*

Using Headings   *140*

Developing Coherence and Unity   *141*

Integrating Sources into Your Text   *141*

Keeping Your Readers in Mind   *142*

Keeping Your Readers Informed   *143*

Handling Quotations   *143*

Punctuating Quotations   *146*

Acknowledging Your Sources   *151*

When to Acknowledge Your Sources   *151*

How to Acknowledge Your Sources   *152*

Avoiding Plagiarism   *157*

Writing Your Conclusion   *159*

Writing the Title   *160*

Writing an Abstract   *161*

Designing Graphics   *162*

Tables   *164*

Graphs   *165*

Drawings and Diagrams   *169*

Exercises   *171*

9 **Revising**   *173*

Preparing to Revise   *174*

Following a Plan   *175*

First Revising Stage: Focusing on the Whole Paper   *176*

Listen to Your paper   *176*

Make an Outline   *176*

First-Stage Revising Process: Student Examples   *178*

Second Revising Stage: Focusing on Parts of the Paper   *182*

Check Paragraphs   *182*

Check Sentences and Words   *185*

Correct Faulty Connections   *192*

Maintain Consistency   *194*

Change Incorrect or Confusing Punctuation   *195*

Focus on Documentation   *196*

Exercises   *196*

10   Preparing Your Final Copy   *198*

Making Your Final Revision   *198*

Computer Programs   *198*

Spelling and Grammar   *199*

Punctuation   *199*

Capitalization   *205*

Abbreviations   *205*

Numbers   *206*

Documentation   *208*

Typing Your Final Copy   *208*

Materials   *209*

Title Page   *209*

Format   *209*

Abstract   *210*

Table of Contents   *210*

List of Illustrations   *211*

Outline   *211*

Appendixes   *211*

Content or Explanatory Notes   *212*

Footnotes or Endnotes   *213*

Glossary   *213*

List of References   *214*

Proofreading and Duplicating   *214*

Cover and Binding   *215*

Exercise   *215*

11   Writing a Paper in the Humanities: The Author/Page Style   *216*

Parts of the Manuscript   *216*

Format   *217*

    Title Page   *217*

    Margins and Spacing   *217*

    Page Numbers   *217*

    Headings   *217*

    Outline   *218*

    First Page   *218*

    Content Notes   *218*

Documentation   *218*

    Parenthetical Citation   *218*

    List of Works Cited   *223*

Documentation Using Footnotes or Endnotes   *236*

Two Sample Research Papers Using the Author/Page Style   *240*

12   Writing a Paper in the Social Sciences: The Author/Date Style   *266*

Parts of the Manuscript   *267*

Format   *267*

    Title Page   *267*

    Margins and Spacing   *267*

    Page Numbers   *268*

    Abstract   *268*

    Headings   *268*

    First Page   *269*

    Introduction   *269*

    Content Notes   *269*

Documentation   *270*

    Parenthetical Citation   *270*

    Reference List   *273*

Sample Research Paper Using the Author/Date Style   *278*

13   Writing a Paper in Science or Technology: The Number System   *295*

Parts of the Manuscript   *295*

Format   *296*

    Title Page   *296*

    Margins and Spacing   *296*

    Page Numbers   *296*

    Abstract   *297*

    Illustrations   *297*

    Headings   *297*

    First Page   *298*

    Introduction   *298*

    Footnotes   *298*

Documentation   *298*

    Textual Citation   *298*

    Reference List   *299*

Sample Research Paper Using the Number System   *301*

APPENDIXES

1   Annotated List of References   *322*

    Brief Contents   *323*

    General Sources   *324*

    Sources in Primary Disciplinary Groups   *329*

    Sources in Specific Academic Disciplines   *333*

**2   Style Manuals and Handbooks
in Various Disciplines**   *362*

Index   *369*

The Bedford Guide
to the Research Process

PART I

Searching

1. Research: Searching, Re-Searching, and Writing
2. Choosing Your Topic
3. Planning Your Search
4. Compiling Your Working Bibliography
5. Recording Information from Library Sources
6. Gathering Information from Other Sources

CHAPTER 1

Research: Searching, Re-Searching, and Writing

Why We Do Research

Writing a research paper is much like writing any other paper: you select and organize your information, analyze it, possibly evaluate it, and then record the results on paper. The main difference between writing a research paper and any other kind of paper is that in a research paper you gain your information through a deliberate, directed search for something you want to know.

If this is your first research paper, you'll find it in many ways more enjoyable to write than other papers you have written because you will be going beyond your own experience to the experiences of others for your information. You will be actively directing your own search; you will be a purposeful collector of specific kinds of information.

"Searching," "exploring," "discovering"—we associate these words with excitement and pleasure, and for good reasons. We like the idea of uncovering what has been hidden, of turning the unknown into the known—whether we are exploring our inner space, like Plato or Freud, or the space beyond us, like Christopher Columbus or Sir Edmund Hillary. Then, after we have made our discoveries, we like to tell others about them. The choice of medium can be anything from film or newspapers to novels and poems. One of the most common media—and the one you will be mastering—is the research paper.

3

With the research paper, as with all exploration, the search is as important as the telling, but when a search is compelling and absorbing for the searcher, there is an almost equally compelling urge to tell or write about it. And not simply to tell about it, but to tell it so well that the reader or listener can participate in the experience and learn as well as the writer what the search resulted in. The more interested you are in your project, the better chance you have of producing an interesting paper. There are other benefits besides this tangible result. Because you direct your own search, you will gain knowledge that is important to you, that can even change your life—as, in varying degrees, all learning does.

One student, Iori Miller, discovered in doing his research paper an area of knowledge that he wanted to continue to explore professionally. When the research paper was assigned, Miller considered plants as a possible subject for his paper. At first, he thought he would concentrate on ferns—he had always admired the different kinds of ferns in the woods near his home and thought he would like to find out more about them. While looking for information about them, he came across a book on cacti and became fascinated by them. He began reading books about cacti and then went to his botany professor for information. His professor took him on a tour of the college greenhouses and identified for him the specimens of the plants he had been reading about. His professor's help and enthusiasm led to Miller's enrolling in a botany course and, the following year, becoming a student assistant in the botany lab. Miller eventually went on to do graduate work in botany and became a botanist himself.

As Miller's search shows, a search like this has no predictable pattern and no predictable results; if they were predictable, there would be no point in undertaking the search. Henry David Thoreau (1817–1862), whom we remember as the author of *Walden*, chose a large subject for his search—he wanted to discover the meaning of life. He decided to live alone in a cabin in the woods to collect his information. Later, in *Walden*, he explained his purpose:

> I went to the woods because I wished to live deliberately. . . . I wanted to drive life into a corner, and reduce it to its lowest terms, and, if it proved to be mean, why then to get the whole and genuine meanness of it, and publish its meanness to the world; or if it were sublime, to know it by experience, and be able to give a true account of it.

Notice that Thoreau's purpose was not only to gather information for himself. He also wanted to "publish" it "to the world"; he wanted to "give a true account of it." During his two years at Walden Pond, Thoreau kept a journal in which he recorded his observations of the animals, the people, the lake, the trees, and the sky and the thoughts that these observations inspired. In his journal, he recorded in dated entries his observations and thoughts as he experienced them. These were his data, his raw material. Natural events, in other words, were the books in which Thoreau did his research on life.

> I start a sparrow from her three eggs in the grass, where she had settled for the night. The earliest corn is beginning to show its tassels now, and I scent it as I walk—its peculiar dry scent. . . . I smell the huckleberry bushes. I hear a human voice—some laborer singing after his day's toil. . . . The air is remarkably still and unobjectionable on the hilltop, and the whole world below is covered as with a gossamer of moonlight. It is just about as yellow as a blanket.

Seven years after he left Walden Pond, he published *Walden*, in which he selected parts of his journal and reordered them topically under such headlines as "Reading," "Sounds," "Visitors," and "The Pond in Winter." This type of organization allowed him to focus on the aspects of his experience that had the most meaning for him and to explain what that meaning was. The observations in his journal, when reviewed, gave new meaning to his subject—the sparrow instructed Thoreau in his subject, life.

> The first sparrow of spring! The year beginning with younger hope than ever! . . . the symbol of perpetual youth, the grass-blade, like a long green ribbon, streams from the sod into the summer. . . . So our human life but dies down to its root, and still puts forth its green blade to eternity.

Charles Darwin (1809–1882), an amateur naturalist from England, set out in 1831 on a five-year voyage around the world on HMS *Beagle*. Like Thoreau, he kept a journal recording his observations of natural life in minute detail. His *Journal of Researches into the Geology and Natural History of the Various Countries Visited by HMS Beagle, 1832–36*—was published after he returned. From the notes in his journal he developed a theory on the formation of coral reefs and a theory of evolution by natural selection. The latter revolutionary theory he explained in *On the Origin of Species*, published in 1859.

Each of these kinds of writing—the journal and the book created from it—has its own organizational form; each has its own value.

Like Thoreau's observations in *Walden* and Darwin's in his *Origin of Species*, what you discover while researching and writing this paper may be important not only to you but also to someone else. Peter DeGress, a student, did a study to find out whether solar energy would be a practical source of heat for his uncle's house. After finding out the costs of installation and computing the savings, he concluded that only solar hot-water heating would save his uncle money. He then drew plans for such a system and presented his results to his uncle as well as to the class.

The aunt of Rhonda Martin, another student, wondered whether a soldier with a name similar to hers who was mentioned in books on the Civil War was a relative. Martin decided to find out. She did much of her research in the genealogical section of the Library of Congress in Washington, D.C. (she happened to live nearby), and she also made a trip to a town in Maryland to look at court documents from the Civil War. She discovered that the soldier was indeed a relative, and she was able to find out a good deal more about where he had lived and worked than the family had known before. Martin's aunt paid her a small amount for her report.

Courtenay Coogan heard her microbiology instructor refer to a little-known organism, *Pseudomonas pseudomallei*, that was causing a hard-to-detect and usually fatal disease in Vietnam veterans. She wanted to find out what research had been conducted on this organism and to determine whether anything could be done to diagnose the disease more accurately. She was able to report to her classmates on the growing danger of this disease and the steps that can be taken to prevent it.

Joan Keller, also a student, examined different types of word processors to see which would be best for her office to buy. Because a word processing system for an office is expensive, she had to do her research carefully and thoroughly. She visited computer stores and talked to sales people to learn the prices and features of computers; she interviewed managers of companies who had purchased computer systems to find out actual time and money benefits as well as their ease of operation and repair records. Through her research she was able to help her company make a decision that would increase staff efficiency as well as save money.

How We Do Research

Searching: Finding Answers to Your Questions

The first stage in writing a paper—searching or exploring—is an activity you began very early in life, probably shortly after you were born. By the age of two you were in high gear, trying to find out everything you could about your world. "The love of the chase is an inherent delight in man—a relic of an instinctive passion," wrote Darwin as he looked back at his journey on the *Beagle*. A two-year-old is probably the pre-eminent human explorer—akin in many ways to the likes of Darwin or Thoreau. Watch a two-year-old on his or her own for fifteen minutes, and you'll get some idea of the single-mindedness, determination, and zest that distinguish the successful researcher. Because of these characteristics, the two-year-old will learn at an astonishingly rapid rate. Later, other search-and-find activities begin to interest us—games of hide-and-seek and treasure hunts. In school we continue our search for information with the help of others. As we get older, we may search for special kinds of seashells, antiques, or buried treasure. As professionals we continue to search: as archaeologists we seek evidence of past civilizations; as ornithologists we look for rare birds; as immunologists we try to find the cure for a disease; as business managers we search for ways to improve a product or service; as lawyers we examine records for pertinent cases. In fact, we often define ourselves or our interests according to the area in which we choose to search.

The search is as important to the searcher as is the written account. Without the interest in the search itself, the product will be of little value or interest either to the researcher or to others. For the true searcher, the product, like the extent of the search, is unpredictable, at least at the beginning. Thoreau's goal was not to write *Walden*; Darwin was not planning to write *On the Origin of Species*. They searched and observed and kept journals. Students, on the other hand, may know they will be writing a report, but what they don't know is the exact *content* of their report.

Choosing Your Topic.   As you begin to choose the subject you will explore, you should be asking yourself not only "What *subject* do I want to explore?" but also "What subject do *I* want to be an explorer of?" You ask these questions because your result will be not only an additional paper but also an addition to your personal store of knowledge— each helps to define you as a person.

Chances are you already have your subject in mind—that is, in your mind. You just haven't uncovered it yet or decided which to choose of the many subjects you have in mind. Take some time to listen to the questions you are asking yourself daily about the subjects you are studying or about what is going on around you. Thoreau asked himself, "What is life?" Darwin asked, "What animals and plants exist in other parts of the world?" Peter DeGress asked, "Can my uncle heat his home with solar energy?"

Finding Sources.   Two of the benefits of writing this paper will be discovering new information and, more important, new ways of finding information. As you begin, you may think first of the process often used by beginning researchers in finding information: going to the library, looking in the *Readers' Guide* and the card catalog, checking out a few books, photocopying a few articles, and then beginning to write. In doing this paper you will learn how to expand this process. No matter what size your community is, you have many sources available to you. Libraries provide books, articles, pamphlets, computer databases, microfilms, videotapes, records, and often other resources. You can probably find experts on your subject on your campus or in your town. For some types of historical research, interviews with people who have had relevant experience may be the best source. The local courthouse or statehouse has documents available to the public; museums store documents and artifacts. The dedicated researcher, in other words, looks under the stones that others merely walk around.

Collecting Information.   When you select for your search one of the many subjects you are interested in, you have your first direction—the first clue in your search. The thoroughness of your search determines the amount of information you have to work with and thus, to a large extent, the quality of your paper. Peter DeGress had to find out the cost of solar space-heating systems and solar water-heating systems. He had to analyze the structure of his uncle's house and family's needs to see how these matched up with available systems. To determine savings, he had to learn about costs of other fuels and returns on other possible investments of the money that would be spent on the heating system. Then he had to compute the effects of these expenditures and savings on his uncle's tax liabilities. Some of this information he could collect directly: as an engineering major, he could study the structure of his uncle's house and take the necessary measurements. For some information he had to rely on other people: he had to read books, pamphlets, and periodicals and make judgments about the reliability of his materials, such as how accurate a pamphlet put out by a manufacturer was or whether an article by a consumer affairs group would be more reliable. And for a technological subject like this, the information had to be up to date; a book published in 1971 was not likely to be of much value. As he collected his information, he recorded it on cards or drew diagrams.

The research paper often requires you to be more an observer of events than a participant in them. You will probably be getting most of your information from the work and experiences of others—experts who may have spent years studying, observing, and examining the same things you want to know about. You'll find this information in books or articles or through interviews. However, you may find that making your own observations or conducting your own experiments is more rewarding or appropriate. Whatever your method of research, your collecting of information will be *purposeful* and *directed*—you'll want to find out more about a specific subject or answer a specific question.

Keeping Records.   In previous papers you've written, you assimilated the information you gathered through your senses or perhaps by listening to others, then re-searched it (found what was significant in it) and wrote it down. Even if you were only recording your experience, you were ordering and selecting and therefore giving significance to some part of your experience rather than another. So the main difference between those papers and your research paper will be the gathering of your information and the documentation of your sources in your writing.

Recording Two Kinds of Information: Keeping a Search Log and Taking Notes.   Since you will probably be using more than your own experience as a source of information, you must learn new techniques for gathering and storing information. You won't be able to rely on your memory to store everything you learn; you'll have to write it down as you go along. And, because you will be learning a process as you gather data, you will be collecting two kinds of information: *what you do* and *what you find*. To keep track of both, you'll need to keep two kinds of records.

First, you'll be keeping a record of what you do—where you go, what kinds of sources you discover, whom you interview, and so on—in a *search log* (much as the captain of a ship keeps a log) so that you will know where you have been and what you still have to do. You can buy a small notebook for this or use a part of your looseleaf binder. You need to have your search log in a form that will be easy to carry with you when you do your research. Besides helping you in your current search, this log will be helpful when you do research in the future. Although logs or journals are commonly used to record various kinds of data, including personal experience, they are sometimes interesting enough to be published (as were Darwin's and parts of Thoreau's) because often the story of the search is as exciting as what is found. When scientists Francis Crick and James Watson discovered the structure of DNA, they explained *what they found* in a scientific article, "Molecular Structure of Nucleic Acids" (1953), in the journal *Nature*. In 1968 James Watson published *The Double Helix*, an account of their search written for the general public that became a best seller. So *what you do* can be as interesting as *what you find*. If you enjoy the search, you will more likely enjoy writing about what you find and thus write an interesting paper. You will probably be "publishing" only the results of your search, though you may share parts of your search log with your classmates as you go along. Keep it as you would a daily journal— record your actions, thoughts, and feelings and the problems you have encountered as well as the successes you have had. You will find suggestions for specific entries in the chapters that follow.

Second, what you find—the information you discover—will go on note cards or on separate pieces of paper so you can organize that information for easy use when you come to write your research paper. Suggestions for taking notes are given in Chapter 5.

Re-Searching: The Search for Meaning

The mere collecting and recording of information is only the first stage. *Re-searching* is looking back over that information and making sense of it, seeing how it fits together and how it links up with what you already know. The two-year-old is searching (exploring); she gathers and stores information but doesn't find the meaning in it as an adult would. In other words, *search* plus *re-search* equals *research*.

Of course, you have gone through this process many times. You re-search when you look for the scores of your favorite baseball team (the searching stage) and then analyze why they played so poorly or so well (the re-searching stage). You use the process when you plan a trip: in the searching stage you decide what route to follow, what supplies to bring, how much time to allot; and in the re-searching stage you decide whether you have the time or the money to go. Or you might decide to buy a new television. As part of your searching stage you would read the ads in the newspaper, ask a friend whether he likes his new set, and perhaps read an article in *Consumer Reports*. Then you would re-search it; you would put all this information together with what you already have observed about televisions and make your decision.

Writing the Research Paper

Exchanging Information.   Writing down the results of your findings is naturally the next step in this process. You're finding out all along—both as you research and as you write—what significance your information has for you and what conclusions you've reached, and you're putting them in a form that will make them available to others. There's a generosity about bothering to write down the results of your search, just as there is a generosity about orally sharing your information and thoughts. Personal relations are enhanced by giving information. (Peter DeGress gave his results to his uncle, Rhonda Martin gave hers to her aunt, and Joan Keller shared hers with her office staff; all of them shared their information with other members of their class.) Communities of interest (scientific, academic, agricultural, political, religious, and sports, for example) are built and maintained through this sharing of information.

Of course, you already know from writing other papers that writing a paper is not just a simple matter of sitting down one night, recording what you know, and handing it in the next day. First you need a written plan—an outline—to organize the information you have collected so that it is logical and understandable. When you sit down to write, an outline will save you time because you won't have to decide what to write next. In your first draft you need only fill in the structure of your outline with details that further shape and make meaning out of your materials. Most people need a second draft to refine the organization and to check the effectiveness of paragraphs, sentences, and words; and a final draft to check the documentation of sources and to solve problems of punctuation, grammar, spelling, and the like. Some parts may have to be rewritten more than three times. Starting early and following a carefully planned schedule will make it possible for you to write a good paper and meet your deadline.

The Importance of Abundance.   Start thinking now of providing more than you need at each stage of your research process. Abundance—even overabundance—is part of nature's back-up system, and you can benefit from it too. Start with a list of more subjects to choose from than you need for your paper. Collect more information than you think you can use. Write more drafts than you plan to. And, if you can possibly manage it, plan to spend more time than you think it may take you to complete the project.

Even when it comes to using paper, be generous. Using both sides of sheets and cards without leaving margins may save you some money, but it will cost you a lot of time. Instead, leave plenty of space so that you can add material if you want to. Smaller amounts of information on more cards or pieces of paper will also make sorting and organizing much easier.

Building overabundance into your process means that you must be willing to throw away what you don't need without feeling that you are wasting something. "Waste not, want not" doesn't apply to writing. Being prodigal may go against our cultural values, but in this case producing more than you need will save you time in the long run and make your product better because it will give you choices. In case something does not work—a subject, source, piece of information, sentence, paragraph—you will have a back-up. Space missions operate on this theory. When people are launched into space, they carry extra equipment with them. So as you begin your exploration, plan for leftovers. You'll end up with a better paper and save time as well.

C H A P T E R   2

Choosing Your Topic

Choosing a topic is often regarded as something that is done only at term-paper or essay-writing time. But we are choosing topics to explore every day. We may explore something as mundane as the taste of a new kind of cheese or as exciting as a mountain. And we're not only choosing topics, we're also rejecting many that we would like to investigate because we don't have time or they aren't important enough. Choosing to study psychology may mean choosing not to study music.

Before you can decide on a specific *topic* for your paper, you will probably want to explore one or more *subjects*, or general areas of study. These subjects interest you because of what you have read or heard or because of what has happened to you or to someone you know. Of course, the intensity of your interest will vary from one subject to another. Now is the time to look at some of those overlooked subjects. Although your choice of subject for a research paper will depend on other things besides your interest in it, interest is certainly the main criterion and the one to consider first. The intensity of your desire to know more about your subject will keep you searching even when obstacles arise— when information seems hard to find, when you are busy with other things, and when the necessary time doesn't seem to be there. The first step in writing a good research paper, then, is to recall some of the subjects that attract you and to choose the most suitable for this occasion.

"But what if I'm assigned a subject to write on," you may be saying. "Then I can't write about what *I'm* interested in." Yes, usually you can. You need to find the part of that subject that relates to something you are interested in. Let's say that in an American history course, your instructor asks you to write a paper on Custer's last stand—the Battle of the Little Big Horn. Before you say that this subject doesn't appeal to you, ask yourself questions about the event that relate to other interests of yours until you find an aspect of it that you think you might like to explore. If you are taking a course in which this subject is relevant, you probably already have some information about it. Questions like the following might occur to you: Was it Custer's fault that the battle was lost? Was he a good military strategist? What was Custer's ability to command men? What was the role of the Battle of the Little Big Horn in settling the West? What is known about Custer's personal life? What fictional treatments have there been of Custer? What films have been made about this battle or about Custer? How does this battle fit into the general policy of dealing with the Indians? After asking yourself questions like this you might come up with the following topics:

   Custer's military strategy
   The role of the Battle of the Little Big Horn in settling the West
   The effect of the battle on relations with the Indians
   The treatment of Custer in films
   The treatment of Custer in fiction

Because any subject can be treated from so many angles, the steps outlined in the following pages for helping you find a subject that intrigues you can be adapted to your own use, even if you are starting with someone else's initial selection.

   Choosing a topic is not a single onetime act, like picking a carton of milk off the shelf. Choosing a topic is more of an evolutionary process that coincides with the beginning of your search. There's a bit of Catch-22 feeling at first: you can't begin your search until you have a topic, but you can't decide on a specific topic until you've done some searching—until you find out (1) what the scope of the subject is, (2) what information is available, (3) whether you can get it in the required time, and (4) whether the time required to explore the subject adequately and write your results corresponds to the time you have. In the early stages of your search, your topic and your information direct each other: your topic tells you where to find your information (for example, in books, from people, or by observation), and your information helps to shape your topic or perhaps leads you to abandon one topic and choose another. Because it's important to reach the stage when you have a clearly defined topic as soon as possible, it is a good idea to begin your search as early as you can.

As you follow the steps given in this chapter, you'll notice that you begin not with choosing a single topic for your paper but with choosing a number of *general subjects* from which you can derive a more specific and manageable topic. Having more possibilities than you need will help you find a better topic. The steps outlined in the following pages are designed to help you find a subject that you will enjoy exploring and writing about and that will result in a paper you and others will enjoy reading. Record the results in your search log, where you will be able to refer to them as a guide as you go through the process of deciding on a topic.

Making a List of Subjects in Your Search Log

Set aside an hour or more, go to a quiet place, and let your mind range over the subjects that interest you. To aid your exploration and stimulate your thinking, ask yourself questions about familiar things such as your experiences, course work, or hobbies. Write down in your search log the subjects that come to you. (Give your entry a title and a date, such as "Subjects for research paper—September 28.") You don't have to be concerned right now about whether a subject would make a good research topic or not. If some subjects are too broad, you may reduce them to specific topics later—you'll be given suggestions for this. Just let your mind wander freely as you contemplate each one of these areas. Don't hurry this step. You are not trying to come up with a final topic; you are trying to find out what interests you and get your ideas on paper. Make a list of at least ten subjects. Here are some examples:

Experiences: What experiences of yours (or someone close to you) have raised questions in your mind that you couldn't answer?

> Thoughts: "I had a friend who was an alcoholic. I wonder why. I wonder if he could have been helped."
> Possible subjects: The causes and control of alcoholism. How friends can help an alcoholic.

School subjects: What subjects have you studied that you wish you had time to learn more about?

> Thoughts: "My psych teacher mentioned gestalt psychology. It sounded interesting, but what is it?"
> Possible subjects: The origins of gestalt psychology. The role of gestalt psychology in mental therapy.

Hobbies: What do you like to do in your spare time? Which of these would you like to find out more about?

> Thoughts: "I planted a few tomatoes last year, but I'd like to have more plants next year—a small garden, maybe. Do I have enough space? Do I have enough sunlight? What would I plant? What plants grow well together? Would I use chemical fertilizers?"
>
> Possible subjects: Planting a small garden. Chemical fertilizers versus organic gardening.

Reading and television: What television programs have you seen that made you want to learn more? What books, newspapers, or magazine articles have you read that made you want to learn more about a subject?

> Thoughts: "I saw a television program on the mind. My grandmother has Alzheimer's disease. I wonder what this means and whether there is a cure. . . . I've been watching a series of programs on China—about Buddhism and Confucianism, about the Chinese use of acupuncture, about the practice of T'ai Chi and other martial arts to keep fit. I've always wanted to know more about China."
>
> Possible subjects: Alzheimer's disease. How to keep the brain from aging. The use of acupuncture in modern China. The practice of T'ai Chi and how it keeps your body healthy.

Now that you've started your list, add to it as possible subjects occur to you. With the added awareness your search has already given you, you'll find that your list will increase.

Choosing Two Possible Topics

Reread your list carefully, putting a check mark beside the subjects that seem most interesting to you. Then reread those you have checked. Pick two that appeal to you most and make each into a sentence beginning, "I want to know more about. . . . " Then for each, complete the following exploratory sentences.

I already know that _____.
I want to find out what _____.
I want to find out where _____.
I want to find out when _____.
I want to find out who _____.

Write these sentences in your search log. Here is an example.

Subject sentence: I want to know more about flying saucers.
Exploratory sentences:

I already know
 that a lot of people say they have seen them.
 that the Air Force says they don't exist.
 that there are a lot of theories about what they are.
I want to find out
 why the Air Force thinks they don't exist.
 why there weren't any reported for a long time until recent
  sightings.
 where they have been seen.
 how they are propelled.
 who has reported seeing them.
 how reliable these people are.

After writing down your sentences, you should revise your subject sentence so that it more accurately reflects what you want to find out. Begin this time with "I want to know. . . . "

 Example: I want to know whether flying saucers exist.

At this point, try rephrasing the sentence as a question in order to focus your topic further. "I want to know whether flying saucers exist" may become, "Do flying saucers exist?" And "I want to find out why the Air Force thinks they don't exist" may become "Why does the Air Force think there are no flying saucers?" These sentences make it clear that you are looking for answers to questions and that your paper will give the answers.

 Your question, "Do flying saucers exist?" now supplies you with a topic—"The existence of flying saucers." The subheadings relating to their existence (such as "why the Air Force thinks they don't exist") will now become more important and a subheading such as "how they are propelled" will be less important, though it may still be included in your search.

The Controlling Idea or Thesis Statement

 After you have done some of your research, you might be able to compose a sentence about the existence of flying saucers, such as "Flying saucers do not exist"; "Yes, there are flying saucers"; or "The existence of flying saucers cannot be proved or disproved." Such a statement will help you further focus your search. Although now you may probably not be able to arrive at the controlling idea that directs your writing stage, you should be alert at each step to the possibility of making your topic more specific. As with other stages, you will find yourself engaged in a back-and-forth process: as you look further into your subject you will be able to define it better; as you define it better you will be able to direct your search more economically. With a controversial topic like flying saucers, you may not feel you can compose a thesis statement until you have collected most of your information. Of course, even as you are writing, you are continuing to focus your topic; focusing is something to be aware of through each stage. (For more information on composing a controlling statement, see Chapter 7.)

Dealing with Special Problems

Maybe you know so little about your subject that you have trouble completing these sentences. Or maybe your mind refuses to get itself in gear and comes up with blanks instead of overflowing with ideas. Here are three ways of solving these problems. If one doesn't work, try the others or try all three, using the same subject.

1. Look up your subject in a general reference source. You can use the *Encyclopaedia Britannica*, the *Encyclopedia Americana*, or an encyclopedia that specializes in one particular area of knowledge. (General and special encyclopedias and other reference works are discussed in Chapter 4.) One student heard "gestalt therapy" referred to in psychology class as a recent development in psychotherapy and decided she would like to look into the possibility of using this therapy as a research subject. The reference librarian directed her to the *International Encyclopedia of Psychiatry, Psychology, Psychoanalysis, and Neurology*. Under "Gestalt Therapy" she found a three-page article explaining the origins of the theory, the philosophy behind it, and its use in therapy. As she read the article, she realized that the techniques used in therapy were what interested her most. They were explained in the following paragraph.

There are several forms which a Gestalt experiment might take (Polster and Polster, 1973). One is the enactment of some important part of the patient's life. Dramatizing a memory or a dreaded encounter provides a stage for inventive action, unhampered by some of the limits, appropriate or not, that the patient might otherwise set for himself or herself during the actual event. It is also a way to explore unfamiliar aspects of the self, as in dramatizing oneself as bully or savior. Directed behavior encourages the patient to expand disregarded behavior or to try out new behaviors as, for example, speaking without qualifications, saying yes more often, and an infinite range of other therapeutically relevant behaviors. By actually performing these behaviors the individual's customary personal boundaries are extended. Fantasy, another form of the Gestalt experiment, is also a means for extending and amplifying feelings about central events in the patient's life. The fantasy is the individual's technique par excellence for representation of an otherwise unavailable world. Once this world is readmitted and assimilated in the supportive framework of the therapy session, the necessity to shun circumstances where these feelings may be provoked is diminished and the patient's confidence is enhanced for successfully traversing dangerous emotional territory. Dreamwork, one form of fantasy, received especially great attention from Perls, particularly in his demonstrations (Perls, 1969, 1973). Pervading the Gestalt view of dreams is the belief that the dreamer has cast himself or herself into each of the elements in his or her dream. These castout parts of the self must be actively reowned and assimilated as relevant ingredients in the patient's experience. Sometimes this involves communication between missing elements in the patient's own personality; some quality of himself or herself which he or she has spurned and projected and which has to be reclaimed. Sometimes the dream reveals a missing or distorted contact which has left the patient with unfinished business with another person.

After rereading this paragraph, she made a list of the techniques that might be used in a therapy session: dramatization, directed behavior, fantasy, and dreamwork. She thought that she might not have time to find out about all of these, so she chose the last one. Her topic became, "How dreams are used in gestalt therapy." As a result of reading the article, she had not only a topic, but also a framework in which to place that topic: she knew a little about the history and the philosophy of the movement, and she had a general idea about the techniques used. In addition, a bibliography at the end of the article—illustrated in Figure 2.1—gave her some sources with which to start her search.

This knowledge from her preliminary research gave her flexibility; she was able to expand or redirect her topic in response to the information that she had found. Although she decided to concentrate on dream techniques, she might have chosen any of the other techniques that looked interesting. She might also have included a brief summary of the history and philosophy of the theory at the beginning of her paper. With this map of her subject, she began her search with confidence. She had a clear sense of direction with flexibility enough to adapt to whatever other information she might find. In her search log she recorded a map of her mental journey so far (see Figure 2.2).

2. Use special categories to help you analyze your subject. We are all familiar with the physical habits we've developed—getting up at the same time, eating the same foods, and so on. We are not always so aware of our mental habits. Our minds get caught in the same daily

FIGURE 2.1   Sample Bibliography

BIBLIOGRAPHY

PERLS, F. S. *Ego, hunger and aggression.* London: George Allen and Unwin, 1947.
PERLS, F. S. *Gestalt therapy verbatim.* Lafayette, Calif.: Real People, 1969.
PERLS, F. S. *In and out of the garbage pail.* Lafayette, Calif.: Real People, 1969.
PERLS, F. *The Gestalt approach and eye witness to therapy.* Palo Alto, Calif.: Science and Behavior Books, 1973.
PERLS, F. S.; HEFFERLINE, R. F.; and GOODMAN, P. *Gestalt therapy.* New York: Julian, 1951.
POLSTER, E. and POLSTER, M. *Gestalt therapy integrated.* New York: Brunner/Mazel, 1973.

MIRIAM POLSTER
ERVING POLSTER

FIGURE 2.2   Search Log Entry

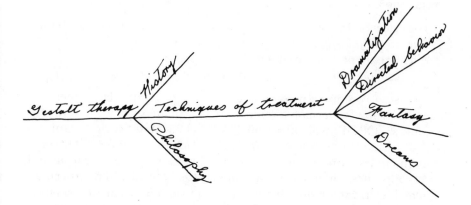

grooves. A characteristic of the good researcher is the ability to see things in a different way. The following exercise helps stimulate your thinking processes by looking at a subject from various points of view. You don't have to be a scientist to find a use in thinking about a subject from a scientific point of view. Just thinking about a subject this way may suggest something completely different to you because it will help you break down your traditional thinking habits and improve your mental agility. Try applying these exploratory categories—personal or psychological, sociological, political, historical, scientific, and any others you wish to include—to any of your subjects. The following examples illustrate how to use such categories to stimulate new ways of thinking.

Subject: Dropping the bomb on Hiroshima

Personal: Who were the people in the airplane that dropped the bomb? What was their reaction? How do they feel about it now? How do the Japanese who survived the attack feel toward the United States?

Sociological: What were the effects on the people of Japan? Did it have an impact on the social structure?

Political: What were the short- and long-term political repercussions in the United States? How did it affect relationships between the United States and Japan after the war? Was the attack justified?

Historical: What was the historical significance of this event? What effect did it have on Japanese history?

Scientific: Was there any scientific value in this act? How was the bomb developed? What medical treatment were victims of the attack given?

Trying to answer such questions on this subject might lead to the following topics.

> The effect on the people who flew in the plane of dropping the bomb
> Why the bomb should not have been dropped
> Why President Truman made the right decision
> The development of nuclear arms in the future

3. Use a computer program. Computer programs have been designed to help you develop a topic. One that many students have found helpful is TOPOI (available from RASSL/Learning Services, University of Texas), based on Aristotle's classification of topics. The program includes almost forty questions about definition, cause and effect, opposites and associations, and matters of fact and opinion—all designed to stimulate thinking about a topic and to define its scope. It asks such questions as these (xxx indicates the topic you have given to the computer):

1. What is the purpose of your paper on xxx?
2. What is the most likely place for xxx to exist?
3. What special experiences made you select this topic?
4. What could be considered a cause of xxx?

The computer's comments and responses are conversational. Here are some examples.

> Hey, that's neat, [your name]. We'll have a good time thinking about xxx.
> Good one, [your name]. Write a little more, please.
> Please ask questions. You'll be surprised by how much I know.

Even if you have never used a computer, you might enjoy using this program or one like it to help you discover useful ways of approaching your topic. Programs for this stage of the process are often classified as "prewriting" or "invention" programs and are constantly being developed as older programs become obsolete.

Remember to record the answers to your questions and the subjects you develop from them in your search log throughout the process of selecting your topic. You'll find that your mind will keep working for you almost indefinitely, and the best ideas may come late in the process.

Choosing a Topic

Choose one of your two topics as the subject in which you will do your research, using your own interest or the approval of your instructor as your guide. Keep your second subject in reserve. When you start a search, you are embarking on the unknown, or at least on what is largely unknown to you—that is the nature of the activity. You must do some planning in advance on the basis of what you know and what others have told you, but until you get there, you don't know whether your plans will work. Therefore, you need both a first-choice topic to begin your search with as well as a back-up topic.

You might want to turn to your back-up topic if any of the following problems develop.

Your topic is so new that little has been written on it. Topics aimed at exploring recent technical developments, newly discovered diseases, or new solutions to old medical problems often prove frustrating because of the lack of information available (for example, "A Substitute for the Insulin Injection" or "A New Development in Contact Lenses").

The answer to your main question can be found only in a single source, so instead of writing a research paper, you would end up paraphrasing or summarizing a book or an article. Such a problem often arises with a process topic that may be covered in a manual ("How to Set Up a Salt-Water Aquarium") or with a general historical topic that may be adequately summarized in a good encyclopedia ("Events Leading Up to the Revolutionary War"). Historical subjects that are more limited or that have produced different points of view may work better (for example, "How Pennsylvania Came to Enter the Revolution" or "The Importance of French Assistance in the Revolutionary War").

Your library does not have the information you need and cannot get it for you.

The information you need is contained in highly technical journals written in language you don't understand; translating these articles would take you too much time (for example, articles from the *IEEE Transactions of Quantum Electronics*).

It might take you more time than you have to find the information you need. You might, for example, have to write to a government agency that cannot promise you a reply in time. Or you might have to get your materials through interlibrary loan. You can avoid the latter problem by checking your library for sources as soon as possible, and if interlibrary borrowing is necessary, finding out how long it will take to get the publication you want.

Sometimes you can anticipate these problems before you choose a topic. Your instructor, who has had more experience than you, can also be helpful. But sometimes it is impossible to know what your problems are until you start your search. Kathy Matthews, in a narrative she wrote explaining her research process, tells what happened to her.

The hardest part of the research paper for me was getting the right topic. I had several criteria to meet: (1) the topic had to be approved by my history teacher; (2) it had to be large enough so that I could write a ten- to fifteen-page paper on it; and (3) it had to be interesting enough to help get me through several otherwise tedious weeks of research. After making lists of subjects I was interested in, I finally settled on "The Effects of Agent Orange on Vietnam Veterans." I figured that periodicals and government documents would be my chief sources of information.

What I didn't know until I started my search was that the campus library had very few government documents. I discovered that all of the military documents on defoliation are still classified and unavailable to civilians. A few newspaper articles had been written, but they seemed to have the same problems I did—little solid information. Fortunately I had a second choice—"The Uses and Abuses of the Artificial Heart (Jarvik 7)." This topic, though I had to get my information primarily from newspapers and periodicals, worked out successfully.

After you begin your search and complete your preliminary bibliography (see suggestions given in Chapter 4), you should be firmly committed to your topic. To turn back later than that would make it difficult for you to finish your paper on time.

EXERCISES

1. Choose one of your subject sentences and read it, along with your exploratory sentences, to a group of your classmates. Read your sentences slowly and clearly to give your listeners time to think about them. Then ask your listeners the following questions:

   Do you think there are other parts of this subject that would be interesting to explore?
   What do you know about this subject that might help me?
   Where do you think I might get more information?

   Write down the answers in your search log.

2. Read part of a recent daily newspaper or newsmagazine. (Members of your class may agree to read the same selection.) As you read, make a list of any interesting research subjects that the articles suggest to you. Choose five, read them to your classmates, and discuss their possibilities as subjects for research.

CHAPTER 3

Planning Your Search

Creating a Search Strategy

Now that you have chosen a subject, you will want to plan your search, much as you would plan a trip. You'll need an itinerary or search strategy showing where you will go, what you will do, and in what order you will undertake the search. Such a strategy will ensure that you conduct your search in the most effective and efficient way possible. Of course, your plans are always subject to change as you learn more about your subject and about the sources available. Like every explorer you may have to change directions. You may find new areas to explore; you may find that some places you had planned to go no longer interest you. Although you need a firm plan to follow, you also need to be ready to alter that plan when new information requires it. So before you begin your search complete the following tasks:

- Make a timetable.
- Compose a preliminary outline.
- List possible sources of information.
- Assemble your materials.

Record the timetable, outline, and list of information sources in your search log. Here are some suggestions to help you.

Making a Timetable

A timetable will help you allocate enough time to each part of your project, so that you meet your deadlines and end up with a good paper. As you make your estimates, take into consideration your writing habits, the amount of time you will be able to spend on the paper, and the recommendations given here (which are based on an average of about two working hours a day). Although it is difficult to make such a plan—it is especially hard to judge how much time to set aside for gathering your information—you need to set up the framework and then revise it as circumstances require.

Before beginning, divide your work into the following stages: searching, re-searching, writing, revising, and typing the final copy (each of these is discussed in a separate chapter). Estimate how long it will take you to do each part, starting with the due date and working your way back to the present. You will thus allot time first to those tasks whose required time is easiest to estimate, and leave the remaining time for searching, the most difficult to predict. Such a timetable will work best if you work a few hours each day or each week, instead of concentrating on your project for a week or two and then neglecting it for a few weeks. If you don't maintain continuity, you will have to re-think your project each time you start to work on it.

The searching stage (see Chapters 4, 5, and 6) is the most difficult to estimate at the beginning because you don't know yet what you need to find, what you will find, and where you need to go to find it. Will you be conducting interviews? You will need to arrange these. Will you be administering a questionnaire? You will have to design and administer it. Because the time required for this stage is so unpredictable, it's a good idea to start your search as soon as possible. The first step will be to compile a preliminary list of sources; then you will need to find out whether these sources are available. You should make these determinations as soon as possible—within a few days of beginning your search. If all goes well, you can proceed with your search. On the other hand, if you decide that your topic will not work, you will have time to change it. The recommended minimum time for searching (assuming you can spend six hours a week) is one month—more if you have it.

At the next stage, re-searching (see Chapter 7), you will have completed your searching and will now be organizing your material, writing a detailed and accurate outline, and developing a controlling idea. Recommended minimum time is six to eight hours, divided between two days.

The third stage is writing the first draft (see Chapter 8). Most people like to write the first draft of a ten- to fifteen-page paper at one or two sittings. If your paper is shorter or longer, adjust your time accordingly. Try to reserve two consecutive days for this work—four or five hours a day. The recommended minimum time for this process is ten hours divided between two days.

Revising, the fourth stage (see Chapters 9 and 10), is the stage in which you will have to make a judgment about your writing habits. Some people revise as they write the first draft; most people write two or three drafts before the final draft. Leave time in between your drafts for "incubation" and for doing other classwork. Two weeks is the recommended minimum time.

Typing the final copy (see Chapters 10 and 11) is the final stage. Your answers to these questions will help you estimate the time required for this step: Will you type the final copy? How good a typist are you? If you have someone type it for you, how far in advance must you give the person the final draft? If you are using your college's computer system, can you arrange for computer and printer time when you want it? Will other papers be due at the same time? When are final exams scheduled? Allow time, too, for proofreading and photocopying. The recommended minimum time is three days for a ten- to fifteen-page paper. Adjust your schedule to fit the length of your paper.

Adapt these suggestions to fit your own needs and count back from the time your paper is due to get specific dates. Mark these dates on your calendar. Here is a typical schedule for an assignment received early in the semester.

Searching: February 15 to March 22
By February 22, complete preliminary list of sources and make final decision on choice of topic.
February 23 to March 22, conduct search.
Re-searching: March 23 to April 1.
Writing: April 2 to April 15.
Revising: April 15 to April 23.
Typing: April 24 to May 1.
Proofreading, correcting, and photocopying: May 2.
Paper due: May 3.

If your paper must be completed in a shorter time, you should scale down this timetable to suit your needs. Here's a suggested shortened timetable of about a month. To finish a paper in this length of time, you may have to spend more time each day and on weekends.

Searching: April 1 to April 14
Re-searching: April 15 to April 18
Writing: April 19 to April 25
Revising: April 26 to 29
Typing final copy: April 30–May 2
Proofreading, correcting, and photocopying: May 2
Due date: May 3.

Composing a Preliminary Outline

Reread your exploratory sentences. By grouping these and rearranging them, make a brief outline to help you organize your search. If your subject is "Do flying saucers (UFOs) exist?" you might have the following exploratory sentences.

I already know
> that a lot of people say they have seen them.
> that the Air Force says they don't exist.
> that there are a lot of theories about what they are.

I want to find out
> why the Air Force thinks they don't exist.
> why there weren't any reported for a long time until recent sightings.
> where they have been seen.
> how they are propelled.
> who has reported seeing them.
> how reliable these people are.

The first step in organizing these headings is to group them. They seem to fall into two main groups: information about sightings of flying saucers and investigations by the Air Force. The headings for these two groups could be "Sightings of UFOs" and "Investigations by the Air Force." It might occur to you that there may have been other investigations, perhaps by newspaper reporters, so you abbreviate your heading: "Investigations." By arranging your subheadings under these main headings, you produce the following list. You may use either the traditional outline numbering system (indicated in brackets) or, because the list is relatively short, just indent the subheadings.

[I.] Sightings of UFOs
> [A.] Who has reported seeing them and how reliable they are
> [B.] Where and when they have been seen
> [C.] What they look like and how they seem to be propelled
> [D.] Where they come from—theories of those who have seen them

[II.] Investigations
> [A.] Air Force investigations and conclusions
> [B.] Newspaper investigations and conclusions
> [C.] Possible other investigations

Adjusting the Scope of Your Subject

Once you have divided your subject this way, you can usually limit it by dropping one or more of the headings or subheadings according to what you find as you begin your search. You might discover, for example, that certain data are limited or nonexistent, or that it takes so long to gather the information on one of your important points, you begin to run out of time. If your topic is flying saucers, for instance, you might need to write the Air Force for information about its investigations or you might want to conduct interviews—both time-consuming—so perhaps concentrating your time and energy on these sources instead of newspaper investigations would be what you decide to do. You should also add to your outline as you discover topics you weren't aware of—for example, you might discover that the sighting of UFOs is not a contemporary phenomenon and that similar stories have been told throughout history.

Listing Possible Sources of Information in Your Search Log

Make a list in your search log of all the places where you think you might find information on your subject. From what you know about your subject, you should have some general ideas about where you will find most of your information. Joe Collins, who decided to evaluate gas-saving devices for cars, knew that he was going to get most of his information from examining and testing the devices himself. In addition, he had seen at least one article on such devices and thought there might be more. Margaret Little, in researching the effects of caffeine, realized that she would not be able to do her own experiments on the subject and would have to rely on reports from original researchers. She guessed she would find her information primarily in periodicals and perhaps books.

Here are some sources that have been successfully used by student researchers. You will find items on this list that don't apply to your subject or you may know of other places where you can get the information you need. You cannot, of course, be completely sure what sources will be helpful until you try them. See Chapter 4 for details on how to use the library.

Library sources
General reference works (encyclopedias, biographical sources, indexes, dictionaries, handbooks)
Specific books on the subject
Periodicals (journals, magazines, newspapers, newsletters)
Government documents
Pamphlets and brochures
Computer databases
Films
Recordings
Videotapes
Reference librarians

See Chapter 6 for details on these sources:

Other sources
    Lectures (public or academic)
    Museums
    Television and radio programs
    Interviews
    Letters
    Questionnaires
    Personal observations, tests, or experiments

The list for a paper on UFOs might look like this:

Library sources
    Encyclopedias
    Indexes
    Periodicals, newspapers
    Specific books on the subject
    Government documents (for Air Force studies)
    Reference librarians
Other sources
    Television and radio programs

The Computer as a Search Tool.   Most topics can be researched in print or microform sources, but computer searching has advantages that will probably result in increasingly greater use of this research tool. Perhaps the greatest benefit is saving time. In a few minutes, you can search through many volumes of print sources. In addition, more and more libraries, especially small ones, are subscribing to computer services instead of to the more expensive print sources.

Some narrowly defined topics require a computer search. For example, because databases can be searched with many more terms, you might use such a search to find sources that describe the effects of tuberculosis on five-year-old girls in British Guiana. Such a narrowly defined topic would be difficult to search in printed indexes with their limited terminology and cross-references.

A final advantage of computer searching is that databases are constantly updated, whereas the information in print indexes is always somewhat delayed. A computer search provides current information on such subjects as recent political events, new scientific discoveries, or contemporary literary criticism. The printed version of the *Readers' Guide*, for example, is updated semimonthly for six months of the year and monthly for the other six months. In addition, it takes some time to get the information printed and mailed. But the information from the *Readers' Guide* on a computer database is available as soon as it's loaded into the computer.

The major disadvantage of using computers for research is the expense. A computer gives you more sources, but you pay more, too. For a short paper, the expense may not be worth it.

If you have a home computer, consider using it not only for word processing but also for searching. With your own personal computer and a modem (plus an access fee, of course), you can search databases without going to the library. If you still want to use the library to find your sources, you have the option of recording your data on your computer. Instead of putting it on cards or paper, file your information on diskettes using almost any number of keywords and phrases (the program SuperFile, for example, will allow you to file information under 250 different keywords). When your search is completed, you can use any of the keywords to locate the information you have gathered and then print it out in any order you wish. Of course, you have to be able to bring sources and computer together, and if you're working in the library, you may not be able to do this. However, you can check out most books and photocopy most articles, so consider trying this method of storing and retrieving information.

Putting Your Sources in Order

After you complete your list, decide what order you will use in exploring these sources. Devise a strategy that will take into consideration the needs of your topic, the materials available, and the requirements of the assignment. Estimate how long each step in your search will take—whether you will have to make advance appointments or request material by mail and how important to your project such information would be. Of course, you will have only a rough idea at the beginning of your search of what your sources might be. As your search progresses, you will revise your strategy to fit your experience. The reordered list for a paper on UFOs might look like this:

Encyclopedias
Government documents (These are an important source that might take some time to obtain.)
Television and radio programs (These may be of questionable importance, perhaps, and they would take time to find and view.)
Indexes
Specific books on the subject
Reference librarians (This source might be consulted earlier if you encounter difficulty.)

A researcher relying primarily on personal observation might have quite a different set of priorities. Marian Glass, writing on the image of the elderly on television, expected to gather her information for her paper from watching television programs. Written sources would be secondary. Her ordered list looked like this:

Television programs (These are an ongoing source.)

Lectures (Her psychology professor had devoted part of a lecture to the way different age groups are portrayed on TV; she would re-read her notes.)

Interviews (She would call immediately to see whether she could get an interview with the local newspaper's reviewer of TV programs. For a discussion of interviewing, see Chapter 6.)

Indexes, periodicals

Pamphlets (These might contain recent studies of television programs.)

Books (Books were the least likely to be useful because the information in them was probably outdated.)

Assembling Your Materials

As you do your research, you acquire two kinds of learning: knowledge about a subject you're interested in, and knowledge about a process—how to search for, find, record, and organize information from your observation and from outside sources. Because you won't be able to contain all of this information in your head, you'll need to keep the following records: (1) the data from your sources, written on cards or on specially prepared paper; (2) an account of the process you use, recorded in your search log.

Taking some time now to decide what materials to use and buying them if necessary will make your work easier and save you time later. Here are some items to consider.

Writing Implements.   Typewriting is much faster than handwriting and it's easier to read. But unless you can take your reading materials out of the library or bring your typewriter in, typing is not practical for you, except, perhaps, for preparing drafts. If you don't type your notes, use pen, not pencil, because pencil smudges easily and is generally more difficult to read.

Writing Materials.   You can write on note cards, in notebooks, or on notebook paper. Cards are easy to carry and easy to sort later; use 4-by-6-inch or 5-by-8-inch cards for notes (3-by-5-inch cards are useful for recording the names of your sources). Some note cards are packaged with spiral bindings and perforated edges so that they can be torn out for sorting. (How to record information on these cards is discussed and illustrated in Chapters 4 and 5.) Or you might choose to write in small notebooks, the size of note cards or a little larger. Finally, you might use ordinary 8 ½ -by-11-inch notebook paper divided into two or three sections widthwise. When you're ready to write your paper, cut the pieces apart and rearrange them.

Efficient Materials and Methods.   In choosing materials, efficiency should be one of your main goals—unless you have an unlimited amount of time to spend on your project. Note cards or pieces of paper, rather than whole sheets of paper, make it possible to write one item of information on each card and subsequently to assemble the information that belongs together in your paper before you begin to write. Most experienced researchers use note cards (though more and more are using computers) because they are easier to arrange and more durable than notebook paper. The following practices are very inefficient and will cost you extra time and money in the long run.

> Taking notes on random scraps of paper
> Writing your notes continuously in a notebook
> Photocopying as a substitute for taking notes

Use photocopying only when you don't have time to read the material in the library or when you are storing your information on a home computer.

EXERCISES

1. On the basis of entries in your search log, write a two- or three-page paper for your instructor giving the following information.

   > The topic of your research paper
   > The reasons why you chose this subject
   > What you already know about this subject
   > What aspects of this subject you plan to find out about

2. Read your paper to your classmates and ask them whether there are other aspects of your subject that interest them and that might interest you. They may also have suggestions about sources of information.

C H A P T E R   4

Compiling Your
Working Bibliography

Where to Start Looking

There is no single best place to start a search for information. You can start by interviewing someone who knows about your subject, by gathering information through observation, by distributing a questionnaire, or by going to the library to extract information from others' thoughts and experiences. Two considerations are important in deciding where to start: you want to get some general information about your subject so that you have a framework within which to operate, and you want to give priority to those types of information that take more time to obtain. Each of the following students started searching in a different place.

Bob Larkin, who wanted to study the culture of the Mayan Indians, began his search in an encyclopedia to see what was generally known about the Indians and to get some bibliographic leads. Judy Farnsworth, who planned to investigate learning disabilities in children, went first to the psychology teacher who had mentioned the subject in class and talked further with him about specific areas she might study. Besides some good advice on how to go about her project, she obtained a list of helpful books on the subject. Moira Jones wanted to examine the disposal of hazardous wastes, so she decided to visit a company engaged in that business. John Exley, whose subject was the use of steroids by college athletes and who wanted to send a questionnaire to college coaches, concluded he had better design and send his questionnaire as quickly as possible in order to have the returns back in time to include them in his paper.

What You Can Find in the Library

For many students, the library is the best place to start a search, and compiling a *working bibliography*—making a list of possible information sources—is the first step. In addition to printed information (including books, journals, newspapers, and pamphlets), your library may have films, records, and videotapes. Some libraries have paintings, photographs, and collections of private papers. Printed matter is often accessible on microforms—either microfiche (a film sheet that usually reduces the size of the material contained on it) or microfilm (35-mm film rolls). Computer services may be available to help you find printed information. To aid you in finding your way, many libraries offer tours, both guided and unguided, and most have a directory or map. Taking advantage of these services will save you time in the long run.

The information given here about libraries applies primarily to academic or other research libraries. Most public libraries will not have all of the specialized indexes, dictionaries, and professional journals that are in a small college library. However, they sometimes have books of general interest that their college counterpart would not have, so you may want to look in both types of libraries.

Making a List of Sources

Before you begin to read and take notes in the library, you should compile a list of possible sources—your working bibliography. It will change as you begin to read; you may drop some sources that are not relevant and add others that are suggested by your reading.

The information given in this chapter will provide a guide for most of the information sources in the library. The detailed discussions of each group of sources will help you decide which of them apply to your project and which you can omit.

As you locate your sources, keep three kinds of records: (1) a record of the sources you have found, (2) an account of where you went and what you did, and (3) notes on your reading for use in your paper.

Recording Information
on Bibliography Cards

Record identifying information about books, periodicals, pamphlets, and other sources that you think you can use on 3-by-5-inch cards, on specially prepared paper in your notebook, or in a file in your computer. This list will be your working bibliography. Because the list will contain only those sources in which substantive information for your paper is found, it won't include titles of indexes (the *Readers' Guide*, for example), but it will include those encyclopedias or dictionaries that provide you with enough information to use in your paper. Encyclopedias and dictionaries used only for background reading or for bibliographic leads are usually not listed in a bibliography. If you do find information in an encyclopedia that you want to use in your paper, record it on 4-by-6-inch or 5-by-8-inch note cards or in your computer. (See Chapter 5 for more suggestions on taking notes.)

Make sure you put down all of the bibliographic information about your sources that you will need later for full, scholarly documentation of your paper. You might want to decide now which of the three main documentation systems you will be using (see Chapters 11, 12, and 13 for details), so that you can record the data on your bibliography cards in the appropriate order. However, although each system orders the bibliographic data in a slightly different way and uses different styles of punctuation, all systems require the following information.

For books, copy call number, author(s), title and subtitle (if any), editor (if any), translator (if any), edition, volume (if part of a series), place of publication, publisher, and date. You will find this information on the title and copyright pages. Copy the facts down exactly as you find them. If only the author and title are given, put those on a card and fill in the other details when you look up the author in the card catalog. (See Finding Information in the Card Catalog, p. 58.)

For articles in periodicals, record author(s), title of article, name of periodical, volume number (omit for popular magazines), date or issue, and page numbers. Add a note indicating where you found this reference; if you found it in an index, give the name of this index—you might want to return to the same index for further references.

It may be tempting to list these titles on a sheet of paper at this early stage, but it's best to put every title on a separate card, even if you don't know yet whether you will use it. Then when you actually find the book, you can add extra information that might help you, such as details from the table of contents, titles of relevant chapters, or the fact that it has a bibliography. And if you decide not to use a book, you'll know why. Eventually, of course, you will arrange the cards in the order in which you record them in your list of citations at the end of your paper. If you're loading your bibliography into a computer, you need only make a list on a sheet of paper and transfer it later to the computer; the computer will alphabetize the entries for you. The main types of bibliography cards are shown in Figure 4.1; the citations in the figures are MLA (Modern Language Association) style. See Chapter 11 for details.

The second step in making a list of your sources is to record in your search log what you did; that is, the institution(s) you used, the bibliographic sources you examined, the date you examined them, and any other comments you might want to include about your search. See Figure 4.2.

FIGURE 4.1   Bibliography Cards

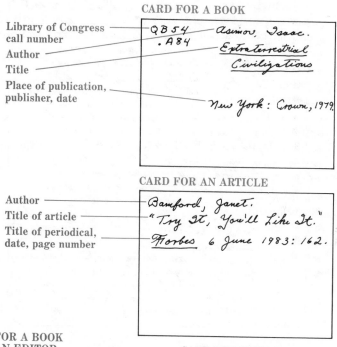

And for the final step, record any information you think you may use and photocopy articles for later reading. Although you will probably take most of your notes later as you read books, articles, and other sources, you may find some information worth recording through your exploratory reading in encyclopedias (see Figure 4.3). (For suggestions on taking notes and for further models of note card, see Chapter 5.)

FIGURE 4.2   Search Log Entry

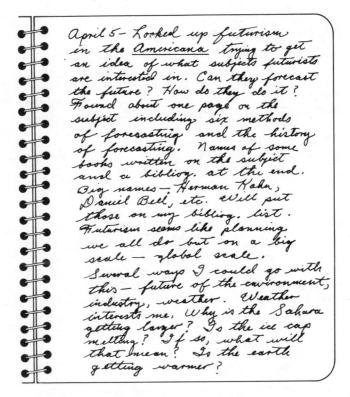

FIGURE 4.3   Brief Exploratory Entry from an Encyclopedia

Author, title of article — *Fitch, "Futurism" Americana, p. 209* — Types of forecast — Subheading from outline

Name of encyclopedia, page number

"Exploratory forecasting" — working from the present; futurists try to predict what will happen.

"Normative forecasting" — using this type futurists imagine a desirable result and try to figure out how to achieve that.

Beginning Your Library Search

Most libraries have a reference section—containing periodicals, encyclopedias, newspapers, and other reference materials that cannot be taken from the library—a section called the stacks where books that can be taken out are shelved, and a catalog area. In addition, some libraries have separate areas for storing microfilm and microfiche; the machines for viewing these materials are usually located nearby. You can begin your library search either at the card catalog or in the reference section, but you should start out in the reference area under any of these circumstances:

if you need general information on your subject, which may be found in encyclopedias, handbooks, or dictionaries.

if you need to do research primarily in current sources, such as periodicals, because indexes to periodicals are frequently kept in the reference room. Periodicals are publications that appear at regular intervals—journals, magazines, newspapers, and newsletters are all periodicals. *Journal* is the term usually used to refer to professional periodicals (*Journal of American Folklore, American Mathematical Monthly*), while a magazine is a periodical with relatively wide circulation and broad appeal (*Reader's Digest, Vogue*). The term *serials* is often used by libraries to refer to publications that appear in successive parts, often at irregular intervals, and that may be issued by organizations and research institutions.

if you need advice about how to conduct your search. Reference librarians are familiar with the kinds of sources available in the library and will tell you where they are located.

This chapter and the next will provide you with most of the information you'll need to search for library material, but you may be unable to locate something on your own or be uncertain at some point how to proceed. Consult the reference librarian in these situations.

As you gain more experience in library research, you will find yourself going back and forth between the reference section and the card catalog to find sources. Through encyclopedia articles you may find relevant book titles, which you will want to look up in the card catalog; in books you may find references to periodical articles, which in some libraries are in the reference room. In addition, you will find in the card catalog or perhaps in a separate list of serials the call numbers for indexes that identify periodical articles for you, although often the reference librarian knows where these indexes are.

To make it easier for you to use this book as a guide, however, the use of resources in the reference room is explained first, followed by a description of the information in the card catalog. Although each person's search strategy is different, a typical library search begins with encyclopedias in the reference room and may very well continue there with indexes, periodicals, pamphlets, government documents, and other sources. The sections that follow in this chapter will guide you through the reference room in this order step-by-step, but when your strategy leads you to the card catalog, look for assistance in the section entitled, Finding Information in the Card Catalog (p. 58). Titles of helpful sources on your subject, including encyclopedias, indexes, and journals, are alphabetically arranged in the annotated list of references in Appendix 1.

Finding Information in the Reference Area

If your topic demands current information, you may want to look at all of the possibilities in the reference room first. The following list starts with the most general sources, moves to more specific sources, and then to special materials. Consulting the sources in this order works best for most search projects, but you can adapt this plan to your own needs.

1. Encyclopedias: general encyclopedias, such as the *Encyclopedia Americana,* a specific encyclopedia, such as the *Encyclopedia of Philosophy,* or both
2. General sources of bibliographic information
3. Biographical indexes
4. Periodical indexes
5. Periodical file or serials list for the library you're using
6. Dictionaries
7. Pamphlets
8. Indexes to government documents
9. Computer databases
10. Sources obtained through interlibrary loan

If, for example, your topic were "The Role of the Ku Klux Klan During the Civil Rights Movement," you would first read and follow suggestions in the rest of this chapter and then check the annotated bibliography in Appendix 1 for relevant titles, making notes in your search log of possible sources. Your list of sources to consult in the reference area, corresponding to the list above, might look like this:

1. *Encyclopedia Americana*
2. *Essay and General Literature Index; New York Times Index*
3. *Social Sciences Index; Sociological Abstracts*
4. Periodical file
5. *A Dictionary of Politics*
6. *Congressional Record* (on microfilm)

Encyclopedias

General Encyclopedias.   Unless your subject is an event or discovery that occurred very recently, the best place for you to start may be a general encyclopedia, in which you might discover facets of your subject that you hadn't thought of. Such discoveries may lead you to expand or narrow your search or to change direction. An encyclopedia article also shows you how your specific topic fits within the framework of the subject as a whole. General encyclopedias attempt to give summaries of knowledge about everything—an impossible task, of course—and in order to make this knowledge easily accessible, most of them are organized alphabetically. Finally, most encyclopedia articles conclude with helpful bibliographies.

The *New Encyclopaedia Britannica* (1985, 32 vols., new printing yearly), which contains the *Micropaedia: Ready Reference* (vols. 1–12), the *Macropaedia: Knowledge in Depth* (vols. 13–29), the *Propaedia: Outline of Knowledge* (1 vol.) and an Index (2 vols.), has attempted to counteract the fragmentation that occurs with alphabetical organization of subjects. The *Propaedia* is a volume-length outline of subjects discussed in the *Micropaedia* and *Macropaedia* in which the editors try to show the interrelatedness of all knowledge. They divide all knowledge into ten areas (such as "Matter and Energy," "The Earth," and "Human Society") and explain in an introductory essay, "A Circle of Learning," their belief that knowledge is circular, not linear. A table of contents at the beginning of the volume directs you to the part of the outline in the *Propaedia* in which the subject you are interested in is located. After each section of the outline, you are referred to relevant articles in the *Micropaedia* and *Macropaedia*.

There are no articles in the *Propaedia* except for introductory essays to each of the ten sections. Browsing in this volume might help you to determine the part of a subject you would like to research and also give you valuable perspective—a framework for your research. For example, if you're interested in the theater but aren't sure what aspect of theater to study, you could look under "Part Six, Art." Under "Section 622. Theatre," you would find a detailed outline followed by a list of articles given in the *Micropaedia* and *Macropaedia*. See Figure 4.4 for an excerpt from this outline and Figure 4.5 for a list of subject headings to be found in the *Macropaedia* and *Micropaedia*. In addition, the *Propaedia* contains a directory of the full names and professional affiliations of the authors of articles in the *Micropaedia* and *Macropaedia* (in the latter volumes authors are identified only by their initials).

The *Micropaedia* contains short articles that summarize a subject and refer you to related articles in the *Macropaedia*. The *Macropaedia* contains longer signed articles on broader subjects with bibliographies at the end. You will find more on a specific subject in the *Micropaedia*, but in

FIGURE 4.4   Part of the Outline for "Theatre" in the *Propaedia*

c. Kinds defined by their system of production; *e.g.*, single-performance productions, repertory systems, stock companies, touring companies

d. Kinds defined by the controlling artist; *e.g.*, actor-dominated productions, dramatist-controlled productions, productions controlled by a nonperforming director

e. Kinds defined by their style: general aesthetic style; styles of particular countries, historical periods, and playwrights

f. Kinds defined by the lack of a unified dramatic structure
   i. Circuses and carnivals
   ii. Pageants, parades, and related forms
   iii. Popular entertainments: music hall, variety, and burlesque productions; nightclub shows; cabaret; musical comedy and revue

Section and outline reference elsewhere in the *Propaedia*
g. Kinds defined by the cultural character of their audience: primitive, folk, and popular theatre
[see 611.B.3.]

2. Methods of theatrical production

C. Elements of theatrical production

1. The production area: theatre buildings, stages, auditoriums
   a. Theatre as place: kinds and uses of theatre buildings, stages, and auditoriums
   b. The historical development of theatres in Western and non-Western cultures

2. Staging and stage design: the arrangement of words, dance, music, costumes, makeup, lighting, sound, and properties for theatrical effect

D. The history of theatre

1. Western theatre

2. Non-Western theatre
[see 613]

FIGURE 4.5   Subject Headings in the *Macropaedia* and the *Micropaedia*

Suggested reading in the *Encyclopædia Britannica*:

MACROPAEDIA: Major articles dealing with the theatre

African Arts	Oceanic Arts	Southeast Asian Arts
American Indians	Pageantry and	Theatre, The Art of the
Central Asian Arts	Spectacle	Theatre, The History of Western
East Asian Arts	Popular Arts	Theatrical Production
Folk Arts	South Asian Arts	

Subject headings arranged in alphabetical order

MICROPAEDIA: Selected entries of reference information

General subjects

dramatic conventions and techniques:	Stanislavsky method	*popular dramatic entertainment:*
agon	stock company	burlesque show
alienation effect	summer theatre	cabaret
lazzo	theatre	carnival
soliloquy	theatre-in-the-round	circus
elements of theatrical production:	theatrical production	conjuring
acting	*movements and tendencies:*	Fasching
actor-manager system	Absurd, Theatre of the	ice show
chorus	biomechanics	masque
courtyard theatre	Cruelty, Theatre of	mime and pantomime
directing	environmental theatre	minstrel show
hanamichi	Fact, Theatre of	music hall and variety
open stage	little theatre	pageant
proscenium	Living Newspaper	revue
régisseur	Open Theatre	shell game
repertory theatre	theatricalism	son et lumière
skene		vaudeville
		Wild West show

the *Macropaedia* that subject is discussed in a larger context—perhaps in several different articles. For example, if your subject were the Italian novelist and playwright Luigi Pirandello, you could look him up in the Index, where you would see references to articles in the *Micropaedia* and *Macropaedia* (see Figure 4.6).

If you looked up the first reference given to the *Micropaedia* (vol. 9), you would find a summary of Pirandello's life and professional accomplishments and a bibliography. The articles in the *Macropaedia* discuss Pirandello's work under two main headings: "contribution to Italian literature" and "establishment of Theatre of Art." "Contribution to Italian literature" consists of an article on Italian literature, including a summary of Pirandello's contribution to Italian theater.

The *Encyclopedia Americana* (30 vols. and a new printing yearly) contains an index volume, which is helpful if you haven't used the same terminology as the *Americana* has for your subject. This encyclopedia is known for its attention to North American affairs and to scientific and technical subjects; in recent editions it has expanded its coverage of international subjects as well. The editors consult with school curriculum designers and make an attempt to keep up with the current needs of American students, a goal that may account for the relatively large amount of space given to biographies. The final paragraph and the bibliography of the *Americana*'s discussion on Pirandello are illustrated in Figure 4.7.

Examples of a bibliography card and a note card derived from an encyclopedia article are shown in Figures 4.8 and 4.9. In Figure 4.8, note that the volume and page numbers aren't given; these are unnec-

FIGURE 4.6   *Encyclopaedia Britannica* Index Entry

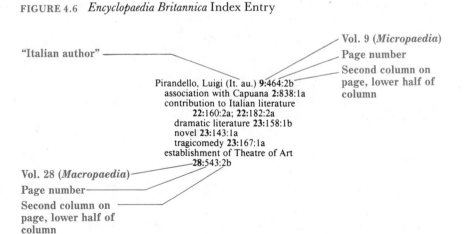

FIGURE 4.7   Last Paragraph and Bibliography from the Pirandello
Entry in the *Encyclopedia Americana*

A few of Pirandello's contemporaries failed to
understand the subtlety of his thought and technique and tended to dismiss his theater as a
clever hoax. Most serious critics, however, expressed great admiration for it and valued highly
his contribution, despite a recurrent weakness in
his dramatic structure. Commentators in Italy
engaged in controversies concerning the validity
of Pirandello's ideas, but even those who accused
him of excessive "cerebral" qualities granted him
a high place as a theatrical innovator, ". . . an artist at the center of our time."

THOMAS W. BISHOP
Author of "Pirandello and the French Theater"

Bibliography

Bishop, Thomas W., *Pirandello and the French Theater*
(N. Y. Univ. Press 1960).
Paolucci, Anne, *Pirandello's Theater: The Recovery of
the Modern Stage for Dramatic Art* (Southern Ill.
Univ. Press 1974).
Pirandello, Luigi, *Naked Masks: Five Plays*, ed. by Eric
Bentley (Dutton 1952).
Starkie, Walter, *Luigi Pirandello*, 3d ed. (Univ. of
Calif. Press 1965).
Vittorini, Domenico, *The Drama of Luigi Pirandello*,
2d ed. (Russell & Russell 1969).

essary in encyclopedias that are organized alphabetically. Significant
words in Figure 4.9 are enclosed in quotation marks.

The *New Columbia Encyclopedia* is an excellent one-volume work providing concise articles in most academic areas. It is a good choice if you
want a short summary of a subject along with a brief bibliography. The
entry on Pirandello gives a brief account of his life, names his main
novels and plays, and lists four authors who have written about him.

FIGURE 4.8   Bibliography Card for an Encyclopedia Article

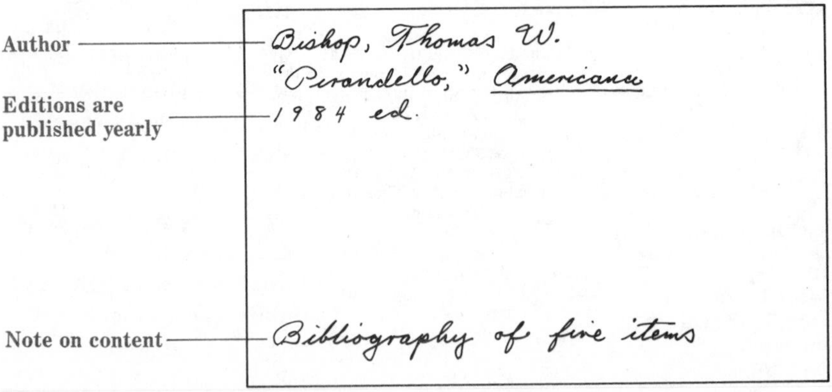

Author ——————————— *Bishop, Thomas W.*
                      "Pirandello," Americana

Editions are   —— *1984 ed.*
published yearly

Note on content——————— *Bibliography of five items*

FIGURE 4.9 Note card for an Encyclopedia Article

Summary of
Pirandello's work

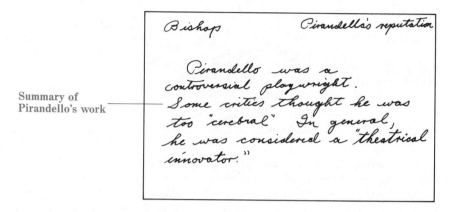

Bishop   *Pirandello's reputation*

Pirandello was a controversial playwright. Some critics thought he was too "cerebral." In general, he was considered a "theatrical innovator."

You may want to consult more than one of these encyclopedias, depending on your purpose: the *New Encyclopaedia Britannica*, for establishing the interrelationships of your subject with other areas of knowledge; the *Americana* for science and technology, American studies, and biographies; and the *New Columbia Encyclopedia* for a brief introduction to your subject.

Specialized Encyclopedias. An encyclopedia dealing only with your subject, such as the *Encyclopedia of Educational Research* or the *Encyclopedia of Anthropology,* may give you specific information unavailable in other, more general encyclopedias. For instance, if you want to know about the religion of the Hittites, who lived about 1,000 B.C., consult the *Encyclopedia of Religion and Ethics*, which contains an extensive discussion along with a bibliography. Other specialized encyclopedias and reference books are listed in Appendix 1.

General Sources of Bibliographic Information

You may be looking for a bibliography on your subject to give you a start in your research; if you are, look in an index of bibliographies—a bibliography of bibliographies. Here are some of the most commonly used general bibliographic guides (again, for indexes and bibliographies on specific subjects refer to Appendix 1 of this book).

Bibliographic Index: A Cumulative Bibliography of Bibliographies is published quarterly with a yearly cumulative index. It cites not only periodical articles that contain bibliographies but also books with substantial bibliographic information and separately published bibliographies. By looking up either a subject or an author, you will find sources that contain bibliographies. Figure 4.10 shows a sample entry under the

FIGURE 4.10   Entry from the *Bibliographic Index*

Main heading — SCHOOL integration — Title of article
— Gerard, H. B. School desegregation; the social science role.
Subheading — Am Psychol 38;876-7 Ag '83 — Date of issue
Hawley, W. D. Effective educational strategies for desegre-
Author — gated schools. Peabody J Educ 59:228-33 Jl '82
Johnson, S. W. and others. Interdependence and interper-
Title of periodical — sonal attraction among heterogeneous and homogeneous
and volume number — individuals; a theoretical formulation and a meta-analysis
of the research. R Educ Res 53:38-54 Spr '83
Page numbers — Patchen, Martin. Black-white contact in schools; its social
and academic effects. Purdue univ. press '82 p377-83
School principal and school desegregation; ed. by George W.
Noblit and Bill Johnston. Thomas, C.C. '82 incl bibliog
— United States
Bibliography. See issues of Integrated education
Subdivision by — Patchen, Martin. Black-white contact in schools; its social
country — and academic effects. Purdue univ. press '82 p377-83

major heading "School" and subheading "integration" and tells you
where you can obtain a list of sources on that subject.

Published in London, the *Guide to Reference Material*, by A. J. Walford
(4th ed., 2 vols.), is a source for international bibliographies with a
British emphasis. Bibliographies for science and technology are listed
in Volume 1 (1980), and those for social and historical sciences, philosophy, and religion in Volume 2 (1982). As the example in Figure 4.11
shows, Walford's annotations are thorough. A third volume on language and the arts is scheduled for publication. Walford's *Concise Guide
to Reference Material* (1981, 1 vol.) covers all subjects.

Trade Bibliographies and Bibliographies of Books

Books in Print is a multivolume index of currently available books. If
an important source book on your topic is not on the library shelf or
has been ordered but not yet cataloged, *Books in Print* will supply you
with complete bibliographic information, including publisher's name
and address. Books are classified by subject, title, and author. The
subject listing for the writer William Faulkner includes numerous titles
of books about him plus bibliographies, dictionaries, and indexes, as
Figure 4.12 shows. *Books in Print* covers publications in the United
States and Canada. Other bibliographical guides are the *Cumulative*

FIGURE 4.11   Entry from the *Guide to Reference Material*

MARTELLO, W.E., and BUTLER, J.E. The history of sub-
Saharan Africa: a select bibliography of books and
reviews, 1945-1975. Boston, Mass., G.K. Hall, 1978. xiv,
158p. $22.

A bibliography, under authors, A-Z, of books, plus
reviews. The reviews were compiled from 18 journals
(including *Africa, Journal of African history* and *Journal of
modern African studies*), 1945-75. Title/author and
reviewer indexes.

Items can be located
by looking up title,
author, or reviewer

FIGURE 4.12   Entry from *Books in Print*

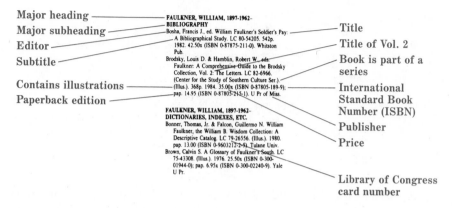

Major heading
Major subheading
Editor
Subtitle
Contains illustrations
Paperback edition

FAULKNER, WILLIAM, 1897-1962-
BIBLIOGRAPHY
Bosha, Francis J., ed. William Faulkner's Soldier's Pay:
A Bibliographical Study. LC 80-54205. 542p.
1982. 42.50x (ISBN 0-87875-211-0). Whitston
Pub.
Brodsky, Louis D. & Hamblin, Robert W., eds.
Faulkner: A Comprehensive Guide to the Brodsky
Collection, Vol. 2: The Letters. LC 82-6966.
(Center for the Study of Southern Culture Ser.).
(Illus.). 368p. 1984. 35.00x (ISBN 0-87805-189-9);
pap. 14.95 (ISBN 0-87805-215-1). U Pr of Miss.

FAULKNER, WILLIAM, 1897-1962-
DICTIONARIES, INDEXES, ETC.
Bonner, Thomas, Jr. & Falcon, Guillermo N. William
Faulkner, the William B. Wisdom Collection: A
Descriptive Catalog. LC 79-26556. (Illus.). 1980.
pap. 13.00 (ISBN 0-9603217-2-5). Tulane Univ.
Brown, Calvin S. A Glossary of Faulkner's South. LC
75-43308. (Illus.). 1976. 25.50x (ISBN 0-300-
01944-0); pap. 6.95x (ISBN 0-300-02240-9). Yale
U Pr.

Title
Title of Vol. 2
Book is part of a series
International Standard Book Number (ISBN)
Publisher
Price
Library of Congress card number

Book Index and the *National Union Catalog* for the United States and other national bibliographies such as *British Books in Print*.

Ulrich's International Periodicals Directory, published annually, provides a subject guide to periodicals likely to have articles on your subject and addresses for ordering if your library doesn't have the particular periodical. Under "Drug Abuse and Alcoholism" are several pages of periodicals from all over the world; Figure 4.13 gives two titles.

FIGURE 4.13   Entry from *Ulrich's*

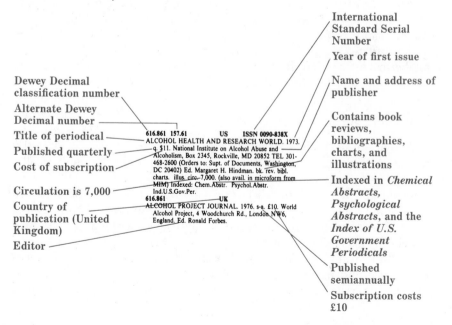

International Standard Serial Number
Year of first issue
Name and address of publisher
Contains book reviews, bibliographies, charts, and illustrations
Indexed in *Chemical Abstracts, Psychological Abstracts*, and the *Index of U.S. Government Periodicals*
Published semiannually
Subscription costs £10

Dewey Decimal classification number
Alternate Dewey Decimal number
Title of periodical
Published quarterly
Cost of subscription
Circulation is 7,000
Country of publication (United Kingdom)
Editor

616.861 157.61   US   ISSN 0090-838X
ALCOHOL HEALTH AND RESEARCH WORLD. 1973.
q. $11. National Institute on Alcohol Abuse and
Alcoholism, Box 2345, Rockville, MD 20852 TEL 301-
468-2600 (Orders to: Supt. of Documents, Washington,
DC 20402) Ed. Margaret H. Hindman. bk. rev. bibl.
charts. illus. circ. 7,000. (also avail. in microform from
MIM) Indexed: Chem.Abstr. Psychol.Abstr.
Ind.U.S.Gov.Per.
616.861   UK
ALCOHOL PROJECT JOURNAL. 1976. s-a. £10. World
Alcohol Project, 4 Woodchurch Rd., London NW6,
England. Ed. Ronald Forbes.

FIGURE 4.14   Entry from the *Essay and General Literature Index*

Author/subject heading

Author

Thoreau's *Journal*

Author of chapter about Thoreau's *Journal*

Thoreau, Henry David
About
Allen, G. W. How Emerson, Thoreau, and Whitman viewed the "frontier." *In* Toward a new American literary history, ed. by L. J. Budd, E. H. Cady and C. L. Anderson p111-28
About individual works
Journal
Howarth, W. L. Travelling in Concord: the world of Thoreau's Journal. *In* Puritan influences in American literature, ed. by E. Elliott p143-66
Bibliography
Glick, W. Emerson, Thoreau, and transcendentalism. *In* American literary scholarship, 1978 p3-16

Chapter in a book

Title of the book

Chapter containing bibliographic information

Title of the book

Paperbound Books in Print, also organized by author, title, and subject, itemizes books available in paperback editions or in both paper bound and hardcover copies. The *Essay and General Literature Index* (from 1900, issued three times a year with a yearly cumulative volume) contains citations to essays and parts of books in the humanities that are generally not listed in other indexes. Material is indexed by author, subject, and sometimes title. Figure 4.14 gives an example.

Biographical Indexes

The *Biography Index* is a good source if you want to know more about the history of the person you are studying. It will refer you to material in American periodicals and books about famous people from all over the world—from basketball players ("Abdul-Jabbar, Kareem") to authors ("Zola, Émile"). An additional index of names by profession and occupation is given in the back, referring you to entries in the alphabetical listings. For further sources of biographical information, see the annotated list in Appendix 1.

Periodical Indexes

Articles in periodicals are indexed in print, microform, or on a database, with the subjects, titles, and authors organized alphabetically. To decide whether you want to look in a magazine or a journal for your information, consider the differences between the two. Journals are usually published by nonprofit professional organizations or academic institutions; before being accepted, an article is usually approved by a panel of experts. The professional status or brief biography of the author that is usually given is a further clue to a journal article's authoritativeness, and the articles are fully and professionally documented. On the other hand, magazine articles are designed to help sell that magazine; their quality and reliability vary, from those in the respected *New Yorker* and *Harper's* to the merely entertaining, as in *Vogue* or *Life*. However, they are much easier to understand because they're not written for the expert. In addition, they may contain more up-to-date information than articles in journals, which, because of their high professional quality and the time limitations of noncommercial publishing, are often slower to produce.

Before consulting a periodical index, check the explanatory material in the front of the book to learn the abbreviations for citing the information you need, such as volume and page numbers, date, and the periodicals that the index includes.

Magazine Indexes.   The *Readers' Guide to Periodical Literature* indexes about 200 magazines, from 1900 to the present, such as *Newsweek, The New Yorker, Rolling Stone,* and *Scientific American*. The semimonthly supplements make it possible to find up-to-date articles on many subjects. Bound cumulative volumes are issued for each year, and some libraries may have back issues available on microfilm or as bound volumes. Articles are indexed by subject and author. There is a book review section at the end of each volume; movie reviews are indexed under "Motion picture reviews—Single Works." The *Readers' Guide* uses subheadings to group related articles under the main subject. In Figure 4.15, for example, the subject paleontology is divided by period and by country. In addition, places in the United States are listed by state. Figure 4.16 shows an author entry.

Magazine Index, available in many libraries online or in microform, covers a greater number of popular magazines—over 400—than the *Readers' Guide*, including, for example, more computer magazines, such as *PC Magazine* and *PC Week*. *Magazine Index* indexes by title, sub-

FIGURE 4.15   Subject Entry from the *Readers' Guide*

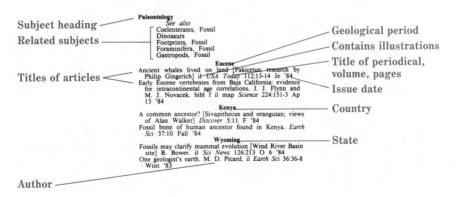

FIGURE 4.16   Author Entry from the *Readers' Guide*

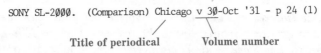

Author ———————————— Wattenberg, Ben J. ————————————— Title of periodical
                              Do Americans believe in anything anymore? il *Esquire*
Title of article ——————————— 102:78-80+ N '84 ——————————— Issue date
Vol. 102, pp. 78–80 ——————— The good news is the bad news is wrong [condensation]
                              il *Read Dig* 124:101-8+ Ap '84
plus additional   GOP tribal politics. il *Newsweek* 104:37-8 S 3 '84 ——— Interview with
scattered pages   about   Wattenberg
                              U.S. still believes tomorrow will be better than today
                              [interview] il por *U S News World Rep* 97:44-5 D ———— Includes picture
                              31 '84-Ja 7 '85

ject, and also by product and brand name. For instance, under "Video tape recorders," articles discussing Sanyo, Sony, and other brands will be found. An entry under "Sony" contains the following information:

SONY SL-2000. (Comparison) Chicago v 30-Oct '31 - p 24 (1)

                    Title of periodical   Volume number

Magazine Index began in 1976. Each microfilm reel goes back no more than five years; outdated material is then transferred to micro-fiche.

Journal Indexes.   In professional journals you can often find arti-cles on your subject written by experts for other experts. Such articles are likely to be more detailed and more authoritative than those in a popular magazine. The disadvantage is that technical terms unfamiliar to the layperson are often used. If, for example, you want to find out the latest developments in heart transplants, you may have to learn the meanings of unfamiliar medical terms. If you need to look up only a few words, you'll probably find the article useful. But if the article re-quires an extensive background that you don't have, you'll probably be more successful with magazines aimed at a less specialized audi-ence. Many professional journals, however, present few problems to the college student. Here are five of the most commonly used indexes to professional journals.

The *Humanities Index* (April 1974-) is published yearly with quar-terly updates and indexes about 275 periodicals on art, drama, litera-ture, history, philosophy, music, film, and folklore. For information before 1974, see the *International Index* (1907–1965) and the *Social Sciences and Humanities Index* (1965–1974), both of which were superseded by the *Humanities Index*. As Figure 4.17 shows, the format of the entries in the *Humanities Index* is similar to the *Readers' Guide*.

The *MLA International Bibliography of Books and Articles on the Modern Languages and Literatures* (1921-) is available in print and also online through DIALOG Database for the years 1968–1984 (eventually all of *MLA* will be available through DIALOG). *MLA* changed its format in 1981, going from three volumes to five and adding a subject index.

FIGURE 4.17   Entry from the *Humanities Index*

Author/subject ———— **MELVILLE, Herman** ———————————————— List of works about
heading   *about* ——   Melville
                    Bartleby the chronometer. H. Schechter. Stud Short Fict
                       19:359-66 Fall '82
                    False sympathy in Melville's Typee. M. Breitwiesser. Am Q
                       34:396-417 Fall '82
                    Melville's Cain. W. Kelly. Am Lit 55:24-40 Mr '83
                    Melville's comic debate: geniality and the aesthetics of
                       response. J. Bryant. Am Lit 55:151-70 My '83
                    Melville's Israel Potter: introducing absurdity and dark irony
                       to the American war novel. O. W. Gilman, jr. J Am Cult ——— Vol. 55, pp. 151-170
                       6:45-53 Summ '83

Now Volumes I and II cover national literatures; III, linguistics; IV, general literature; and V, folklore. The five volumes are issued and bound yearly in one volume and are subtitled *Classified Listings with Author Index*. A second annual volume is the *Subject Index*. To find entries in the *Classified Listings*, look either in the *Subject Index* (organized alphabetically) or in the *Classified Listings*, finding first the appropriate section or national literature, then the time period of your subject (for example, the nineteenth century), and finally the author (if your subject is a writer) listed alphabetically. Figure 4.18 shows the references you will find if you look up "Science Fiction Film" in the *Subject Index*.

Each volume in the classified section is numbered with roman numerals (I-IV) and each entry with arabic numerals. Figure 4.19 presents the entry you would find for the Menzies reference—number 310 in Volume IV—in the *Subject Index* (Figure 4.18).

FIGURE 4.18   Entry from the *Subject Index, MLA International Bibliography*

Main heading ————————— **SCIENCE FICTION FILM** ——————————— Vol. IV (general
Primary subheading ————— **General literature. Film: SCIENCE FICTION FILM.**   literature), citation
                                Menzies, William Cameron as director. IV:310.   no. 310
Secondary ————————   Treatment of contact with alien beings; study example: Kubrick,
subheading   Stanley: *2001: A Space Odyssey*; Clarke, Arthur C.: *2001: A Space*
                                Odyssey . IV:324 (I:4072).   — Vol. IV, citation
                             Treatment of mechanized environment; role of computer. IV:374.   no. 324 (also in Vol. I,
                             Treatment of space travel. Sources in literature. IV:509.   citation no. 4072)
                             Treatment of terror; the imaginary. Discusses film festival in Spain:
                                Madrid. IV:447.
                             General literature. Film: SCIENCE FICTION FILM and
                             television.
                             Bibliography. IV:653.

FIGURE 4.19   Entry from the *Classified Listings, MLA International*
              Bibliography

                                                                  — Volume number
                                                                  — Number of item in
Citation number ————— [310] DiFate, Vincent. "William Cameron Menzies and the Dreams of   that issue
Illustrated ————————   Childhood." *Starship*. 1982-1983 Winter-Spring; 19(1 [43]): 28-31. [Il-
                        lus. †Science fiction film. Menzies, William Cameron as director.] — Page numbers
Dagger denotes   — Issue number
heading used as
subject descriptor
(see Figure 4.18)

The *Public Affairs Information Service Bulletin* (PAIS)(1915-) indexes 1,400 worldwide publications in six languages in such subjects as economics, political science, business, law, finance, education, and social work using the *Readers' Guide* index entry format. PAIS is published semimonthly, with cumulative volumes issued four times a year and bound volumes annually.

The *Social Sciences Index* (April 1974-) consists of yearly volumes updated quarterly, and contains guides to about 250 English-language periodicals on sociology, psychology, environmental affairs, economics, political science, geography, and anthropology. Like PAIS, it also uses the *Readers' Guide* citation format. (From 1907 to 1965, this index was called the *International Index* and from 1965 to 1974, the *Social Sciences and Humanities Index.*)

The *Social Sciences Citation Index* (1972-; also available online), useful for subjects in the social, behavioral, and related sciences, is divided into four parts—Citation, Source, Permuterm Subject, and Corporate indexes—any of which may be used to begin a search. Perhaps you have the name of an authority in your field from an encyclopedia article or one of your textbooks. If you look up the name in the Citation Index, you will find the name of other writers who have cited this authority and who are probably dealing with the same kinds of subjects. In this way you can build a bibliography of experts in your subject area. For example, you may have heard your instructor mention Fritz Perls, an American psychologist who developed his own approach to your subject, gestalt therapy. To discover others who are currently writing in that same area, you would look up Perls in the Citation Index and see those who have cited articles by Perls (see Figure 4.20).

Let's say you are interested in the 1977 article by Perls, "Gestalt Therapy," and decide to look up the first author—Bassoff—listed as citing Perls's article. Looking in the Source Index under E. S. Bassoff, you would find an entry showing that in his article in the *Personal Guidance Journal* he cited nineteen other articles besides the one by Perls. Figure 4.21 gives the title of Bassoff's article ("Healthy Aspects of Passivity and Gendlin Focusing") and the citations for the twenty articles to which he referred. These citations will give you a lengthy list of possible articles on your subject. Of course, you can look up as many of the other authors listed under the entry for Perls as you wish.

The Permuterm Subject Index enables you to search a subject by pairing significant related words. If you are interested in the relationship of crime and adolescence, the Permuterm Subject Index will provide authors who have written on the subject (Figure 4.22); for publication details, look up these names in the Citation Index.

The Corporate Index, which lists authors by organization or country, enables you to determine whether anything has been published on your topic in South Africa, for instance, or at the University of Florida.

FIGURE 4.20   Entry from the Citation Index, *Social Sciences Citation Index*

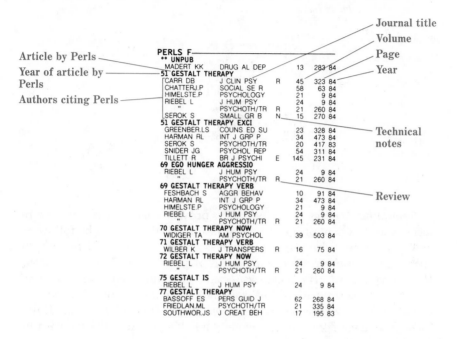

FIGURE 4.21   Entry from the Source Index, *Social Sciences Citation Index*

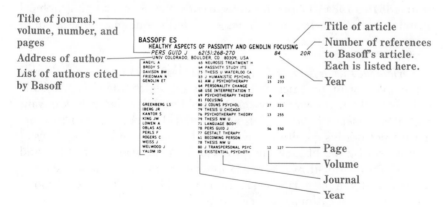

Indexes for Specific Disciplines.   Indexes for journals in specific disciplines are listed and annotated in Appendix 1. Look in one of these specialized indexes—such as the *Music Index* or the *Index Medicus*—if your topic is highly technical or if you have trouble finding references in the general indexes.

FIGURE 4.22   Entry from the Permuterm Subject Index, *Social Sciences Citation Index*

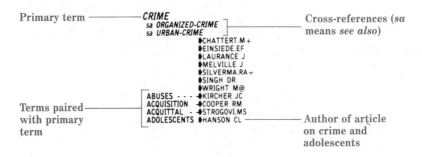

Primary term ——— CRIME
                    sa ORGANIZED-CRIME
                    sa URBAN-CRIME
                                  ◆CHATTERT.M+
                                  ◆EINSIEDE.EF
                                  ◆LAURANCE J
                                  ◆MELVILLE J
                                  ◆SILVERMA.RA+
                                  ◆SINGH DR
                                  ◆WRIGHT M@
                    ABUSES - - - ◆KIRCHER JC
Terms paired   ACQUISITION ◆COOPER RM
with primary   ACQUITTAL - ◆STROGOVI.MS
term   ADOLESCENTS ◆HANSON CL

Cross-references (*sa* means *see also*)

Author of article on crime and adolescents

Newspaper Indexes.   Newspapers provide current accounts of subjects as well as contemporary views of historical events. The following newspapers publish their own indexes (items are indexed by subject only): the *Christian Science Monitor, Los Angeles Times, New York Times, Wall Street Journal, Washington Post,* and London *Times.* The *National Newspaper Index* (on microfilm) is a guide to articles in the *Christian Science Monitor, Los Angeles Times, New York Times, Wall Street Journal, Washington Post.* Each film indexes two and a half years, and the *Index* is updated frequently; old films are on microfiche.

The *Personal Name Index to the New York Times Index,* by Byron J. Falk, Jr., and Valerie R. Falk, indexes names appearing in that newspaper from 1851 to 1984. These volumes provide a short cut to biographical search in the *Times,* because names are listed in one place instead of in many different volumes by year.

Periodical File or Serials List.   This list of periodicals—which may come in a print or microfiche format or which may be available online—will tell you whether your library has the periodicals you want and, if so, where the periodicals are located. It lists in alphabetical order the periodicals the library owns, the beginning and ending dates of acquisition by the library, the physical form they are stored in, and their location. If call numbers are not given, the journals are shelved alphabetically in the periodical section of the library. Figure 4.23 shows three different locations for periodicals.

Dictionaries

The massive book open on a stand or low shelf in the reference area is probably *Webster's Third New International Dictionary of the English Language* (1981). If it looks well-worn, it is probably the earlier 1961 edition. This

FIGURE 4.23   Entry from a Periodical File

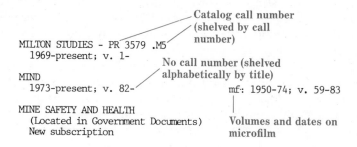

unabridged dictionary contains more words than any other American dictionary. It covers "the current vocabulary of standard written and spoken English" and is especially good for pronunciation and usage.

If the way a word has been used over the years is important in your search, see the *Oxford English Dictionary* (13 vols.). Known as the OED, this dictionary illustrates the history of each word it defines by giving quotations in historical order beginning with the first-known usage. Supplements keep the OED up to date. Figure 4.24 shows the changing meanings of the word "educate." One of its uses in the early seventeenth century—to rear children and animals by supplying their physical needs—is now obsolete. But it's interesting to notice that Shake-

FIGURE 4.24   Entry from the *Oxford English Dictionary*

Educate (e·diŭke⋅t), *v.* [f. L. *ĕducāt-* ppl. stem of *ēducāre* to rear, bring up (children, young animals), related to *ēdūcĕre* to lead forth (see EDUCE), which is sometimes used nearly in the same sense.] *trans.* or *absol.*

† **1.** To rear, bring up (children, animals) by supply of food and attention to physical wants. *Obs.*
1607 TOPSELL *Four-f. Beasts* 229 The Epirotan & Sicilian horses are not to be despised, if they were well bred & educated. **1651** WITTIE tr. *Primrose's Pop. Err.* 292 A boy of a good habit of body, with large veines, well and freely educated. **1690** [see EDUCATED]. **1818** [see 2].

2. To bring up (young persons) from childhood, so as to form (their) habits, manners, intellectual and physical aptitudes.
1618 BOLTON *Florus* I. i. 3 Himselfe delighting in the Rivers and Mountaines, among which he had beene educated. **1818** CRUISE *Digest* VI. 336 A devise .. to the intent that with the profits he should educate his daughter. **1839** tr. *Lamartine's Trav. East* 168/1 The principal amongst them [Greeks] have their children educated in Hungary. **1875** JOWETT *Plato* (ed. 2) V. 40 The youth of a people should be educated in forms and strains of virtue.

b. To instruct, provide schooling for (young persons).
1588 SHAKS. *L. L. L.* v. i. 84 Do you not educate youth at the Charg-house on the top of the Mountaine? **1863** MARY HOWITT tr. *F. Bremer's Greece* I. i. 13 It has educated, and it educates to this day, a great portion of the Athenian female youth of all classes. **1863** A. TYLOR *Educ. & Manuf.* 40 It costs 8*d.* per week to educate a child.

3. To train (any person) so as to develop the intellectual and moral powers generally.
1849 KINGSLEY *Lett.* (1878) I. 198 In my eyes the question is not what to teach, but how to Educate. **1875** JOWETT *Plato* (ed. 2) V. 120 Elder men, if they want to educate others, should begin by educating themselves. **1886** *Pall Mall G.* 10 July 4/2 Our artists are not educated at all, they are only trained.

speare's use of the word as early as 1588 was much the same as our use of it is today. After listing the word, the OED gives the pronunciation, part of speech, derivation, and grammatical use. Each numbered section provides a meaning of the word followed by the date, author, title of work, and quotation illustrating the word.

The word you want may be in a special dictionary, such as the *McGraw-Hill Dictionary of Scientific and Technical Terms.* Some dictionaries, such as the *Dictionary of Symbols* by J. E. Cirlot, are much like encyclopedias, with extended entries on a single subject. To find the dictionary best for you, consult *Dictionaries, Encyclopedias, and Other Word-Related Books* (2 vols.), edited by Annie M. Brewer.

Pamphlets

The library's pamphlet file contains uncataloged printed material. This material varies in size from pamphlets of a few pages to small paperbound books of a hundred or more pages, published by local government agencies, business firms, or special interest groups. Most libraries store pamphlets or serial publications in file drawers, commonly known as vertical files. Contents of the files are usually arranged alphabetically according to subject.

To discover whether pamphlets have been published on your subject, consult the *Vertical File Index: A Subject and Title Index to Selected Pamphlet Materials,* published monthly with a cumulative subject index issued quarterly. This index tells you the name of the pamphlet, the source, and the cost so that you can order the pamphlet directly if your library doesn't own the item. It's a good idea to order pamphlets as soon as possible because the length of time it takes to receive them is unpredictable. Figure 4.25 shows two of the many kinds of pamphlets you might find through this source.

FIGURE 4.25   Entries from the *Vertical File Index*

INVESTMENT trusts

Directories

Your guide to mutual funds 1984-1985 directory. 36p '84 No-Load mutual fund assn 11 Penn Plaza Suite 2204 N Y 10001 $2 send payment with order

Publisher of pamphlet

JOYCE, James

James Joyce's hundredth birthday, by Richard Ellmann. 27p il '82 U S Lib of Cong Central services div Washington D C 20540 single copy free

A lecture delivered at the Library of Congress on March 10, 1982.

The pamphlet is a reprint of a lecture by Ellmann.

Indexes to Government Documents

If the subject of your search pertains to history, government, or law, federal government documents can provide interesting firsthand reports of committee findings, bills passed, and much other information about what goes on in Congress and elsewhere in the government. Many college libraries are depositories for government documents (a library must have at least 15,000 titles in its catalog in order to qualify as a depository). One depository in each state (a regional depository) receives all government documents; other depositories (selective depositories) choose the documents they wish to receive. Selective depositories may obtain any document they do not have from the nearest regional depository. Although some government documents can be checked out of the library, most do not circulate, and they may be stored in either print or microformat. Small collections of government documents might be kept in the reference area, but large collections will probably be located in their own room or department.

Libraries with large collections of government documents usually do not list them in the card catalog and therefore do not use the classification systems used for other material. (Libraries with limited numbers of government documents may, however, integrate them into their regular cataloging system.) Instead, government documents in depository libraries are assigned a SuDoc (Superintendent of Documents) number that looks like this: Y 10.2:W29/2. Consult the librarian for indexes to the documents and their location. Here are the chief indexes.

The *Monthly Catalog of U.S. Government Publications,* issued by the Government Printing Office, describes all of the publications sent to depository libraries. The contents are indexed in the back of the *Catalog* by author, title, subject, series, stock number, and title keyword. These cumulative indexes are issued semiannually and annually. Documents published before 1971 are indexed somewhat differently and may best be located in two commercial publications: the *Cumulative Subject Index to the Monthly Catalog, 1900-1971* (15 vols.), by William W. Buchanan and Edna M. Kanely, and the *Decennial Cumulative Personal Author Index* (3 vols.), edited by Edward Przebienda, covering the years 1941 to 1970. As the title indicates, you can locate information in the Buchanan–Kanely index by looking up a subject; you can also find some authors by looking up "Addresses, Lectures," where speakers' names are listed in alphabetical order. Przebienda indexes material only by author.

The *Congressional Information Service* (CIS) index is issued monthly in two parts—Abstracts and Indexes—with quarterly and annual cumulative volumes. Items are indexed by subject, name, title, document

FIGURE 4.26   Entry from the *Congressional Information Service* Index

Public Law number   **J862–12**   **STATE AND LOCAL FISCAL**   92nd Congress,
(*J* means *joint* study ⌐   **ASSISTANCE ACT OF 1972.**   second session
by both houses)   Sept. 27, 1972.   92-2. $3.75
                                     ix + 885 p.
Government Printing _____ Y4.In8/11:St2/2/972. ─────────── SuDoc number
Office number   ──15790(73).   72-603225. ── Library of Congress
                                     Supplemental report on H.R. 14370, showing the   card number
                                     distribution of funds as agreed to by the con-
                                     ferees.

number, and committee chairman. To find information in this volume, look up your subject in the Index and find the number of the document you want; then find the abstract in the Abstracts volume. Figure
4.26 presents a sample abstract entry from the CIS index. Recently the
CIS made its information available on microfilm. A reference such as
CIS/MF/4, for example, indicates that the material is available on four
reels of microfilm.

The *American Statistics Index* (ASI) is a guide to government publications containing statistical information. It follows the same format as
the *Congressional Information Service*.

The *Congressional Record,* a daily record of proceedings in the House
and Senate, is usually shelved in the reference room or in the government documents section. Published daily, the *Congressional Record* is indexed biweekly, with a yearly bound cumulative issue. Material is indexed by author and subject. It is available on microfilm from 1873.

Computer Databases

Hundreds of databases now contain bibliographic information
available to libraries that subscribe. For a long-term intensive research
project, you may want to take advantage of this service if your library
offers it. A fee, from $5 to $100 based on the computer time required,
is usually charged. A search may take up to two weeks, depending on
the number of searches being requested and the computer and personnel time available. Some libraries suggest that students plan for at least
a two-week wait. *Introduction to Reference Work,* Vol. 2, by William A.
Katz (1982) describes library computer services and provides an annotated list of databases. The following databases are among the most
commonly used in college libraries:

ERIC (Educational Resources Information Center)
PSYCHINFO
SOCIAL SCISEARCH and/or SCISEARCH (*Social Sciences Citation
    Index* and *Science Citation Index* online)
MEDLARS/MEDLINE (*Medical Literature Analysis and Retrieval Sys-
    tem* online)
NTIS (National Technical Information Service)

An effective computer search depends to a great extent on the accuracy of the terms you use to describe your project. These terms called *descriptors,* must match the descriptors used to file the data. Librarians familiar with the terminology can tell which terms work best. Often students are asked by the library staff to fill out a search request form and to have an interview with the librarian to explain their needs. Here are some examples of information you may be asked to give.

1. Give a narrative description of the subject or problem to be searched. Be specific, defining terms in the context of your request. Provide both scientific or technical terms and common vocabulary synonyms as well as alternate spellings for words.
2. List at least one printed index you used to search for information on this topic, the subject heading(s) you used, and the title(s) of article(s) you found.
3. Give the time period to be covered (e.g., ''since 1980'').
4. Specify whether you want references in languages other than English.

For the computer search excerpted in Figure 4.27, the librarian applied the terms *pornography* and *children* to a search of the *Social Sciences*

FIGURE 4.27 Printout from an Online Search

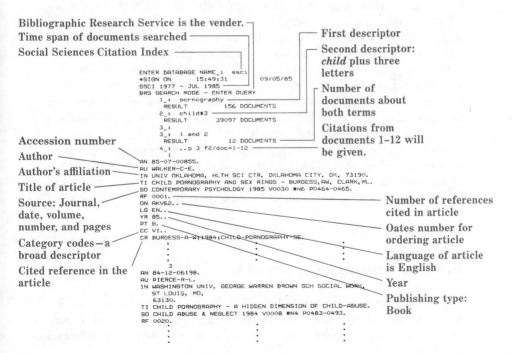

Citation Index. The vendor, or owner of the database files whom the library paid for the right to search, was BRS (Bibliographic Retrieval Service). As the search begins, the librarian has already selected a group of databases—"Social Science and Humanities Databases"—and is about to choose a specific file from this group. Thus, in about thirty minutes 4,500 journals from 1977 to the present will have been searched for you, a search that would take much longer with the printed version.

Sources Obtained Through Interlibrary Loan

If you find that some of the most promising articles or books are not available in your library, your reference librarian may be able to get them through interlibrary loan. A computer network, such as OCLC (Online Computer Library Center), which links the catalogs of subscribing libraries, may be able to assist you in finding a library that has the source you want. If you want a book, arrangements may be made to borrow it for you. You may also arrange for photocopies of articles in periodicals to be sent to you, for which you will probably pay a small fee. Before you ask for such a service, however, determine the relevance of your article by reading an abstract of it in an index of abstracts if one is available for your subject. You will find indexes of abstracts along with other indexes in Appendix 1. Although with more than 300 subscribers from academic and nonacademic libraries OCLC is the largest of these networks, other online networks are available to libraries that want to participate including RLIN (Research Libraries Information Network), a network of large academic research libraries such as Cornell, Harvard, Stanford, and the University of California; WLN (Washington Library Network), a network of Pacific Northwest libraries; and UTLAS (University of Toronto Library Automation System), a Canadian libraries system.

Before you leave the reference room, take a few minutes to review your records. You should have a list of possible sources on cards or note paper, and, in your search log, a record of where you went and what you did, including names of indexes you searched.

Finding Information in the Card Catalog

The card catalog contains a list of all the books in the library and is often located on the first floor. Some library catalogs are on a computer, some on microfilm, but most consist of alphabetically arranged

3-by-5 cards in catalog drawers. Many card catalogs are divided into two sections, with cards organized by author and title in one section, by subject in another. A book in such a system will have three or more cards filed for it: an author card, a title card, and one or more subject cards. Each book in the library is given a unique call number so that it can be easily distinguished from all other books. This call number appears on the book and on the pertinent cards in the catalog. Two classification systems, Dewey Decimal and Library of Congress, are in common use.

Dewey Decimal System

This system classifies books by using numbers and decimal points. All information is divided into the following ten groups:

000–099	General Works	600–699	Technology
100–199	Philosophy		(Applied Sciences)
200–299	Religion	700–799	The Arts
300–399	Social Sciences	800–899	Literature
400–499	Language	900–999	History
500–599	Pure Science		

Each of these classes is further divided into groups of ten, each of these groups into more subdivisions, and so on. Decimal points are added to increase the number of subdivisions. Here are the ten main subdivisions of Technology:

600	Technology	650	Management
	(Applied Sciences)	660	Chemical Technology
610	Medical Sciences	670	Manufactures
620	Engineering	680	Miscellaneous
630	Agriculture		Manufactures
640	Home Economics	690	Buildings

Under a specific number and its divisions (for example, 610.73, which includes books about nursing) is a combination of letters and numbers that represents the individual book's author and title. Ronald Philip Preston's *The Dilemmas of Care* has been classified this way:

Medical Sciences — 610.73 — Nursing
First letter of author's last name — P939d — First letter of book title
Cutter number, derived from author's name

Library of Congress System

This system was developed to make even more categories possible than are allowed under the Dewey Decimal system. Instead of the ten basic divisions of knowledge of the Dewey system, the Library of Congress system maintains twenty basic divisions corresponding to the letters of the alphabet (note: I, O, W, X, and Y are omitted, and E and F are both reserved for American history):

A	General Works	K	Law
B	Philosophy, Psychology, Religion	L	Education
		M	Music
C	History and Auxiliary Sciences	N	Fine Arts
		P	Language and Literature
D	History and Topography (except North and South America)	Q	Science
		R	Medicine
		S	Agriculture
E-F	History: North and South America	T	Technology
		U	Military Science
G	Geography and Anthropology	V	Naval Science
		Z	Bibliography and Library Science
H	Social Sciences		
J	Political Science		

An additional letter subdivides these divisions. Medicine, for example, is divided into the following categories:

R	Medicine (General)	RL	Dermatology
RA	Public Aspects of Medicine	RM	Therapeutics
RB	Pathology	RS	Pharmacy and Materia Medica
RC	Internal Medicine		
RD	Surgery	RT	Nursing
RE	Ophthalmology	RV	Botanic, Thomsonian, and Eclectic Medicine
RF	Otorhinolaryngology		
RG	Gynecology and Obstetrics	RX	Homeopathy
RJ	Pediatrics	RZ	Other Systems of Medicine
RK	Dentistry		

Other letters and numbers that follow the decimal point provide further subdivisions. Here is the call number for *Rehabilitation Medicine* by Howard A. Rusk:

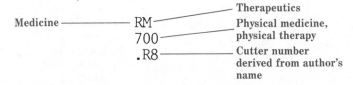

The *Library of Congress Subject Headings,* usually located near the card catalog, can be consulted to find out whether the words you have used to identify your subject are the same terms that the library has used to classify that material. For example, if your subject is "solar power," you will not find books under that subject in the card catalog. In the *LC Subject Headings*, you'll be referred to "Solar energy":

Solar power
See Solar energy

Then, under "Solar energy," you will find other subject headings that might be helpful (see Figure 4.28). (Refer to the front pages of the *LC Subject Headings* for a guide to the meaning of the symbols used.)

Now you are ready to look up your selected subject headings in the card catalog. Under "Solar energy" you will probably find several subject cards; one of them might look like the sample in Figure 4.29.

FIGURE 4.28   Entry from the *LC Subject Headings*

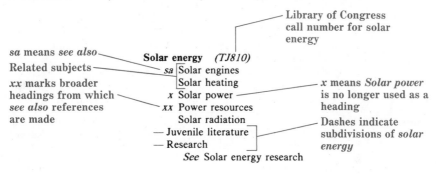

FIGURE 4.29   An LC Subject Card

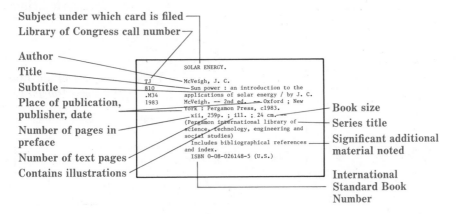

At the end of the listing of books specifically on your subject, you'll find cards on related subjects, subdivided by dashes and further headings, such as a card for economic aspects of solar energy (Figure 4.30). Or you might find cards like Figure 4.31, referring you to such reference books as bibliographies, indexes, or dictionaries.

In the author/title section of the card catalog, you can look up books you have found in your search and enter these on your bibliography cards. Be sure to include the call numbers of the books.

Before you begin your search for the articles and books in your working bibliography, group your cards according to the location of the books and articles in the library to save yourself some time. Put your periodical cards in alphabetical order according to the title of the periodical and your book cards in order of the call numbers.

FIGURE 4.30 An LC Subject Card with Subject Subdivision

SOLAR ENERGY--ECONOMIC ASPECTS--
UNITED STATES.

HD 9681 .U62F44

Feldman, Stephen L.
On the economics of solar energy : the public-utility interface / Stephen L. Feldman, Robert M. Wirtshafter. -- Lexington, Mass. : Lexington Books, c1980.
xi, 256 p. ; 24 cm.
Bibliography: p. 239-256.

1. Solar energy industries--United States. 2. Public utilities--United States. 3. Solar energy--Economic aspects--United States. I. Wirtshafter, Robert M., joint author. II. Title

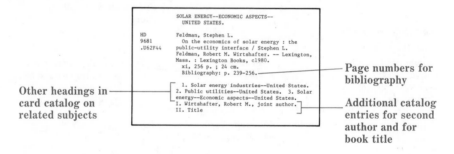

FIGURE 4.31 An LC Subject Card with Form Subdivision

SOLAR ENERGY--BIBLIOGRAPHY.

Ref. TJ 810 .U546x 1976

United States. Energy Research and Development Administration. Technical Information Center.
Solar energy, a bibliography. [Oak Ridge, Tenn.] : U.S. Energy Research & Development Administration, Office of Public Affairs, Technical Information Center ; [Springfield, Va.] : available from the National Technical Information Service, U.S. Dept. of Commerce, 1976.
2 v. ; 28 cm. (TID-3351-R1P1-P2)
CONTENTS.--[1] Citations.--[2] Indexes.

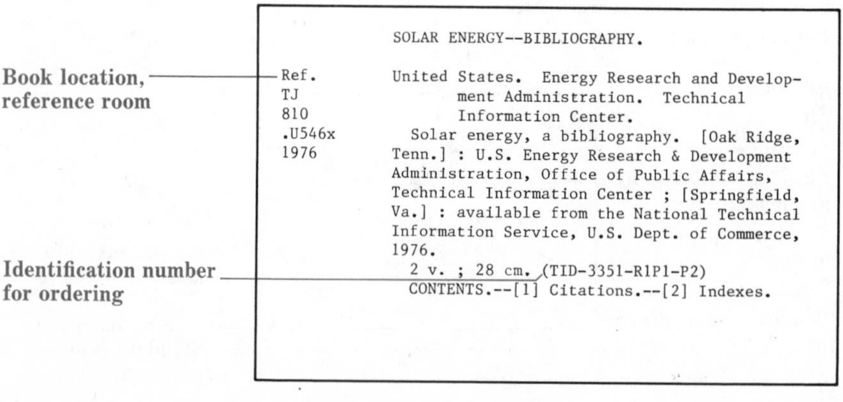

Taking Stock

You are now ready to find the periodicals that have the articles you want and to locate the books you need on the library's shelves. Help in evaluating these sources and taking notes will be given in Chapter 5, but before you begin that process, it would be wise for you to answer the questions, Where am I? Where have I been? Where am I going?

As you followed the steps in compiling your bibliography, you were constantly finding references to related subjects. Beginning with the encyclopedia, you were given a number of directions to take. When you looked through the indexes, you found more possibilities. Again as you searched the card catalog, you were presented with subject headings from which to choose. By this time you had to make a number of choices of direction; some of these decisions you made consciously, others unconsciously. Now, before you begin to locate your sources, review your progress and note where you are headed.

Widening or Narrowing?

First review your original outline or list of subtopics and add possibilities you may have found in encyclopedias, indexes, periodical listings, and the card catalog. Then choose from this expanded list the subtopics you want to cover. In deciding which ones to include, consider their relevance to your main topic, your interests, and the time and sources available to you. The list you make now will guide you as you look up and examine your sources. Use the subtopics from your outline as headings for your note cards.

Focusing a Topic

A subject—any subject—is a little like a Fourth of July sparkler: it gives off sparks or light in all directions. Sometimes when you're starting to investigate a subject, these sparks seem to be multiplying at an uncontrollable rate. Marvin Kohl started to write a paper on pornography. He wanted to know answers to these questions: What is pornography? Is it harmful? Should anything be done about it? He went first to the *Encyclopedia Britannica*'s Micropaedia where he found, besides a brief definition, two reasons for laws against pornography: it corrupts morals and causes crime. In the Macropaedia he found a discussion of the following subjects: censorship, laws against pornography and obscenity, a history of such laws, laws in other countries, and book-banning. He then looked up his subject in the *Encyclopedia Americana* and found that this source concentrated on American obscenity laws and referred to congressional hearings. To keep track of all of these ideas and others that were occurring to him, he drew a diagram (Figure 4.32) to show how one subject suggested another. From this diagram he selected the topics he was most interested in: laws passed in the United States and elsewhere and effects of pornography.

His next step was the *Encyclopedia of Psychology* in which he found an article that referred to reports of the Commission on Obscenity and Pornography. In the *Readers' Guide* he spotted a reference to an article that attacked pornography on the grounds of violation of women's rights. Next the reference librarian recommended the *Encyclopedia of Crime and Justice,* which, as it turned out, was an excellent suggestion because the article on pornography discussed the two aspects of the subject he was mainly interested in—behavioral and legal. It was a lengthy article with a long bibliography. On the basis of this article, he decided to concentrate on photographic pornography. Kohl was now ready to compose a working title and a preliminary outline.

The Social Effects of Photographic Pornography

Possible bad effects (to be verified or disproven)
Involves the exploitation of children
Leads to the exploitation of women
Causes increase in crime
Results in moral corruption

Possible good effects (to be verified or refuted)
Can be used in sex education and treatment programs
Helps in preventing some crimes

Laws relating to pornography
Legalization of pornography in Denmark
Laws against pornography in the United States

He next read over his outline to make sure that the topics and subtopics were listed in the order of most to least important. On review, Kohl thought he might have trouble covering all these topics in the time available; but he decided that if necessary, he could always drop "Laws relating to pornography" and still produce an interesting paper.

Refer to the summary of steps below in assessing your position and deciding which direction to take.

1. List all the possible subtopics you might cover.
2. Choose the ones you want to include in your search.
3. Re-examine your purpose and restate your topic.
4. Rewrite your list of subtopics according to your revised topic in order to make a working outline; that is, put the subtopics in logical order and group them under headings to demonstrate their relationships.

FIGURE 4.32 Focusing a Subject

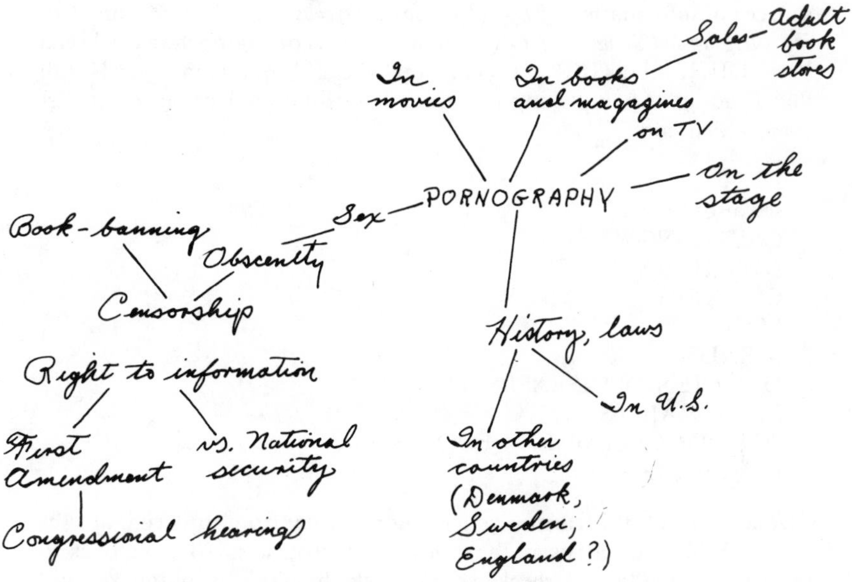

This kind of decision making is, as you have found, a continual part of your search. Searching, or exploring, always means going into new unknown territory. It means setting out on a Lewis-and-Clark expedition with some general guidelines and an idea of the ground to be covered but also with the need to constantly reassess your strategy and direction.

Keeping a Search Log: Student Examples

Be sure to record in your search log what you did. Such a record will make it possible for you to resume your search quickly even if you have to stop for other assignments for a few days. The following students' accounts of their searches were written on the basis of records kept in their search logs.

Michelle Stigliano's Bibliographic Search. Michelle Stigliano's account of the beginning of her search on "The Treatment of Anorexia Nervosa" shows how the focus of a topic can change as the search proceeds. She gradually realized how she wanted to shape her topic as she looked at the subject listings in the card catalog, consulted indexes to periodicals, and browsed in books. Notice that in her case it helped to work back and forth between the reference area and the card catalog.

I started my search with the card catalog. Looking in the subject headings section under "anorexia nervosa," I found three possible sources of information: *The Golden Cage, Psychosomatic Families,* and *Eating, Sleeping and Sexuality.* At the end of the cards on anorexia, a card read "see: DIET, HUNGER." Looking up "diet," I found many cards with that heading. After picking out several possibilities I came to the last card, which said:

DIET
see also:
GASTRONOMY
NUTRITION
COOKERY
FOOD
MENUS
DEFICIENCY DISEASES
FOOD HABITS
SCHOOL CHILDREN—FOOD
BEVERAGES

The items on this card were leading me away from my original subject, so I decided to look in the indexes and abstracts and come back to the card catalog later. I checked through the library's list of indexes and abstracts and picked three that would probably list sources relevant to my topic: *Abridged Index Medicus, Bibliography of the History of Medicine,* and *Nutrition Studies Abstracts.* Copying the references for all the articles became tedious, but as I read the titles, I realized that I was not really sure whether I wanted to evaluate the treatments of anorexia or go into the personality characteristics of the victims and their families. So instead of continuing through the lists of periodicals and writing down every possible source, I decided it would make more sense to stop and do some browsing through the books I had selected to determine which topic I wanted to pursue.

Looking at the table of contents in *The Golden Cage* by Hilde Bruch I found myself most interested in Chapter 4, "How It Starts," and after reading it I realized I had found the area I wanted to concentrate on— how it starts. I went back to the periodicals and was able to pick out the ones that would help me on this topic.

Vaurice Starks's Bibliographic Search.   Vaurice Starks's search for a working bibliography on her topic, "The Hazards of Smoking to the Smoker and to Others," went smoothly at the beginning. Here is her account.

When I went to the library to begin my search, I wasn't sure where to start. There were so many possibilities—the card catalog, indexes, and encyclopedias. I decided to start with the card catalog.

I pulled out the drawer labeled "Smithsonian I–Social." I slowly flipped through the cards, pausing when I got to the word *smoking*. There were several book titles relating specifically to my subject; two of these were Harold Diehl, *Tobacco and Your Health: The Smoking Controversy,* and Ruth Winter, *The Scientific Case Against Smoking.* Some titles didn't indicate a relationship to my subject, but when I read the details of the contents on the card, I thought they might be useful (for example, *The Stop-smoking Book for Teens* by Curtis Casewit). There was a summary on the card that said, "Examines the physical and psychological implications of smoking cigarettes."

In order to keep track of the books I wanted to look up, I listed them on index cards. I found this convenient because I could put together all the cards for books located on the same floor. I checked the location of the books and took the elevator to the second floor. It took me quite a while to find books because some of them were misshelved. I ended up finding five out of the seven books I wanted. When I went down to the circulation desk to see if the other two were checked out, I was told that they would be returned in two weeks. I filled out a reserve form and the librarian said she would notify me when the books came in. By this time I was tired so I went home.

The next day I went to the orientation session given by the librarian for our class. I found out that the library has indexes and abstracts on just about everything. I was accustomed to using only the *Readers' Guide to Periodical Literature.* After Judy, the librarian, showed us examples of index entries on slides, she directed us to a table where she had arranged indexes and periodicals on our various topics. I asked her what indexes would be helpful for me and she showed me *Pollution Abstracts* and the *Public Affairs Information Service Bulletin* (PAIS). (Later on my own I found the *Index to Nursing and Allied Health Literature* and looked up my topic in it and also in the *Readers' Guide*.) I found a number of articles about smoking. At first I had trouble translating some of the code numbers in the indexes, but Judy showed me that 67: 7–8, M'81 meant volume 67, pages 7 and 8 in the March 1981 issue.

After deciding which of these articles were pertinent to my topic, I wrote them down on index cards too. Besides the name of the article, I wrote down who wrote it, the name of the periodical, the volume, the page numbers, and the date. I also included a brief summary of what the article was about when this was given in the index or collection of abstracts. Then I went off to see if the periodicals I wanted were in the library. I found the titles listed in alphabetical order on microfiche, which I had placed in a machine that magnified them. The library had all the magazines I was looking for. I was lucky.

Starks still had some focusing to do, but this took place later. As she read her materials, she realized that, because she did not smoke, she was more interested in the hazards to "passive smokers"—those who are in physical proximity to smokers—and concentrated on the dangers to them.

EXERCISES

1. Using the notes in your search log, write a narrative account of your search up to this point. Use the straightforward approach of Stigliano or Starks. Or make a list in your search log of all of the metaphors for searching that occur to you, such as exploring a cave, climbing a mountain, going to the moon, or snorkeling. Then write an account of your library search using one of those metaphors as a framework. Attach a copy of your working bibliography and a brief working outline.
2. Make a list of other sources that Michelle Stigliano and Vaurice Starks might have used.
3. Write a two- or three-page essay in which you state the subject of your search and discuss the following points: why you chose your subject; what the most difficult parts of your search have been so far; what you have learned about a library search that you didn't know before; and how the search for this paper has been different from other library searches you have done.

C H A P T E R   5

Recording Information
from Library Sources

The Library [is] a wilderness of books. . . . It is necessary to find out exactly what books to read on a given subject. Though there may be a
thousand books written upon it, it is only important to read three or
four; they will contain all that is essential, and a few pages will show
which they are.

—*H. D. Thoreau: A Writer's Journal*

If you have followed the suggestion in Chapter 1 to build abundance
into your search process, you will have perhaps not the thousand books
that Thoreau mentions but many more books and articles on your list
than you will need or can use. The next step is to locate them in the
library so that you may begin the process of evaluation—selecting
those sources that are the most useful and reliable.

Locating Books and Periodicals

Books, unless they are reference books such as encyclopedias, dictionaries, and the like, are shelved in the stacks according to their call
numbers. These stacks are open in most college libraries, that is, you
may locate books yourself and take them to the checkout desk. (In some
large public libraries, you must hand in your book requests and wait
for your books to be delivered to you.) An advantage of open stacks is

69

that you may see other books on the subject that interest you while you are looking for the ones on your list. To simplify your search for books, arrange your bibliography cards in order according to the classification system used by your library. If your library uses the Library of Congress classification system, put all of your PF cards together, your QP's, and so forth, then arrange them in alphabetical order, according to library practice.

Bound volumes of periodicals may be located in a separate room or in the book stacks by call number (see Chapter 4). You may want to photocopy short articles from them to read later (be sure to record complete publication data on these copies so that you can identify them). Microforms may also be stored separately, along with the machines for using them; some of these machines may print copies of the microforms.

Once you have located your sources, you are ready to evaluate, read, and take notes. Skillful reading and notetaking are crucial to the writing of a good research paper.

Evaluating Your Sources

As you evaluate your working bibliography you will find out which sources will be the most useful and reliable for your paper. You have probably already begun this process by noticing the copyright date (if currency is important to you), by paying special attention to authors who have been recommended, and by reading abstracts of books and articles. The evaluation process, which, like other parts of searching, is a continuous one, is especially useful at this stage, when you have assembled your bibliography and are about to begin reading. The following suggestions will help to eliminate those sources that are not worth your time to read.

Some sources may be of limited value to you, others so unreliable as to be misleading and deceptive, and the value of still others may be hard to determine until you begin to read them. But you should keep in mind that the integrity of your paper depends to a great extent on the reliability or authenticity of your sources. If your subject is controversial, you will want to make sure that you use unbiased sources or, at least, that you are aware of their biases. Although all standards of reliability are relative and subject to error, the *copyright date, author, periodical* in which an article appears, *recommendations and reviews,* and *content* provide you with the information necessary to make a reasonable judgment. Although you may not be able to judge the content adequately until you start reading, you can learn about it to some extent beforehand. If you examine the following guidelines, you will have a good idea of the reliability and usefulness of your sources by the time you are ready to locate them in the library.

Copyright Date

The publication, or copyright, date of a book or article is important for any research project. In the sciences, for instance, researchers build on the information of their predecessors because knowledge in these subjects is increasing at a rate that produces obsolescence almost overnight. For a paper on the uses of artificial satellites, for example, most sources more than five years old are of limited value; new uses for satellites in communications and new reports from satellites used as observatories are reported almost daily. In the social sciences, too, the date may be crucial: a study on the methods of achieving school integration should look at contemporary data; currently, instead of busing, many school districts are integrating through the use of "magnet schools." Although sources in the humanities tend to age more slowly than those in the sciences, new documents or new information sometimes emerges that makes old sources obsolete. For example, a study focusing on Virginia Woolf's later writing would be limited without an examination of the latest volume of her diaries, which are being issued at irregular intervals.

You will usually find the publication date on the copyright page (the page following the title page) or sometimes on the title page itself. The number of dates may be confusing, but the significant date, the one you would use in your bibliography, is the latest copyright date, which is the date of the last revision. Additional printings do not necessarily indicate changes in the text—only new *editions* acquire new copyright dates. Figure 5.1 shows two examples of copyright pages.

Once in a while you may come across a book that does not give a

FIGURE 5.1   Sample Copyright Dates

Latest copyright date

Symbol for copyright, Universal Copyright Convention

Copyright © 1960, 1966, 1967, 1968, 1969, 1973, 1975, 1978, 1981 by the Trustees of the Merton Legacy Trust
Copyright © 1959, 1961, 1963, 1964, 1965, 1981 by The Abbey of Gethsemani, Inc.
Copyright 1953 by Our Lady of Gethsemani Monastery

Date of last revision

Reprinting dates; no changes made in text

PUBLISHED, JUNE, 1943
SECOND PRINTING, DECEMBER, 1958
THIRD PRINTING, APRIL, 1961

publication date. In that case, check the card catalog; a copyright date may be given on the card. (The abbreviation *c* before a date on a catalog card means *copyright*.)

Author

The status, experience, and professional position of an author are clues to the reliability of the writing. You may learn about an author's background in such sources as *Who's Who in America* (there are similar books for other countries). Those in academic disciplines and professions may be found in the appropriate subject volume of the *Who's Who* series, which includes American history, arts and literature, commerce and industry, economics, electronics, engineering, finance and industry, government, law, music, nursing, opera, politics, religion, technology, and theater. For biographies of writers, consult *Contemporary Authors* (updated volumes appear regularly) and the *Directory of American Scholars*. Credentials of scientists can be checked in *Modern Scientists and Engineers* and *American Men and Women of Science*. All these sources are usually shelved in the reference area.

You can also tell something about the professional status of writers by how often they are mentioned by other experts. For example, if your subject is in the social sciences, see the *Social Sciences Citation Index* for names of other writers who have cited the author of a book or article on your list (Chapter 4 describes this index in detail). Although these citations are not recommendations in themselves, their appearance in professional sources is some indication of the author's importance. As you proceed with your reading, watch for references to other writers; then look up these names in the index that applies to their discipline (the *MLA Bibliography*, for example, if they are writing on literary subjects) and study their publishing record.

Professional Journals

Articles in professional journals are usually more trustworthy than those in widely circulating magazines. Published by professional associations or by academic institutions, they are approved for publication by specialists in a field and are written for an audience knowledgeable in that field. As a result, such articles are usually well-documented and carefully reasoned. However, articles in some commercially published magazines and newspapers, though they are not as formally documented as those in scholarly journals, can also supply bibliographic information and can be equally reliable.

Every periodical possesses its own point of view to attract its audience. If you use an article that discusses only one side of an issue, you should at least be aware of that bias and try to find other points of view. Moreover, whatever the bias of an article, you should always judge the writing by the presentation of facts and the conclusions based on them. *Magazines for Libraries* evaluates both journals and magazines and explains the kinds of articles most often published by them as well as any detectable biases. It also gives the circulation size, which may indicate a limited audience. See Figure 5.2 for reviews of two magazines with different political views.

Also be on your guard against bias by reading the masthead of a magazine or periodical (usually found on the same page as the table of contents) to see who publishes it. Many lobbying organizations, such as the Sierra Club or the National Rifle Association, issue their own publications in which the point of view of their organization is promoted.

Recommendations and Reviews

The reliability of a book or article may also be determined by the source that recommended the material to you. College faculty, librarians, and others knowledgeable about your subject are dependable

FIGURE 5.2   Reviews from *Magazines for Libraries*

The Nation. 1865. w. $21. Blair Clark. Nation Co., 333 Ave. of the Americas, New York, N.Y. 10014. Illus., index, adv. Circ: 30,000. Sample. Vol. ends: June & Dec. Microform: UMI.
Indexed: PAIS, RG. *Bk. rev:* 4, 1,500 words, signed. *Aud:* Hs, Ga, Ac.

No liberal magazine in America is better known than this, other than its sometimes look-alike cousin *The New Republic.* Contributors include almost all major liberal figures from Ralph Nader and Robert Sherrill to the late Martin Luther King, Jr. The articles are concerned with foreign affairs, local and national politics, disarmament, education, law, etc. There are excellent regular reviews of books, theatre, films, and the arts. There is some advertising, but the magazine depends almost entirely upon subscriptions.

National Review; a journal of fact and opinion. 1955. bi-w. $15. William F. Buckley, Jr. William A. Rusher, 150 E. 35th St., New York, N.Y. 10016. Illus., index, adv. Circ: 110,000. Sample. Vol. ends: Dec. 31. Microform: UMI.
Indexed: RG. *Bk. rev:* 5–8, 800 words, notes, signed. *Aud:* Hs, Ga, Ac.

The intellectual voice of conservatism in America, this is the outspoken critic of most liberal or progressive ideas. In coverage and scope it is somewhat similar to *The New Republic* and *The Nation.* Here the analogy ends. First and foremost, it is the child of William Buckley, its controversial editor who has brought a degree of respectability to the conservative school. He blasts both reactionary right and progressive left with a telling wit and a style that is sometimes flippant, sometimes penetrating, but always readable. All contributors represent a depth of thought and opinion that brings out the respectable aspects of the conservative cause. It must be noted that the conservatives have yet to produce as many major journals as their liberal counterparts, but the emergence of publications such as *Conservative Digest* and *The Alternative* indicates that this lack may be remedied in the future. *National Review,* however, always will be a major voice of conservatism, and because of its intellectual approach should be in every library, from senior high school to academic. (C.W.)

sources. Bibliographies in printed sources, such as encyclopedias or books by known professionals, are usually reliable. The presence of a book or periodical in a college library may also recommend it because such material is often chosen by instructors in the field or by librarians who have studied reviews. However, some books of doubtful validity do make their way into college libraries, so double-checking may be necessary.

Book Review Digest provides excerpts from book reviews by professionals writing in about two hundred periodicals, such as *Commentary*, the *New York Review of Books*, and *Science* as well as in scholarly journals such as the *American Journal of Sociology* and *Modern Language Journal*. The reviews cited have appeared in at least two periodicals and within eighteen months of a book's publication. Although you may not find it necessary to look up a review of every book you find on your subject, you might want to research further a book that deals with a controversial subject or that is central to your paper. Figure 5.3 presents excerpts from reviews of a book on the history of neurosis from *Book Review Digest*.

If you do not find the work you are looking for in the *Book Review Digest*, you might try the *Book Review Index*, which indexes almost four hundred and fifty publications, from the *Atlantic Monthly* and the *New York Times* to scholarly journals, such as the *Journal of Asian Studies* and the *American Historical Review*. Because the *Index* functions only as a referral, you must look up the original review in the source cited. Two other helpful works that index reviews are the *Index to Book Reviews in the Humanities* and the *Index to Book Reviews in the Social Sciences*.

FIGURE 5.3   Reviews from *Book Review Digest*

Author	DRINKA, GEORGE FREDERICK. The birth of neurosis: myth, malady, and the Victorians. 431p il $21.95 1984	Title
Library of Congress call number	Simon & Schuster — 616.85 L. Psychiatry 2. Neuroses 3. Medicine—Europe ISBN 0-671-44999-0 LC 84-10563	Contains illustrations Number of pages
Classification subjects	This is a "history of the study and treatment of nervous disorders in the nineteenth century." (Atlantic) Bibliography. Index.	Library of Congress card number
Quotation from the review in the *Atlantic*	"Rousseau's noble savage was one of the myths and railway spine was one of the maladies confronting the physicians Dr. Drinka describes. Some of those early neurologists were as eccentric as their patients, but while some of their theories seem quite daft, others have been proved correct by modern researchers using instruments unavailable to the pioneers. It is a fascinating and often amusing story that Dr. Drinka has to tell, and he presents it well." — *Atlantic* 254:128 S '84. Phoebe-Lou Adams (120w)	Contains bibliography and index Reviewer Number of words
Periodical, volume, page number, and date	"This study of pre-Freudian Victorian notions about neurosis and psychopathology ranges widely, exploring the works of Charcot, Krafft-Ebing, Janet, and other major neurologists and psychiatrists. . . . This is a fascinating area that lends itself to further work; the material will therefore be of interest to a broad range of scholars. It is therefore unfortunate that the book tends to be rambling and unfocused, without a clearly developed thesis, jumping back and forth between difficult clinicians in a confusing way. Henri F. Ellenberger's The Discovery of the Unconscious [BRD 1971] is a more coherent overview of the development of modern psychiatry."	
Year of review in *Book Review Digest*	*Libr J* 109:1854 O 1 '84. Paul Hymowitz (120w)	
	Ms 18:14 O '84. Margaret McDonald (700w)	No excerpt given from this review

FIGURE 5.4   Review from *Choice*

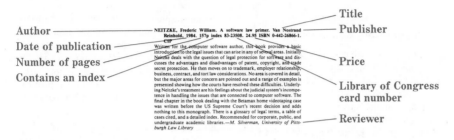

Author

Date of publication

Number of pages

Contains an index

Title

Publisher

Price

Library of Congress card number

Reviewer

Choice, an American Library Association monthly publication used by many librarians and faculty to evaluate books for academic libraries, is another good source for checking the reliability of your sources. Unlike the *Book Review Digest* or the *Book Review Index*, *Choice* contains complete, short reviews by experts, as well as bibliographic essays that discuss books written on a subject of current interest; these essays are indexed in *Library Literature*. Figure 5.4 provides an example.

Content

The most important indication of the reliability of an article or book is, of course, its content. Primary sources are usually more valuable than secondary sources. They may be either firsthand accounts (autobiographies and eyewitness reports); original research based on questionnaires, interviews, observations, personal experiences, or experiments; or poems, novels, plays, and other original creations of an author. However, secondary sources—articles, books, speeches, and so on—derived from primary sources are also important; in fact, an expert's commentary on primary sources is sometimes more valuable to a nonexpert than information gained through primary research. For a college writer, a combination of these two kinds of sources is desirable. Use the following questions to help you evaluate the content of a source.

1. If information is gathered through original research, are the problem and the search strategy or method clearly stated?

A scientific article detailing an experiment usually follows a four-part format: an introduction stating the problem and reviewing previous work on the subject, an explanation of methods and materials including how the research was conducted, a description of the results, and a discussion or conclusion analyzing those results. The methods and materials section provides the details that make evaluation possible. Figure 5.5, from an article in the *Journal of the American Medical As-*

FIGURE 5.5 Methods Section of a Scientific Article

METHODS
Laboratory Communications

Each of the laboratories in this study was contacted by a "doctor" interested in doing hair analysis on his patients. All responded with instructions for submitting specimens, and most included literature on the supposed value of the test. Additional viewpoints were gathered from articles and advertisements in chiropractic journals and health food industry trade publications.

Preparation of Hair Samples

The specimens consisted of shoulder-length hair from two apparently healthy 17-year-old girls. The hairs varied in length up to about 15 cm. One sample weighed 60 g, while the other weighed 36 g. Each was rinsed 20 times in tap water, allowed to dry, cut into 1- to 2-cm lengths, and mixed thoroughly so that hair from different locations would be selected for inclusion into each laboratory specimen. Twenty-six specimens of 0.5 to 2.0 g each were then prepared from each hair sample according to instructions from each laboratory; some were measured into envelopes, some were measured using a teaspoon, and others were prepared with a balance card supplied by the laboratory.

One sample per subject was sent to each laboratory, under an assumed name, and this process was repeated using different names about three weeks later, so that 52 reports were obtained. Each report presented mineral levels in parts per million or milligrams per 100 g, and indicated in some way whether these values were "low," "normal," or "high" compared with the laboratory's standards. Tables 2 and 3 summarize the values for each mineral. The Figure illustrates portions of the reports from five laboratories.

Statistical Analysis

The degree of concordance between matched pairs for each mineral in the four samples sent to each laboratory was assessed using Cohen's κ, a standard coefficient of agreement.[7] A κ value of 1.00 would signify perfect agreement. A value of .75 or more is usually regarded as a high level of agreement; .41 to .74, moderate agreement; and .40 or less, low agreement. The 13 laboratories scored as follows: laboratory A, .70; laboratory B, .42; laboratory C, .24; laboratory D, .40; laboratory E, .73; laboratory F, .83; laboratory G, .28; laboratory H, .83; laboratory I, −.06; laboratory J, .66; laboratory K, .78; laboratory L, .62; laboratory M, .90.

sociation, shows how such details are explained. The problem being investigated is whether commercial hair analysis is a scientific process. From the methods section, readers can judge whether the writers selected their samples carefully and evaluated their statistics fairly.

In a less scholarly publication such as *Consumer Reports* the experiments are simpler and less formal in presentation, but they contain the same information. Margaret Little used the article "Caffeine: How to Consume Less"—from which the excerpt in Figure 5.6 was taken—as well as scholarly articles in her paper on caffeine (see Chapter 13). Notice that the purpose of the study, methodology, results, and discussion of the results are all given.

2. If the information you find in a book or article is based on someone else's original research or experience, are the sources and method of

research explained well enough to validate the findings? Or are the secondary sources authoritative enough to be convincing without further explanation?

An article "Whose Brain Is It, Anyway?" by David Holzman, in the *Washington Post Magazine* (Feb. 12, 1984), shows the strengths and weaknesses of a popular source. Holzman claims that the "triune brain theory" of Paul MacLean, once "used to explain the evolution of the human brain" by such authorities as Carl Sagan, is now being questioned. The validation used by Holzman is given in part in the following sentence: "Of more than 25 brain scientists interviewed about MacLean's triune brain, only a few say they subscribe to the view and

FIGURE 5.6   Extract from *Consumer Reports*

The triangle test

Methodology —

One way to detect flavor differences is through a method called a "triangle test." Panelists are given three coded samples of a food or beverage and are asked to identify the one that's different in flavor from the other two. Our panelists were chosen from volunteers among CU's staff. They included frequent and infrequent soft-drink users, smokers and non-smokers, males and females.

On each of five test days, panelists received three soft-drink samples and were asked to identify the "odd" one by taste. All samples were identical in color, temperature, and quantity.

For the first three days, panelists received samples of *Coca-Cola* and *Pepsi Cola*. The flavor of these two leading cola drinks differs only slightly. And both contain caffeine. The purpose was to familiarize panelists with the triangle test and let them practice detecting small flavor differences. They were not told the identity of the brands nor that the tests were practice sessions. They were simply asked to pick out the odd sample.

If the panelists had *not* been able to detect a difference between *Coke* and *Pepsi*, one-third would still have been likely to pick out the odd sample by chance alone. But the percentage of correct answers each day was much higher than that. On the third day, 66 percent of the panelists were able to pick the odd sample correctly, indicating excellent ability in discrimination.

On the fourth day, the panelists tasted samples of two orange sodas, *Sunkist Orange* and *Nehi Orange*. *Sunkist* contains added caffeine, while *Nehi* is caffeine-free. However, there are also other differences in the formulas. This session was designed to give the panelists practice in tasting orange flavors, and to check their performance. This time, 48 out of 77 panelists—or 62 percent—identified the odd sample correctly.

Purpose —

The key test—to determine whether caffeine might affect flavor—came on the fifth day. Each panelist received three samples of *Nehi Orange*, but some samples had caffeine added in an amount

comparable to that in *Sunkist*. Only the presence or absence of caffeine could explain a flavor difference.

Results —

Our results showed that 34 out of 76 panelists—or 45 percent—correctly identified the odd sample. The outcome was statistically significant (the chance of getting that many correct responses by random guessing is only one in 40). However, it was well below the previous day's performance in discriminating between *Nehi* and *Sunkist*, suggesting that caffeine has only a subtle effect on the flavor of an orange soda.

Discussion —

Our tests indicate that a large panel with practice in identifying flavor differences can detect a slight flavor effect of caffeine in orange soda. Our results apply only to orange soda. We can't say what effect caffeine might have on colas or other soft-drink flavors.

A complete surprise, however, was an apparent sex-related difference in our test results with caffeine. Through the first four days of tests, there were no significant differences between male and female panelists in their ability to detect flavor differences. But a striking reversal of this pattern occurred in the triangle test for caffeine.

Only 9 out of 32 women—or 28 percent—correctly chose the odd sample of *Nehi Orange*, a result that could be expected from random guessing. Among the men, 25 out of 44—57 percent—made the right choice. The chance of that many correct choices occurring by guessing is one in 870. Accordingly, while it's highly unlikely that the men's performance was due to chance, the results suggest that women as a group could not detect the addition of caffeine to *Nehi*.

If confirmed by further research, that finding has some obvious implications for soft-drink producers. For one thing, if caffeine is added for flavoring, why include it throughout a brand line if half the population may not be able to detect its flavor? More important, if caffeine poses even an uncertain risk of birth defects, should women who may not be able to taste it be exposed to it needlessly?

all but one of these say it is accurate in only a general sense." Only two of these scientists are quoted and named. Nor does Holzman explain how the brain scientists were chosen or how representative and reliable they are. However, the audience for this article probably is interested only in the ideas discussed and does not want to read and evaluate the methodology. They are willing to trust the *Washington Post Magazine*, the author, who is identified as "a Washington science writer," and the author's logic. An article like this cannot be dismissed, but it needs corroboration by other sources if it is to be cited as evidence.

3. Is consideration given to both sides of a controversial subject? If not, can you find another source that supplies the opposing point of view?

Of course it is impossible to find completely unbiased sources. All of us have our own ways of looking at events because of our past experiences. Even the objectivity of science has recently come under criticism; for example, see Jackson Albrecht's article, "Social Context of Policy Research," in *Sociological Methods & Research* (Feb. 13, 1985) in which he speaks of "the myth of value-free science." Universities, he points out, often have their research funded by government agencies or business firms. Politics often determines what research will be funded within the government. "Researchers," he declares, "carry their values into any study they begin." What is the solution? He urges scientists to "openly [declare] their assumptions and biases, stating the research objectives of the funding agency, investigators, and audience, and describing the location, time, and context of the study." As a student, rather than a professional researcher, you may have difficulty discerning subtle influences of values, but you should be aware of the more obvious ones. It is wise, for example, to examine carefully studies by tobacco companies that describe the effects of tobacco on health. Also remember that you as a researcher and an individual have your own biases and you should recognize them.

4. Are statistics used accurately and are they interpreted fairly?

The use of statistics is like the use of other evidence in research: their collection and interpretation is subject to bias. In his book *A Primer of Statistics for Non-Statisticians*, Abraham N. Franzblau warns:

> First and foremost, the consumer [reader of statistics] should beware of statistics with a built-in bias—statistics, in other words, which aim to serve a vested interest. He should look routinely to the source of every statistic offered and carefully scrutinize the purpose for which it was compiled. He should be wary of sales inducements, clouded contexts, partial truths, and slanted findings. . . .

The consumer of statistics should also beware of large conclusions drawn from small facts. How was the sample selected? Was it large enough? . . . Are the generalizations which are made justifiable?

It's often difficult for the nonexpert to determine whether statistics are being used fairly. Many times, though, plain common sense will come to your aid. Suppose you find in your research the following "evidence": in random interviews a reporter asked five people on the street whether they think the government is handling a current crisis well. The implication in the story is that their views are representative of many other people—how many is never stated. But common sense tells you that this is not a fair sample of the beliefs of a whole country or even a small part of it. Experienced poll-takers take samples according to tested poll-taking techniques. But even they recognize that they are not likely to be completely accurate in making claims for large groups on the basis of evidence from small groups. Consequently, they allow for margins of error. The figures of a professional, experienced poll-taker should be regarded as good evidence, but no sampling is as reliable as a survey of the whole group. Frequently, you will not be able to examine the way statistics were gathered and compiled, so you will have to rely on the credibility or reputation of your source.

5. Is a single example or anecdote used as proof for a generalization about a group?

One example might be: "Cigarette smoking isn't harmful. My grandfather smoked every day and he lived to be eighty." One person's experience may be considered, but, it cannot be used alone as representative of a group. Individual experiences and examples are valuable for making generalizations understandable but not for proving them. In other words, each piece of evidence should be given appropriate weight.

Source Evaluation: Student Examples

The examples that follow demonstrate how three students evaluated their research sources.

Robert Close's Source Evaluation. For his paper "Does Dowsing Work?" (see Chapter 11), Robert Close chose a subject treated with great skepticism by scientists, so he had to check his sources carefully, especially those reporting that dowsing did work. Finding the publication dates of his sources, he observed that most of them fell within the last five years. The two *Harper's* articles in his bibliography were published in the fifties, but they presented interesting information on both sides of the subject. One author believed dowsing works, one did not. The magazine, then, was obviously neutral. The credibility of *Harper's* was further underscored when Close looked it up in *Magazines for Libraries*. This guide "highly recommended" *Harper's* and praised the "excellence" of its writers. Close trusted the articles in the *Encyclopedia Britannica* and the *Encyclopedia Americana* because of the reputation of these references.

Next Close decided to look up the reviews of two books central to his research, *The Divining Hand* by Christopher Bird, and Francis Hitching's *Dowsing: The Psi Connection*. In *Book Review Digest* he found references to two reviews of Bird's book, one in the *Library Journal* by Fred O'Bryant, and one in the *New York Times Book Review* by Doris Grumbach. He found both reviews to be favorable. O'Bryant, calling *The Divining Hand* "a fine reference," described the book as a "lengthy and detailed compendium of examples and anecdotes galore, copious illustrations, and extensive bibliography, and enough data and theory to provide nearly endless thought." Grumbach's more detailed review referred to *The Divining Hand* as "an encyclopedic work" that "is surely destined to become the sourcebook for future research on the subject."

Unlike *The Divining Hand*, Hitching's book was not listed in *Book Review Digest*, which meant that it had not been reviewed by at least two periodicals. But according to *Book Review Index, Dowsing: The Psi Connection* had been reviewed by *Library Journal*. The review called it a "fairly comprehensive book on dowsing" and suggested purchase "if you have a significant parapsychology collection."

Close decided to find out more about Hitching by looking him up in *Contemporary Authors*. According to this source, Hitching is British and is a member of the Royal Archaeological Institute; two other books by him had been published by reputable publishers, Morrow and Holt (*Dowsing* itself had a well-known publisher—Doubleday). Hitching was quoted in *Contemporary Authors* as saying, "I am more interested in what science hasn't explained than what it has."

While Close was looking in *Contemporary Authors*, he checked the background of John Wyman, author of a historical study on dowsing. Wyman was described as a history professor at the University of Wisconsin with a number of scholarly books and articles to his credit. The last writer Close checked was J. Harvey Howells, who, according to *Contemporary Authors*, was a novelist, playwright, and magazine contributor. After moving from Scotland to Maine, Howells spent seventeen years in advertising; then at the age of forty-three he began to write novels, television plays, and articles for popular magazines before publishing *Dowsing for Everyone*. His background was less scientifically and academically oriented than Close's other sources, but the content of his book revealed sound research.

Although Close thought the professional credentials of his authors were good indicators of their reliability, he knew that he did not have scientific evidence to prove that dowsing worked; his writers were primarily literary researchers rather than scientists. Yet there was enough evidence provided by a few scientists, many other nonscientific observers, and personal experience that he couldn't dismiss dowsing as patently untrue. He decided to present his research, showing that proof had not yet been provided by either side.

Jean Carroll's Source Evaluation. In her paper on agoraphobia (Chapter 12)—the abnormal fear of open spaces—Jean Carroll recognized that she had to rely on the credibility of her professional sources because she did not have the expertise to evaluate the validity of the subject matter. The articles in the journals were written by professionals, and she was satisfied that they were reliable. To find out more about the authors, she looked in the *Social Sciences Citation Index*. All the authors were cited in at least six articles. Two, D. W. Goodwin and J. Wolpe, were cited more than thirty times. The only popular source she used was the *Washington Post*, which she knew to be a reputable newspaper, a view that was confirmed in *Magazines for Libraries*. In addition, the information in the *Post* was based on an interview with an agoraphobic, the kind of information that a newspaper handles especially well.

Margaret Little's Source Evaluation. Margaret Little's paper (Chapter 13) required a somewhat different type of validation. It relied to a great extent on statistics concerning the amount of caffeine in various foods and drinks and on observations of people who had used caffeine. Little had to be sure that the tests and experiments carried out with caffeine were carefully conducted. Her statistics were primarily found in three groups of sources: professional journals in psychology, health, and medicine; publications of government and professional organizations, such as the Federation of American Societies for Experimental Biology and the U.S. Department of Health and Human Services; and articles from newspapers and magazines, such as *Consumer Reports*, which had conducted its own tests and explained them in detail and was rated highly by *Magazines for Libraries*. The newspaper she had used—the *New York Times*—was generally well regarded and was rated high in reliability by *Magazines for Libraries*. The first two groups were established professional sources.

Reading

Finding information is a little like searching for gold. First you have to search to find out where the likely places are—you can't dig everywhere—and then you have to dig carefully and thoroughly. When you have finally located sources of information, you need to read efficiently. You can save time by scanning the whole article or book to see whether it is worth reading at all and, if it is, by deciding which parts you want to scan and which you want to read closely. Then you must read carefully the material that you have decided is important and record the relevant material in your notes.

Scanning a Book

To scan a book, look first at the title and subtitle. Of course you have already written down the title, but you may not have noticed the subtitle, which is often more descriptive of the contents. *Wishes, Lies, and Dreams* by Kenneth Koch is a rhythmic and evocative title, but it does not indicate what the book is about as clearly as the subtitle—*Teaching Children to Write Poetry*. Record both on your bibliography card. Next read the table of contents to discover the scope of the book and to see whether any chapters or parts of chapters deal with your subject. If you are doing a report on the capacity of the human brain, you might look at Carl Sagan's *The Dragons of Eden: Speculations on the Evolution of Human Intelligence*. The table of contents contains two chapter titles referring to the brain:

I
The Cosmic Calendar · 11

II
Genes and Brains · 19

Consulting the index to a book is another quick, useful way of determining contents. In Sagan's book, index entries on the brain include:

Brain
density of information content, 45–46
differences between the sexes and among the races, 34–36
human, possible improvements in, 199–204
information content of, 26, 41–47
mass in humans, 33–36
microcircuits, 42, 43
third ventricle of, 63, 64

The table of contents gives you a general idea of what is in a book; the index gives specific citations or references. Be sure to make a note on your bibliography card of the chapter or page numbers that contain useful information. You may want to come back and read them later.

If the book seems to discuss relevant material, read the preface or introduction (some books have both). The preface usually explains the author's reason for writing the book and perhaps its organization or focus. Carl Sagan's preface gives the hypothesis on which his book is based: his belief "that man is descended from some lowly-organized form." The introduction may not be labeled as such; it may be just a part of the first chapter. The introduction prepares readers for the substance of the book by telling them what they need to know in order to understand the book's contents. In Sagan's introduction, preceding the first chapter, he defines his audience ("the interested layman"), states his fundamental premise (that the workings of the brain "are a consequence of its anatomy and physiology, and nothing more"), and explains that he will outline the evolution of human intelligence. After reading such an introduction, you would be able to decide whether you wanted to continue.

In some cases, you might also want to glance at the conclusion, especially if you plan to read a substantial part of the book. Like the introduction, the conclusion may not be labeled; it may be just the last part of the book. In *The Dragons of Eden*, the last chapter, Knowledge is Our Destiny, sums up the author's beliefs, forecasts the discovery of extraterrestrial intelligence, and suggests how the brains of extraterrestrial beings might be constructed.

Finally, if the book has a bibliography note this fact on your bibliography card. Then check the bibliography to see if any of the sources listed seem relevant to your research. If you find any, record them on separate bibliography cards so that you can look at them later.

Scanning an Article

To scan an article, note first the biographical facts about the author, often given at the beginning or sometimes at the end; these facts will help you further evaluate the article. Then read the first paragraph or first page, which usually states the scope and argument or thesis of the article. Finally, you may want to glance at the last paragraph, which usually states the results or conclusions reached. Scanning these elements will give you a kind of map to follow, making it easier to understand the article if you decide to read it closely.

Suppose you are writing a paper on early women poets and you locate an article by Elizabeth A. Nist in *College English*. The first page is reproduced in Figure 5.7.

First, at the bottom note the author's credentials; her professional position and publications are given. The first paragraph of the article

FIGURE 5.7   Scanning an Article: The First Page

"Men might consider that women were not created to be their slaves or vassals, for as they had not their origin out of his head, (thereby to command him), so it was not out of his foot to be trod upon, but in a (medium) out of his side to be his fellow-feeler, his equal and companion."

When and by whom was this written? It sounds like some turn of the century suffragist, or, with a little more contemporary diction and syntax, it could be a Bible-belt feminist during the ERA campaign of the 1970s. Probably it goes as far back as some pioneer woman in Nebraska or Utah in the 1870s, but, at the very least, surely it was written after 1700, because even Virginia Woolf admits that "nothing is known about women before the eighteenth century and certainly no woman wrote a word of that extraordinary Elizabethan literature when every other man, it seemed, was capable of song or sonnet." The contents of all our anthologies of British literature suport Virginia Woolf's surmises.

But our opening quote did not come from the "modern" women's movement. It was published in 1640 in London in *The Women's Sharpe Revenge . . . Performed by Mary Tattle-well and Ione Hit-him-home, Spinsters*. A little digging shows these pseudonymous co-authors were not alone in their opinions or their talent for forcefully expressing them.

Women wrote and wrote well during the Elizabethan period. A surprising number of manuscripts have been preserved, but they are not readily available to readers and scholars. Most are held in the British Library, private collections, or university rare book collections and can generally be read only on microfilm. Even though a few good anthologies of women's literature have been published in the past ten years,[1] most professors and teachers of literature remain unaware of these works.

---

1. Three recent anthologies of early women writers are particularly outstanding: Ann Stanford, ed., *The Women Poets in English* (New York: McGraw-Hill, 1972); Mary R. Mahl and Helene Koon, eds., *The Female Spectator: English Women Writers Before 1800* (Bloomington: Indiana University Press and Old Westbury, N.Y.: The Feminist Press, 1977); and Fidelis Morgan, ed., *The Female Wits: Women Playwrights of the Restoration* (London: Virago Press, 1981).

Elizabeth A. Nist teaches at Utah Technical College. She has published essays, stories, and poems in many journals, and a book of her poems, *Now Is My Springtime,* was published in 1974.

College English, Volume 46, Number 7, November 1984

---

is a quotation that can be skimmed quite quickly by reading the first line and glancing over the rest, just for a general understanding. The main point comes in the fourth paragraph—particularly in the first sentence. Here the author tells about the good poetry women wrote in the sixteenth century. Finally, a footnote supplies you with a short bibliography of anthologies of early women writers. If these interest you, enter them on your bibliography cards.

Turning to the end of the article, you notice four concluding paragraphs (Figure 5.8). The first sentence of this group of paragraphs is almost the same as the thesis statement at the beginning: "Women wrote and wrote well during the Elizabethan period." The second paragraph is a summary of the article, the third paragraph comments on the importance of these women, and the last paragraph makes an appeal for equality of women. After reading the introduction and conclusion of this article, you have a good idea of what it is about and what

FIGURE 5.8   Scanning an Article: Concluding Paragraphs

It is obvious that Elizabethan women did write, and they wrote well. This essay presents only eleven of the more than fifty women whose work is known. Yet even from these few examples we get a glimpse of the variety and importance of their writings.

They have given us some wonderful lyric poetry that celebrates not only their joys but, even more significantly, expresses their sorrows and their pain. In their prose we not only have firsthand accounts of life at that time, but realistic and practical accounts. We also have the first attempts to create real-life characters and dialogue in English, along with realistic subplots. In drama we have the first play by a women in English, attracting the attention and respect of the other writers of her time.

These writers speak for themselves. Surely a true picture of our cultural heritage cannot be constructed without their contributions, but, despite the fact that all of these works were published in the sixteenth and seventeenth centuries (many in repeated and popular editions), they are virtually unknown by modern scholars.

That no women wrote before 1800 is a myth, and until women like Margaret More Roper, Mary Sidney Herbert, Elizabeth Cary, and Mary Sidney Wroth stand alongside their husbands, brothers, and uncles, the myth will continue. As Mary Tattle-well said, "Men might consider that women were not created to be their slaves or vassals . . . but out of [their] sides to be [their] fellow-feelers, their equals and companions."

the author's point of view is. If you wish, you can read the rest of the article later.

In scanning, you save time by not reading everything—instead, you read fast to find out where to read slowly and carefully. Try not to be distracted by interesting but irrelevant material unless you are in the early stages of your search and have time to change direction. In addition, do not waste time by reading sources that merely repeat factual information you already have. Of course, you may want to read several accounts of an important or controversial event, such as the assassination of John F. Kennedy, for a variety of viewpoints, but if you are looking for general information on, for example, the Battle of Bunker Hill, an encyclopedia article will give you the necessary facts that other sources would merely duplicate.

Close Reading

Close reading means reading each word and sentence to learn the author's exact meaning. The following suggestions will help you to read efficiently as well as thoroughly.

Reading with a Purpose.   When you locate a chapter, a book, or an article that you want to read completely, read with a clear sense of what you want to find out. To sharpen this sense of purpose, read with certain questions in mind derived from rephrasing parts of your outline: Does dowsing work? If so, how does it work? What is it primarily used for? You might look for the answer to one question in one article or book and the answer to another question somewhere else. Of course, at the same time be ready to encounter and absorb information that you were not able to anticipate with your questions. Reading for a paper on nutrition, Jeffrey Smerko began to encounter warnings about advertisers' misrepresentations on health food products, so he decided to add a section in his paper on this subject.

Entering the Mind of the Writer.   Withhold judgment until you have enough evidence. When you are reading an article on one side of a question, try to follow the thoughts of the writer in order to understand how conclusions were reached. If you make up your mind too soon on a controversial subject, you may overlook important information.

Reading for Main Ideas.   With the main idea or purpose of the author in mind, try to associate each paragraph and sentence with this main idea. If you seem to be getting off the track—if an idea does not seem to fit—stop and figure out whether you or the writer is at fault.

Defining Technical Terms.   Do not look up a word that you can figure out by the context unless you have plenty of time. Your goal is to keep your concentration intact.

Paraphrasing.   This is the test that determines whether you have understood the writer, whether you have made the writer's thoughts part of your own thinking and expanded your own knowledge not only factually but also conceptually. Failure to achieve this understanding usually results in one of the following problems. First, much of what is termed plagiarism (copying another's words and ideas) results not so much from design as from failure to comprehend the original. What you don't understand you can't put into your own words and so the alternative is to use the words of the original writer simply because there are no other words available. Then when the source is not acknowledged, plagiarism results. Second, if you use quotations too frequently, your paper becomes a patchwork of other people's words, and the writer's voice—your voice—is not heard.

Taking Notes

Good notes are the bridge between reading and writing; they make it possible for you to retain all of the material you read. But they have a further advantage: with good notes, not only will you have easy access to what you've read, but you will also have begun the writing process.

Photocopying is not a substitute for the mental activity that occurs when you take notes. Although it is a convenient device for taking restricted material out of the library so that you can read it later, photocopying really adds an extra step to the process because you will eventually need to take notes from the photocopies. If you attempt the short cut of writing your paper directly from books or photocopied articles, it will be harder for you to write a good paper. The temptation to use the words of the original may eliminate the step of making the ideas part of your own thinking.

Good notes also tell you where you found your information so that documenting your sources later on will be easier. Because taking notes is time-consuming and sometimes laborious, it is tempting to think that you will be able to recall the necessary bibliographic information when you need to assemble and record your sources. Try to resist this temptation. You will collect so much information that you will have trouble remembering it all, and it is unlikely that you will always remember the sources. Here are some general suggestions for taking notes using note cards or paper (if you use a computer, these suggestions will, of course, not apply):

Put an abbreviated form of the source name at the top of each card, on the left or right side. When you have finished taking your notes, stack all cards from the same source together.

Put a heading from your working outline (see Chapter 3) at the top of each card opposite the source. Before you start to write, group all cards with the same outline heading.

Put the page number of the source somewhere on your card, either in the corner by the source name or at the bottom of the card. If you take notes from more than one successive page, be sure to mark the page break in your notes, so you will be able to identify the exact page in your citation.

Use only one side of each card. Because you will write from your cards, you might find it helpful to spread them out and study their contents without turning them over. If a single note covers more than one side of a card, use another card, numbering the cards consecutively in the heading.

Put only information that belongs in the same part of your outline on the same card, even if that means you will write only one or two lines on a card. If your subject, for instance, is the use of solar power for home heating and your source includes information on both design and cost, put the data on different cards so that you can later sort them by subject.

Write with pen, or type (pencil is hard to read and smudges when the cards rub together).

Figure 5.9 illustrates headings for note cards.

FIGURE 5.9   Note Card Headings

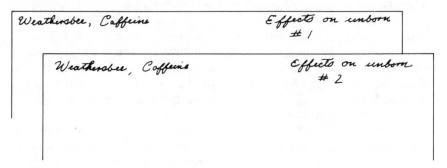

Recording Your Information

Notetaking and close reading are interrelated. You need to read carefully, of course, in order to take notes; at the same time, note taking is a significant aid to reading with comprehension and retention. It isn't easy, especially at the beginning of your search when you are still defining your topic, to decide what is relevant to record on note cards. Instead of being too concerned about what to record, remember the researcher's safety policy: when in doubt, choose abundance and plan to write down much more than it seems you need.

There are three main forms of recording information: paraphrasing, summarizing, and quoting. At first you will probably find yourself quoting quite a bit simply because you are not as familiar with your subject as you will be later. However, you will still save time by summarizing and paraphrasing as much as you can because these represent conversions of someone else's ideas into your own—a step closer to writing your paper. In addition to recording information on your cards, add comments and questions of your own, either on the same card or separately. These comments will also help you integrate your information and make it part of your own thinking. Be sure, though, that you differentiate between what is taken from your sources and what is your own thinking. One way to do this is by putting brackets around your own words or thoughts.

Paraphrase

Paraphase is a kind of translation. If you can paraphrase something, you know you understand it. When you paraphrase, you put the message that appears in someone else's language into your own but always be sure to credit the actual author in your notes and paper. Paraphrase when you need the details of the original but don't want to use the same words—you want to use your own words so that your paper conveys the sound of your own writing style. Margaret Little, in her paper on caffeine (see Chapter 13), found this sentence in one of her sources: "Stone Age people are believed to have discovered the principal caffeine-containing plants and to have made beverages from them." She wrote the paraphrase, as illustrated in Figure 5.10, on her note card. In her paper this note became part of the first sentence:

> Since Stone Age people discovered plants containing caffeine and made a beverage from them, caffeine has been used as a stimulant (1).

You might also want to paraphrase when your source is technical or scientific and you know that your audience is unfamiliar with that kind of language. Little's audience was her college writing class, and most of them were not science majors. In an article in *Medicine and Science in Sports*, she found the following passage:

> Since muscle glycogen depletion is considered responsible, in part, for exhaustion during prolonged exercise, slowing the rate of glycogen utilization should improve endurance performance (5,8,12). It has previously been established that the elevation of plasma FFA [free fatty acids] results in an increased rate of lipid metabolism and a diminished depen-

FIGURE 5.10   Paraphrasing: A Sample Note Card

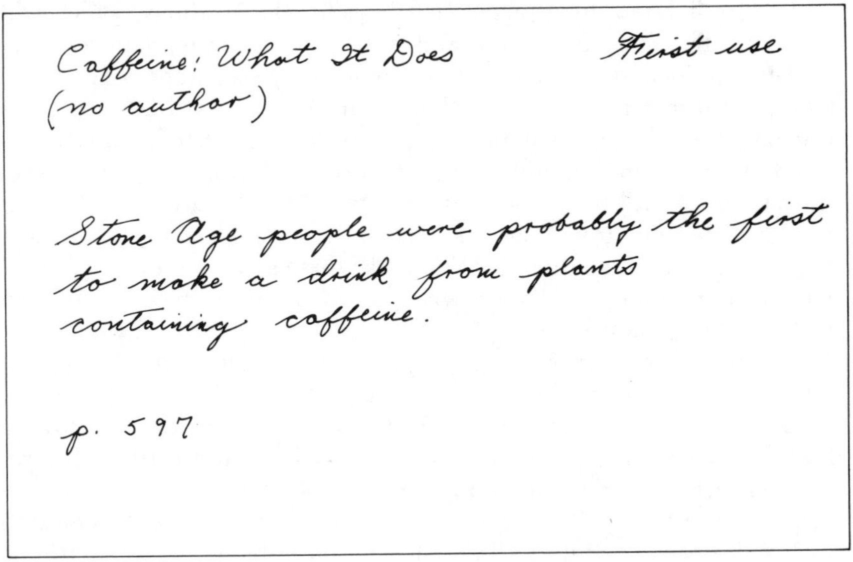

Caffeine: What It Does   First use
(no author)

Stone Age people were probably the first
to make a drink from plants
containing caffeine.

p. 597

dence on muscle glycogen in exercising skeletal muscle (5,9,14). In the present study, as in previous investigations, the ingestion of caffeine resulted in a 50 to 100% increase in plasma FFA (1,7,14).

On her note card, Little wrote this paraphrase:

During exercise tests, the ingestion of caffeine raised the levels of fatty acids in the blood. Since high levels of fatty acids have been shown to slow the rate of carbohydrate depletion, which in turn leads to exhaustion, caffeine seems to help athletes' endurance.

In her paper, this information was reduced to a phrase in the section on the benefits of caffeine:

In addition caffeine has been found to enhance the speed and accuracy of physical tasks such as typing (4) and to increase endurance during exercise by reducing carbohydrate oxidation and increasing fat metabolism (22).

Summary

Summarizing takes more concentration than other forms of note taking because you must reduce a long passage (a paragraph, page, or several pages) to a sentence or a few sentences. It requires the ability to generalize—to extract the main ideas from a passage along with any significant details. You can see the difficulty in generalizing when you ask a child to explain the movie she has just seen. She will recount one detail after another without generalizing to show how all the details are related.

To summarize a long piece, first look for the headings, which will announce the topics discussed, and then try to find the main sentence or the main idea in each paragraph. In newspapers and popular magazines, paragraphs are so short that often they are not built around a central idea or main sentence. You may have to read several paragraphs to detect the general thought that ties them together. The rest of the paragraph will usually consist of details or elaborations of the central idea. Pick out any of these details that you want to mention in your paper. Take a moment to reflect, to make these ideas and details part of your own thinking, and then write down a summary in your own words of what you have read.

If your article or book is photocopied, you can aid your reading and note taking by underlining or highlighting the main points as you read. Figure 5.11 presents an excerpt from the article "Caffeine: How to Consume Less" in *Consumer Reports*, cited by Margaret Little in her report on caffeine (see Chapter 13). Because of the heading, A Few Surprises, Little looked for the surprises—the unexpected data. Working with a photocopy, she underlined the general statements about caffeine

FIGURE 5.11 Underlining Sample

A few surprises

You expect to find caffeine in colas, and food-science literature suggests that top sellers such as *Coca-Cola* and *Pepsi Cola* will score high in caffeine. They didn't. Their caffeine content was near the lower end of the range for caffeinated soft drinks.

Even more surprising, though, were some of our test results with the non-colas. Among the brands highest in caffeine were three citrus-flavored beverages—*Mountain Dew, Mello Yellow,* and *Sunkist Orange.* Their caffeine content was close to that of a cup of instant coffee. *Diet Sunkist,* on the other hand, turned out to be caffeine-free.

Only two colas—one sugar-free brand and one regular cola—contained no added caffeine. The Royal Crown Company last year began marketing *RC-100,* which is promoted as "100 percent sugar-free, 100 percent caffeine-free." And *Cragmont Cola,* Safeway's house brand, had virtually no detectable caffeine; it's made with decaffeinated kola-nut extract. Among the 10 leading soft-drink brands in sales, only two, *7-Up* and *Sprite,* contained no caffeine.

Why is caffeine added to so many soft drinks in the first place? The answer seems to depend on whom you ask.

Several representatives of soft-drink firms told CU that caffeine was added as a flavoring agent or flavor enhancer. "What it does is suppress the syrupy-sweet after-taste," said an official of the Sunkist Soft Drink Co., which makes *Sunkist Orange.* "The bitter note that caffeine provides cuts the sweetness, and gives you a more rounded flavor."

But the "Food Chemicals Codex," a compendium of official industry information about food additives, does not mention any flavor function of caffeine. It says that caffeine is used for "central stimulation in cola-type beverages." Critics of the industry tend to dismiss the flavor role. They say caffeine is added to soda for its stimulant effect, to give people—and product sales—a lift. And, of course, the history of soft-drink promotion is replete with references to the "refreshing lift" or "zing" or "life" one is supposed to get from imbibing.

content in soft drinks and some of the details that she thought she could use in her report.

Figure 5.12 illustrates how Little summarized the material on her note card. Most of the summary was used in Little's paper; the following passage combines information from this and other note cards:

> Although people expect to find caffeine in their cola drinks, it may be surprising that three drinks without ''cola'' in their names—Mountain Dew, Mello Yellow, and Sunkist Orange—contain more caffeine than many so-called colas. On the other hand, two colas—RC-100 and Cragmont—do not have any (6).

You can see that you do not need to use everything you write down; you can combine the material you read into a new piece of writing that is yours. Having a comfortable cushion of extra background material as a basis for your own words will help make your paper distinctively yours.

FIGURE 5.12   Summarizing: A Sample Note Card

> Caffeine: How to . . .   Caffeine in soft drinks
> (no author)
>
> Coke and Pepsi contain less caffeine than
> most other caffeinated drinks (surprise!),
> and RC-100 and Cragmont Cola don't
> contain any. Of the 10 soft-drink sellers, only
> two — 7-Up and Sprite — have no caffeine.
> So why do companies add caffeine? To
> improve the flavor, they say. But "critics
> of the industry" say it's added as a
> stimulant. (Of course, that means to improve
> sales.)
>
> p. 597

Quotation

When you quote, you are using the exact words of someone else. However, because one of your purposes in writing a paper is to tell something in your own words, it doesn't make sense to overuse the words of other people. (You don't want to have to title your paper, "A Collection of Quotations on the Use of Solar Energy.") Therefore, use quotations only when the exact wording is significant or necessary (see Chapter 8 for further suggestions on using and punctuating quotations). On the following occasions, a quotation is the best choice: (1) when you need to say exactly what was said in the original, (2) when the language of the original is metaphorical or highly individualistic; or (3) when the person quoted is an authority on the subject. Sometimes all three conditions apply.

Verbal precision is often important in technical subjects, such as law or medicine. Margaret Little, taking notes on an article by Dr. E. R. Lutz on the effects of caffeine on the human body, quoted some of his words in order to provide a precise medical description of the symptoms (see Figure 5.13).

Highly individualistic or metaphorical language cannot usually be paraphrased adequately, as in Yogi Berra's statement, "It ain't over till it's over." Language that has great emotional appeal or is associated

FIGURE 5.13   Quoting: A Sample Note Card

Lutz, Restless Legs   Effects of caffeine

Five percent of coffee drinkers have "restless legs syndrome," a type of muscle spasm. The symptoms are "unpleasant, creeping sensations in the lower legs between the knee and ankle" and restlessness in the arms and shoulders. Symptoms result from sedentary pastimes, but victims feel the most discomfort in the evenings and at night.

p. 693

with grand historical moments is also often quoted: "Give me liberty or give me death" (Patrick Henry) or Martin Luther King, Jr.'s, "I have a dream" speech. Poetry or highly metaphorical prose is difficult to paraphrase or summarize. In the following passage from *Moby Dick* by Herman Melville, the metaphors and poetic sounds of the words make it impossible to separate the words from the meaning.

> It was a clear steel-blue day. The firmaments of air and sea were hardly separable in that all-pervading azure; only, the pensive air was transparently pure and soft, with a woman's look, and the robust and man-like sea heaved with long, strong, lingering swells, as Samson's chest in his sleep.

The interest of a quotation may lie in the fact that it was spoken by an authority on the subject or by a well-known person, such as the president of the United States. "A man paints with his brain and not with his hands" is an interesting observation, but it has more significance when the reader knows that it was said by Michelangelo.

An authority may be someone with firsthand experience. Jean Carroll wrote down the exact words of a person who had had a phobic attack (see her paper "The Causes and Treatment of Agoraphobia," Chapter 12). Figure 5.14 shows part of what Carroll recorded in her notes.

FIGURE 5.14   Quoting: A Sample Note Card

Mansfield, Wash. *Post*   Interview

Mansfield interviewed Marjorie Goff, 64 yrs old, who described her first attack one Saturday in 1946 in a beauty shop where she regularly had her hair done. "I was sitting under the dryer, and all of a sudden this feeling swept over me. I'm losing my mind, I thought. I'm going crazy. My heart started beating fast. My legs felt weak. My body trembled. It was the most incredible feeling of fear. I wanted to scream, to run out of there. I got up with all the pins in my hair, slapped a five-dollar bill on the counter, and ran all the way home."

p. 91.

Personal Comments

As you consult your sources, you are consciously or unconsciously making connections between what you have read before and what you are reading now. You are analyzing, making judgments, and asking questions. While these thoughts are fresh in your mind and you still remember clearly the readings on which they are based, write them down to use when you are composing your paper. Of course, you might write down brief comments as you record information from your sources, but there may be times when you want to make more lengthy or general observations on your work. Putting these comments on note cards will enable you to order them along with your other cards. As she was reading sources for her paper on agoraphobia (see Chapter 12), Jean Carroll recorded her thoughts, indicating by brackets that they were her own (see Figure 5.15).

Another kind of personal card is a description or evaluation of a source. Instead of summarizing content, you describe what an article or book contains and then perhaps evaluate it. Such an account is called a *descriptive abstract*. Suppose you find a book early in your search and you aren't sure whether you want to use it. Write a descriptive abstract of the book and file it with your note cards for later reference.

Figure 5.16 presents a descriptive abstract of a book titled *Biofeedback: How to Control Your Body, Improve Your Health and Increase Your Effec-*

FIGURE 5.15   Personal Observation: A Sample Note Card

Cause of agoraphobia   Mar. 12

[I haven't been able to find any cause
yet for agoraphobia. Or, rather, there
seem to be many theories about the cause.
Which is right? If they can't find the
cause, can they find a cure? I'm
beginning to realize that this is a
very complicated illness.]

FIGURE 5.16   Descriptive Abstract: A Sample Note Card

Stern and Ray   Descr. abstract
EF 319.5
B5 S73

S. & R. define biofeedback, describe procedures used, and
then explain how it can be used to treat problems and
illnesses such as high blood pressure, asthma, epilepsy,
and headaches. Authors are psychologists who seem to
have done a lot of research. Info. is in easy-to-read
language. Their reference notes gave several good
sources; I've added these to my bibliog. I'll explore
these first because they are primary sources and I
think they'll go into more detail than S. and R.
Good glossary; I may use if I run into trouble
with vocabulary in some of the more tech.
sources. May come back to this for gen.
overview.

tiveness, by Robert M. Stern and William J. Ray. After reading the
preface and the table of contents, and after scanning the first chapter,
"What Is Biofeedback?" and the reference pages, you might record
your comments on a card for future reference.

As you take notes, write quotations in complete sentences or weave the pertinent lines in with your own words. Make sure, though, to quote your source accurately, including all marks of punctuation (see Chapter 8 for details). If you omit any words, use the marks of ellipsis (. . .). If the ellipsis marks fall at the end of a sentence, you need the three dots of ellipsis plus a period. Any addition of your own within a quotation, such as a comment or mark of punctuation added for clarity, should be enclosed in brackets.

Avoiding Plagiarism

If you take notes carefully and record your sources accurately, you will be able to document your sources when you write your paper. You must give others credit when you use their words or when you paraphrase or summarize their original ideas. Failure to do so is called *plagiarism*, which means literary theft, and may lead to a legal suit if the plagiarized material is published uncredited. In college, plagiarism is also unacceptable. The best way to avoid plagiarism is by converting the ideas of your source into your own words—as summary or paraphrase—as you take notes or, if you quote directly, by making sure that you use quotation marks. Whenever you write down any information from a source, be sure to note where you found it so that you can cite that source in your paper. If someone else's words are on your note cards without identification, you may end up with the same words in your paper, which is unarguably plagiarism. You may also slip into plagiarism by failing to take notes at all and instead trying to write your paper directly from photocopied material or from books. Without the intermediate stage of putting the information into your own words on cards, it is easy to use the words of the original source without realizing it.

But, you might ask, do I have to document every bit of information I put into my paper? Must I have a footnote for every sentence? Because a good bit of what you write will be yours and some of it will be general knowledge, you will not need to document every sentence in your paper, but you must, as a careful researcher, record your sources on your note cards so that you will know to whom to give credit. Suggestions for documenting your paper will be given in Chapter 8.

The preceding sections on paraphrasing and summarizing show how to take notes that do not plagiarize. You will not get into trouble if you make the information part of your own thinking and then put it down in your own words. Trouble arises when you take notes mechanically, without actually understanding what you are writing. Plagiarism usually appears in one of the following three forms:

1. Word-for-word transcription of the entire passage.
2. A paraphrase using the basic sentence structure of the source with a few of the words or phrases of the note taker substituted for those of the source.
3. A paraphrase using the note taker's sentence structure and many of his or her words but with key words of the author used without quotation marks.

Here are some examples of note taking illustrating the last two of these types of plagiarism. The notes are based on this passage from *The Greek Experience*, by C. M. Bowra.

> The essence of the heroic outlook is the pursuit of honour through action. The great man is he who, being endowed with superior qualities of body and mind, uses them to the utmost and wins the applause of his fellows because he spares no effort and shirks no risk in his desire to make the most of the gifts and to surpass other men in his exercise of them.

In the following paraphrase, the writer keeps the basic structure of the original and merely changes a few of the words. This is plagiarism.

> The main idea in the heroic outlook is striving to achieve honor by being active. The great man, having the highest qualities of body and mind, uses them to the greatest extent and is applauded by his comrades because he will pay any price in his desire to make the best of his gifts and to do better than other men in his use of them.

The following note uses the note taker's sentence structure, but borrows key words and phrases without quotation marks. This also is plagiarism.

> The Greeks believed that the hero had superior qualities of body and mind. In his desire to make the most of his gifts the great man would spare no effort in his desire to use his gifts in surpassing other men.

An acceptable paraphrase would be as follows:

> Heroism to the Greeks meant the demonstration of superiority through great deeds. The Greeks believed that the hero was a man who was superior to other men and who was willing to use his great qualities even if he risked his life doing so. He deserves the praise he gets from his fellowmen.

Or a combination of paraphrase and quotation may be used:

> The Greeks' idea of heroism was "the pursuit of honour through action." The hero has "superior qualities of body and mind" and he will take any risk in order to demonstrate his heroism to his fellowmen.

These paraphrases can now be integrated into a paper with no danger of plagiarism. Of course, the source must be cited; instead of using a footnote, the writer might give the author's name in the text as part of the introduction to the passage. Notice that single words do not have to be put between quotation marks unless they show an original or distinctive use by the source; the word *superior* as used in the first acceptable paraphrase does not indicate a special use of the word and so no quotation marks are necessary. Notice also that quoted material must be given exactly as it is in the original; in the second example the writer uses the British spelling of *honor*.

EXERCISES

1. Photocopy a short article or part of a long article from an encyclopedia or periodical on a subject related to your topic. On note cards, summarize the material on the photocopy in a short paragraph and paraphrase some of it. Intersperse a few words from the original if you wish (being careful to use quotation marks), but the notes should be primarily in your own words. In class exchange your notes and photocopy with another class member; then write a comment to the person whose paper you have, answering the following questions: (a) Are the summary and paraphrase accurate? (b) Do they avoid plagiarism?
2. Record the following in your search log:

   The most interesting bit of information you have learned about your subject so far.
   The most frustrating experience you have had so far in your research.
   The most enjoyable part of your research process until now.
   Exchange your observations with your classmates.

3. Write an evaluation of at least three of your sources, including both a book and an article, if possible. Explain in detail how you arrived at your evaluation and the sources that guided you.
4. In your search log, write a summary of the progress you have made in recording and evaluating your sources.

CHAPTER 6

Gathering Information from Other Sources

Although we often think of research as something that we do only in libraries, we do most of our research outside them. We can't limit our search—whether it's going to the moon, exploring caves, finding out about our own city, or just studying our own family tree—to books. We want to know. We may find diaries, letters, or personal papers that no one else has yet seen, or we may discover information too recent to be in print. We are limited only by our inability to see what is there for us to discover and to figure out how to find it.

You can collect information outside the library by

- interviewing
- designing and administering questionnaires
- recording oral history
- reading diaries, letters, and personal papers
- examining court and other government records
- observing, exploring, and experimenting

Interviewing

The holdings of a library record the experiences and thoughts of people as they have been collected in the past. In interviews you discover people's current thoughts, ideas, and attitudes. You can interview authorities—those who, like college professors, have been purposeful collectors of information—or talk to people about their own beliefs and experiences.

Although there are several kinds of interviews—the employment interview, the doctor-patient interview, the counseling interview, the journalistic interview, and others—you will be conducting the informational or research interview.

Personal Interviews

Personal interviews are usually more productive than telephone interviews or personal letters. Everyone has special information of some kind, and most people enjoy sharing it with others. When you're thinking about people to interview, look first in your home or college community, then widen your net.

Finding People to Interview.   First talk to people in your neighborhood or school. To locate instructors in your subject, consult the college directory, which will tell you the department they are affiliated with. If you want to know about running a business, talk to the small restaurant owner or store owner in your neighborhood. Are you writing a paper about the influence of foreign cars on the American market? Ask the local car dealer for his or her point of view. What does your uncle remember about World War II? What was it like for women when they couldn't vote? The elderly woman who lives down the street or in the nursing home may be able to tell you.

Use the telephone to inquire in your community. The phone book contains names of people and organizations who can help you. Most communities have a chamber of commerce, an association of business people and merchants that exists to promote the business interests of a community; chambers of commerce usually publish a membership directory, another useful information source. In the yellow pages, look up "Social Service Organizations" to find phone numbers for groups like the Mental Health Association and the American Heart Association; organizations of ethnic groups, such as the Spanish Community Association, the Polish American Congress, Inc., or the Chinese Culture Services Center; political lobbying and information groups, such as the Consumer Product Safety Commission, Common Cause, or National Organization for Women; nonpartisan political information groups, like the League of Women Voters; and educational groups, such as the American Association of University Professors or American Association of University Women. For a partisan point of view, call the local office of your congressional representative or senator and, of course, your local Democratic or Republican party organizations (you can call or write the national headquarters too). For national organizations that might be located in your area, consult the *Encyclopedia of Associations* in the reference room of the library; this source organizes associations alphabetically and geographically and includes social service, educational, hobby, government, scientific, cultural, and many other kinds of groups, both national and international. Whatever your interest, there is likely to be an organization of like-minded people.

Your phone book also has a special section that provides city and county government numbers. See the listings in areas such as environmental management, citizens' information, alcohol and drug programs, community affairs, status of women committees, consumer affairs, and recreation. You might find people at your local newspaper office or radio station, public school system, or police department who would be glad to talk to you. If you are interested in business or management, don't forget that your college or university is also a business, with managers, public relations officials, and others who may be willing to talk to you.

The thought of picking up the phone and calling someone you don't know may be intimidating, but remember that an interview can result in a valuable experience. Stuart Levin, for instance, called a local radio station, explained that he wanted to learn about the career possibilities in broadcasting, and was invited to talk to one of the managers. After a helpful discussion, he was given a tour of the station and invited to sit in on his favorite disk jockey's program.

Making the Appointment.   When you reach the person you want to talk to, state your name, the purpose of your call, and the specific information you are seeking: "My name is Steve Gorbush, and I'm a student at Valley State. I'm writing a paper on the New York Stock Exchange, and I wonder if you would have time to answer a few of my questions about it." In arranging a time for meeting, be sure to mention the times you will not be able to meet because of classes or other obligations, and then ask the person to set a time convenient for him or her. Indicate how long you need to talk (a half-hour is generally sufficient for such an interview) so that your interviewee knows how much time to allow. Be sure to find out the exact location of the interview and any directions that you may need for getting there—you want to arrive on time.

Preparing for the Interview.   A good interview requires good preparation. First, clearly define your purpose. What do you want to find out and how do you want to use this information? Review your working outline to see what you need to find out from the person you interview. And do some reading on your subject first—you will better understand the information given to you if you can put it in a context, and you won't waste time asking questions that you can just as well find the answers to in a book or article.

Then write out a list of questions whose answers will serve your purpose. Concentrate on the kinds of questions that can best be answered in an interview, such as questions on current topics like computer security or U.S. policy in the Middle East if that's the person's area of expertise, or questions that can be answered from the interviewee's experience, such as the amount of capital needed to start a small business. Or instead of writing down questions, you may want to jot down subjects to cover. This list will serve as a reminder to you in case the interview begins to stray from your subject. At the same time, though, be prepared to let the interview branch out into areas that perhaps you weren't able to foresee but that might supply valuable information.

Find out as much as you can about the person you are going to interview. If you are interested in the way a lawyer handles *pro bono* or public service cases, try to find out what cases the person you will be interviewing has handled. At the very least, you should know the person's complete name and job title, place of employment, and area of specialization. Decide how you will record the information you obtain. You might take notes during the interview, tape-record the interview, or simply listen and write down your notes later. All three have advantages and disadvantages. Writing can distract the speaker and also keep you from concentrating fully on what is being said. Tape-recording can inhibit the speaker even more, but it is more accurate and complete than taking notes. Tape recorders, though, can also fail and leave you with no record at all. If you decide to tape your interview, practice with your machine beforehand so that you can operate it unobtrusively. Also, out of courtesy, ask your interviewee in advance for permission to tape-record.

Although some professional interviewers have trained themselves to listen carefully and memorize what is said at least in short interviews, most rely on a pen or pencil and a pad of paper. Be sure you take along extra pens. Some interviewers write on note cards, but most professionals find that it is more efficient to transcribe notes onto note cards after the interview in order to clarify sketchy notes and weed out irrelevant information. The best procedure for you is to take notes in your search log, then transfer relevant information to your note cards later.

Conducting the Interview.   Arrive a few minutes early so that you are calm and relaxed and have a chance to look at your surroundings—they may give you some ideas for questions. A geologist, for example, may have photographs or rock samples decorating his office that would be of interest to you. Questions about these provide an informal, relaxed way to begin the interview. You might also begin with some questions about the background of your interviewee in order to give both of you time to get used to each other. Assume an attitude that tells your interviewee that you are interested in what he or she has to say. You do not want to act apologetic for taking the interviewee's time, but neither do you want to act as though you are a trial attorney interrogating a witness. Make the interview as conversational as possible, and let your interviewee set the direction as long as he or she does not stray too far from your subject. During pauses, always use your questions as a prompt. If you take notes, take them as unobtrusively as possible, using abbreviations and other means of shorthand when you can. Record the exact words of the speaker when something is said that you would like to quote in your paper. Unless you use a tape recorder, as a courtesy, verify direct quotations with your interviewee before you leave. At the end of the time you have both agreed on, thank the person you've been talking with, and leave.

Following Up. As soon as you can, review your notes and add what you didn't have time to write down during the interview. This is also the time to decipher the scribblings that won't be legible the next day. Everything will seem so fresh right after the interview that it is tempting to believe you won't forget what took place, but a few days later, you will have forgotten many details. Transfer relevant information to your note cards as soon as possible. Oral historians and sociologists who conduct interviews generally use tape recorders, but they also write down significant information on note cards as soon as possible after the interview. In addition, they keep a field log or journal in which they record information not included on tape, such as the surroundings, dress and demeanor of the person interviewed, feelings of the interviewer, and the like. If your purpose is to collect data from the interviewee, such details are irrelevant, but do record them if you think they might be useful.

It's also a good idea to make a bibliography card for your interview because an interview is considered a source and should, in most systems of citation, be recorded in your list of works cited at the end of your paper. Besides the interviewee's name, include his or her position or area of expertise, and the place and date of the interview. You might also want to include a few biographical details.

Finally, within a day or two, write a brief thank-you note to the person who has taken the time to help you.

Ed Kovalcik's Interview with His Professor. The following account of a personal interview was taken from a student's search journal.

I was sitting at my desk after my computer science class waiting for Professor G. to finish talking to the students crowded around his desk. I had made an appointment at the last class meeting to talk to him after class tonight. I wanted to ask him about the future of computers. What changes did he see coming? Where was the use of computers going? I felt the tension making my body a little stiff, making my heart beat a little faster. Why hadn't I interviewed a friend or relative? Too late to back out now. Then the last student's question was answered and Professor G. came over and sat down near me.

There was a strong feeling of uneasiness in the air. It was my first interview—maybe it was his, too. I started out with some questions about his academic background. He said he had gotten his bachelor's and master's degrees in mathematics from the Polytechnic Institute of Brooklyn and his Ph.D. from New York University. After a few more questions about his education, the anxiety in my voice and body began to ease and my confidence rose. This isn't too bad after all, I thought.

Knowing that he taught at the university only part-time, I asked him about his full-time job. He explained that he was in charge of research and development at COMSAT (Communications Satellites) Laboratories. "Right now we're working on a communications scheme that allows corporations to send up their information on a time-sharing basis." He continued to explain this process using words like "transducers," and "multiplexers." He was going so fast that I stopped taking notes and waited for him to slow down. He went to the chalkboard and drew a diagram depicting a theory for centralizing radio waves and pointing out the savings that could result for business. When he came back to his desk I began to question him about the future of computers—the subject I was most interested in. "Well, I believe that the smaller computers will become more widely used," he said. "And networking minicomputers to do the work of mainframes will save money for business."

I was now on firmer ground. "Networking" and "mainframes" were my language. Computer questions came streaming from my mind and out of my mouth. Among other things, Professor G. told me that ADA, a new computer language developed by the government, would be a popular language in the future. He also said that some of the older languages like FORTRAN and COBOL were holding on stronger than ever because of senior programmers' aversion to change. Furthermore, because most computer programs still in use were written in these outdated languages, the expense of rewriting the programs would be astronomical. "Computer programmers aren't cheap, as they once were thought to be," he pointed out. "It's the hardware that is inexpensive today."

I began to run out of questions and we were running out of time. "Well, I guess that's it. Thank you," I said. "I appreciate your taking the time out of your busy schedule to talk to me." "I enjoyed it," he answered, shaking hands with me.

As I walked back to my dorm, I felt a sense of exhilaration. I had conquered a new experience. I had gotten to know a person through a new medium for me, an interview.

FIGURE 6.1   Bibliography Card and Note Card for an Interview

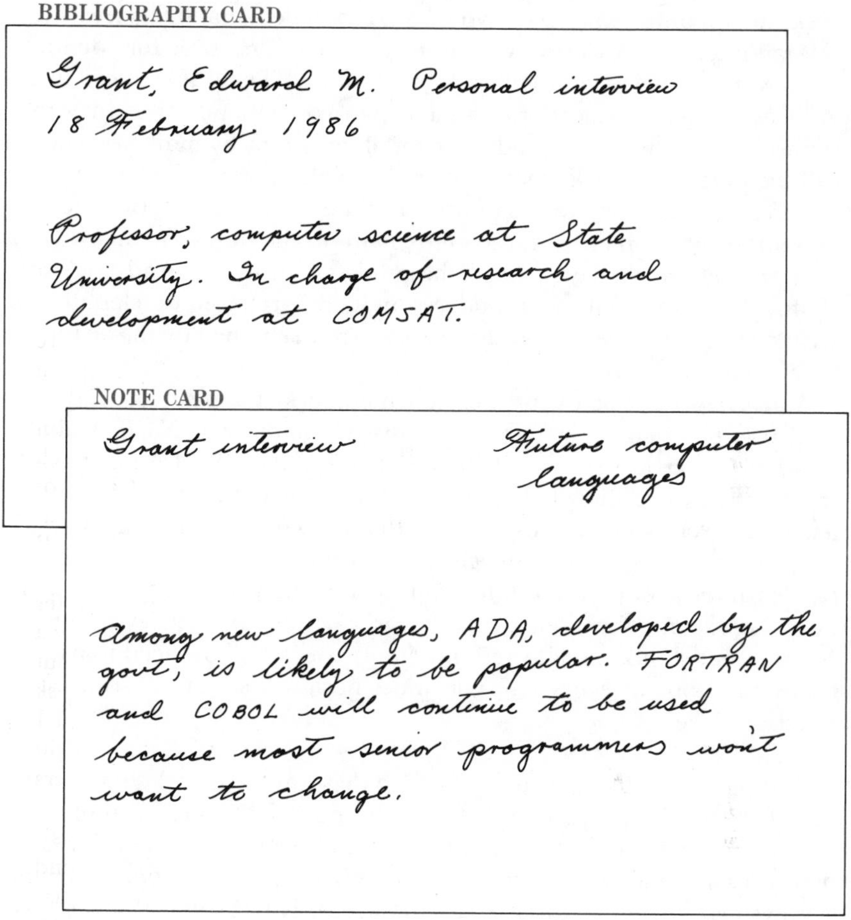

BIBLIOGRAPHY CARD

Grant, Edward M. Personal interview
18 February 1986

Professor, computer science at State
University. In charge of research and
development at COMSAT.

NOTE CARD

Grant interview   Future computer
                                            languages

Among new languages, ADA, developed by the
govt, is likely to be popular. FORTRAN
and COBOL will continue to be used
because most senior programmers won't
want to change.

After this interview, Ed Kovalcik made a bibliography card and several note cards (Figure 6.1).

Telephone and Mail Interviews

Telephone and mail interviews are usually much more structured
than personal interviews because you cannot observe the person's reactions to your questions and adjust your line of questioning accordingly.
Of course, you can tell something from the tone of voice. For a telephone interview, you may not need an appointment. You might, for
example, call a professor during her office hours and say, ''I wonder if
you would have a few minutes to give me your reaction to the Simpson-
Mazzoli bill that just passed in the Senate. You mentioned it in class the

other day when you were talking about immigration problems.'' If you need more than a quick answer to a single question or two, call and make an appointment, just as you would for a personal interview.

Mail interviews can save you time and make it possible for you to interview someone in another state or country. They also allow interviewees to answer questions at their own convenience. But they take time as well. Before you send out a set of questions by mail, you should call the person and ask whether he or she will respond. Then carefully draft your questions. You may want to send the same questions to several different people. Be sure you explain on the questionnaire or in a covering letter when you need the answers returned. And enclose a stamped envelope with your address on it. Be prepared to telephone or write with a reminder if your answers are not returned by the deadline.

Surveying.   When you interview members of a group (your fellow students, train engineers, the residents of Smalltown, North Dakota, or whatever group you want to find out about), you are not usually trying to acquire knowledge about a subject—the best treatment for leukemia. You would ask experts for that kind of information. Instead, you want to know some of the characteristics, behavior patterns, or attitudes of the group. You might want to know how many cars they own, how they spend their leisure time, or whether they believe physical punishment should be allowed in schools. Because you need to ask the same questions of everyone, you must design a set of questions or a questionnaire.

Polling.   Polling is usually done to develop statistical data about a group. Questionnaires may be self-administered (and distributed by mail or in person), or they can be administered by an interviewer in person or by phone. You should remember that data from polls and surveys are extremely difficult to analyze; it is hazardous for the novice pollster to draw firm conclusions about a group unless everyone in the group is questioned. In fact, it is hazardous for anyone; figures are sometimes used to prove what pollsters want them to prove. However, experts can do an ''inferential statistical test'' to confirm that results of surveys are typical of the group as a whole. (For details, see Carol A. Saslow, *Basic Research Methods* [Reading, Mass.: Addison-Wesley, 1982].)

If you are not an expert, the best thing for you to do is plan and describe your methodology carefully so that your reader has a basis for judging your reliability. For example, suppose that you want to know how many students in your school exercise daily. You do not have time to question everyone, so you decide to take a sample. How many students should you ask? Obviously, the larger the sample, the more reliable it is. Still, even a large sample may be faulty if you ask only students going in and out of the gym or studying in the library. Because you want a random sample, you must ensure that every part of the student population is represented. Obtaining a random sample requires that you identify the different groups of the student population according to sex, age, number of courses taken, or other significant groups and then sample at random each of these groups. Likewise, you must take your samples at various locations and at different times of the day. Try to think of other ways to make your survey more representative.

Designing a Questionnaire.   When you ask for people's opinions on something, you may have a feeling that you are getting the *truth*, that you are finding out what is really going on in people's minds. But designing a questionnaire that is effective is not easy. If you have never designed a questionnaire before, it would help to do some reading on questionnaire development or to talk to an expert. But if you keep your questionnaire relatively simple and short, you should be able to compose a serviceable one. Before you begin, ask yourself the following questions.

1. What do I hope to find out from the results of this questionnaire?

Unless you have a lot of time to spend designing the questions, keep your results brief—no more than five items, if possible—and write them down. Use them to focus your questions. Suppose you are doing a survey of health clubs in your area. You might make the following list of what you want to find out: (1) the kind of body-building equipment the clubs have; (2) the exercise facilities they own (swimming pools, tennis courts, and so on); (3) the type of relaxing equipment they have (saunas, steam rooms, and so forth); (4) the kind of instruction that is available and the qualifications of the instructors; and (5) the fees and bonded status of the clubs.

2. What people will most likely be able to give me the information I need?

The answers to the questions on health clubs can easily be given by the managers of these clubs; furthermore, much of the information can be verified by a tour of the premises. However, if your questions are different—say you want to find out about the quality of the services offered—the patrons would be able to supply that information better.

3. What kinds of questions will give me the information I want?

You can use open-ended questions, two-way questions (those that require choosing one of two alternatives), multiple-choice questions, or questions requiring a specific answer. Open-ended questions are easy to ask, but they are more difficult to answer as well as to interpret. "What do you think of the registration procedure at the university?" is likely to produce vague answers. The advantage is, of course, that you may get interesting answers you could not anticipate. Two-way questions are more focused ("Do you prefer objective tests or essay tests?") and you receive quantifiable answers, but they do not leave room for replies that might fall somewhere between the two questions. A person who is asked, "Do you believe abortion should be legal?" might want to respond, "Well, yes and no." If you think your subject cannot be reduced to only one of two answers, use multiple-choice questions. They are easily quantifiable and do not take much time to answer. One kind allows variations of degree ("Abortion should be outlawed. Circle the answer you prefer: Strongly agree, agree somewhat, neither agree nor disagree, disagree somewhat, strongly disagree"). You can have as many alternatives as you wish, although five are the most common.

You can also use multiple-choice questions when you want to find out the extent of the respondents' knowledge (this is the type of multiple-choice question often used in school tests). For instance, you might want to learn how much the students in your school know about foreign affairs or perhaps about U.S. history or geography. Such questions must be carefully thought out so that the answer you want to obtain does not seem obvious. To avoid this problem, provide three or more answers that seem like genuine answers; for example, "In what state did the Wright brothers make the first airplane flight? Ohio, North Carolina, or Alaska." Most respondents would eliminate Alaska immediately, thus leaving only two possible choices. "Ohio" might be a better choice than Alaska because the Wrights lived and worked there. The correct answer, of course, is North Carolina.

The hardest question to respond to is the one that requires a specific answer: "Who said, 'The only thing we have to fear is fear itself '?" or "How many feet are there in a mile?" If the question deals with behavior rather than knowledge, it might not be as difficult: "How many hours of sleep do you get each night, on the average?"

Be cautious in using questions about behavior that respondents might find threatening. Results from such questions are less reliable because people don't like to admit doing things that others might disapprove of. One way to improve reliability is to use open-ended, rather than two-way or multiple-choice questions. The question "How often do you drink beer?" might in some contexts carry with it the threat of criticism. If given a range, then, the respondent is likely to choose the lowest figure or none at all; in this case it would be better to leave the question open-ended (that is, allow the respondent to name a figure) rather than offer a range. Such a question is also "loaded." It assumes that the behavior exists and is thus less threatening than the question "Do you drink beer?" which may sound like an accusation, and the respondent may be tempted to answer "No." So the first question, "How often do you drink beer?" asked without a given range, or open-ended, is likely to produce more accurate answers. Another way to improve the accuracy of potentially threatening questions is to ask the respondent about the behavior of others: "Does your roommate smoke? How many cigarettes a day?" Such questions might be a better way to find out about the behavior of members of a group than asking the members directly about themselves.

Although the loading of the question above is in the interest of validity, some loaded questions originate in the bias of the questioner and thus are designed to produce biased answers. "Do you believe in supporting the defense of our country by funding the _____ bill?" suggests that a "no" answer would come only from someone unconcerned with national defense or from an unpatriotic citizen. Because few people want to think of themselves as unpatriotic, most of the answers would probably be "Yes."

You can see that the wording of questions is crucial to the validity of a questionnaire. In summary, if you are writing a questionnaire for the first time, it is a good idea to keep it short, word your questions so that you get the information you want, and check your questions for bias. When writing your paper, explain your procedures to your readers; that is, tell them how many people you questioned, what groups these people belonged to, and the purpose of your questioning as well as the results you obtained. Include a copy of your questionnaire in the body of your paper or in the appendix.

Michelle Morrissey's Telephone Survey.   Michelle Morrissey, a student volunteer in a program to teach English as a second language (ESOL), wanted to find out why so many tutors who took the training course either did not tutor or dropped out soon after training. She planned to prepare the results for the Literacy Council of Northern Virginia (LCNV), who trained the tutors, so that they could improve their program. Before she formulated her questions, she read books on preparing questionnaires and consulted with the LCNV staff and with another LCNV volunteer who was a statistician to discover what information they wanted her to gather. Here is part of the introduction to Morrissey's paper.

> After deciding to do a survey, I had to decide what type of survey would suit my purposes best. There are three major types of survey: the direct interview survey, the mail survey, and the telephone survey. The direct interview survey was eliminated because the tutors were too widely dispersed geographically, and the mail survey was unsuitable for such a

small survey (300 tutors). The telephone survey, on the other hand, was ideally suited to LCNV needs because it is quick and inexpensive and allows for great flexibility in scheduling interviews. I decided to do a short preliminary survey to find out whom I would be interviewing and to make an appointment for a later call. I then divided this group into three subgroups—active tutors, tutors who have taught but are not teaching now, and trainees who never tutored—then designed a questionnaire for each of these groups. This procedure was time-consuming, but it permitted me to proceed with confidence with the longer interviews because the interviewees knew they were going to be interviewed and had given me a preferred time to call.

Morrissey included a copy of the short screening questionnaire that she used to identify those she would interview later at length (see Figure 6.2). Figure 6.3 illustrates the questionnaire Morrissey designed for those trainees who had never tutored.

After analyzing the results of her questionnaire, Morrissey recommended the following measures: more stringent screening of prospective tutors, the setting up of information sessions before trainees commit themselves, and the establishment of a tutoring center instead of tutoring in homes.

FIGURE 6.2   Preliminary Questionnaire for a Telephone Survey

PRELIMINARY SURVEY SAMPLE FORM

Michelle Morrissey

Identifying information (already known):

Date and hour of call_____

Name:_____ Sex_____

Address:_____ Phone_____

Date of training session_____

Questions to ask:

Hello, my name is Michelle Morrissey. I am calling on behalf of the Literacy Council of Northern Virginia. We are doing a survey of ESOL tutors, and I have a few questions to ask you.

Are you tutoring now?   Yes_____   No_____

If no: Have you tutored at all since you took your training?

Yes_____   No_____

These are the only questions I am going to ask you now, but I may be calling you again in a few weeks for more questions. When is the best time to reach you? Weekday evening_____   Saturday daytime_____

Sunday afternoon_____   Anytime_____

Thank you very much. Good-by.

FIGURE 6.3 Questionnaire for a Telephone Survey

QUESTIONNAIRE FOR GROUP III

Date of training session_____

Name_____ Phone_____

Hello, my name is Michelle Morrissey. I am calling on behalf of the Literacy Council. You may remember that I called you earlier. I have a few questions to ask you. Is this a convenient time? If not, when? _____

Are you a member of LCNV now? Yes____ No____
Are you employed outside your home? Yes____ No____ If yes, PT____ FT____
If yes, are you a teacher or otherwise working in education? Yes____ No____
If not employed, are you retired? ____ staying at home? ____ seeking
   employment? ____
Do you have any preschool children at home? Yes____ No____
   of school age? Yes____ No____

In which age group do you belong? under 35?____ between 35 and 49?____
   between 50 and 60?____ over sixty?____

Did you take the LCNV training with the intent of tutoring? Yes____ No____

If no, why did you take the training?_____

If yes, why did you change your mind?_____

Would you be interested in tutoring eventually? Yes____ No____

If yes, would you want to attend a refresher course first? Yes____ No____

If yes, would you be interested in tutoring at a center where a group of
   tutors work with many students, either one-to-one or in small groups?
   Yes____ No____

If yes, would you use baby-sitting facilities if offered at the center?
   Yes____ No____

If yes, would you prefer to work there in the morning? ____
   in the afternoon? ____ in the evening? ____

Can you suggest any ways to improve the training? _____

Even though you have not tutored, do you feel the training was useful to
   you in other ways? Yes____ No____

If yes, specify:_____

That's all. Thank you very much for your assistance.

Tape-Recorded Interviews

Not all interviews with groups are structured as rigidly as Morrissey's. Studs Terkel in his book *Working* interviewed people to find out their attitudes toward their jobs. He explains in his book why his interviews were relatively long and unstructured:

> I realized quite early in this adventure that interviews conventionally conducted were meaningless. Conditioned clichés were sure to come.

The question-and-answer technique may be of some value in determining favored detergents, tooth-paste, and deodorants, but not in the discovery of men and women.

Because Terkel's interviews were open-ended—without a time limit—he could use a tape recorder effectively. His respondents got used to it with the passage of time and talked as though it weren't there. Terkel's books—*Division Street, Hard Times,* and *Working,* in which he records the edited results of many taped interviews—have been called oral histories. *Oral historiography* or *folklore research* are terms used to refer to the study of the past through the recollections of living people recorded on tape or in questionnaires. Oral historical research has developed rapidly in the past few decades and has its own methodology and theoretical framework. You might want to conduct some interviews of grandparents, aunts, or uncles this way to learn about your family history. Or observe the groups around you—they are living sources of historical information.

Students have recorded on tape the activities and customs of many groups, including city bus drivers, tattoo artists, coal miners, palm readers, neighborhood children, railroad workers, store owners, and musicians of all kinds. Projects can also be designed by asking a particular group to talk about a specific topic, such as weddings, folksongs, folk remedies, crafts, recipes, poetry, holiday customs, or rituals (baptisms, marriages, or funerals). Perhaps you can find someone on the college faculty who has done work in oral history and is willing to talk to you about a project. Further sources of information are *Folklore: A Handbook for Study and Research* by J. H. Brunvand (New York: St. Martin's Press, 1976) and *The Tape-Recorded Interview: A Manual for Field Workers in Folklore and Oral History* by Edward D. Ives (Knoxville: University of Tennessee Press, 1980).

Reading Diaries, Letters, and Other Personal Papers

Many families have writings of various kinds hidden away in boxes in the basement or attic that could provide information about family history. Sometimes personal papers providing local historical information are given to public libraries or local historical societies. Such papers can be used to supplement tape-recorded interviews or used independently like other written sources. One student wrote a biography of her great-grandmother, who married a West Point graduate in 1899 and kept diaries and letters that described in detail her military wedding and her life as an army wife. She wrote of a tour of duty in Idaho when the mines were put under military control after a strike and of her husband's death while riding horseback with the king of Italy. By researching the parallel historical events, the student was able to show how the life of her great-grandmother was part of the history of the United States.

Examining Government Records

State and County Records

It can be fascinating to trace the history of the place where you live. Is there a historic event in your area that you would like to explore, perhaps a flood or a battle? Would you like to find out the history of a town or of a piece of land? Is there a trial or a court case you would like to learn more about? Marit Beecroft was interested in the history of a large park: some of the park had apparently been farmland, whereas other parts of it were preserved as former Indian camping grounds. She found records of land sales and old maps in the county courthouse and traced the history of the area.

Perhaps you would like to learn more about one of your ancestors. State and county records contain large numbers of documents including census figures, wills, deeds, tax rolls, military rolls, election results, and records of births, deaths, and marriages. Such records can help provide political, social, and economic information about the past as well as about specific persons. (Except for a few records that are sealed, such as adoption records, all court records are open for public examination.) County courthouses store records for their own jurisdictions; a state may maintain a separate archives building for its records.

If you want to examine these records, just go to the office of the clerk of court in the courthouse. Provide the name of the documents you want to see (for example, "land titles" if you are researching a piece of land) and they will be brought to you. If you do not know the name of a document, or if you are not sure what areas you want to explore, you can look in the indexes—usually found in the clerk of court's office—to see what information the court has available and for what dates. If you want photocopies to take with you, most courts will provide them, although they tend to cost more than those at your local photocopier.

Federal Records

The National Archives.   Do you like adventure? Do you like to explore the unexplored? discover the unexpected? If so, searching in the archives may be for you. Billions of pages of "permanently valuable" national records are stored in the National Archives Building in Washington, D.C., in seven regional Archives branches, and in the six presidential libraries. These buildings contain documents—some bound, some loose in boxes—that record life in the United States over the past two centuries, and if you are over sixteen, you can look at them. Besides documents, the archives contain photographs, maps and charts, films, and recordings. If your subject has anything to do with diplomatic relations, land or Indian policies, law, foreign or domestic trade, navigation, military history or affairs, immigration, agriculture, transportation, communications, and many other areas, consider the National Archives. Consultants will help you find the information you are looking for, and although they will not do specific research for you, Archives staff members will answer concise requests for information by mail. You will find specific information about archives holdings in the following publications; these may be ordered from the Government Printing Office but check at your library first.

> *Guide to the National Archives of the United States.* Available for purchase from the Superintendent of Documents, U.S. Government Printing Office, Washington, D.C. 20402

> *Select List of Publications of the National Archives and Records Service.* Available free from the Publications Sales Branch (NEPS), General Services Administration, Washington, D.C. 20408

If you are not able to visit the National Archives Building in Washington, D.C., you may be near one of the regional branches in Boston, New York, Philadelphia, Chicago, Atlanta, Kansas City, Fort Worth, Denver, San Francisco, Los Angeles, or Seattle.

Although holdings do vary, in general the regional branches contain many documents, including records from the district courts, U.S. courts of appeals, the Bureau of Indian Affairs, and the Bureau of Customs, and they provide the researcher with reading rooms, microfilm reading equipment, and photocopying machines.

Of special value to college students is the collection of documents on microfilm stored in regional branches and available through interlibrary loan. These include some of the most significant government records in subjects such as history, economics, public administration, political science, law, and genealogy. To learn whether what you need has been recorded on microfilm, send for the *Catalog of National Archives Microfilm Publications* from the Publications Sales Branch (NEPS), General Services Administration, Washington, D.C. 20408. Your library may also have this catalog—look in the title section of the card catalog or ask your reference librarian.

Recent Government Papers.   Most government files dated before 1960 have been placed in the National Archives. But if the information you want is in government files dated after 1960, you must search in the current files of government agencies. Under the Freedom of Information Act (FOIA) of 1966, most government files are open to the public. To obtain information of this kind, you must write a letter to the Freedom of Information officer affiliated with the government agency that you think holds the files you need and ask for a specific document or information on the subject you are interested in. (If you send your request to the incorrect agency, your letter will usually be forwarded to the correct one.) The more precise you are in specifying the documents you want or their time period, the less time it will take to honor your request. Perhaps you are interested in what the government has done about the problem of acid rain—such papers are probably filed with the Environmental Protection Agency. Or you might be writing a paper on an author who was active in anti-Vietnam demonstrations, like Normal Mailer, and you want to know whether the Federal Bureau of Investigation has a file on him. Write to the FBI and ask for such information under the FOIA. You will get an answer—though not necessarily the documents—within ten days; if you don't receive the documents, you will be told the status of your request. Use the same process to retrieve papers from any government agency. If the documents you require have a security classification, the agency must decide whether they can be declassified. If they can be declassified, they will be copied and sent to you. The first fifty pages are provided to you without cost; for any pages above that number you will be charged ten cents each. The length of time it takes for such a search varies, so place your request early. You can find the address of government agencies in the *United States Government Manual,* which your library should own, or in a District of Columbia telephone book.

Rhonda Martin's Records Search.   Rhonda Martin wanted to find out the background of a legendary figure in her family. Three theories existed: he came to America as a Hessian horse soldier during the American Revolution; he was a Virginian in the Virginia militia during the American Revolution; he arrived as a youth in Pennsylvania from Germany in the 1700s. Martin did her research at the Library of Congress, the National Archives, and the Pennsylvania Archives. At the Library of Congress, she read the Hessian Horse Soldiers and passenger ships lists for 1750 to 1770. No one with the name of her ancestor was listed. From the census records in the National Archives, she discovered where a man by that name lived from 1790, when the first census was taken, until his death in 1823; all of the locations were in Pennsylvania. From the research files of the Daughters of the American Revolution, she learned that a man of the same name had fought in Virginia during the American Revolution but that he had never lived in Pennsylvania. She decided to start from the present and work back.

In the Pennsylvania Archives (Harrisburg, Pa.), she located deeds (called indentures) showing that he owned land in Greene County and that he sold "seventeen acres and one hundred and thirty-two perch of land" to his son for seventy-one dollars and twenty cents (a perch equals 30¼ square yards). In 1798 he paid $1,300 as his glass tax, the first tax ever levied, based on the number of glass windows in his home. From these and other details, such as names of wife and children, living places, and land purchases, Martin was able to compose a brief biography. He had never lived in Virginia and the names of his wife and children were different from the names of the wife and children of the Virginia militiaman. Thus she was able to trace the ancestry of those living now back to an indentured servant who had come to the United States when he was seventeen and died in 1823; she was able to prove that the last of the hypotheses was correct.

Observing, Exploring, and Experimenting

All of us observe, explore, and experiment and draw conclusions on the basis of our findings; these are daily activities. We observe and count the kinds of birds in our backyards; we explore a park or a neighborhood; we experiment with a new recipe. However, we usually do not keep records and put our conclusions into writing. Students in the social sciences, natural sciences, and psychology may want to do these kinds of research in a systematic way. The usual order is identifying the problem, planning a search strategy, collecting and measuring data, analyzing the results, and drawing conclusions.

In doing this kind of research, first formulate a question you want to answer. Can gold be found by panning in the local streams? Which grocery chain has the lowest prices? How polluted are the local rivers or the air we breath? How much violence is there in children's TV programs? After deciding on a question to answer, decide on a plan for collecting your information; then collect your data, analyze it, and draw conclusions and perhaps make recommendations. The final step is a scientific paper in which you "report [your] original data in an organized fashion" (Robert A. Day, *How to Write and Publish a Scientific Paper* [Philadelphia: ISI Press, 1983]). You will find further information on writing a scientific paper in Chapter 13.

The following student research projects have used some of the strategies discussed in this chapter.

1. Sandra Sweitzer observed a prison art class, given for the purpose of rehabilitation. Besides observing the members of the class, she interviewed the instructor, the students, the sheriff, and some members of the class. She concluded that the art class had important therapeutic effects on the prisoners; its benefits as a tool for rehabilitation were more difficult to assess. Her paper, in modified form, was published in a local newspaper.

2. Doris Hill compared prices at three grocery chain stores. She selected ten staple grocery items and checked their prices at these stores periodically for four weeks. She also interviewed patrons at random. After computing her evidence, she discovered much lower average prices at one of the stores. Location and size of the stores as well as varied economic levels of the shoppers were described in her analysis of the reasons for the difference in prices.

3. Tom Davis set out to find the location of knapping rocks in his area. *Knapping* is the term used by geologists and anthropologists to refer to the breaking or shaping of rocks. Indians knapped rocks to make implements, but only certain, glasslike rocks can be used in this way. Tom studied geological maps from the army map service and other geological evidence to determine possible locations of glassy stones, such as semiglassy quartzite, and then visited the areas to confirm his findings. Besides semiglassy quartzite, he found miscellaneous materials such as crushed stone, quartzite gravel, glassy quartz crystal and chert, and manmade glass. His paper containing his methodology and conclusions also included a geological map of the knapping rocks in his area; the map is available to local knappers with the warning that "To protect archeological evidence, these cobbles must be knapped or gathered only in disturbed areas and streambeds."

4. Mark Olin wanted to know whether the five streams in his county were polluted. He collected water samples, grew cultures in petri dishes, and counted and identified the bacteria. After determining that the levels of the bacteria *E. coli* constituted dangerous pollution, he concluded that two of the streams qualified as polluted. Olin then studied maps to find out the source of the pollution. Besides writing his paper, he sent a letter to the county board summarizing his findings.

All of these projects grew out of the personal interests of these students. They gathered their information carefully and thoroughly, then analyzed it to make it meaningful to them and their readers.

EXERCISES

1. Choose partners from your class and interview one another. Follow the suggestions given for interviewing given in this chapter. Your purpose for interviewing will be to find out everything you can about your partner's research project. Take a few minutes to make a

list of questions to ask. Make it about a ten-minute interview. After the interview, write down what you learned. If you have time, check the facts with your partner for accuracy.

2. Design a short questionnaire—four or five questions—to discover the opinions of students on a topic of current interest. If all the class members agree on the same topic, you will be able to compare results and discuss the advantages and disadvantages of certain questions. If possible, agree on a single set of questions and, before using it to survey the student body, have class members complete the questionnaire and critique its effectiveness. The class could then distribute the questionnaire to a sample of the student body and analyze the results.

3. Using a tape recorder, interview the oldest member of your family about one of his or her most memorable experiences. Make this interview as professional as you can so that you can practice this kind of interviewing technique. Write an account of the interview in your search log; include the preparations you made, the questions you asked, the reactions of your subject to the interview, what you would do differently the next time, and what worked well. Using this data, write a short report for your classmates and instructor on interviewing with a tape recorder.

4. Interview an expert in the profession you wish to enter when you graduate. Ask the person what skills are required for such a position and whether he or she has any suggestions on preparing for this profession.

PART II

Researching and Writing

7. Re-searching and Outlining
8. Writing Your First Draft
9. Revising
10. Preparing Your Final Copy
11. Writing a Paper in the Humanities: The Author/ Page Style
12. Writing a Paper in the Social Sciences: The Author/Date Style
13. Writing a Paper in Science or Technology: The Number System

Re-searching and Outlining

Reviewing Your Information

You collect your information in bits and pieces in the order of what may be available first or what may turn up first. Until you have all of your information, you don't know what the shape of your paper is likely to be. When you have all of your material, you can begin to shape it, much as a sculptor creates a form out of marble or wood. In re-searching, you examine what you collected and determine what you can make out of it: you give your material form and meaning.

The first steps in researching are to read over your notes, ask yourself the following questions, and record the answers in your search log (limit your answers to one or two sentences).

1. What was my purpose in doing this research?
2. Did I realize my goal or did it change?
3. If my goal changed, what is my purpose now?
4. What did I learn from my research?
5. What conclusions can I draw from this knowledge?

Answering these questions will help you to shape and give meaning to all of the material you have collected. In answering questions 1, 2, and 3, you reassess your purpose and relate it to the answer to question 4, what you have learned. The answer to question 4 is a summary of the information you have collected. In answering question 5 you make a generalization or an inference based on the information you have collected; that is, the evidence leads you to an opinion, a judgment, or an evaluation. Making such generalizations are part of everyday life, so you are familiar with the process. For instance, you decide which is the best car for you to buy after looking at several cars, examining their features, checking the prices, and driving them. Or you study the schedule of courses, look up the requirements, weigh your needs and desires, and determine which courses will best suit your needs.

Florence McMullen, a student in an anthropology class, selected as her topic, "Teaching anthropology to elementary school students." She answered the re-searching questions in the following way.

1. My purpose was to observe a group of sixth-graders enrolled in a class in cultural anthropology and study the educational procedures.
2. I changed my goal and my topic.
3. Instead of concentrating on educational procedures, I decided to study the cultural values of the students in the class.
4. I learned that these students value the following qualities:

    Intellectual achievement
    Social equality, especially between males and females. However, some traditional behavior patterns still exist (boys and girls tend to sit in separate groups; girls primp and comb their hair in class; boys are noisier and more active).
    Contributions of technology to personal comfort (television sets, hair dryers, microwave ovens, etc.)
    Peace or lack of conflict between individuals and groups

5. I concluded that the cultural values of children have changed in significant ways since I was a child.

Writing a Summary Sentence or Thesis Statement

After you have answered these questions, you should find it easy to write a sentence or two—sometimes called a thesis statement—that summarizes your paper or states what your paper "proves." Composing such a sentence helps you to find meaning in the information you have collected. Although your summary sentence may change as you write your paper, this statement provides an organizing force for you at the beginning: all parts of your paper must uphold or validate this statement. If you find, as you write, that your material is inconsistent with this statement or irrelevant to it, you can either change your statement to include the new information or discard the new material, leaving your original statement intact.

McMullen's summary statement included her answers to the last two questions; it was both a summary of the information she had found and a conclusion that she had drawn from this information: "In the last twenty years, the changing cultural values of children are shown in the following observed characteristics: respect for learning and intellectual achievement, new perceptions of male/female roles, acceptance of material goods as contributing to the quality of life, and a longing for worldwide peace." Notice that she has discarded as a topic the educational procedures used in this class. Consequently, any notes she has on this subject will not be used.

When you begin to write your paper (see Chapter 8), the answers to these five questions form the framework for your paper. The statement of your purpose and your summary statement form the basis for your introduction; the development of your summary statement forms the body of your paper; and the generalizations you make about your material shape your conclusion. With a good idea of what the beginning, middle, and end of your paper will be, you will be able to write confidently and expeditiously.

Although you are not ready to write yet (you still have to order the details that go into the body of your paper), you may be interested in seeing how McMullen used the answers to these questions in her introduction and conclusion. Here is her introduction.

> I observed a group of sixth-graders in a suburban public school. Although I intended at first to record and study the educational procedures used, I became interested in the way the children approached their study topic, cultural anthropology. I realized that they were applying their own cultural values in their study of the cultures of past civilizations. Intrigued by their ethnocentric reactions, I decided to study them in the same way they were studying others. By watching them, I was able to define the cultural values of their (our) society and observe how these values seem to have changed since I was in school.

The following excerpt from McMullen's paper shows how the answer to the last questions formed her conclusion.

> From observing these sixth-graders, I conclude that children's cultural values have changed since I was the age of these students. For one thing, they seem to value intellectual pursuits more; they were pleased to be in this special class with an advanced curriculum. When I was in elementary school, children tried to hide any intellectual achievements for fear of teasing or other negative reactions from their peers.

Making an Outline

With your thesis statement as a guide and with a clear idea of the general shape of your paper, you can now turn your attention to the body of the paper. The information you have gathered must be organized logically so that it makes sense to both you and your readers.

You have been using a list of topics and subtopics to guide your search. Now that you have all of your information, you can expand this list if you want. You can even convert it into a formal outline; that is, an outline with a prescribed logical and syntactical form (explained below). Some people prefer to write using a simple list of topics and subtopics, but others prefer the clarification that designing a formal outline provides. Whether you use an expanded list or a formal outline, be prepared to alter it as you write your first draft. Your list or outline is your attempt to impose form on the chaos of material that continually exerts its own power. From this tension between form and raw material, your paper takes shape.

The Purpose of an Outline

A formal outline delineates the parts into which your paper is divided as well as the relationship between those parts and will serve as a guide during the writing process. Later, placed at the beginning of your paper or used as the basis for a table of contents, it guides the reader.

At this point you should have a number of cards labeled with each part of your working outline. Your next task is to sort these cards into groups that correspond to these headings. You may find that some cards do not quite match the headings; put those cards aside for now. After you have all of your cards sorted, read again those that did not correspond to your existing headings. Jot down on a separate sheet of paper one-word descriptions (headings) for these cards so that they will fit into your outline. Don't hesitate to discard those that you think do not belong in your paper—you can expect to have superfluous material. Pencil these new headings into your outline and write the corresponding headings on each card.

In a paper on soil erosion, the following headings and subheadings were part of Joseph Masters's working outline:

Strategies for erosion control
    Agronomic strategies
    Mechanical strategies

As he went through his notes he found note cards on soil management that he had not found a place for in his outline. After deciding that they belonged under "Strategies for erosion control," he labeled them and added them to his outline:

Strategies for erosion control
    Agronomic strategies
    Mechanical strategies
    Soil management

Your next step is to decide on the order of the cards within your headings; as you do this, you may want to create some subheadings. To make the process easier, read each group of cards carefully and, on a sheet of paper, jot down the specific subject of each card. Then fit these headings into your working outline, changing the wording where necessary and adding subheadings where they fit.

Mavis Olson used a simple working outline as she gathered information for her paper on physical fitness programs in the workplace:

History
Benefits of fitness programs
    Employee benefits
    Employer benefits
Facilities needed
    Space
    Equipment
Setting up a program

After gathering information, she constructed the following summary, or thesis, sentence and formal outline with additional subheadings.

Summary sentence: Companies should consider developing physical fitness programs for their employees.

  I. Introduction: History of industry-provided recreation
 II. Objectives of employee fitness programs
    A. To benefit employees
      1. By improving mental and physical health
      2. By reducing boredom, absenteeism, and fatigue
      3. By promoting employee efficiency
    B. To benefit management
      1. By providing recruitment appeal
      2. By improving employee-employer relations
      3. By lowering organizational health costs
III. Design of facility
    A. Fitness center design
      1. Architectural layout
      2. Order of construction
      3. Estimated costs
    B. Equipment
      1. Types of exercise equipment
      2. Estimated costs
 IV. Conclusion: The future of fitness programs in the workplace

The Logic of an Outline

An outline organizes the material in your paper into logical divisions. As you sort your cards, notice how the material helps you to create an outline at the same time that the outline helps you to shape your material. It is a back-and-forth operation. The logic demanded by the structure of the outline helps you to organize your material and also provides a way to ensure that you haven't omitted anything important. If you have, you may have to do a little more reading now, before you begin to write. In outlining the objectives of employee fitness programs, Mavis Olson found that her notes dealt almost completely with employee benefits; she had noted only that management used recreation programs as a recruitment lure. When she constructed her outline containing this information, she saw how unbalanced it was.

II. Objectives of employee fitness programs
   A. To benefit employees
      1. By improving mental and physical health
      2. By reducing boredom, absenteeism, and fatigue
      3. By promoting employee efficiency
   B. To benefit management: by providing recruitment appeal

She had included only one benefit for management. It seemed logical to Olson that management would have to find more benefits in order to fund such programs. After doing some more reading, she found two more benefits: improving employee-employer relations and lowering organizational health costs.

In making an outline, you not only ensure that you have enough information, you also design an orderly presentation for your paper. It is this logical structure that makes it easier for your reader to understand what you are trying to convey. Implied in the outline structure are these propositions:

1. All topics at the same level are of equal, or nearly equal, importance. All headings numbered with roman numerals, for example, constitute the major divisions of the paper and deserve equal emphasis. Joseph Masters's original outline on soil erosion had these divisions:

   I. Water erosion
     [subheadings]
  II. Wind erosion
     [subheadings]
 III. Strategies for erosion control
   A. Agronomic strategies
     [subheadings]
   B. Mechanical strategies
     [subheadings]
   C. Soil management

As he looked at his notes and outline, he realized that his paper really had two main parts: kinds of erosion (water and wind) and ways of controlling them. To reflect this he changed his outline by converting two former main headings to subheadings and adding a new main heading to balance "strategies for erosion control." His outline then looked like this:

  I. Types of erosion
     A. Water erosion
     B. Wind erosion
  II. Strategies for erosion control
     A. Agronomic strategies
     B. Mechanical strategies
     C. Soil management

2. Each topic, if divided, is split into at least two parts that, at each level, add up to the whole. Thus, Mavis Olson's outline shows under "II" two objectives of employee fitness programs. We can assume that her paper will not contain any other objectives or that no other information will appear under this heading. Note that it is not logical to divide something into one part. If you find that you have only one subtopic under a single heading, no divisions exist and you should combine the topic and subtopic. Olson's outline first began:

  I. Introduction
     A. History and philosophy of industry-provided recreation

She realized that if "A" were the only subdivision, it must be the main heading and so she combined the two:

  I. Introduction: History of industry-provided recreation

Avoid using the labels "Introduction" and "Conclusion" without giving them any designated content. It is easy to avoid thinking about what will go into the first and last parts of your outline by using terms that mean only "beginning" and "end." If you use these terms, combine them with a phrase indicating their content, as Olson did.

3. To reflect the relationship among categories in the outline, headings at the same level should have the same grammatical structure. For example, all of Olson's categories designated by roman numerals are nouns. But the "A" and "B" subheadings under "II" are infinitives and the headings under each of these are prepositional phrases:

  II. Objectives of employee fitness programs
     A. To benefit employees
       1. By improving mental and physical health
       2. By reducing boredom, absenteeism, and fatigue
       3. By promoting employee efficiency
     B. To benefit management

. . . . .

  III. Design of facility

. . . . .

4. The outline shows an orderly progression. In Olson's outline, the progression of the main headings seems to be in the chronological order that would be followed in setting up an employee fitness program. Objectives would come first; then facilities would be designed. Her subheadings use either order of importance (II. A) or chronological order (III). To check your outline for a logical sequence, write down the major headings in a list to see whether they are of equal importance and whether they are logically arranged. Then look at each group of subheadings in the same way. Olson had the most difficulty with the order of subheadings under "II. A." Was health more important than efficiency? She decided that from the point of view of the employee it was.

You can see that an outline, besides helping you to organize your paper, helps you clarify the relative importance of its parts. To write an outline, first decide on the major divisions—the main parts into which you intend to divide your paper. After you have decided on your major categories, divide each of them in a similar way. Think arithmetically; make the parts add up to the whole with nothing left over.

The Form of an Outline

Most outlines use alternating numbers and letters along with indentation. Major divisions are indicated by roman numerals; first subdivisions, by capital letters; and second subdivisions, by arabic numerals. Further subdividing is seldom required in papers written for college classes. If you find you need more subheadings, indicate them by small letters, then by arabic numerals in parentheses, and finally by small letters in parentheses. The order should look like this:

I.
   A.
      1.
         a.
           (1)
             (a)

If you glance back at Olson's outline, you'll notice that the period following each roman numeral is aligned; then, each subdivision is indented, with all divisions of the same order arranged in a vertical line and with the letter or number of each subdivision directly under the first letter of the first word in the larger category:

I.
II.
III. Design of facility
   A. Equipment
      1. Types of exercise equipment
      2. Estimated costs
   B.

Place a period after each number or letter, but do not put a period after the topics in a topic outline. (Of course you would put periods after the sentences in a sentence outline.) Capitalize the first letter of the first word of each topic. Such arrangement and punctuation make your outline easier to read and reinforce its logic.

Types of Outlines

The most common type of outline is, like Olson's, the topic outline, which uses single words or phrases. Sometimes, however, a sentence outline is used to define the categories more precisely. In order to make a sentence outline, you must have your material very clearly in mind. Although such precision is not always possible before writing, creating such an outline does force you to be clear about what you want to say. As a result, the actual writing of your paper will be much easier. The following sentence outline helped Farah Farhoumand compose a stronger paper.

Topic: The growing problem of child abuse in the United States
Summary sentence: Child abuse is a growing problem with diverse causes and remedies.

I. Child abuse is increasing in the United States.
   A. Statistics are difficult to analyze because child abuse is defined differently by different experts.
      1. Some experts define it as severe battering.
      2. Others consider it to be any use of physical force that causes physical injury.
      3. Still others define it as mental as well as physical abuse.
   B. Statistics show that child abuse is increasing.
      1. The Department of Health and Human Services reported that child abuse cases doubled during the last two years.
      2. Large cities, where reporting is more accurate, report dramatic increases in child abuse.
      3. Researchers estimate that the number of reported cases is only a fraction of the real number.
II. Experts differ as to the causes of child abuse.
   A. According to some, the mental and emotional illness of parents causes child abuse.
   B. Others believe that parents' aggression is learned behavior.
   C. Another theory is that child abuse is caused by social, cultural, and economic factors.
   D. A few believe that children with behavioral problems can contribute to their own abuse.

III. Remedies are as varied as the causes.
  A. Recognition of the problem and reporting of cases is essential.
  B. Psychologically disturbed parents should be treated.
  C. Children should be separated from their parents and treated.

The decimal outline is often used in technical writing because it is easily expanded into many subdivisions. Sometimes almost every paragraph is numbered for easier reference. For example, the second edition of the *MLA Handbook for Writers of Research Papers* uses the decimal system, which allows additional subdivisions and the numbering of each one. By citing divisions and subdivisions in the index instead of page numbers, the editors make it easier to locate information. The decimal system also makes it easier to see at a glance the relative importance of a heading. Notice how these systems correspond.

Using numerals and letters	Using decimals
I. First major topic	1.0
A. Major subtopic	1.1
1. Minor subtopic	1.1.1
a. Subsubtopic	1.1.1.1
b. Subsubtopic	1.1.1.2
2. Minor subtopic	1.1.2
B. Major subtopic	1.2
II. Second main topic	2.0

Diana Holford used the decimal system in her paper surveying home computers. Here is part of her outline.

1.0 Qualities of a good home computer
  1.1 Memory
  1.2 Display
  1.3 Screen format
  1.4 Graphics resolution
  1.5 Printers
    1.5.1 Impact
    1.5.2 Dot matrix
    1.5.3 Thermal
  1.6 Keyboard
    1.6.1 Pressure sensitive
    1.6.2 Typewriter
  1.7 Storage
    1.7.1 Cassettes
    1.7.2 Floppy discs

    1.8 Software languages
        1.8.1 BASIC
        1.8.2 FORTRAN
        1.8.3 Others
2.0 Six popular computers

The Arrangement of Your Cards According to Your Outline

If you add to your outline or if you change its order or wording, be sure that you change the corresponding words or symbols in the upper corner of each card. Resort and regroup them if necessary. You will then be ready to write your paper easily and efficiently.

EXERCISES

1. It is a good idea to get help in your researching from other members of your writing class. Your instructor will help you divide into groups, preferably of four or five. Using your search logs, read aloud to the group the answers that you have written to the questions given in the beginning of this chapter. Read slowly. After you have finished, ask your classmates to write down what they understand to be your purpose. Then ask each of them to read what he or she has written. After they have read, discuss your purpose with them. Did everyone understand it? If not, what was the difficulty? Can your classmates help you clarify it?
2. To make sure the format and content of your outline are logical, complete the following procedures:

    Write the headings of each level, one below the other, on a separate sheet of paper. Start with the primary headings (I, II, etc.) and move on to capital letter headings, and so on.
    Check the logic of your form and structure by asking yourself these questions about each group:

    a. Are all the headings in a group of equal importance?
    b. Does each group of headings or subheadings divide equally and without overlapping the heading under which they are listed? Headings labeled with capital roman numerals, for example, should summarize the contents of all the subheadings in that group.
    c. Taken together, does each group explain adequately the heading under which they are grouped?
    d. Have you used the same grammatical structure (parallelism) for each group?

CHAPTER 8

Writing Your First Draft

As you *conducted your search*, you were satisfying your own curiosity. Now, as you *write*, you will be satisfying your readers' curiosity. You will also be satisfying the desire we all have at times to tell someone else what we have done, thought, or discovered. If you can maintain the enthusiasm for sharing your information that you have when you talk to your best friend, you will automatically eliminate many of the problems that arise in writing a research paper.

Preparing to Write

Preliminary Planning

Materials. Make the writing process as physically easy for yourself as you can. Use the writing instrument that is most comfortable for you. If you can, you should use a typewriter or a word processor because with either of these you can write faster and revise more easily. Whatever you use to write with, plan to use plenty of paper. Wide margins (one-and-a-half or two inches) and double- or triple-spacing will give you plenty of room to add words and sentences. And if you write on only one side of the paper, revising will be easier because you will be able to see more than one page of your writing at a time; you'll also be able to cut apart your pages and rearrange the parts if you wish.

Place. Do your composing in a place where you can be free of distractions and, if possible, where you can leave your papers and cards arranged, ready to work on them at any time.

Schedule. Review the timetable you constructed as you were planning your search (see Chapter 3). Write down the total time you scheduled for your writing and divide it into parts, allowing time for revising and incubating. Take account of your own writing habits: if you revise as you go along, you will take more time on the first draft and probably less time on subsequent drafts. Also use your timetable to help you change any habits that may not be benefiting your writing. Procrastination often prevents writers from spending as much time on revising as they need to. Making a realistic timetable and following it will help you improve your writing procedure and, consequently, your writing.

The following schedule for a ten- to fifteen-page paper provides for three drafts. Your paper may require more. Or you may find that you have two complete drafts with some pages or paragraphs rewritten several times. Make adjustments for your own writing habits. The schedule also includes an incubation period. Many writers have found—perhaps you have too—that their minds work on a problem or a piece of writing even when they aren't giving it their conscious attention. To allow your mind time to do this work is the idea behind scheduling some time for incubation.

Writing the first draft: focus on getting down all the information you need to make your points clear. Ten to fifteen hours (four or five hours for each writing period)

Incubation period: from one to seven days (if you leave your paper for a longer time, you may forget too much)

Writing the second draft: focus on organization and paragraphing. Ten to fifteen hours

Incubation period: four to twenty-four hours

Writing the third draft: focus on sentences, words, punctuation, and format. Eight to ten hours

Typing the final draft: three to five hours

Proofreading and photocopying: two to four hours

Try not to rush during the period you have set aside for writing. Writing progresses best when you don't have to feel anxious about finishing; hurried writing is not usually good writing. Of course you will have a deadline to meet. But following your timetable will make it possible for you to have enough time to do your best and meet your deadline too.

Focusing on Your Audience

When you tell a friend about a concert you have attended or a movie you have seen, you use a vocabulary that you know your friend will understand. You include all of the background information your friend needs in order to understand what you are talking about; you use an organizational plan that will make it easy for your friend to follow your explanation; and you use grammatical structures that make your meaning clear.

All these techniques are part of the process of verbal communication that you use daily, whether you are aware of using them or not. In writing a paper of this length you will want to be sure that you use these techniques with precision and care. Your friends may be able to ask you for clarification; they may know you well enough to understand you even if you are sometimes vague. But you have to write your paper with the assumption that there will be no chance for your audience to ask you to explain your meaning. Writing a paper takes more planning and more careful execution than talking or writing to a friend. Still, the same desire to tell, the same eagerness to make it possible for your readers to understand you, and your own interest in and enthusiasm for your subject are the most important prerequisites for writing a good paper, just as they are for communicating in any medium.

The main thing you will have to decide about your audience is how much knowledge they have about your subject. Will they be familiar with the vocabulary? If your topic is *"Pseudomonas pseudomallei* infections in humans" and you are writing for your microbiology class, you will be able to write such a sentence as "The disease is often mistaken for tuberculosis or mycotic lung infections because of the cavitations on the lungs seen in x-rays" without translating the terms. But if you are writing for your English class, you should either put such words in a glossary, define them when you use them, or translate the sentence itself into layperson's terms. How do you decide which of these solutions to use? Here are some guidelines, but they are not hard and fast rules.

1. Include a glossary if you use more than five technical words frequently in your paper (for more suggestions on composing a glossary, see Chapter 10). Do not use words in your glossary that are just as difficult as the word you are defining. Defining *flagella* as "helical protein appendages that allow bacteria to be motile" is probably not going to help your readers.

2. Define words in the text or in a footnote if you have only four or five words unknown to your audience. You can put such definitions in parentheses immediately after the word.

Sheet erosion (a landslide or mudflow) occurs extremely rapidly and results in greater losses of soil than any other type.

You can put the definition into a sentence that becomes an introduction to the subject.

A computer network can be thought of as a collection of independent computers; it can include systems as simple as two word processors linked together or as complex as a nationwide research system consisting of many computers connected by telephone lines.

Or you can use a content note or footnote.

A trained analyst examines each photograph for details such as terrain, structures, ground disturbance, discarded material, and signatures.[1]

---

[1]The term ''signature'' is used to denote a particular pattern, shape, tone, or color that consistently indicates the presence of an object or material in an aerial photograph, even though the object itself may be indistinguishable.

3. Use words that will be understood by your audience and integrate definitions into your writing when necessary. At this level, you may be somewhat limited in your ability to discuss highly technical subjects. If you are, don't write:

The disease is often mistaken in x-rays for tuberculosis or mycotic lung infections because of the cavitations on the lungs.

But write:

The pittings or small depressions in the lungs caused by the disease and seen on x-rays often lead to mistaken diagnoses of tuberculosis or parasitic fungus infections.

Obviously, technical language or a higher vocabulary level usually requires fewer words and is often more precise. Therefore, you want to use the highest level that you think your audience can understand. But avoid using technical language just to impress your readers.

Besides suiting your vocabulary to the level of your readers' understanding, you will also have to consider how much they know about your subject and how much they need to know in order to understand what you are trying to say.

Establishing Your Own Style and Tone

With your first words you establish a relationship with your readers, much as you would if you introduce yourself personally. The reader gets a sense of you as a person and of the tone you will use in your paper. Your tone may be serious, friendly, humorous, angry, or concerned—just about any emotion or combination of emotions is possible. It's important, though, that you are conscious of the tone you are using and that it fits your subject and the results you want to obtain. Most research papers are serious, but they need not be dull. Whatever your attitude as you write, it will probably assert itself in your writing. A serious but relaxed and friendly attitude usually works well. Humor may work with some subjects, but you have to use it with care; it would not work well, for example, in a paper on the problems of alcoholism or the prevalence of teenage pregnancy. Sometimes the syntax, or the arrangement of words in the sentence, may make your writing hard to understand; write simply, saving complex sentence forms for complex ideas. Notice the following sentences from a paper on the results of environmental impact studies:

> Currently, field tests are being scheduled by the Envionics Corporation to coincide with the receipt of incremental site assessments which will be forwarded from the Environmental Photographic Interpretation Center (EPIC) upon completion.

Fortunately, the writer of this passage realized before she went very far that she was trying too hard to sound authoritative and that the result was unclear writing. By omitting unnecessary use of the passive voice and unneeded words, she composed a much clearer passage.

> The Envionics Corporation will conduct tests for potential hazards as soon as they receive the site assessments now being completed by the Environmental Protection Agency.

An overly formal style in which you try to avoid using "I" or "you" can lead to such awkward constructions as the following:

> As has been said, not all of these writers had a political purpose in writing.
> As can be seen from Table 2, all cotton grown in the West is now under irrigation.

Instead, you can strengthen your writing by using simple and clear language.

> As I have already pointed out, not all of these writers had a political purpose in writing.
> Table 2 shows that all cotton grown in the West is now under irrigation.

Using your own style and writing clearly will help to give your paper unity and coherence. This unity will be reinforced if you are consistent in the verb tense you use. Use the present tense for routine or customary activities.

Most pregnant girls learn about the agency through referral by a church or other organization. The first contact is usually made by phone call, during which an interview is set up.

Use the present tense, too, for references to what is in print or in law.

Section 104 of the Copyright Law *prohibits* the public performance, for profit, of copyrighted music without permission of the copyright holder.

Ziswiler *points* out that "conservation" applies to animal species, not to individual animals (100).

But use past tense when you are relating a past event, such as an interview.

Mrs. Rumford *explained* that the adoptive couple must go through one to three years of intense interviewing and observation before they are accepted or rejected as adoptive parents.

Of course, you will be able to make changes when you revise, but you can save yourself time by writing as simply and clearly as you can from the beginning. Start with a style that you feel comfortable with, and you will be able to give your complete attention to what you say rather than to how you say it.

Writing Your Introduction

The first part of a paper is its introduction, but whether you label it as such depends in part on the discipline in which you are writing. Papers in the humanities usually do not use a heading. The *Publication Manual of the American Psychological Association* and the *Handbook for Authors of Papers in American Chemical Society Publications* recommend against using "Introduction" as a heading because the position of the material at the beginning is sufficient. However, "Introduction" is recommended as a heading in the *CBE Style Manual*, published by the Council of Biology Editors.

In the introduction you tell your readers what they need or would like to know about your subject before you begin your specific discussion of it. You might explain your purpose for writing or state the problem you have studied. In writing some papers (especially if you are doing original research), you may want to review published writing on the same subject.

You have already prepared for writing your introduction in Chapter 7 when you answered this question in your search log: "What was my purpose in doing this research?'' Here are some other questions you can ask yourself as you think about how to begin your paper:

1. How did I happen to get started on this subject?
2. What would my reader like to know before I explain what I found?
3. What does my reader need to know in order to understand my paper?
4. What am I trying to prove?
5. What would my reader like to know about this subject?

Include in your introduction the answers to any of these questions that are relevant to your subject. The answer to the first two questions can provide background or a discussion of the problem you are trying to solve. The answer to the third question may be a brief history of the subject or a summary of what has already been written about it. The answer to the fourth question can be your hypothesis or your thesis statement. You can give your thesis statement in the introduction or at the end, where it appears as your conclusion.

Beginning with an Anecdote

Lee Atkinson began a paper about life on Mars by explaining how he became interested in his subject. Notice that his story leads into the question that he will answer in his paper.

> One warm summer day after classes, I made it home just in time to see the noon news. ''Viking I has landed and is sending pictures back to earth from Mars,'' the newscaster said, speaking with the usual deep voice of broadcasters. ''Here is the first picture sent back. Notice the can-like object to the left. Scientists say it did not come from Viking.''
> It looked like a beer can and my mind started whirling. Could there be life on Mars?

Beginning with Background

A paper on the treatments of alcoholism began with some historical background on the use of alcohol.

> As a sign of trust and friendship in the early days of civilization, two men would draw their blood and mingle it with each other's. As time passed, alcohol began to be almost as important as blood. It was called ''aqua vitae''—''water of life''—partly because it was often safer to drink than water. Trust was established and friendships and agreements were sealed with a cup of wine.
> Today alcohol has become a social drink, but for many people social pressures and everyday problems can cause serious drinking problems.

These people have a disease called alcoholism. The alcoholic's only hope for recovery is to stop drinking completely. How the alcoholic can do this is the subject of this paper.

Beginning with a Definition

Tom Davis's report resulting from a field exploration for knapping stones began with a definition to help his nonscientific audience—the members of his class—understand his paper.

Knapping is the art of making cutting tools by the controlled fracturing of stones. Glassy minerals, such as obsidian, chert, or flint (see glossary, p. iii), are fairly easy to knap because their smooth texture allows us to predict how they will break. A semiglassy mineral, such as quartzite, is much harder to knap because its graininess makes its fractures less predictable. . . . To find the best places for knapping in the area, I first searched the geological literature, including maps, at the U.S. Geological Survey Headquarters Library. After noting the deposits that are either very large or that were said to contain quartzite cobbles, I knapped cobbles at a site in each deposit. This paper describes the locations of major deposits of knappable stones in the area and the compositions of these deposits. By using the marked map in the appendix, the knapper should be able to locate these sites easily.

Beginning with a Summary

A paper on the problems of health care in the United States began with a question and then stated four answers, which became the four main parts of the paper.

Why is our health care system failing? Those who advocate a national health insurance law have cited four reasons: (1) there are not enough doctors and medical facilities, and those we have are not well distributed; (2) medical services are fragmented and poorly coordinated; (3) many people cannot afford adequate medical care of insurance; and (4) the cost of medical care is rising.

Beginning with a Review of the Literature

Sometimes, a writer may want to start with a brief review of what other writers have written on the subject, as this writer does in a study of Mark Twain's pessimism.

Literary critics have made much ado about Mark Twain's pessimism. What caused it and whether it existed from his early years are questions not yet answered conclusively. On the one hand there are those like

DeLancey Ferguson who see him as "a born worrier" (184). Henry Seidel Canby goes to some lengths to explain what he calls Twain's neuroticism (252–54). On the other hand, Bernard De Voto traces his problems to a guilt complex fed by family misfortunes for which he blamed himself (301). But the most likely cause of his problem, was, I believe, his feeling of shame for having yielded to the materialism of the Gilded Age.

You can see that an introduction can serve a number of purposes: it can define a word that is crucial to the understanding of the paper; it can state why the writer undertook the study; it may state the purpose of the research; it may briefly outline the body of the paper. In short, the introduction tells readers what they need or would like to know before reading the body of the paper; it introduces them to the paper. Choose the kind of introduction that fits your subject and purpose. You might want to try two or three different kinds to see which works best.

Getting Started without a Plan

If, after trying a number of possibilities for getting started, you still have a blank page in front of you, just begin writing anyway. Start talking on paper about your topic as if you were talking to a friend. You can rewrite your introduction later. Or take out your notes and begin writing the body of your paper. You may have a better idea of how you want to write your introduction after you have written some or all of your paper.

Writing the Body of Your Paper

In the body of your paper, you tell what you have discovered about your subject. If you are conducting an original study or experiment, you explain the methods you used as well as the results you obtained. If you are using secondary sources—information from others' studies and experiments—the body is where you give the information you have found. This is where you present the evidence that makes your thesis statement true.

Using Headings

The use of headings within the body varies according to the discipline you are writing in. Papers in the humanities usually do not use headings within the body. If you have done primary research, such as a scientific experiment or a field study in social research, you would present your findings under at least three headings (the introduction would have no heading): materials and methods, results, and discussion or conclusions. You can use secondary headings under these that correspond to your outline. If you are writing a technical report, use the headings corresponding to topics and subtopics in your outline. A research paper using secondary sources will usually follow the humanities or technical paper format. In organization, these two are similar, following an outline like those discussed in Chapter 7. (Note that papers using secondary sources can use any of the three main documentation systems illustrated in Chapters 11, 12, and 13.)

Developing Coherence and Unity

Following the outline you have designed before writing your paper (see Chapter 7) will help you to write a paper in which all of the parts are connected clearly and logically. Each part should logically follow the one before it. You should set up expectations for your readers—first in your topic, then in each part of your paper—which you then fulfill. Each paragraph is a kind of promise which is fulfilled in the next paragraph; each sentence is a promise fulfilled in the succeeding sentence. This linkage creates the feeling of coherence in your paper. Your introduction has already pointed to what you will discuss or prove in the body of your paper. You must now make sure that you do this. If you look back at the sample introductions given earlier in this chapter, you will see that you know after reading them what will follow. Read your introduction over again and see whether it prepares your readers for what you will write in the body of your paper. As you complete the discussion of each subtopic in the body of your paper, stop and see whether it moves smoothly and clearly from the preceding section.

Your outline should also provide unity for your paper. That is, you want to make sure that you don't include irrelevant information. If you deviate from your outline as you write, make sure you have a good reason for doing so—perhaps you have left something out of your outline. You'll have a chance to check your first draft for coherence and unity when you revise your paper (see Chapter 9 for suggestions).

Integrating Sources into Your Text

A transformation takes place as you write your paper. The information on your note cards, based on the words of a number of writers and speakers plus any information you have collected through your own observation, becomes a unified paper written in your own style and your own words. The paper becomes your message to your readers about the discoveries you have made during your search. The following suggestions may help you to make this transformation. With your note cards arranged according to your topics and subtopics, read your cards slowly and carefully, one subtopic at a time. When the material in one group of cards becomes part of your thinking—when it is integrated with the rest of your knowledge and experience—you will be ready to write. Then write as if you were passing the information on to your readers. The words should come from what is now in your own mind, rather than from the words on the cards. Write as much as you can without looking at your note cards; refer to your cards primarily for exact quotations or statistics or to note the source of information that needs documenting.

Keeping Your Readers in Mind

Instead of feeling that you are mechanically filling up pages for an assignment, maintain the sense of direct and active communication with your readers as you write. Your sources can become participants in this discussion of your subject; what they have to say is part of the story you are telling. Recall the way you tell someone about a conversation you have heard on a subject on which perhaps several people have disagreed. You will be saying something like, "John said this, but Jim disagreed because . . . . And Mary didn't agree with either of them. I thought there was some truth in what they all said. . . ." You will want to give a similar sense of a lively discussion on a topic of interest to you and to your readers, perhaps something like the way one student, Joan Ostby, reported writing part of her paper.

For her paper on Hart Crane's poem *The Bridge*, Ostby entitled a part of her outline "Evaluations." She read over her note cards with this heading and thought about them for a few minutes. There was some ambiguity and disagreement among the critical comments. She looked at her own notes and comments on the poem. She reflected on what had been written by critics about the poem and how she felt about it. When her thinking became clear, she sat down and wrote; she first summarized the views of the critics, quoting from some of them, and then gave her own evaluation. Notice how she varies her introductions of authors and their views.

The reviews of The Bridge are by no means unfavor-

Quotation with source in parentheses.

able; yet most of the critics seem to feel that it was a noble effort that did not quite succeed. It is termed a

Combination of paraphrase and quotation with author introducing the sentence.

"magnificent failure" by some (Horton 142). Allen Tate writes that The Bridge failed because "a great talent is engaged upon the problem of stating a position that is fundamentally incapable of definition." As a symool, the bridge, he believes, "stands for no well-

defined experience" (210). In <u>Hound and Horn</u> he

expresses his disapproval of the romanticism of the poem

View by another ——(132). Howard Moss objects also to the symbol of the
critic: reference in
text, page number bridge because he believes that it remains a static
in parentheses.

symbol--even though Crane tries to activate it. It is,

Page number
identifies source he says, "metaphysical on one hand and mechanical on
for two previous
sentences. the other. It rarely achieves balance between fact and
Reference not
needed for each vision" (42).
sentence.

—Although these criticisms are probably justified,
Introduction to
paragraph giving the poem seems to me to fail because it lacks integra-
Ostby's view.

tion. The "bridge" itself is supposed to be a symbol

of unity, connecting the past, present, and future. But

the poem as a whole does not present that feeling of

unity. The poetry is not consistently good, and the

transitions between sections are sometimes rough. It

Quotations from does not seem, either, that he has projected the "abso-
the poet being
discussed. lute ideal" "free from my own personality" that was

his design.

Although other critics are quoted, Ostby maintains her own control of the ideas expressed. They are merely aids to her in telling readers her view of this poem. (For detailed information on citing sources, see Acknowledging Your Sources, p. 151.)

Keeping Your Readers Informed

The Ostby excerpt illustrates how to combine paraphrases and quotations and at the same time how to let readers know when they are getting information from sources and when they are getting the writer's own opinions. It also shows how to cite those sources so that parenthetical citations disturb the writing as little as possible. When you can put the name of the author and even the book or article title in the text, you need only the page number in the citation.

Handling Quotations

When you indicate that you are using someone else's language by putting the words in quotation marks, you must make sure that you quote accurately; the spelling of each word and each mark of punctuation must be just as they are in the original. When you make changes in the original to make it fit your own language and style, you must indicate these changes to your reader. The instructions that follow for using quotations from your reading include suggestions on how to show such changes.

1. Let your own voice dominate. In order to keep your own style and tone you will want to use direct quotations sparingly, and, when you do use them, you'll want to integrate them carefully into your paper. If you have followed the suggestion of paraphrasing and summarizing as you read your sources (see Chapter 5), and if you have read each group of notes before starting to write, you should find it easy to use your own words. However, if you write directly from an article or book, the words of the source may dominate your thoughts and you might write a passage like this:

> "Don't Worry Baby" "became the first pop standard created by Brian Wilson" (Leaf 52). The song was a "staggering, textured tour de force of harmony, dramatic falsetto, and revolving melody. As an expression of teenage yearning and emotional insecurity, it was unsurpassed in the history of rock" (Priess 24).

The voice of the writer in this passage is lost among quotations of little or no significance. There seems to be little purpose in using the words of Leaf; the following paraphrase of the first sentence would work just as well: " 'Don't Worry Baby' was Brian Wilson's first pop standard." And the writer does not prepare us for the quotation from Priess nor does she let us know why she is using it. If the writer thought that this was an especially interesting or significant quotation, she could have introduced it this way: "One critic called it 'an expression of teenage yearning and emotional insecurity' and expressed his great enthusiasm for the piece by referring to it as 'staggering, textured tour de force of harmony, dramatic falsetto, and revolving melody' that was 'unsurpassed in the history of rock.' " This way the passage takes on more of the writer's style, and we hear *her* quoting Priess's words.

2. Integrate quotations into your paper by introducing the original author. All short quotations should be worked into the fabric of your own writing, by giving the name of the original author or by identifying the author in some other way, perhaps as an authority. The use of quotation marks is not enough to alert the reader to the fact that the words used are not yours. Quotation marks are visual cues, but you need verbal cues as well. Usually, if the words are important enough to be quoted verbatim, the reader wants to know who said them. This passage provides that necessary information:

> Most social learning theorists hold that child abuse is learned behavior. According to Lystad, parents who severely punish their children pro-

duce aggressive children who "in turn tend to punish their children more severely" (336).

3. Integrate quotations by making them fit grammatically. Sometimes you will have to omit words of the quotation at the beginning or end or even insert words of your own into the original (see the use of brackets, p. 148). You must make sure, though, that you indicate the changes by punctuation. For example, you can add a word for clarity.

ORIGINAL

"Orthodoxy, of whatever colour, seems to demand a lifeless, imitative style." (George Orwell, from *Shooting an Elephant and Other Essays*)

WORD ADDED

"[Political] orthodoxy, of whatever colour, seems to demand a lifeless, imitative style."

Or you might omit words from the beginning of the quotation and change verb tense when necessary.

ORIGINAL

"And thus, in the days ahead, only the very courageous will be able to take the hard and unpopular decisions necessary for our survival in the struggle with a powerful enemy. . . ." (John F. Kennedy, from *Profiles in Courage*)

INTEGRATED PASSAGE

Kennedy concluded that "only the very courageous [would] be able to take the hard and unpopular decisions necessary for our survival in the struggle with a powerful enemy. . . ."

4. Quote only significant or interesting words. Although the words of someone else intrude on your style, there are times when those words are what you want to use. One of these times occurs when the words of your source seem the best way to state an idea. Margaret Sharp found these words in her notes; the source was an interview with the manager of an adoption agency.

"Most girls intend to keep their children. It's rare that a girl comes to the agency intending to give up her baby. Those who do are usually older, more mature girls—nineteen or twenty years old. The average age of girls is fifteen years old. Out of 140 cases, we've placed 43 babies."

When the information appeared in her paper, most of the original was paraphrased; only one word was quoted directly.

Associated Catholic Charities took care of 140 young women and their newborn babies last year. Mrs. Rumford explained that most of these "girls"—except for the older ones, the nineteen- or twenty-year-olds—did not have adoption in mind when they came.

It's clear from the context that the word in quotation marks is Mrs. Rumford's. It is the only word that is hers, but the author wanted to report her use of this term in order to underline the plight of these young women by indicating that they were mere "girls." Quoting the whole passage would not have been necessary and would have detracted from the emphasis on one word.

5. Use long quotations when you want to hear the voice of your source. The following passage illustrates why you might want to quote a long passage and what the effect is when you do. It also shows how you can prepare your readers for a long quotation. Alice Drake, in her paper on how writers write, wanted to explain how Eudora Welty, the fiction writer, began her writing career. Drake decided that using Welty's writing style would add to the account, so she introduced her and let her tell it in her own words.

How do great writers start? Is there some sign at the very beginning of what is to come? Eudora Welty, in her biography *One Writer's Beginnings*, described her start this way:

The earliest story I kept a copy of was, I had thought, sophisticated, for I'd had the inspiration to lay it in Paris. I wrote it on my new typewriter, and its opening sentence was, "Monsieur Boule inserted a delicate dagger into Mademoiselle's left side and departed with a poised immediacy." I'm afraid it was a perfect example of what my father thought "fiction" mostly was (85–86).

Punctuating Quotations

To make your quotations effective and easy to understand, punctuate them carefully. In addition, you must indicate either by quotation marks (for short quotations) or by indentation (for long quotations) whenever you are borrowing words from someone else.

Introducing Quotations.   Use a comma or a colon to introduce a quotation that can stand alone grammatically: a comma for a short quotation and a colon for a long quotation (see p. 148 for illustrations of long quotations).

According to one psychologist, "Child abuse is a phenomenon of uniform symptoms but of diverse causation" (Gil 347).

But when you integrate the quotation into your own sentence structure, you do not need any introductory punctuation.

One psychologist has stated that child abuse ''is a phenomenon of uniform symptoms but of diverse causation'' (Gil 347).

To introduce a line of poetry or to emphasize a short quotation, use a colon.

A famous soliloquy of Hamlet begins: ''To be, or not to be: / That is the question.''

Sigmund Freud asked the question: ''What does a woman want?''

Quotation Marks. Always place quotation marks outside commas or periods.

''With me,'' William Faulkner told the students, ''a story usually begins with a single idea or memory or mental picture.''

When you put a citation at the end of a sentence, the citation is considered as part of the sentence but not part of the quotation. Therefore, place the quotation marks after the quoted material and the period after the citation.

Lincoln Steffens promoted ''the Henry George plan for the closing up of all the sources of unearned wealth'' (*Autobiography* 493).

Always place semicolons and colons outside quotation marks except when they are part of the quotation.

We meet Lena in the first sentence of *Light in August* ''sitting beside the road, watching the wagon mount the hill toward her''; she had come ''all the way from Alabama a-walking.''

Hotchner writes of Hemingway's ''superb skill at instruction'': Hemingway ''guided me every step of the way, from when to pull up to set the big hook in his mouth to when to bring him in close to be taken.''

Place a question mark inside the quotation marks if the quoted material is a question, outside if the quoted material is part of a sentence that is a question. The following quoted material is a question.

According to Young, aphasics can answer the question ''Were you drinking tea?'' but cannot tell where they live.

In the next example, the quoted material is not a question; the sentence that contains the quoted material is a question.

Do you know who said, ''That's one small step for a man, one giant leap for mankind''?

When an unfinished quotation ends the sentence, the three ellipsis points must be used in addition to a period. Notice the order: ellipsis points, quotation marks, citation, and period. (For further explanation of ellipsis points, see p. 149.)

Halberstam calls the study on the bombing of North Vietnam prepared by the Policy Planning Council "a pure study" that "reflected the genuine expertise of the government . . . ." (435).

Long Quotations.   Indent quoted material of more than four lines ten spaces from the left margin; do not use quotation marks. The right margin remains the same as the rest of the text. If your quotation is only one paragraph or a part of a paragraph, don't indent the first word more than the rest. The following quotation begins in the middle of one paragraph and follows with an entire paragraph, the first line of which is indented three additional spaces.

As The Great Gatsby closes, Carraway speculates about Gatsby's
death and life:

> I thought of Gatsby's wonder when he first picked out
> the green light at the end of Daisy's dock. He had come a
> long way to this blue lawn, and his dream must have seemed
> so close that he could hardly fail to grasp it. . . .
>
>   Gatsby believed in the green light, the orgastic fu-
> ture that year by year recedes before us. It eluded us
> then, but that's no matter--to-morrow we will run
> faster, stretch out our arms farther. . . [ellipsis dots
> in original]. And one fine morning--

When you quote material within a long quotation, use double quotation marks.

In Tillie Olsen's story "I Stand Here Ironing," the narrator describes her attempt to "make up" for not having paid enough attention to her daughter as she was growing up:

> Now when it is too late (as if she would let me hold and comfort her like I do the others) I get up and go to her at once at her moan or restless stirring. "Are you awake, Emily? Can I get you something?"

Single Quotation Marks.   Use single quotation marks to enclose a quotation within a short quotation.

Hart points out that "Given a problem and the necessary raw inputs, and 'left alone' to deal with it, our neocortex obligingly will solve it."

Brackets.   When you add clarifying words or phrases to a quotation, enclose them in brackets.

Hamlin Garland admitted that he abandoned polemics after "the destruction of the People's party and the failure of this novel [*A Spoil of Office*]."

Use brackets when you have to add words to make the quotation fit the grammatical structure of your sentence.

Cooper held that to "encourage the rich to hold real estate [was] not desirable" (*The Redskins* 8).

Use brackets to indicate you have underlined part of a quotation for emphasis.

She pointed to what Lincoln said in his Gettysburg Address: "Fourscore and seven years ago our *fathers* [emphasis added] brought forth on this continent, a new nation. . . ."

Use the Latin word *sic*, which means "thus," to indicate that your quotation or the spelling of a word is accurate, even though it may appear to be incorrect.

At the end of *Huckleberry Finn*, Huck writes that he is going "to light out for the Territory" because his Aunt Sally is "going to adopt me and sivilize [sic] me."

If you do not have brackets on your typewriter, leave a space before and after the material you want to bracket and add the brackets later in ink.

Ellipsis Points. Use three ellipsis points or spaced periods with a space before and after each point to indicate that you have left out part of a quoted passage.

J. Z. Young maintains that "the important feature of brains is . . . the information that they carry" (2).

When you omit material at the end of a sentence, place the period at the end as you normally would, with no space between it and the last word, and then add the three ellipsis points—a total of four periods in all.

According to *Time* magazine "the persistent growth of euphemism in a language represents a danger to thought and action. . . ."

When you omit a sentence or more in the middle of a passage, you need four periods. Be sure that you have a complete sentence both before and after the ellipsis points.

Faulkner explained in an interview at West Point that "every experience of the author affects his writing. . . . He has a sort of lumber room in his subconscious that all this goes into, and none of it is ever lost."

Use a line of spaced periods to indicate omission of a whole paragraph.

> Paul Taylor of the *Washington Post* pointed out the increasing difficulty of the uninsured to get care at hospitals:
>
>> One set of concerns is strictly medical; the other involves access and equity.
>> . . . .
>>
>> Relman and other critics also fear that the country is heading toward a two-tiered network of hospital care—private hospitals for paying patient, public hospitals for the poor and uninsured.

Poetry.   Punctuate poetry as you would prose. When you are quoting more than one line of poetry within a sentence, separate the lines with a virgule or slash (/) with a space before and after the virgule.

> To substantiate his view he quoted Blake's lines: "We are led to believe in a lie / When we see *with* not *through* the eye."

If you are quoting more than three lines of poetry, begin your quotation on a new line, ten spaces from the left margin, and double-space as you would with any other quotation.

```
Ogden Nash is recalled for his witty and sometimes philosophical
poetry:
                I think that I shall never see
                A billboard lovely as a tree.
                Indeed, unless the billboards fall
                I'll never see a tree at all.
```

However, if the lines are unusually long, you may indent them fewer than ten spaces.

When a poem has unusual spacing or when some of the lines are indented to follow a pattern, be sure to follow the spacing of the original.

> In the concluding verse of "Invictus," William Ernest Henley enunciated his philosophy of self-determination:
>
>> It matters not how strait the gate,
>>   How charged with punishments the scroll,
>> I am the master of my fate:
>> I am the captain of my soul.

Indicate the omission of one or more lines of poetry by typing a line of spaced periods in place of the omitted lines.

> In his poem "To a Skylark" Shelley addresses the bird as a being that knows more than humans:

Teach us, Sprite or Bird,
   What sweet thoughts are thine:
. . . .
Teach me half the gladness
   That thy brain must know.

Acknowledging Your Sources

When to Acknowledge Your Sources

You must give credit in your paper for ideas or information that belongs to someone else, whether you quote it, summarize it, or paraphrase it. Explaining where you got your material is part of the information about your subject that belongs in your paper. It gives readers a chance to judge its reliability and accuracy and also makes it possible for them to look up more about the subject if they want to. Failure to give the source is literary theft or plagiarism. (For suggestions on avoiding plagiarism, see p. 157.)

But give citations only when they are necessary. Every footnote or endnote number or parenthetical citation disturbs the flow of your writing to some extent. You do not need to cite your source in the following instances:

1. When your information is common knowledge.

> Mars was the Roman god of war.
>
> Dwight Eisenhower became president in 1953.

Although it may be difficult sometimes to identify what is common knowledge, in most cases you should not have trouble. Any date, like the one given in the example, that can be verified in an encyclopedia, newspaper, or almanac need not be documented, even though many people might not remember it.

2. When the information is accepted as true by most people.

> Alcoholism impairs the functions of the brain, liver, stomach, and lungs.

This kind of information may be harder to identify. You may be gathering information on a subject you know little about and everything is new to you. In doing research for a paper on drugs, you may read that most former heroin addicts are unable to stay away from heroin permanently. Is this common knowledge among doctors and heroin users? When you aren't sure whether it's common knowledge, and when your readers are people at the same level of knowledge as you who might question the validity of your information or wonder where you got it, you should document it.

3. When the statements or observations are your own.

> No one should be locked into full-time custodial care when alternative means of treatment are available.

You should always cite your source in these instances:

1. When the information is exclusively the idea or discovery of one person or a group of people. All direct quotations and most paraphrases and summaries of factual information fit this description.

> As crime rates rise, more prisoners stay longer in prisons that are already crammed well past their planned capacity (Jenson 1980).

The statement that "more prisoners stay longer" in crowded prisons needs to be documented by citing the person who has the figures to back up this information.

> In 1981 only 8 percent of architects reported using computers; in 1986, 32 percent of architects are expected to be using computers in their work ("Computers" 20).

You should give the source of any figures unless you compiled them.

2. When your readers might like to find out more about the subject.

> In his "Health Care for All Americans" bill, Senator Kennedy proposed the creation of a comprehensive plan to control health care expenditures (Riegle).

3. When your readers might question the accuracy or authenticity of the information. Ask yourself whether your readers are likely to ask "Where did you find that?" or "Who said that?"

> One species of mammal becomes extinct each year (Ziswiler 17).

4. When you use a direct quotation of one word or more.

> In his later years Lowell called Rousseau "a monstrous liar" (*Letters* 466).

How to Acknowledge Your Sources

The documentation within your text can be placed in footnotes or within parentheses; the documentation at the end of your paper will be a list called Works Cited, References, or Bibliography. Your choice of documentation style depends either on your subject or on the preference of the person or organization you are writing for. Check with your instructor to find out what style is required for your paper. The style commonly used by writers in the humanities (English, foreign languages, history, and philosophy) is known as the author/page style and is recommended by the Modern Language Association in the *MLA Handbook* (1984). This style is frequently used by writers in other disciplines, too, so if you are in doubt as to which style to use or if your instructor does not express a preference, the author/page style will probably be acceptable. Chapter 11 gives detailed guidelines for using this system as well as two sample papers illustrating its use.

A variant of this style is the use of footnotes at the bottom of the page or endnotes on a separate page at the end of the paper. Until 1983, footnotes or endnotes were advocated in the *MLA Handbook*, and many writers in the humanities still use them. You'll find suggestions for using them also in Chapter 11.

The author/date system is favored by writers in the social sciences, biology, earth sciences, and business and is recommended in the *Publication Manual of the American Psychological Association* (1983). Details for using this system and a sample paper are given in Chapter 12.

A third major documentation style is the number system, preferred by writers in the applied sciences, medical sciences, and engineering and outlined in the *CBE Style Manual,* published by the Council of Biology Editors (1983). The use of this style is explained and a sample paper is provided in Chapter 13.

The three major systems—author/page, author/date, and the number system—recommend that documentation information be given in parentheses within the paper with a list of references placed at the end. The following guidelines give some of the most frequent uses of these systems. You will find details for each system in Chapters 11, 12, and 13.

While you are writing your first draft, be sure to give the source in parentheses so that you will know where the material came from when you write your final draft. No matter what citation system you use in your final draft, give at least the author and page number of every summary, paraphrase, or quotation as you write your first draft.

Author/Page System. If you use the author/page system of citation, you need to supply the author's last name and the page number of the work, either in your text or in parentheses. Readers who want to know the name of the work and the publication facts can look those up in the list of works cited at the end of your paper. Place the parenthetical citation as near as possible to the information you are documenting, either where a pause occurs or at the end of the sentence.

When should you put the author's name in your text and when should you put it in the citation? To decide the answer, consider the needs of your readers. If the name of the author is a significant part of the information you are giving, give the name in your text, leaving only the page number for your citation.

> According to Van Doren (4), early American fiction writers were often charged with corrupting the public morals.

Here the page number is placed after the name of the author instead of after the information given because a pause occurs there.

When the information you are giving or the point you are making is more important than the author, place the author's name as well as the page number in the parenthetical citation.

> The Alliance adopted the free silver plank in its platform of 1887 (Hicks 132).

Note that there is no punctuation between the author and page number and that the period marking the end of the sentence comes after the parenthetical citation.

However, if you have included more than one work by an author in your list of works cited, you will have to include a brief title in your citation.

> As early as 1884, both major parties recognized labor in their platforms (Destler, *American Radicalism* 141).

You might refer in your text to a whole work; in that case you would not need a parenthetical citation.

> In *My Ántonia,* Willa Cather allows the narrator to overshadow the heroine.

When you have a long quotation set off from the rest of the text, place the citation in parentheses two spaces after the punctuation mark at the end of the quotation.

> In *The Jungle,* Upton Sinclair depicted the horrors of slaughterhouses in passages like this:
>> The fertilizer works of Durham's lay away from the rest of the plant. Few visitors ever saw them, and the few who did would come out looking like Dante, of whom the peasants declared that he had been into hell. To this part of the yards came all the "tankage," and the waste products of all sorts; here they dried out the bones— and in suffocating cellars where the daylight never came you might see men and women and children bending over whirling machines and sawing bits of bone into all sorts of shapes, breathing their lungs full of the fine dust. (129)

In the author/page system, as in the other systems, you would not put any documentation in footnotes or endnotes. The only notes you might use are content or explanatory notes to explain a point further or cite other bibliographic sources. If you use these, you would put them at the end of the paper before the Works Cited section. In the text you would place a superscript numeral, like this,[1], to refer your readers to a note at the end of the paper in a section labeled Notes:

> [1] See also Schlesinger (717), who points out that Adams was fascinated with politics throughout his career.

Leave one space between the superscript number and the beginning of the note.

Explanatory or content notes are explained further in Chapter 10; you will find other examples of their use in the sample papers in Chapters 11 and 12.

Author/Date System. For those who use the author/date system (writers in the social sciences, biology, business, economics, linguistics, and earth sciences), the date of the information cited, as well as the name of the author, is important and must appear either in your text or in a parenthetical citation. The list of sources appears at the end of the paper arranged in alphabetical order and usually titled References. A few of the most commonly used citations are given here; you'll find others in Chapter 12, along with a sample paper.

As you would want to do with any of these systems, make sure you introduce your source rather than just giving a quotation or paraphrase with a citation at the end.

If you use the author's name as part of your text, place the date in parentheses following the name:

> Wellington's study (1982) clearly showed that . . .

If the date is important enough to be included in the text, you should need no citation:

> Wellington's 1982 study showed that . . .

Perhaps you will want to put both the author and date in the parenthetical citation:

> At least one authority (Wellington, 1982) has pointed out that . . .

Note the comma between the author's name and the date.

Some instructors and some publishers prefer that page numbers be given with each citation. In any case, when you quote directly from someone else's work you *must* give a page number. When the author and the quotation are separated, the date is usually given directly after the name of the author; and the page number follows the quotation.

According to Lowe (1979), prison "should be the last alternative" (p. 14).

With a quotation of more than forty words, indent the whole passage five spaces from the left margin. If there are any paragraphs within the passage, indent the first line of each one five more spaces.

```
Barlow and Seidner (1983) reported the following results:
     The majority of relationship problems are connected with the
     phobia.  This seemed clearly true in the first client where
     the relationship was basically very strong. . . . Neverthe-
     less, relationship issues improved considerably as phobia
     improved.  This girl was referred for further therapy con-
     cerning interpersonal relationships and career choices fol-
     lowing treatment.
          The second client, on the other hand, came from a se-
     verely disturbed family with constant conflict.  The mother
     held the family together by trying to accommodate everybody
     but was hospitalized occasionally for periods of amnesia
     lasting several days during times of particularly intense
     family stress.  (p. 525)
```

Note the location and punctuation of the page number for a block quote—two spaces after the final period.

Number System.   The number system is used by writers in chemistry, physics, mathematics, medicine, and nursing and by some writers in biology. (A few chemistry journals use the author/date system.) With this system, citations start with "1" and are numbered consecutively throughout the paper. If a reference is repeated, its original number is repeated. Items in the list of references at the end of the paper are given in numerical order. Some writers use a variation of this system: the list of references is in alphabetical order and, consequently, the numbers in the text are not in serial order. For more details on the use of the number system of citation and a sample paper, see Chapter 13.

A citation using the number system appears this way.

Paroxysmal tachycardia occurs more often in young patients with normal hearts (5).

In a variation of the number system, some writers use both the number and the name of the author(s).

Paroxysmal tachycardia occurs more often in young patients with normal hearts (Krupp and Chatton 5).

Avoiding Plagiarism

Plagiarism is using others' words or ideas without attribution (see Chapter 5 for suggestions on avoiding plagiarism while taking notes). The use of summaries, paraphrases, and quotations from other without citing the source is plagiarism; using verbatim quotations without enclosing them in quotation marks is also plagiarism.

Plagiarism results from a writer's failure to integrate information from sources into his or her own thinking. Such failure often originates in inadequate paraphrasing and summarizing when you take notes; attempts to shorten the process and write directly from sources can lead to plagiarism. Besides the academic and legal penalties for plagiarism, one of the most unfortunate results is the writer's loss of the pleasure that comes from discovery of knowledge (plagiarism is evidence of the lack of such discovery) and the subsequent pleasure of telling about it.

Plagiarism is usually recognizable because the borrowed material is written in a different style from that of the author of the paper. Sometimes the borrowed material alternates with the writer's words with resulting distortion and lack of clarity. Often terms that were explained earlier in the original are not explained in the paper. Writers involved with their audiences do not write this way. But the writer who uses others' writing instead of his or her own is not concerned primarily with communicating to the reader, and most readers can sense this. Figure 8.1 is an example of plagiarism in the introduction to a paper. You will find it difficult to understand, even though it is the beginning of the paper, and you will probably lose interest rather quickly. The plagiarized passages are underlined.

Although the writer cites a source, his citation is given only at the end of the last sentence. Therefore, a reader has to conclude that everything else is his own. Yet it is obvious that to make such sweeping generalizations about large periods of history, the writer would have had to engage in years of research and would need to produce a book-length work to give the details on which they were based. The scope is beyond a student writer at almost any level. Lack of clarity and coherence are the result of stitching together unexplained generalizations from another writer with a few words of the writer's own.

Plagiarism is a rhetorical as well as an ethical problem. It results from interconnected failures in thinking, note taking, and writing. Here are some suggestions for avoiding plagiarism.

1. Make a schedule when you start work on your paper and follow it as closely as possible. When you find yourself rushing to meet a deadline, it is easy to get careless and save time by using someone else's words.

FIGURE 8.1 Plagiarism

ORIGINAL

The long epoch from the Second Awakening to the war with Spain was also a century of great tribulation, an "ordeal of faith" for church-going America. . . .

On the intellectual level the new challenges were of two sorts. First, there was a set of specific problems that had to be faced separately: Darwin unquestionably became the nineteenth century's Newton, and his theory of evolution through natural selection became the century's cardinal idea. . . . Accompanying these specific problems was a second and more general challenge: the rise of positivistic naturalism, the cumulative result of modern methods for acquiring knowledge. In every discipline from physics to biblical criticism, myth and error were being dispelled, and the result of this activity was a world view which raised problems of the most fundamental sort. (Sydney E. Ahlstrom, *A Religious History of the American People* [New Haven: Yale University Press, 1972], pp. 763–64)

PLAGIARIZED VERSION

The long epoch from the Second Awakening of 1785 and the war with Spain in 1898 was a century of tribulation and ordeal for religious Americans. During this period, but most notably between the years 1865–1900, many intellectual clergymen created a new Liberal Theology built on the tenets of Darwinism and positivistic naturalism, while the unlettered population remained staunchly conservative based on the orthodoxy of the Puritans.

The intellectuals dealt with two challenges, each of them separately. First, there was Darwin, who had become by (1865) the Newton of the nineteenth century, whose theory of natural selection had become the century's cardinal idea.

The second was a more general challenge: the rise of positivistic naturalism, or the cumulative result of modern methods for acquiring information. In every discipline from physics to biblical exegesis, myth and error were being dispelled, and the resulting world view raised fundamental problems concerning faith and the deterministic principles held by the church (Ahlstrom 763–64).

2. Choose a topic that you want to learn about and will want to tell others about. If you are genuinely interested in your subject you will want to use your own words to explain it.

3. Make sure you understand the materials you are reading; if you don't understand them, don't use them in your paper. If you don't comprehend your information, you will have to use someone else's words to explain it.

4. Take notes only after you have integrated your reading into your own thinking. Use paraphrasing and summarizing as much as possible in order to ensure that the material has become your own.
5. Before you write, review your notes carefully and make sure you understand how and where they will fit into your paper. If you don't see the connection between your information and your overall purpose, it will be difficult for you to use your own words.
6. Avoid writing directly from your sources. It's difficult not to use the words you see right before you.

If you follow these guidelines, it's unlikely that you will find yourself plagiarizing. Even more important, you will have the pleasure of writing a paper that you yourself will enjoy reading.

Writing Your Conclusion

The last question you answered in your search log as you began your research was, "What did I learn from my research?" If your research was successful, your learning will have changed your thinking in some way; you will see things differently. In your conclusion, record how your thinking has changed. You shouldn't have to strain to find out what these changes are. These changes in your thinking are what your readers would like to know. The examples that follow show how the thinking of these writers changed and how that thinking was recorded in their conclusions. A conclusion may be only a sentence or two, or it may be several paragraphs.

A conclusion may summarize. In her paper, "Two Proposals for a National Insurance," Mary Simione sums up the main differences between two proposals. Notice the detailed summation in the first paragraph followed by a more concise one.

> Senator Kennedy's plan would be more inclusive and comprehensive than President Carter's. Senator Kennedy advocated monitoring the quality of every level of health care while President Carter left the quality of the physician's work virtually uncontrolled. Although the initial cost of Senator Kennedy's plan was higher than President Carter's "Catastrophic Coverage" plan, his "Health Care for All Americans" act offered equal and quality service to the entire population; the Carter plan just provided supplemental care for the poor and elderly.
>
> Senator Kennedy has worked on restructuring the entire health system; President Carter attempted to solve the problems by guaranteeing care for the portion of the population that doesn't receive it now.

Some papers recommend change. In a paper on prison overcrowding, Linda Thornberry concluded:

> Long-term incarceration is necessary only for a very small percentage of incorrigible criminals. Nonviolent offenders, especially those serving two years or less, are prime candidates for alternatives to imprisonment. The alternatives that exist should be used in order to avoid prison overcrowding as well as to increase the chances of rehabilitation.

A conclusion may evaluate and predict. Joe Collins made a study of gas-saving devices and concluded:

> The vast majority of devices being marketed as mileage improvers are frauds. Because most of them don't work, it is hard for legitimate devices to gain public acceptance. Some devices which could improve mileage can't get to market because they can't conform to some government regulations.
>
> Any significant breakthroughs in mileage will probably come from the auto makers because they are the only ones with enough capital to invest in massive research and development programs. But in these times of trouble for them, even they may not have the funds without government assistance.

A conclusion fits the paper that it was written for. It grows naturally out of what came before it. If you find yourself thinking, "I'm supposed to write a conclusion, but I don't know what to say," take some time to reread your paper and think about it. What is it that you want your readers to know above everything else? What is the main idea that you would like your readers to remember? What thoughts would you like to leave them with? Tell them as clearly as possible.

Writing the Title

You may already have a working title, but after you have written your first draft, you may be able to decide on the final version. Your summary or thesis sentence can help you in composing a good title, but it contains more than you need in a title; a thesis sentence includes not only your subject but also what you are going to say about that subject. The title, on the other hand, is not a complete sentence—it doesn't have a verb; and it gives only the specific subject of your paper, not your conclusions about that subject.

Mavis Olson's summary sentence was "Companies should consider developing physical fitness programs for their employees." She decided on the title, "Developing Physical Fitness Programs in the Workplace." The following examples show how thesis statements can become titles:

Thesis sentence: Computer crime can be stopped with expensive security programs.

> *Title:* Solving the Problem of Computer Crime

Thesis sentence: The Gilded Age shows Mark Twain's cynical attitude toward democracy.

> *Title: The Gilded Age:* Mark's Twain's Comment on Democracy

Thesis sentence: The adoption agency performs an important service for both the mother and the adopting couple.

> *Title:* The Role of the Adoption Agency

Thesis sentence: The vast majority of devices being marketed as mileage improvers are frauds.

> *Title:* Getting Taken for a Ride With Gas-Saving Devices

The title can be imaginative but use humor or cleverness with care.

Writing an Abstract

An abstract or summary is often placed at the beginning of a paper in the social sciences, in the biological and applied sciences, and in engineering and business. There are two kinds of abstracts, each serving a different purpose: the first, the descriptive abstract, tells what a paper *does*; the second, the informative abstract, tells what a paper *says*. The descriptive abstract describes what the purpose of the paper is and explains how the purpose is achieved. It will talk *about* the paper. The informative abstract, on the other hand, is a summary—a condensed version of the paper. Most papers, however, would not have both kinds of abstracts.

An abstract may be a few sentences long (the descriptive abstract is usually short) or it may be several paragraphs long. The informative abstract of a ten- to fifteen-page paper is usually about three-quarters of a page long. It may appear on the title page single-spaced (if it's short), on a separate page at the beginning of the paper, or at the end of the paper. If you are asked to write an abstract, be sure you understand what kind it is supposed to be.

To write a descriptive abstract, read your outline or table of contents carefully and then convert the outline into cohesive sentences. Notice the following descriptive abstract; it *describes* what is in the paper.

This paper analyzes the volunteer program at State Museum and relates volunteer tasks to management functions. Specific areas for improvement are proposed. Finally the role of the volunteer coordinator is discussed, and recommendations are made for improving volunteer performance.

The informative abstract usually starts with the thesis statement or a summary and then gives details. It, too, should follow the outline or table of contents, but it gives the content of the paper as well as the paper's basic structure. The following informative abstract was included in a paper titled "The Uses of Computers in Architectural Design."

Computers are increasingly being used in architectural practices. The initial cost of the equipment can be as much as one-half million dollars or more, but this expense can be amortized in two to six years depending on the expense of the system and its full integration into the business. Before a computer is installed, the buyer often must remodel to find space to install the system. Once the system is installed, there will be a temporary slowdown in productivity; however, once it is integrated into the business, the gains will be evident.

Although many architects are choosing to install a computer system in their business merely to keep up with the competition or to impress clients, most investors find that computer-aided design cuts down on repetitive drawings and therefore increases productivity. Because the computer can produce high quality, accurate drawings, it reduces design problems.

Abstracts make it possible for readers to find out what your paper is about without reading the whole paper. Some readers in business and government will read only the abstract. Readers of journals may read the abstract of an article to find out whether they want to read all of it. Margaret Little's paper in Chapter 13 has an informative abstract as part of the paper's front matter.

Designing Graphics

Are you an artist at heart? Or do you think putting pictures on paper is not one of your talents? Graphics are a visual form of communication that anyone can use to clarify meaning. What we can "see" we tend to understand better—literally as well as symbolically. Illustrations can be tables, graphs, charts, diagrams, photographs, maps, or drawings. They are most frequently used in papers in the social sciences, in earth and applied sciences, and in engineering, but they can be helpful additions to any paper. Tables and graphs help you explain quantitative information; pictures and illustrations make hard-to-understand ideas easier to comprehend. If your paper is in history or geography, you can use maps; if literature is your subject, you may be able to use photographs or drawings; if your paper is on a business topic, you may want to use graphs, organization charts, or flow charts. To decide which of these are appropriate for your paper, look for information that can be quantified or visualized.

Conventionally, illustrations are either tables or figures. Tables, which are statistics or terms organized in columns and rows, are usually titled at the top; figures, which include all other types of illustrations, are usually titled at the bottom. The source of the information for the table or figure is given at the bottom; if the title is also at the bottom, the source should appear below the title, and the word Source should precede the source information. If information comes from more than one source, these sources should be given in footnotes at the bottom of the illustration. If the graphic itself was taken from another source, the source should be identified in parentheses after the title; for example, Figure 1. Pedestrian Deaths (*Daily News*, 2 June 1985; 18).

Several kinds of footnote symbols are commonly used in tables and graphs: superscript lowercase letters (a, b), superscript numerals (1, 2), and symbols such as asterisks, daggers, and so on. Most style manuals suggest that you use different symbols for illustrative material from the ones you use in your text to avoid confusion. Because any symbols you use in your text are likely to be superscript numerals, you would want to use one of the other systems for your table and figure footnotes. The *MLA Handbook* and APA *Manual* recommend superscript lowercase letters; scientific papers show a variety of symbols; technical writers usually use superscript numerals.

Be sure to introduce and explain your illustrations in your text and then refer your readers to the figure or table by number.

> U.S. cotton production over the last 45 years shows a continuing shift to the West and Southwest, away from the traditional cotton growing regions of the Delta and the Southeast (see Figure 5, page 3).

Or make the reference a part of your sentence.

> Table 4 shows the dramatic increase in exports of goods from Japan.

If you have three or more illustrations and are using a format with a table of contents (see Chapter 9), you should have a separate page titled List of Illustrations in the front matter of your paper, following the table of contents. If all your illustrations are tables, you can title your page List of Tables; if all are figures, call it List of Figures.

Tables

Tables present statistics and other information in a readable, understandable way by organizing them into columns and rows. Short, simple tables that can be read as part of the text need not be numbered or titled. Such *informal tables* also need not be framed with ruled lines nor contain internal ruled lines. In her paper on health care, Mary Simione first wrote the following sentences:

> We are paying more for medical care now than we ever have before. As a percentage of the gross national product (GNP), health expenditures grew from 5.25 percent in 1960, to 8.6 percent in 1975, to 9.1 percent in 1980 (Riegle 96).

She decided that the figures in the second sentence could be compared more easily if they were in table form, so she changed her paper to read:

> We are spending more of our gross national product (GNP) for medical care now than ever before, as the following figures show (Riegle 96).

GNP	1960	5.25%
GNP	1975	8.60%
GNP	1980	9.10%

Formal tables, like informal tables, compare data by aligning them in columns and rows. However, formal tables are not part of the text, although they are usually placed in the text near the passage that refers to them. They are always numbered and titled. In addition, they often contain more statistics and receive more emphasis through the use of horizontal lines and extra space. Formal tables can share a page with other text or can occupy a separate page. If you design a table, be sure to label all columns, using parallel grammatical structure, and give the source at the bottom of the table.

Perhaps the easiest way to make a formal table is to type it on your typewriter or computer and put in the horizontal lines with the underlining keys. Then using a ruler with a metal edge, draw the vertical lines with pen and dark ink. Your table will look more professional, however, if you make all the lines with pen and ink. To make your lines straight, tape your typed copy to a sheet of graph paper and tape them both to a window (unless you have a drafting table with a light underneath). You will be able to see the graph lines and can easily draw the box lines for your table.

If you find yourself in an artistic mood, you might try creating your lines with charting tape, a product sold under such names as Presto Graphic Tapes or Letraset Transfer Rules at office and art supply stores and most college bookstores. As with the ink-lining process, you should place your typed paper over a sheet of graph paper and tape

FIGURE 8.2 Preparing a Table

TABLE 1.

Cotton Exports of the United States and the USSR*

in Thousands of Bales

Country of Destination	Exporting Country					
	US 1967/68	USSR 1967	US 1972/73	USSR 1972	US 1978/79	USSR 1978
France	154.9	66.4	151.1	202.0	63.6	443.4
Germany, F. R.	104.0	82.1	188.3	49.3	96.3	111.3
Netherlands	37.4	10.1	48.8	3.2	18.0	23.3
United Kingdom	130.9	68.3	92.9	93.2	72.1	90.3

Source: Cotton and World Situation. Economics, Statistics and Cooperative Service. USDA: August 1980.

*U. S. = crop year; USSR = calendar year

them both to a window in order to apply the tape. Trim the tape with a razor blade or an X-Acto Knife (worth the small investment if you do several tables). The charting tape and transfer rules, which come in different widths and colors, are especially useful with long or complicated tables. Figure 8.2 shows a table that illustrates the bold effect of lines using charting tape or transfer rules.

If you plan to put your table on part of a page in your text, make the table on a separate sheet of paper; then trim the margins to fit the space where it will go and attach it with paper glue or rubber cement. If your table is very large, you may wish to reduce the size photographically before inserting it in your paper.

Graphs

Graphs (sometimes called charts) have more pictorial appeal than tables. They frequently show movement—trends or cycles. The three main types are bar graphs, line graphs, and circle or pie graphs. Graph paper, available in different sizes and patterns, makes construction of bar and line graphs relatively simple. After plotting your graph on blue-lined graph paper you can photocopy it and the blue grid marks will not be visible.

Bar graphs enable readers to compare and understand figures quickly and easily. The bars can be drawn vertically or horizontally. In general, vertical bars are used for altitudes and amounts and horizontal bars for distances, but you do not have to be overly concerned about which type to use as long as you label the items in your graph carefully. If you have graphic capability on your computer, be sure to use it. If not, here are a few guidelines for creating bar graphs.

1. Use a scale that shows your data to best advantage; you may have to experiment a little to find the best increments. Mark the intervals on graph paper, and then draw your bars.
2. You do not need grid lines on the final graph unless the bars would be so far away from the figures that the amounts would be hard to determine. You need only tick lines on the side to indicate the amounts.
3. Draw bars equidistant from each other, with the width of the spaces less than the width of the bars.

FIGURE 8.3   A Segmented-Bar Graph

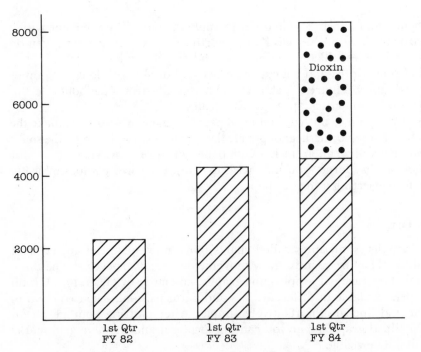

Figure 1. Growth in sample data (in milligrams).

The bars on a bar graph can be grouped; see, for example, the multiple-bar graph in Margaret Little's paper, p. 311.

You can also divide the bars in your bar graph, as Susan Titus did in the segmented-bar graph in Figure 8.3. For creating contrasting patterns in multiple- and segmented-bar graphs, you can use shading films, such as Zipatone and Letratone, which come in a variety of patterns on self-adhering sheets. Cut the film to fit the area you want to cover, then press it on the graph until it adheres. This graph was made for a report on soil contamination. In the first two years of gathering samples, no dioxin (polluting substance) was found. Dioxin increased dramatically in the last year (1984). The contrasting patterns add interest to the graph and show the contrasts more clearly.

Line graphs show movement or change, usually over a period of time. The independent variable—or the constant measurement, which in the graph in Figure 8.4 is the time interval—is placed horizontally, along

FIGURE 8.4   A Line Graph

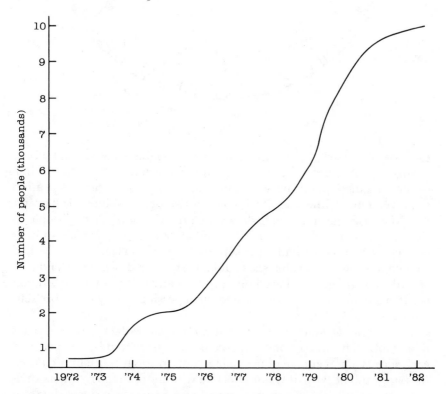

Figure 3. Annual attendance for Prince William Park for the last ten years.

Source: Records kept by park rangers.

FIGURE 8.5   Pie Graph Template

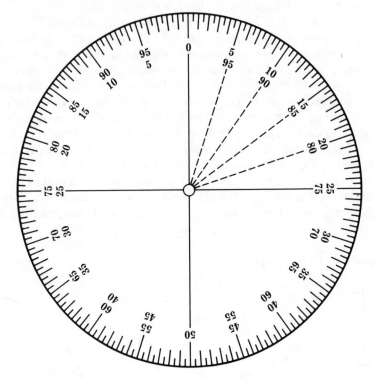

the base of the graph, and the dependent variable—the one subject to change—is placed vertically. Use points to mark the amounts; the line connecting these points draws the eye along, creating a visual sensation of movement. A line graph can contain two or more lines. For example, Marrit Beecroft's graph shows the attendance of all the people in Prince William Park between 1972 and 1982 as a single group only. If the necessary records had been kept by the park service and if she had wanted to show the results, she could have broken down the attendance records into subgroups based on age or an any other subgroup. If you use more than one line, you have to distinguish them by using broken, dotted, or colored lines.

Pie or *circle graphs* are useful if you want to show the relation of parts to a whole. The whole, or 100 percent, is represented by the pie, and each slice is a percentage of the whole. This graph is more limited than the bar graph because it is not effective with more than five or six divisions (you can, however, group several small parts in a single slice and label it "other").

To construct a pie graph you will need a compass to draw a circle and a protractor to divide the circumference into segments (3.6 degrees equal 1 percent). Or you can trace Figure 8.5 and use it to find the points on your circumference that correspond to your percentages. Begin at twelve o'clock (at zero on the figure) with the largest segment and proceed around the circle clockwise in descending order of size (unless you have a good reason for using another arrangement, such as maintaining uniformity with related graphs). Label the segments horizontally inside each slice, if there is room. In your labels include percentages and, if desired, the absolute quantity.

Drawings and Diagrams

Even simple drawings can help explain complicated structures and movements. In a paper on the Viking spacecraft, Lee Atkinson included the drawing in Figure 8.6 to show how the moon's gravity was used to direct the spacecraft. The drawing illustrates the route of the spacecraft. First directed toward the moon, the spacecraft was drawn into its gravitational pull, which then directed the craft toward Mars.

FIGURE 8.6   A Sample Drawing

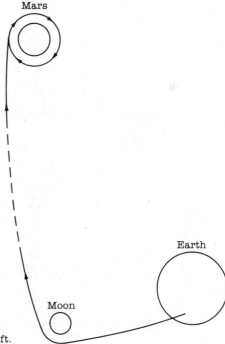

Figure 1. Path of the Viking Spacecraft.

Diagrams are more useful than photographs if you want to show only selected details. Peter DeGress drew the diagram shown in Figure 8.7 to demonstrate the placement of a collector in his design for a solar hot-water heating system.

A *flow chart* shows the stages of a process. You can use boxes to enclose the information for each stage, or you can use diagrams or drawings, as you might if you were to show the operation of a machine. The flow chart by Donna Ellis (Figure 8.8) shows the process of developing a telecommunications device, a process she discussed and evaluated in her paper. In making her report, she indicated the steps in the process, starting with ''block diagram'' and ending with ''prototype testing and qualification.'' The percentages indicate how much of the process in terms of time and money has been completed at each stage. When you have completed the circuit design, you are halfway through the process.

FIGURE 8.7   A Sample Diagram

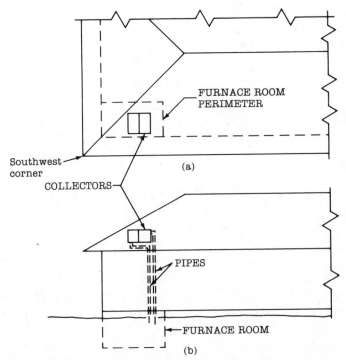

Figure 1. Top (a) and front (b) views of collector placement area.

FIGURE 8.8 A Flow Chart

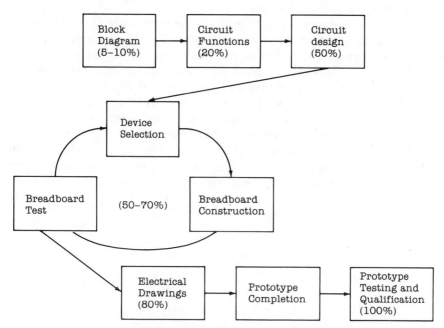

Figure 1.   Electronic system development process. Percentages
indicate the amount of development completed.

Source: P. Korda, RCA Price Operations.

EXERCISES

1. Choosing from the types of introductions given in this chapter,
   write two different introductions for your paper. Then choose the
   one you like best. Be prepared to explain your choice to your classmates.
2. Write a profile about a page long of the person you see as the typical
   reader of your paper. Include descriptions of his or her interests,
   level of education, knowledge of your paper's subject, and any other
   pertinent information.
3. Make a table from the following information: Maxim Junior College students came last year from three states. But the proportions
   in the two classes differed. Of first-year students, 28 percent came
   from North Dakota, 25 percent from South Dakota, and 47 percent
   from Minnesota. Of second-year students, 17 percent came from

North Dakota, 16 percent from South Dakota, and 67 percent from Minnesota.

4. Construct a multiple-bar graph from the information in Exercise 3.

5. Using the information you have collected for your research paper, design a graphic that will explain data more clearly than words do. Look for quantifiable data to make tables and graphs. Look for images that might form the basis of drawings or designs.

6. Using your thesis or summary statement as a source, record in your search log a list of at least three possible titles for your paper. Be thoughtful, but don't avoid putting down whatever might come to mind. These are not your final choices. Discuss your alternatives with other members of your class, perhaps in a group of three or four. Ask for reactions and suggestions for alternatives.

CHAPTER 9

Revising

I have to rewrite everything many, many times just to achieve mediocrity.

—William Gass, novelist

I never reread a text until I have finished the first draft. Otherwise it's too discouraging. Also, when you have the whole thing in front of you for the first time, you've forgotten most of it and see it fresh.

—Gore Vidal, novelist

I write my first version in longhand (pencil). Then I do a complete revision, also in longhand. . . . Then I type a third draft on yellow paper. . . . Well, when the yellow draft is finished, I put the manuscript away for a while, a week, a month, sometimes longer. When I take it out again, I read it as coldly as possible, then read it aloud to a friend or two, and decide what changes I want to make and whether or not I want to publish it.

—Truman Capote, novelist and nonfiction writer

I find it easier to discover mistakes or lack of smoothness when I read my paper aloud to myself. That's why I prefer to write and revise my papers when I am all alone. At times I like to read my papers to other people, so I can get an objective opinion about what I have written. It's sometimes easier for another person to hear something wrong than it is for me. When I revise I am constantly crossing out and adding on, so my papers contain a lot of writing in the margins and many arrows.

—Wendy Cohen, student

Revising is not something that you have to do because you failed to do the first draft properly; it is a natural and necessary part of the writing process. It means revisualizing or reseeing your material. Although the amount of change made varies from writer to writer and depends on the nature of the project, sometimes extensive changes are necessary. Figure 9.1, a page from Wendy Cohen's first draft, shows part of her revising process. She changed the order, combined and reworded sentences, and added more material. Sometimes revising requires more changes; sometimes, fewer.

All writers develop their own strategies at each stage of the revising process. Students, like professional writers, need to find out what works best for them as well as what does not. "I've always done it this way," doesn't mean "this way" is the best. Even though you want to produce the best possible paper, you also want to learn a process that you can use for any paper. Trading information on revising practices with your classmates is a good way to pick up ideas that you might want to try.

Preparing to Revise

As you already know from revising short papers, revising can mean that an idea that was only partially developed in an early draft becomes clear; it can mean that new ways of thinking about your subject occur to you; it can mean that you refocus your topic. If you have allowed yourself an incubation period (as suggested in Chapter 8), your mind has unconsciously been at work on your paper. Revising, then, is not so much a matter of correcting what you have already written as it is a second stage of the writing process. If you leave wide margins and keep two or three spaces between the lines, you will be able to rearrange words and sentences easily. If you want to add a whole paragraph, or even a whole page, you can put it after the appropriate page and number it by adding a letter to the page number; for example, the page after page 2 would be page 2a. Make a note on your manuscript to show where page 2a is to be added when you recopy. Or if you want to take a paragraph out and insert it somewhere else, you can cut it out and place it where you want it, using transparent tape or staples. Some people like to use different colored paper for each draft so that they don't confuse one draft with another. You can use colored mimeograph paper, which is inexpensive, for separate drafts; or you can use plain white paper for one draft and yellow paper for another.

FIGURE 9.1   Revising the First Draft

> *combine with first paragraph on next page*
>
> Nearly 600,000 of the nearly 1,000,000 teenage females who become
> pregnant each year elect to complete their pregnancies. / Teenage
> pregnancy ~~is on the uprise~~ *has been on the rise* since the 1960s and currently ~~results~~ *occurs* in
> 1/10 of the entire populat(oi)n of teen women each year. ~~These women~~
> ~~are at high risk of death because of their pregnancy and its com-~~
> ~~plications than women between 20-35.~~ Adole(s)cents ~~under the age of~~ *15 and older*
> ~~14~~ are in danger from complications related to pregnancy ~~and its~~ *and at higher*
> *risk of death* ~~complications~~ than women between *the ages of* 20 *and* 35. ~~Women between 15 and 19~~
> ~~die 35 percent more frequently than mothers in their early twenties~~
> ~~because of complications.~~ *Pregnant* /Teenage women ~~who undergo pregnancy~~ *also*
> deliver low weight babies twice as often as women in their twenties,
> and ~~experience infant death~~ *their babies die* nearly twice as often as *babies of* mothers in
> their twenties.

Following a Plan

Because you are re-viewing and re-seeing your entire paper, it's a good idea to make a plan for revision that focuses first on large elements—the paper's faithfulness to its purpose and to its organization—and then on smaller parts of the paper—paragraphs, sentences, individual words, and documentation. Too much early concern with the structure of sentences and the choice of words can waste your time if the paragraphs containing them are eventually enlarged, shortened, or eliminated altogether.

Revising with a Word Processor.   Revising, or any stage of writing, is physically easier with the use of a word processor. You can easily move parts of a manuscript from one place to another or omit them altogether by pressing a few keys. Such physical ease also benefits writers psychologically; all of us tend to do more of whatever is easier to do. In the revising process, computers are most helpful with the later stages of editing. Software is available to count the number of words in your sentences and to point out such structures as passive verbs and trite phrases, but only you can decide whether the changes are necessary. Availability of software varies according to the brand and type of computer you are using, but most computers can use programs to help you find spelling and typing errors. If you are in a special computer-assisted instruction class (CAI), you will, of course, be getting help from your instructor on using the computer in the research and writing process.

When planning your revision with a word processor, print a copy of your paper before you start so that you can see more of your manuscript at one time. You can also make notes on your hard copy, or you can even cut and rearrange parts as you would with hand- or typewritten copy before you begin revising the file of your diskette.

First Revising Stage: Focusing on the Whole Paper

Listen to Your Paper

If possible, read your paper twice—once aloud and once silently. The first time you read it (or have someone read it to you), assume the role of your audience. Read the title first, as though you were hearing it for the first time, and then read your paper straight through. Just listen to the sound of it and make mental notes of your reactions. You can make notes on paper, too, but you don't want to be distracted right now with details. Do you have enough information? Do you have too much? Is the line of argument clear? Do you find yourself hesitating or stumbling over words or phrases (these may be places that are difficult to understand)? Does the paper move clearly from one subject to the next and from one paragraph to the next, or do you find yourself trying to figure out your own meaning? Does the tone sound appropriate for the audience and is it consistently maintained? After hearing your paper, make a note of any changes you might want to make or any places that seemed unclear. You may not want to make these changes, however, until you have completed the second, silent, reading of your paper.

Make an Outline

Now read your paper once more, this time with a pad of paper and pen or pencil in hand. First read your thesis statement or summary sentence so that you have it clearly in mind as you start. Then read one paragraph at a time, and in a few words summarize what each one says. (As an alternative, you can write a summary sentence of each paragraph.) When you finish you will have a rough outline, which you can check against your working outline to see whether it corresponds. Where you find discrepancies, you may be able to see the reasons immediately and make the necessary changes. But it's a good idea to consciously check your paper for each of the following characteristics of a good paper to make sure that your paper contains them.

1. Check your paper's unity. Your paper has unity when everything in it is included in your thesis or summary statement. It has unity when every idea in your outline fits within your thesis statement. If you find in your outline something outside the scope of your original concept, you will have to either broaden your topic or eliminate the ideas that don't fit. If your summary statement is ''Sex education programs in the schools have benefited teen-age students,'' your outline should show only these benefits. However, if according to your outline, you have included some negative results and some needed improvements, you have more in your paper than you planned for. If you want to keep the negative results but show overall benefits, you could reword your summary statement to read: ''Although sex education programs in the schools need some improvement, they have already resulted in important benefits to teen-agers.''

2. Check your paper's organization. Make sure the order of your outline is logical. Try to identify the order: Have you used chronological order? comparison and contrast? order of importance? order of size (large to small or small to large)? Or have you proceeded from problems to solutions? from causes to effects? from the general to the specific? Other kinds of order are possible, as well as combinations. After identifying the order you have used, make sure you have followed it throughout your paper. Also check the order of subheadings. If your summary sentence is ''Although sex education in schools needs improvement, it has already resulted in substantial benefits for teen-agers,'' you may have the following main headings:

> Benefits of sex education in schools
>> Reduction of the number of teen-age pregnancies
>> Other benefits
> Some problems of sex education programs
> Suggested reforms of current sex education programs

You have to decide whether this is the best order. You have three main topics: benefits, problems, and reforms. If benefits are most important, as indicated by the fact that you put them in your main clause in your summary statement, then you have a most-to-least-important organization. You also have chronological order: you start with current benefits, move to analysis of problems, and then suggest what can be done in the future.

3. Check your paper's completeness. Your paper should contain everything you need to support your thesis. The major headings in your outline should be a good indication of whether you have covered everything. If your summary statement is "People should know how protein functions with other foods, what foods contain protein, and what it does for the body," obviously you have to explain each of these subjects. Or, if you are arguing, as one student did, that "the courts have been inconsistent in their decisions on cases involving affirmative action," you have to cite those court cases, and possibly statistics on them, to prove your statement.

4. Check your paper's coherence. The links between points in your outline should be clear; the reader shouldn't be surprised when you shift to another subject. Such shifts or transitions are often prominently marked by the repetition of key words; by the use of transitional words such as *therefore, however, before,* and *for example*; or by the use of headings. Sometimes, however, transitions are more subtle; a time sequence, for example, may be enough to provide coherence between parts. Sometimes the visual break itself between a section or a paragraph is sufficient. If you add transitional words or phrases just because you think you should, rather than because logic or sense demands them, you may tell your readers what they already know. A common example is the use of *In conclusion* at the beginning of a concluding paragraph that obviously sums up what you have said. Putting yourself in the place of your readers will help you to discover where coherence is lacking.

First-Stage Revising Process: Student Examples

Wendy Cohen's Process: Limiting the Scope of the Paper.   Wendy Cohen started with what seemed to be a manageable topic: the care of pregnant women. After doing some preliminary reading, she had five main headings to help her direct her research:

1. Misconceptions and myths about pregnancy
2. Day-to-day care
3. Common problems
4. Problems of high-risk pregnant women
5. Diseases of pregnancy

She read eagerly and extensively because she was very interested in her subject. When she reached her deadline for ending her search for information, she knew she had a lot of material, but she didn't realize how much until she began to write it down. When she finished she had over seventy handwritten pages. Because she knew that revision in itself would be a sizeable job, she decided that she could not meet her deadline unless she limited the scope of her paper.

First, Cohen made a detailed outline—a map to see where she was. Under "Day-to-day care" she listed "nutrition, effect of emotional health, work, sleep, sex, exercise, clothing, and travel." Under "Diseases of pregnancy," she listed "rubella, syphilis, herpes, gonorrhea, Rh disease, diabetes, and anemia." She seemed to be on her way to writing a book, but she didn't have time to write one. Obviously, she had to leave out something, but she didn't know what. In fact, she didn't really want to leave out anything; she wanted all the work she had done to show up on the pages of her paper. But Cohen finally decided to be realistic and limit her paper to the parts of her subject that she was most interested in—that is, to the care of women who were most likely to have problems in pregnancy and the diseases that caused some of these problems. She excluded the first three headings in her first outline. This was the final outline of her paper:

I. The importance of the prenatal period to mother and child [the introduction]
II. The risks of teen-age pregnancy
III. The risks of pregnancy for women over 35 years of age
IV. The dangers of disease during pregnancy
    A. Rubella
    B. Toxemia—Preeclampsia
    C. Rh disease
    D. Venereal disease
V. Recommended uses of drugs and vaccines in high-risk pregnancies

Cohen was now ready to write a second draft based on this outline. Because she had done so much research on her subject and knew it so well, she was able to write her second draft easily and confidently. By revising each section as she went along, she was able to complete her paper in three complete drafts—the minimum number for most writers.

Martha Cross's Process: Shaping and Focusing the Paper. Martha Cross wrote a paper on the criminal justice system. Her summary sentence was "The criminal justice system—consisting of law enforcement, judicial process, and corrections—does not adequately control crime.'' This was her working outline:

1. Law enforcement
2. The judicial process
   Attorneys
   Courts
3. Corrections
4. Evaluation

After completing the first draft of her paper, she reread it paragraph-by-paragraph and made the following informal outline:

1. The police department
   Lack of emphasis on law enforcement
   Lack of sufficient staff and budget
2. The adversary system
   Use of inexperienced public defenders
   The greed of private lawyers
3. The courts
   Delayed hearings
   Inequities in sentencing
   Full dockets
   Overuse of plea-bargaining
4. Correctional systems
   Overcrowded prisons
   Lack of sufficient staffing
   Lack of meaningful work
   Denial of simple amenities in order to punish
5. Lack of help for victims
6. Evaluation and solutions

With her new outline in hand, she checked her paper for the following characteristics.

1. Unity. Here she noticed a problem. Heading 5, ''Lack of help for victims,'' did not fit into her summary statement. Her concern for victims had developed as she wrote her paper. At the beginning she had written:

> According to James Campbell, criminal justice means ''effectively controlling the increasing levels of deviant behavior in a manner consistent with our ideas of fair and humane treatment'' (11). As a crime-controlling agent, our current criminal justice system does not work.

However, near the end of the paper she had written:

> Protection of victims should be a main concern of the justice system. Criminals have more rights than the victims. That is not justice! The of-

fenders should pay restitution to the victims. The victims are the neglected ones, not the criminals.

Cross found that she had shifted the focus of her topic as she wrote—a common occurrence in writing a first draft. In the beginning she was writing about justice for criminals, and at the end she was writing about justice for victims. She had to decide whether she wanted to broaden the focus of her paper to include justice for both criminals and victims or to leave out an issue she felt strongly about—the rights of victims. Before making this decision, she thought she would wait until she had checked *all* four points.

2. Order. Cross next checked the organization of her paper. It followed the chronological order of handling criminal cases—arrest, trial, and imprisonment. Each point she made fit into this order, except for one—"Overuse of plea-bargaining" under "The courts." She began her discussion of plea-bargaining with this sentence: "The prosecuting and defense attorneys should not use plea-bargaining as freely as they do." Obviously she needed to move this decision to the section on the adversary system.

3. Completeness. The issue of completeness coincided with her unity problem. Her statement that "Criminals have more rights than victims" was vehement and heartfelt, but she had given no evidence to prove it. In fact, she realized she would have trouble proving such a sweeping generalization. To add more details here would require more research and change the whole focus of her paper; she would have to leave out much of what she had already written. Reluctantly, she decided to stay with the original design of her paper and leave out the section on lack of help for victims.

4. Coherence. Transitions occur between all elements of a paper—between sections, between paragraphs, and between sentences. Cross was looking now for transitions between sections. She had three major transition points: (a) between number 1, the police department, and number 2, the adversary system; (b) between number 2, the adversary system, and number 3, the courts; and (c) between number 3, the courts, and number 4, the correctional systems. Major divisions of a paper are often like minipapers; hence, you can achieve a transitional effect by indicating the completion of the discussion of one subject and by wording that looks forward to the next section or paragraph. Or the new section can look back by using a word or phrase that connects the two and shows their relationship.

Cross looked at her transitional sentences. This is the way sections two and three began (the transitional words are italicized):

The adversary system *also* needs to be modified.

The courts are *also* in need of radical changes.

In addition, she used the word *also* as a transitional word within sections: "The judges *also* create inequities within the court system." The transition to section four had no transitional words at all:

> There are many faults with the current system of corrections.

Obviously her transitions needed some attention. She needed some variety in her transitional words as well as different language to show the relationships between these sections. She changed the transition between sections two and three to the following sentence:

> Although improvement in the adversary system would help to improve the justice system, changes in the courts are needed even more.

Then Cross rewrote the transition between sections three and four (between the courts and the correctional systems) in this way:

> If these suggestions were followed, the improvement within the judicial process would be noticed within a year.

Thus she ended the section on the judicial process with an evaluation and a recommendation. The beginning of the section on the correctional system looked back at the first two sections and then focused on its own theme—corrections:

> However, the problems within police department and the judicial process seem relatively easy to solve when compared with the problems of changing the offenders.

She was now ready for the second stage of revising.

Second Revising Stage: Focusing on Parts of the Paper

Check Paragraphs

Read each paragraph in your paper to make sure it is integrated, unified, and complete. The following examples show how students have rewritten paragraphs to improve them.

1. Improve integration of sources. Whether you summarize, paraphrase, quote, or use your own ideas, your writing should flow as though it came from one source—you. It will be integrated if you make it part of your thinking rather than just copy from cards or articles. Here is a passage from the first draft of a paper on alcoholism.

> Studies have shown that family behavior patterns are often important in the transmission of alcoholism from parent to child. Some of these

patterns are parental conflict about drinking, parental disagreement about drinking practices, and parental abuse of alcohol (3, p. 42). Scientists have claimed that problem drinking among males can be predicted just by looking at their age, socioeconomic class, ethnic origin, and religious affiliation (4, p. 163).

In rereading his paper, the writer noticed that the sentence beginning "Scientists . . ." moved away from the subject of family behavior patterns and even contradicted what he had written in the first two sentences about family patterns as a primary cause of alcoholism. He had gotten the information for the first two sentences from one source and the information for the last sentence from another, and he hadn't integrated them. He rewrote the paragraph to show the relationship between these ideas and to clarify them. He also combined the first two sentences, with this result:

> In transmitting alcoholism from parent to child, such familial behavior patterns as parental conflict about drinking, parental disagreement about drinking practices, and parental abuse of alcohol have been important (3, p. 42). However, some scientists believe that alcoholism is more of a social phenomenon and claim to be able to predict problem drinking among males just by looking at the age, socioeconomic class, ethnic origin, and religious affiliation (4, p. 163).

2. Keep the paragraph unified. The writer of a paragraph makes a promise to readers to explain something. Usually this promise is made in the first sentence (often called a topic sentence). Readers expect that everything in the paragraph will help to carry out the promise so that the paragraph will be unified. When the writer fails, readers are disappointed and confused. The following paragraph makes a clear promise, but it isn't kept.

> The real task for the black community and society as a whole is to develop incentives that will be more attractive to teen-agers than having babies. Many people feel that teaching their child to say "no" to sex is the solution to the problem, but it is not. Saying "no" is an important part of solving the problem but not the solution in itself. According to Noel, parents must help teen-age girls develop more self-confidence and improve their ability to make their own decisions (92). If they learn these skills, they are not so likely to succumb to peer pressure, not only in sexual matters but in other areas of their lives. Dr. Marion Howard, director of a teen services program, recommends the following guidelines for parents (Noel 94):
>
> Learn to listen.
> Try to avoid judging the child.
> [Etc.]

This paragraph promises to talk about the responsibility of society in dealing with the problem of teen-age pregnancy. But it shifts to the problem of peer pressure and suggests ways for parents to help their child make decisions. The subject of this paragraph is really how improvement in the relationship between parents and child can help the child withstand the peer pressure that leads to pregnancy. This writer rewrote the beginning of the paragraph to make the promise match the content.

> As part of the solution to the problem of teen-age pregnancy, professionals have suggested educating the parents so that they can communicate better with their children (Noel 92). Many parents feel that teaching their child to say "no" to sex is the solution to the problem; but, although saying "no" is part of the solution, it is not the solution itself. According to Noel, parents must help teen-age girls develop more self-confidence and improve their ability to make their own decisions (92). If they learn these skills, they are not so likely to succumb to peer pressure, not only in sexual matters but in other areas of their lives. Dr. Marion Howard, director of a teen services program, recommends the following guidelines for parents (Noel 94):
>
> > Learn to listen.
> > Try to avoid judging the child.
> > [Etc.]

Now the paragaph is unified around the idea of what parents can do about this problem.

Sometimes the writer introduces an irrelevant idea into the middle of a paragraph:

> Since most of a prisoner's complaints are aired in prison disciplinary hearings, the organization of such hearings is interesting to examine. *In a correctional institution, administrators normally have several forms of enforcing discipline, such as the withdrawal of privileges afforded the average inmate. More severe discipline such as isolated confinement can be instituted for serious offenses.* In 1973 the Supreme Court determined that the state must provide twenty-four hours' written notice of charges, that prisoners have the right to call witnesses, and that an impartial body be chosen to consider the case. But prisoners are not allowed to cross-examine witnesses and there is no provision for legal counsel.

The italicized sentences introducing the idea of how administrators enforce discipline do not belong in this paragraph, which is about the organization of disciplinary hearings. The reasons for calling such hearings should be discussed in an earlier paragraph.

3. Include enough information. If a paragraph leaves unanswered questions in readers' minds, more information is probably needed. The first draft of a paper on subliminal advertising contained the following paragraph:

> As a result of Vance Packard's book, *The Hidden Persuaders,* six state legislatures and the U.S. House of Representatives introduced legisla-

tion to ban subliminal techniques. In the 1960s, public discussion on the subject virtually disappeared; the proposed legislation was never enacted.

It was not the book but what Packard said in his book that led to the legislation. Readers are likely to wonder what that was. The writer rewrote the paragraph this way:

> As a result of Vance Packard's accusations in *The Hidden Persuaders* that advertisers practice the "psychoseduction" of consumers and "play on our subconscious," six state legislatures and the U.S. House of Representatives considered legislative action to ban subliminal techniques. . . .

4. Make the paragraph coherent. When a paragraph has coherence, each sentence fulfills the promise of the preceding sentence and in turn predicts what will follow. Thus each sentence is a link in the chain of sentences that forms the paragraph. This linkage allows readers to understand you easily and quickly. But when you set up readers' expectations and then don't fulfill them, the result is confusion. Readers may be able to sort out the order, but it will take some time. And they shouldn't have to do your job. A paragraph is like a conversation between the writer and readers with the readers making mental responses or asking questions after each sentence and the writer setting up those responses or questions and then answering them.

In the following coherent paragraph, the reader's mental response is given in brackets so that you can see how each sentence satisfies the issue raised in the previous one:

> The main reason for the computer industry's vulnerability to microcomputer-assisted crime is that businesses do not want to spend money. [Reader: How does that encourage crime?] The necessary precautions are not being taken for a system whose usefulness relies heavily on security. [Reader: What precautions are not taken?] Businesses must have auditing systems so that they will know who is using their system. [What else?] They must keep back-up files to replace those that are erased and altered. [Anything else?] Finally, they must be willing to prosecute computer criminals, instead of refusing for fear of bad publicity. [The word *finally* signals the end of the paragraph.]

Because the expectation set up by each sentence is fulfilled by the succeeding sentence, readers can read the paragraph quickly, without confusion.

Check Sentences and Words

Read your paper once again, focusing on the sound and meaning of the sentences. When a sentence seems unclear or when it does not flow easily and naturally, you may be able to see the problem immediately and correct it. But if you have trouble identifying the source of the difficulty, the following suggestions will help you improve it.

You'll notice that your sentences may need attention in more than one place because a breakdown in one place often causes breakdowns in others. A sentence with major problems needs more than the change of a word of two; it needs complete rewriting. Sometimes, too, your sentences may be free of errors, but still need improvement.

The following suggestions show how you can improve the strength, unity, and coherence of your sentences by using strong verbs, by structuring your sentences for emphasis and clarity, and by eliminating unnecessary words.

1. Use strong verbs. Writing conveys the energy of the writer, just as the voice conveys the energy of a speaker. And, just as you soon find your mind wandering from the words of a speaker who is dull or monotonous, you soon lose interest in reading sentences that lack vitality and strength.

Verbs generate energy for your sentences and give your sentences the life that keeps your readers reading. If you use too many weak verbs, such as verbs in the passive voice or linking verbs (forms of the verb *to be* such as is, are, was, and were), you make your writing lifeless and dull. You can use a computer program to find such verbs for you, but you still have to decide whether they are the best choices. In general, you should use the passive voice only when the receiver of the action is more important than the doer or when you don't know who the doer is. Linking verbs are useful, of course, but avoid overusing them. The following examples show problem sentences that students found in their papers, along with analyses and revised versions.

FIRST VERSION

A decision was made by the president to begin the bombing at once.

Was made is in the passive voice. The real action in the sentence has been weakened by putting it in the form of a noun—*decision.* To improve this sentence, put the main action of the sentences into a verb form—*decide.*

REVISED VERSION

The president decided to begin the bombing at once.

FIRST VERSION

The adversary system is in need of improvement.

The linking verb *is* undermines the vitality of this sentence. The use of the noun *need* instead of the verb form further weakens the sentence.

REVISED VERSION

The adversary system needs improvement.

2. Revise sentences that are too long. The meaning of your sentences is conveyed partly by their structure. A sentence that is too long can get monotonous and fail to emphasize anything. But counting the number of words in a sentence won't tell you whether a sentence is too long. A sentence is too long when it lacks a central, emphatic idea or when the connections between words become so unclear that readers can't follow the meaning to the end. One remedy for a long, unwieldy sentence is to divide it, as the following example shows.

FIRST VERSION

According to Alvin Bronstein, the executive director of the ACLU's National Prison Project, "prisons were instituted in a Jacksonian hope that human improvement was possible if a criminal's unfortunate upbringing could be overcome in an antiseptic and healthy setting," but obviously today's prisons do not meet such standards.

None of the ideas in this sentence stands out. If the writer wants to emphasize the last part of the sentence she can put it into a short simple sentence of its own. The contrast with the longer preceding sentence would then make both sentences more effective.

REVISED VERSION

According to Alvin Bronstein, the executive director of the ACLU's National Prison Project, "prisons were instituted in a Jacksonian hope that human improvement was possible if a criminal's unfortunate upbringing could be overcome in an antiseptic and healthy setting" (19). Obviously today's prisons do not meet such standards.

Another remedy for a long sentence is to shorten it.

FIRST VERSION

Probably the greatest incentive that could lead the Soviets into a decision to invade the Gulf would be that it would be an ideal place from which to project power since currently their greatest logistical constraint is that they lack a warm water port, and the Middle East leads to everywhere in the world as the term used to describe it—"historical bridge between East and West"—implies.

Notice how the subordinate clauses follow one after another ("that could lead . . . ," that it would be . . . ," "that they lack . . . ,") making it difficult for readers to keep track of the connections. Readers may lose interest. The verbs *could be* and *is* are weak. The writer needs to find the main action word (here it is in the noun *decision*) and make it into the main verb of the sentence. The addition of a *because* clause would show the relationship of the other ideas to the main clause.

REVISED VERSION

The Soviets might decide to invade Iran because such a move would give them a warm water port and a base of power in the Middle East—an area Kingston has called the "historical bridge between East and West."

3. Combine short sentences by using subordination. A short, simple sentence is emphatic; it highlights one idea. When you have too many short sentences together, you are telling your readers that every idea in them is of equal importance. You are failing to show readers the relative importance of ideas and the relationships between those ideas, thus leaving them to figure out the relationships on their own. In addition, groups of short sentences usually repeat the same pattern (subject, verb, object) and repeat words, especially pronouns. Although, with care, use of one or two short sentences can be effective, too many of them make your writing monotonous and lifeless. Signs of sentences that might be improved by combining are successive short sentences, sentences that repeat words, and sentences that begin with pronouns. Notice the repetition of the same word (or a pronoun that refers to that word) at the beginning of each of the following sentences.

FIRST VERSION

The first law was known as the "28-hour law." It protected livestock shipped by rail. It stated that cattle had to be exercised in pens if their journey was to be longer than twenty-eight hours.

The writer revised this draft in order to put the ideas he believed to be less important into subordinate (or less important) structures. His revision is clearer and stronger.

REVISED VERSION

The first law, passed in 1906 and known as the "28-Hour law," required that livestock be shipped by rail and that they be exercised in pens if their trip was longer than 28 hours.

4. Use coordination to show equal relationships. Sometimes you want to show the equality of ideas; you want to "coordinate" rather than "subordinate" ideas. Joining two or three clauses of the same kind can be effective, as the following example illustrates.

FIRST VERSION

Many people believe that a child's sexual values develop slowly from observation, imitation, and guidance at home. Teaching sex education in school would only be a waste of time and energy because attitudes, values, and outlooks are already established at home.

Some of the ideas in these sentences are almost the same, so some could be eliminated. It seems clear that the second sentence is also part of what "many people feel." Why not combine and coordinate them?

REVISED VERSION

Many people believe that a child's sexual values develop slowly from observation, imitation, and guidance at home and that teaching sex education in school would only be a waste of time and money.

5. Use parallelism for emphasis. Parallelism is a form of coordination that uses repetition of structures and often words for emphasis. The writer sets up a pattern that gains its effectiveness from building to a climax, like Lincoln's conclusion to the Gettysburg Address: "that government of the people, by the people, and for the people, shall not perish from the earth." Here three prepositional phrases are linked and the word *people* is repeated. In Julius Caesar's famous statement about conquering Gaul (France)—"I came, I saw, I conquered"— three short clauses beginning with *I* build from the simple "I came" to the strong "I conquered." Use parallelism to create this emphasis when you can.

Problems can arise when you set up the pattern and do not follow it through. You must continue with the structure you started with (such as prepositional phrase, subordinate clause, noun, or adjective) and you must repeat the word, when there is one, that signals the parallelism. These structures are usually joined with coordinating conjunctions such as *and* or *but*. These examples show how a sentence can be strengthened by parallelism and how to remedy faulty parallelism.

FIRST VERSION

In the remedial reading clinic he learned how to coordinate his eye movements, how to scan for information, and how frequent reviewing for key ideas helps.

Although *how* is repeated, the pattern set up is the repetition of *how to*.

REVISED VERSION

In the remedial reading clinic he learned how to coordinate his eye movements, how to scan for information, and how to review for key ideas.

FIRST VERSION

Other advantages [of the aircraft] include day or night operation in all types of weather, continued operation for 11 hours and twice as long if

refueled in flight, and if systems malfunction, its computer switches all
operations to back-up computer circuits.

A long, complicated sentence like this needs the clarifying force of parallelism. First notice the use of a noun instead of a verb (*operation*) to
carry the action in the first two elements and the use of a weak verb,
include. In revising, the writer should try first to restore strong verbs.
More than one solution is no doubt possible; the writer's choice would
depend to a great extent on what comes before and after this sentence.
This would be one possibility.

REVISED VERSION

The aircraft can also operate in all types of weather, can fly for 11 hours
(twice as long if refueled in flight), and, if systems malfunction, can
switch to back-up computer circuits.

6. Eliminate unnecessary words. Make every word count. When
you add unnecessary words, you make your readers, who have to read
them and disregard them, do your work for you.

FIRST VERSION

This illustration shows the financial impact with respect to FY83 salaries.

With respect to is one of a number of phrases, such as *with regard to* and *at
this point in time* that can be shortened to one or two words.

REVISED VERSION

This illustration shows the financial impact of FY83 salaries.

7. Avoid needless repetition of words. You can repeat words effectively for emphasis, but when you don't want to emphasize, the repetition is irritating. Needless repetition of words in successive sentences
usually means that the sentences can be combined.

FIRST VERSION

They have fur which is a dense coat of underfur covered by longer guard
hairs. This fur is shiny and varies in color from black to dark brown, but
may also have white-tipped hairs scattered throughout.

The words *fur* and *is* are repeated; also the main verbs (*is*) are weak
linking verbs. Notice also the unneeded phrase *in color.* If you read these
sentences aloud, you will hear their deadness. The writer needs to locate the subject of these sentences and the main action word and then
build a sentence around them. The subject, of course is *coat of underfur,*
and the main action word is *varies.* These will form the core of a revised
sentence.

REVISED VERSION

Their dense, shiny coat of underfur, covered by longer guard hairs, varies from black to dark brown with scattered white-tipped hairs.

8. Avoid using jargon. Jargon is the language of a particular group, usually a professional group. Doctors, lawyers, teachers, computer programmers, truck drivers, musicians, and baseball players all use jargon to talk to each other. Jargon is the shorthand that makes it possible for the members of these groups to communicate more easily with each other. But jargon is also a way to show who belongs to the group and who doesn't. In the effort to prove membership, writers often use awkward constructions and unclear language. Overuse of the passive voice and linking verbs is common. Student writers can easily pick up this jargon as they read the sources used in writing their papers. In your paper you should use specialized terms only when clarity demands that you do, not to show that you know the language of a certain group. Now is the time to change any jargon you have used to plain English, as the following examples illustrate.

FIRST VERSION

Similar experiments to those performed on nonhumans have yielded congruent results with humans.

The phrase *have yielded congruent results* can be simplified.

REVISED VERSION

Experiments similar to those performed on nonhumans have shown the same results with humans.

FIRST VERSION

The exponential growth of computer power, along with exponentially expanding telecommunications capacity and availability, has served to fuel an insatiable appetite for using information in the management function of organizations.

Not only is this writing difficult to understand, it makes the reader feel that even trying to understand it is not going to be worth the struggle. What does *appetite for using information* mean? A possible revision:

REVISED VERSION

The rapid growth in the use of computers along with the expanding use of telecommunications facilities has resulted in an increased demand among managers for exchanging information.

Correct Faulty Connections

Just as sections of your paper and paragraphs must be coherent, the parts of a sentence must be clearly connected. Each word in a sentence must link up with some word or words in order for the sentence to read smoothly and to make sense. The basic linkage is between subject and predicate or verb. Secondary linkages are between nouns and verbs, adjectives and nouns, and pronouns and nouns. Making these links correctly helps your readers to understand your sentences more easily.

1. Make subjects and verbs agree in number. The subject determines whether a verb is singular or plural. Most writers don't have trouble when the subject and verb are next to each other (*Jack is my brother*), but when the subject and verb are separated by a phrase or clause, it's easy to lose track.

FIRST VERSION

Many experts believe that specific instructions to prepare youngsters for the many responsibilities of marriage is now needed more than ever before.

The subject *instructions* is separated from the verb *is* by several words; the word *marriage* comes immediately before it, but the writer has to remember what the subject is and make the verb agree.

REVISED VERSION

Many experts believe that specific instructions to prepare youngsters for the responsibilities of marriage are now needed more than ever before.

2. Connect participles with nouns or pronouns. Participles are verb forms used as adjectives; they must, then, link up with a noun. When this link is broken, a participle is said to be "dangling."

FIRST VERSION

After studying this definition, a discrepancy is immediately recognized.

When a participle (a verb form) appears in a phrase at the beginning of a sentence, readers expect it to modify or connect with the first noun in the main clause; that noun will explain who or what is doing this action. In this sentence, *studying* is linked with *discrepancy,* a link which obviously doesn't make sense. Thus the sentence doesn't tell who is doing the studying.

REVISED VERSION

After studying this definition, I immediately recognized a problem.

Note that the change results in another improvement: the verb becomes active instead of passive.

FIRST VERSION

So far, I am ahead of my research deadline, making the rest of my schedule relatively free of pressure.

When the participial phrase comes at the end of a sentence, readers expect it to connect with the nearest noun. But here, *making* seems to connect with the whole idea in the first clause. It's clearer to have a single word for a participle to refer to or to rewrite the sentence completely.

REVISED VERSION

Because I am ahead of my research deadline, the rest of my schedule will be relatively pressure-free.

3. Make pronouns agree in number with the nouns they refer to. Because a pronoun represents a noun, it should be the same number (and also the same sex, if that's relevant) as the noun it's representing. The following examples show this lack of agreement.

FIRST VERSION

A child needs to be educated beginning at birth; teaching should not have to be delayed until they enter school.

The pronoun *they* refers back to *child* and should be in the singular to agree. Either the noun or the pronoun can be changed.

REVISED VERSION

Children need to be educated beginning at birth; teaching should not have to be delayed until they enter school.

FIRST VERSION

The serious runner may alter his or her lifestyle considerably, for he or she begins to center his or her life around running. One must abstain from doing many things that one previously did.

His and *her* are used to avoid sexism, but the repetition becomes awkward. To avoid this awkwardness, the writer makes another shift to *one*. The best solution here is to use the plural for both noun and pronouns.

REVISED VERSION

Serious runners may alter their lifestyles considerably. As they begin to center their lives around running, they must abstain from doing many things they previously did.

4. Make pronoun reference clear. Since pronouns are substitutes for nouns, readers must know which nouns those are.

FIRST VERSION

Industrial recreation is a growing career opportunity. Because of this, I would like to learn more about it.

What does *this* refer to? What does *it* refer to? Industrial recreation? A career opportunity?

REVISED VERSION

Because industrial recreation offers many career opportunities, I would like to learn more about it.

Note that combining these sentences eliminates extra words and sharpens the meaning by subordinating the less important idea.

Maintain Consistency

1. Keep the same person throughout a sentence. Sometimes the perspective of a sentence is shifted by changing the pronoun from first person (*I* or *we*) to second person (*you*) or to third person (*he, she,* or *it*). Of course you may want to refer to different people and use these different pronouns; but don't shift when you are referring to the same person or group.

FIRST VERSION

Many people lease cars because, compared to financing, the payments are much lower. The only drawback is the fact that at the end of the leasing term you do not own the car.

The first sentence is written in the third person, *Many people.* The second sentence changes to the second person *you.*

REVISED VERSION

Many people lease cars because, compared to financing, the payments are much lower. The only drawback is the fact that at the end of the leasing term they do not own their cars.

2. Keep the same point of view throughout your paper. Most research papers are written primarily in the third person. But the use of the first person (*I*) is no longer forbidden, as it once was. Of course, you do not want to overwhelm your readers with constant use of *I* and especially with the overuse of *I feel* or *I think*; and you also want to avoid using *we* as a polite form of *I.* But if you have conducted an experiment, for example, it is appropriate to use the first person in explaining it. James Watson and Francis Crick begin their article announcing their discovery of the structure of DNA with these words: "We wish to suggest a structure for the salt of deoxyribose nucleic acid (D.N.A.)." They continue to use *we* freely throughout the article.

If you are writing instructions, you should use the second person (*you*); research papers, on the other hand, are rarely how-to papers. If you have written such a paper, however, make sure that you have not shifted from *you* to *one* or *they*.

3. Keep the tense consistent. Of course, if you are talking about past events, use the past tense; if you are talking about the present, use the present tense. When you are referring to one of your written sources, use the present tense: "Young *concludes* that . . ." because what he has put into print still exists. Note the following example.

FIRST VERSION

The defendants appealed the decision, but the Court of Appeals affirmed. Then the Supreme Court reverses the decision and holds that double-celling does not violate the Eighth Amendment.

The verbs in the first sentence are correctly in the past tense. But the first two verbs in the second sentence shift to the present tense. The third verb, *does,* is correctly in the present tense because it expresses something true now.

REVISED VERSION

The defendants appealed the decision, but the Court of Appeals affirmed. The Supreme Court, however, reversed the decision and held that double-celling in this Ohio prison does not violate the Eighth Amendment.

Change Incorrect or Confusing Punctuation

Punctuation is part of the structure and meaning of your sentences. Periods and question marks define sentences; internal marks of punctuation such as commas and semicolons are crucial to the meaning and the sound within the sentence—they are not just decorative symbols. Try reading the following sentence using the marks of punctuation as sound clues. As you will gradually discover, the sound suggested by the punctuation doesn't fit the meaning.

Although these definitions include groups such as the Hells Angels, who operate nationwide, engage in illegal activities and use violence to enforce their rules; and other organized outlaw groups, this paper will deal with the best-known organized criminal group, the Mafia.

Punctuated this way it is clearer:

> Although these definitions include groups such as the Hells Angels—an organization that operates nationwide, engages in illegal activities, and uses violence to enforce its rules—and other organized outlaw groups, this paper will deal only with the best-known organized criminal group: the Mafia.

Sometimes problems occur with a short sentence. Try to read this sentence aloud.

> His death was not the end however it was the beginning of a new medical era.

Try punctuating it both of these ways, and then read the sentence aloud to hear the difference.

> His death was not the end, however; it was the beginning of a new medical era.

> His death was not the end; however, it was the beginning of a new medical era.

The meaning changes with the punctuation. If you don't let your readers know, they will have to punctuate the sentence themselves.

When you construct your sentences, use the marks of punctuation with as much consideration of their meaning as you do your words. You will find detailed suggestions about punctuation in Chapter 10.

Focus on Documentation

Check your documentation to make sure it is correct and complete. If you use the number system, you may have to renumber your parenthetical citations and the order of your references after you revise your paper. Detailed documentation conventions are given in Chapter 11 (author/page system), Chapter 12 (author/date system), and Chapter 13 (number system).

EXERCISES

1. In a group of three or four of your classmates, read the first few pages of your paper, depending on the amount of time you have, to the other members of your group; or have another member of the group read your paper to you. Read slowly. When you have finished, ask each of the members of your group to write a sentence summarizing what you have read. Read and compare the results, and then decide whether what you want to say in your paper is clear.

2. Find two examples of passive voice in your paper and change the verbs to active voice. After observing the difference in effect, decide which voice you want to use.

3. Find two or three sentences in your paper that you think might sound better if they were combined. Decide first which idea is the most important. Then combine the sentences, putting the most important idea into the main clause and the other ideas into subordinate clauses or phrases. Assess the results and decide whether you made the best decision.

4. Using the same sentences you worked with in Exercise 3, rewrite them, putting another idea in the main clause. Decide which version is the best.

5. Number the paragraphs of your draft in the margin. Then exchange papers with another member of your class. Read the paper silently and as you read, write on a separate sheet of paper the main idea of each paragraph.

   Return the paper to your partner. Reread carefully your own paper and your partner's list of the topics of your paragraphs. If any of the topics your partner has listed do not correspond to your own idea of what the paragraphs contain, consider rewriting the paragraphs to make them clearer.

6. Record your revising process in your search log. Evaluate your process and decide how you could make it more efficient.

7. Find a classroom partner. Interview each other about your revising processes (see the excerpts by the professional and student writers at the beginning of this chapter). If you have time, discuss the whole writing process starting with the first draft. When you have finished, report your discoveries to the class. Then, as a group, evaluate the most common revising practices and decide which ones might be improved.

Preparing Your Final Copy

After revising your first draft (following the suggestions in Chapter 9), you are now ready to complete your paper. Four steps remain: a final revision to correct spelling, grammar, and mechanics; the preparation of preliminary elements (*front matter*); the preparation of supplemental elements (*back matter*); and typing and proofreading the final copy.

Making Your Final Revision

After the extensive revision of your first draft, your copy is likely to be so messy that you will have trouble reading it. You will need a clean copy so that you can concentrate on details: checking your documentation to make sure you have the correct authors and page numbers; then with the help of the suggestions on the following pages, checking spelling, grammar, and such mechanical elements as capitalization, abbreviations, and use of numbers.

Computer Programs

If you have access to a computer, you may be able to get some mechanical help. Programs such as Grammatik and The Word Plus flag possible grammar and spelling errors. The Word Plus can also check for punctuation, capitalization, and typographical errors. Another program, RightWriter, provides checks on word frequency, sentence length, trite phrases or jargon, and other potential sytlistic problems. Look in your computer store for the latest software of this type and for the kind that is compatible with your computer; new programs are constantly being developed. Remember, though, that even the best software can only point out possible errors—only you can make decisions and judgments.

Spelling and Grammar

Spelling.   Pay special attention to the correct spelling of homophones, words that sound the same but have different spelling and meanings (*their, there*; *led, lead*; *to, too, two*). If you are a chronic misspeller, your task will be easier if you have a list of words you frequently misspell to guide you (if you don't have such a list now, think of keeping one in the future). Reading your work aloud will also help you to find misspellings. Consult your dictionary for any spellings you are uncertain of. If you are tempted to think that spelling is not important because your readers can figure out what you mean, remember that your readers should not have to assume a responsibility that is yours.

Correct Word Usage.   Prepositions (words like *by, for, in,* and *on*) can be troublesome because their meanings are not easily defined and because dialects vary in their use of some prepositions. (Do you say "standing on line" or "in line"? According to standard English usage, you should say "standing in line.") If you are not sure which preposition to use, check a handbook or a dictionary.

Punctuation

Punctuation is a matter of convention. If we are to talk to each other on paper, we must agree on what these marks mean or what sounds they create in pitch and rhythm. For example, if you know the different sounds created by the use of a comma and a semicolon, you will be able to hear the difference in meaning between the following sentences:

> I am not passing judgment on the conduct of the war, rather I wish to explain the reasons for continuing it.

> I am not passing judgment on the conduct of the war; rather I wish to explain the reasons for continuing it.

Notice that as you read the first sentence, your voice dropped only a little after *war* because you were expecting an added-on phrase, perhaps like the pattern in this sentence: "Let's go by train, rather than by plane." However, as you read the second sentence, your voice probably dropped more after *war* and there was a greater pause because of the signal given by the semicolon; then you moved on to the second clause of the sentence. In contrast, the first sentence misled you. You may have had to read part of the second clause of the sentence before you realized that the comma did not signal the addition of a minor sentence structure, such as a phrase. If so, you had to quickly reread the sentence in order to understand it. Writers must follow the conventions of punctuation to avoid confusing readers.

The following guidelines are intended to help you understand how marks of punctuation are used to create sound and meaning. But because these guidelines are attempts to describe what experienced writers do most of the time, they cannot make allowances for all of the variations that are possible. Therefore, your ultimate objective should be to develop a sense of how marks of punctuation make your sentences sound, so that instead of consulting a rule when you punctuate, you can listen to the meaning the punctuation gives to your sentence.

Period.   Use a period

- At the end of a sentence that makes a statement. In a sentence ending with a quotation, even if it is only a single word, always place the period *before* the quotation marks: *He closed his concert with Beethoven's "Moonlight Sonata."*
- After most abbreviations: *Ms., p.m.* Omit the period after abbreviations of some organizations known better by their initials: *UN, IRS, NBC.*
- After numbers or letters introducing items in a list when these are stacked, as in an outline:

  A. To benefit employees
    1. By improving mental health

  (Parentheses usually enclose numbers used to itemize elements within a sentence: *He made the following decisions: (1) to . . . and (2) to. . . .*)

Question Mark.   Use a question mark

- After a direct question: *What causes soil erosion?* Do not use a question mark after an indirect question: *He wanted to find out what causes inflation.* Place the question mark within quotation marks when the quotation is a question: *I couldn't answer the question, "Who wrote* Rabbit, Run*?"* Place the question mark outside the quotation marks when the whole sentence is a question: *When are you going to say "I quit"?*

Comma.   Insert a comma

- After a long introductory clause or phrase: *Because he has fought for a lost cause, he serves as a symbol for Adam's ancestors.*
- Before *and, but, or, for, nor, so,* and *yet* (coordinating conjunctions) when they connect two independent clauses (clauses that can stand alone as sentences): *Hospital costs have risen 170 percent, and physicians' fees have risen 60 percent.*
- Between coordinate adjectives: *The long, dry, dusty climb up the canyon wall exhausted the hikers.*
- After words introducing or following direct quotations: *"Most people favor presidential primaries," he reported.*

Pair of Commas.   Use a pair of commas

- To separate clauses or phrases that are not essential to the meaning of the sentence; these clauses and phrases are sometimes called nonrestrictive elements: *The idea of property rights, especially the rights to possession of land, can be traced to Locke.* But do not use commas to set off elements of a sentence that are essential to its meaning: *The two candidates who received the most votes ran in the run-off election.*
- To set off a contrasting phrase: *Carson City, not Reno, is the capital of Nevada.*

For use of the comma with quotations, see Chapter 8.

Semicolon.   Insert a semicolon

- Between two independent clauses not linked by a coordinating conjunction. Remember that *however* and *therefore* can't take the place of coordinating conjunctions; therefore (as in this sentence), a semicolon is needed when either introduces the second independent clause.
- When two independent clauses linked by a coordinating conjunction contain internal punctuation: *The politician of the earlier novels was controlled by the money of the business man—he was a hireling; but here he has become a big businessman himself.*
- Between items in a series when there are commas within the items: *The following cities recorded temperatures below zero for the period studied: Butte, Montana; Bismarck, North Dakota; Boise, Idaho; and Escanaba, Michigan.*

For use of the semicolon with quotations, see Chapter 8.

Colon.   Use a colon

- To introduce items in a series when the words introducing the series form a complete clause: *A business letter must have the following parts: return address, inside address, greeting, body, and complimentary close.* Notice that the word before the colon (*parts*) identifies the kind of items that will be listed. Notice, too, that a significant pause follows the word just before the colon. If you use a colon between a verb and its object or between a preposition and its object, you cause an unnecessary break in your sentence: *The courses offered in literature included: Eighteenth-century Poets, Victorian Novel, and American Short Story.* A colon here causes an undesirable break between the two main parts of the sentence—the verb and its objects.

- To separate titles from subtitles: *Eight American Authors: A Review of Research and Criticism.*
- To separate two main clauses when the second explains the first: *I knew the man who answered the door: he was my father.*

For use of the colon with quotations, see Chapter 8.

Quotation Marks. Use quotation marks

- To enclose direct quotations: *"Who are you, anyway?" he demanded.*
- To enclose titles of short pieces (poems, short stories, articles, parts of books, pieces of music, and speeches).

Single Quotation Marks. Use single quotation marks

- To enclose quoted words within another quotation: *The speaker began: "Ladies and gentlemen, let us recall Patrick Henry's words, 'Give me liberty or give me death.'"*

Punctuation of quotations in the text of your paper is discussed fully in Chapter 8.

Ellipsis Points. Insert ellipsis points (spaced dots)

- To indicate omission in a quotation: *Thoreau wrote in* Walden: *"It would be some advantage to live a primitive and frontier life . . . if only to learn what are the gross necessaries. . . ."* When omitted words come at the end of a sentence, four dots are used—a period and the three ellipsis points. Unless confusion would result from not using them, ellipsis points are usually not needed when words are omitted at the beginning of a quotation: *John Kennedy called courage "that most admirable of human virtues."*

Other uses of ellipsis points are explained in Chapter 8.

Brackets. Use brackets

- To insert explanatory material or editorial comment into a quotation: *James Fenimore Cooper wrote, "The class to which he [the gentleman] belongs is the natural repository . . . of the principles of a country."*

- To enclose *sic,* a Latin word meaning *thus,* placed after an error in a quotation to indicate that the error was in the original: *He wrote that "President Crater's [sic] administration was marred by numerous errors."*

Other uses of brackets with quotations are discussed in Chapter 8.

Apostrophe.   Use an apostrophe

- To form the possessive: *the boat's rudder* (singular); *the boats' rudders* (plural); *Mr. Jones's house* (singular ending in *s*). Note: Do not use an apostrophe in the possessive pronouns *its, hers,* or *theirs*: *The house lost its roof in the storm.*
- To indicate an omitted letter in a contraction: *can't, it's* (meaning *cannot* and *it is*). Be sure to place the apostrophe where the omission occurs. Note: An occasional contraction in a research paper can be the right word choice, but too many contractions detract from the serious tone that you want to maintain throughout your paper.

Dashes.   You can use dashes

- To indicate an interruption or a shift in direction at the end of a sentence: *The president restrained his anger until the end of the meeting— well, almost until the end.*
- In pairs to set off words and phrases from the rest of the sentence. Dashes differ from comma pairs and parentheses, which de-emphasize what they enclose, by emphasizing the words they set off: *He had one reservation—and it was a big one—about the decisions they had to make.*

Note: When typing dashes, use two hyphens with no space before or after.

Parentheses.   Use parentheses

- To separate less important information from the rest of the sentence so that the flow of the sentence is disrupted as little as possible. Use them in the following circumstances: (a) when citing sources in your text: *(Adams 105)*; (b) when adding explanatory material: *He was elected president of the OAS (Organization of American States)*; (c) when enclosing figures or letters that introduce sequential elements: *Leasing a car has three advantages over buying: (1) you need only a small down-payment; (2) you can buy the car at a depreciated price at the end of the leasing term; and (3) your insurance premiums are lower.* Note: The use of numbers in (c) to introduce the clauses signals their beginning and emphasizes them. But they also interrupt the flow of the sentence, so use them sparingly.

Hyphen.   Insert hyphens

- To divide a word at the end of a line. Avoid breaking a word at all, if possible. When necessary, divide a word between syllables: *syl-lables*. Use your dictionary if you are in doubt. Do not leave one or two letters alone on a line: *a-lone, lone-ly*.
- To join words: *self-evident*. Divide hyphenated words only at the hyphen: not *self-ev-ident*. It's not always easy to tell when a word should be written as a compound (*per-cent*), as one word (*percent*), or as two words (*per cent*) because some words that used to be two words are now hyphenated or written as one. (*Percent* is now the most common spelling.) Your dictionary can help you. However, you should join words with a hyphen in the following cases: (a) when an adjective that is created by joining two or more words precedes the noun it modifies, as the following examples illustrate: a noun and participle: *death-defying leap*; an adjective and noun: *a low-percentage risk*; a number and a noun: *a four-way stop*; a phrase of three or more words: *a once-in-a-lifetime chance*. But do not hyphenate two modifiers when the first is an adverb ending in *-ly*: *a heavily wooded site*. (b) when a noun is created from a verb and a preposition: *My car needs a tune-up*. Do not use a hyphen when you use a verb followed by a preposition: *The mechanic agreed to tune up my car*.

Slash or Virgule.   Use this mark of punctuation

- To indicate the end of a line of poetry when it is run in with the text: *Hamlet's speech beginning, "O, that this too too sullied flesh would melt, / Thaw, and resolve itself into a dew!" is often cited as an indication of his despair.*
- To indicate a choice: *The best sellers in recent months have been in science fiction and/or romance.* The *and/or* use of the slash can easily be overdone—usually you should use either one or the other. Sometimes it sounds better to repeat *or*: *I may decide to major in science or math or both.*
- To separate the numerator from the denominator in a fraction: *2/3*.

Note: There is no space before or after the slash except when it is used to separate run-on lines of poetry.

Underlining.   Underlining in typewritten copy appears as italics in print. Use underlining

- To indicate titles of separate publications, such as books, plays, newspapers, pamphlets, and periodicals as well as nonprint titles, such as the names of television and radio programs, records, films, musical compositions, paintings, sculpture, ships, and planes.

- To distinguish words being discussed from words that are part of the text: *He doesn't seem to know what monophobia means.*
- To show emphasis: *"I said I did not want to go."*
- To distinguish foreign words not yet Anglicized: *He explained to the class the use of the deus ex machina in Greek and Roman plays.* Words that have been Anglicized shouldn't be underlined: *The main item on the menu was quiche.*

Capitalization

When you capitalize a word, you give it special distinction. To preserve this distinction, capitalize as sparingly as possible. You already know that the first letter of a sentence is capitalized, including the first letter of a quotation that is a sentence. Listed below are other frequently used examples of capitalization (but note that documentation systems often follow different capitalization conventions).

- The first, last, and all principal words of book titles. Do not capitalize articles: *a, an,* and *the*; prepositions: such as *in, by, of, before*; and coordinating conjunctions *and, or, but, nor, for,* unless they are the first or last words of a title: *He was reading* Of Time and the River. Note that the divisions of a book or literary work are not always capitalized when referred to in the text: *preface, introduction, appendix, chapter 4, act 1, stanza 3.*
- Periodical, journal, and newspaper titles. Do not capitalize the introductory definite article unless it is part of the name: *the New York Times,* but: *The New Yorker.*
- Most derivatives of proper names: *Freudian slip*; but: *china doll, roman numerals.*
- Regions of the country: *Hemingway and Fitzgerald both grew up in the Middle West*; but not directions such as north, south, east, and west: *Americans went west in large numbers during the Gold Rush.*
- Titles preceding personal names: *Professor Rosabeth March*; but not titles following names: *Rosabeth March, professor of history.*
- Titles of college courses: *He taught History of the American Revolution*; but not names of subjects unless they are proper nouns: *She changed her major from French to biology.*

Abbreviations

The use of abbreviations varies according to the style you are using. Here are some general guidelines for use of abbreviations in your text. For illustrations of abbreviations with specific styles in reference lists or works cited, see the sample papers in the chapter discussing the style you are using (Chapters 11, 12, or 13).

Use abbreviations in the text of your paper

- When the abbreviation is commonly used as a word itself: *A.D. 200* or *AD 200* (anno Domini, in the year of the Lord, or since the beginning of the Christian era); *a.m., p.m.* or *A.M., P.M. (ante meridiem,* before noon; *post meridiem,* after noon); *IQ* (intelligence quotient); *UN* or *U.N.* (United Nations).
- After spelling out the complete term the first time it is used and giving the abbreviation. This convention applies especially to terms that may be frequently used in your text: *Rapid Deployment Force (RDF); Department of Transportation (DOT); miles per hour (mph).*
- For personal and professional titles: *George Brown, Ph.D; Mark Stevens, Jr.; Prof. Julia Lawson.*
- In technical or scientific writing for units of measurement when they are accompanied by numerical values (usually without punctuation): *20 mm* (millimeters), *50 l* (liters).

Note: A recent dictionary may list abbreviations in alphabetical order as it does words—or it may present a list of abbreviations in a separate section—and it will also indicate whether you should use periods with it.

Do not abbreviate in the text of your paper:

- Latin terms, except when they are used in parenthetical material: *for example,* not *e.g.; that is,* not *i.e.; and so forth,* not *etc.; versus* or *against,* not *vs.*
- Personal titles preceding the surname only: *Governor Cuomo;* but: *Gov. Mario Cuomo.*
- Names of countries, states, counties, cities, and the like (except *USSR*): *the United States; Annapolis, Maryland* (in addresses in correspondence use abbreviations.)
- Geographical words such as street, avenue, drive, road, and the like (remember to capitalize them when they are part of a name): *Rodeo Drive, Lorcom Lane.*

Numbers

For the use of numbers in parenthetical citations, see Chapter 8. For the use of numbers in reference lists, see the chapter discussing the documentation system you are using (Chapters 11, 12, or 13); the lists of references or works cited at the end of the sample papers illustrate the principles you will read about. The conventions or style for numbers within the text varies from one discipline to another and even from one organization to another. Newspapers, businesses, and government agencies often have their own conventions. Conventions used by the three main academic divisons—humanities, social sciences, and applied sciences—are given here for the most common situations.

Numbers in the Humanities and Social Sciences.   General rule: Use words for whole numbers from one through nine and numerals for all other numbers. However, when a number over nine occurs at the beginning of a sentence, spell out the number. If a sentence begins with a number requiring several words it's best to recast the sentence.

FIRST VERSION

1,039 new employees were hired during the past week.

REVISED VERSION

During the past week, 1,039 new employees were hired.

Use numerals for

- Numbers over nine: *29, 138, 2,986.*
- Dates: *June 19, 1950.*
- Street addresses, decimals, fractions, percentages, and times of day: *312 Perkins Lane, $20.18, 3-1/2, 5%, 8 a.m.*
- A series of numbers: *8 days, 4 hours, and 30 minutes.*
- References to pages and other parts of literary works: *page 42, chapter 3, act 1, lines 295–98.*

Use a combination of words and numerals for

- Large numbers: *3.2 billion.*
- Consecutive modifying numbers: *three 2-way radios.*

Note: A comma is usually placed in large figures after every third digit, counting from the right: *2,098* and *3,229,894.* Exceptions are address numbers: *2100 Vacation Lane;* four-digit years: *1986*; and page numbers: *page 2389.*

Numbers in the Earth and Applied Sciences.   There is wide disparity in style and format among the sciences, partly because of the different kinds of measurements that are used in the different branches of science. The most commonly used conventions for numbers (given here) should be adequate for most college papers. If you wish to publish, you should follow the style of the publication you plan to send your manuscript to. General rule: For numbers one through nine, use words; for all others, use numerals (as in the humanities and social sciences). Note these distinctive uses of numbers in science papers.

- Numbers with four digits have no punctuation and no spaces: *3597.*
- Numbers over four digits contain a space between each group of three, beginning with the decimal point and going in either direction: *14 583* and *500 243 489.*
- A number preceding a unit of measurement is given in numerals: *3 mm.*
- Dates are written without punctuation: *9 June 1983*; *12 January.*
- Time is expressed in the 24-hour system: *0830* and *2259.*
- Measurements are given in the metric system, and the decimal system is usually used instead of fractions (except in equations).

Documentation

Check your parenthetical or endnote documentation carefully against your note cards to make sure authors, titles, and page numbers are correct. Details about documentation are given in Chapters 11, 12, and 13.

Typing Your Final Copy

Your final copy will usually contain these elements in the following order (remember that your paper may not contain all of these and that some style manuals may recommend a different order of elements).

Front matter (or preliminary elements)

Title page (explained in this chapter, p. 209)
Abstract (see Chapter 8, p. 161)
Table of contents (explained in this chapter, p. 210)
List of illustrations (explained in this chapter, p. 211)
Outline (see Chapter 7, p. 123)

Text of your paper
•Back matter (or supplementary elements)

Appendixes (explained in this chapter, p. 211)
Content notes (explained in this chapter, p. 212)
Endnotes (explained in Chapter 11, p. 236)
Glossary (explained in this chapter, p. 213)
List of references (see Chapter 11, 12, or 13 for the appropriate documentation style).

A preface is usually unnecessary in a college paper. If you want to acknowledge special help, use a content note. If someone has provided you with information orally, use the proper citation format for your documentation system.

Materials

If your paper is typed, use 8½-by-11-inch white paper of good quality and a new black ribbon. Most instructors prefer that you avoid using onion skin or erasable paper. Erasable paper smudges easily and does not photocopy well. If your instructor will accept a good-quality photocopy, you can use white correction fluid or correction tape to correct errors without having to retype your paper. Handwritten manuscripts, if your instructor will accept them, should be legibly written with black or blue-black ink on lined paper with margins. (Be sure to observe the same margins on all sides, including the bottom, as you would use when typing. See the section on typing format below.)

If you use a word processor, use a typewriter-quality printer rather than a dot matrix or other high-speed printer. The forming of the words by dots makes the readers' eyes work harder; in addition, some letters, such as *q*'s and *g*'s, are difficult to distinguish.

Title Page

A short paper (up to ten pages) does not usually need a title page; a blank sheet of paper in front of the first page will help keep it neat. If your paper is longer, if it is a technical report, if it has front matter, or if your instructor prefers, use a title page. It should contain, on separate lines, the title of your paper, your name, the instructor's name, the course title, and the date. Although you can use any attractive format, the most common and probably the easiest is centering these items a little above the middle of the page. Only the first letter of each important word of the title should be capitalized; the words should not be underlined. If your title is long, use two lines and divide it where a pause seems natural (see the title page of the sample paper on page 241).

If you do not use a title page, leave a one-inch margin at the top, and then place your name, the name of the professor, the course title, and the date in the upper left corner of the first page, using double-spacing. After another double-space, center the title; then quadruple-space and begin your text (see the sample paper on page 256).

Format

Margins vary according to the documentation format you are using. Please see details in the chapter illustrating your format—Chapter 11, 12, or 13. Double-space the text of your paper, including indented quotations. Indent the first line of each paragraph five spaces. Number pages consecutively throughout the paper, using arabic numerals without punctuation (use small roman numerals for front matter). Place numbers in the upper right corner. Page headings vary according to the documentation system you are using.

Abstract

Place your abstract on a separate page with the heading, Abstract, centered. Capitalize only the first letter (unless you are writing a technical report, in which case you would usually capitalize all letters). Double-space your abstract (see Chapter 8 for an explanation of writing an abstract).

Table of Contents

A table of contents (TOC) is often part of a technical report or a research paper prepared for education, business, or government organizations or for private research groups. Each audience may have different interests and needs. Employees or the public may want to learn what research has been done at an institution; managers may want a general view of the research on the subject presented in the report; experts may want to find out the details of a research project. The table of contents, which is really an outline in a different format, provides readers with a detailed summary of the report as well as page numbers, so that specific subjects can be quickly and easily located. The headings used in the TOC make reading and understanding the text of the report easier.

You can easily transfer the headings and subheadings of your outline to the TOC, although you don't need to include any subheadings below the third level. Every heading or subheading that you list in your TOC must appear word-for-word as in the report. The numbers or letters that you use with the headings in your outline are usually not included in the TOC; instead, typography or indenting indicates the different levels of headings. (For suggestions on typography in headings, see Chapter 12.) If you do include numbers and letters with the headings in the body of your paper, they should also appear in the TOC.

You can prepare the TOC after typing the final copy of your paper so that you can insert the correct page numbers. An alternative would be to type it at the beginning and insert the page numbers later. Note that the front matter should be numbered with small roman numerals.

Although the order, contents, and typography of a formal report can vary, the form for the table of contents described here will be acceptable in most cases. If possible, confirm this form with the person for whom you are writing the report.

In main headings of the TOC, the first letters of main words are usually shown in capital letters and begin at the left margin; subheadings are indented and usually only the first letter of the first word is capitalized. Spaced periods often connect these headings to the page numbers at the right margin; but some writers, preferring a less cluttered look, do not use the periods. Double- or triple-space headings to make them easier to read. If you use an outline numbering system, use it only for the body of the paper, not for the front or back matter.

See p. 304 for an example of a table of contents in a research paper.

List of Illustrations

If your paper includes both figures and tables (any graphic that is not a table is considered and labeled a figure), combine them in one list called List of Illustrations or simply Illustrations and subdivide that list into parts labeled "Figures" and "Tables." If you have only one kind, title it accordingly—List of Figures or List of Tables. A list of three or fewer illustrations can be placed on the same page as the table of contents, just below the contents. If you have more, list them on a separate page (see the list for the sample paper on page 305).

Outline

An introductory outline is optional. You do not need an outline if you have either an abstract or a table of contents. If your instructor wishes you to submit an outline, place the word Outline at the center of the page as your heading. (See Chapter 7 for spacing and punctuation of outlines.) The outline you prepared for your first revision (see Chapter 9) will probably need no changes; however, if you have made changes in the order or content of your text, adjust your outline to reflect them. Proofread it carefully to ensure that the headings are parallel and that the mechanics (capitalization, punctuation, and use of numbers and symbols) are correct.

Appendixes

The appendix or appendixes contain information that isn't necessary to the body of your paper and may be difficult to integrate into your text, but that is important and helpful to your readers. Any of the following might appear in an appendix: sample questionnaires, maps, worksheets for feasibility studies, excerpts from documents, interview questions, correspondence, photocopies of documents, details of an experiment, lengthy tables or lists of statistics, and so forth. An appendix is useless, however, unless readers know it's there; when you are discussing a point amplified in an appendix, refer to it: *(see appendix, p. 19)*. You may number appendixes as a continuation of your text

FIGURE 10.1   A Sample Appendix

Appendix 1.   Project Data Sheet.

WORKSHEET A--PROJECT DATA

PROJECT *Drain Down DHW System*

Location *Washington, D.C.*   Latitude   = *40°*

Building Heating and/or (Hot Water Load)

Design Heat Loss Rate, q_d = *N/A* Btu/h

Winter Design Temperature (97-1/2%), t_w = *N/A* °F

Average Hot Water Consumption   = *60* gal/day
(may vary on a monthly basis)

Average Cold Water Supply (main) Temp., t_m = *55* °F

Hot Water Supply Temp., t_s = *140* °F

⋮   ⋮

(with arabic numerals) or, if the appendix is the last section of your paper, you may use a separate numbering system consisting of capital letters to identify the main groups of information and arabic numerals to identify the separate items of those groups; for example, A1, A2 (for two questionnaires used) and B1, B2 (for statistics and calculations based on the questionnaires). Peter DeGress included worksheets in the appendix of his feasibility study on solar heating (see Figure 10.1).

Content or Explanatory Notes

Writers who use parenthetical documentation rather than endnotes may still use content or explanatory notes to amplify or explain information they have given in the text. You can use content notes to cite further sources of information on a subject, to give details or statistics that may be interesting but are not essential to your paper, to explain procedures you have used, to acknowledge contrary evidence, or to mention the names of those persons or organizations that provided you with special help. Such notes should be used sparingly; if the information is not important enough to be included in your text, you may not need it at all.

If you use a content note, type a superscript number in the text ([1]) to refer readers to the note. The note itself may be positioned in any of the following places, depending on the citation style you are using.

1. In the author/page style, notes are placed on a page titled Notes, following the body of the manuscript.

2. In the author/date style, notes are also placed on a page following the body of the manuscript, but they are titled Endnotes.
3. In the number style, footnotes are positioned at the bottom of the page on which the superscript number or symbol is given.

It's likely that any of these styles will be acceptable in a college class unless your instructor has a preference. Center the title (Notes or Footnotes) on the page following the text. Double-space before beginning the first note. Indent the number for each note five spaces and raise it one half-space above the line. Double-space throughout—both within entries and between entries. A content note would look like this (for author/date style, do not leave a space after the superscript number):

> [1] However, in his introduction to the American edition of *Fabian Essays,* Bellamy states that he favored not only government ownership of the productive mechanism but also equal distribution of the product.

Footnotes or Endnotes

Although most writers find it easier to document their papers by putting brief citations in parentheses within the text and a list of references at the end, some writers, especially those in the humanities, prefer to use footnotes or endnotes either with or without a separate list of references. This system of documentation is explained in Chapter 11.

Glossary

If you are writing a technical or scientific paper for an audience that includes nonexperts, you will probably need a glossary—a list of technical or scientific words and their definitions. Two or three technical words can easily be defined within your paper by putting the definitions in parentheses following the term. But too many of these will clutter your paper and can annoy those readers who are already familiar with the terms.

In compiling such a list, you will have to assess carefully the level of your audience in order to decide which words or terms to include. Then you will have to define those terms; in effect, you will have to translate them into words that your audience will understand. The definitions should contain two parts: first, the class to which the item belongs and, second, the ways in which it differs from other items in the same class. In the glossary for his paper about the stock exchange, Craig Mayes defined *floor reporter* as "an employee of the Stock Exchange who monitors trades at trading posts and posts price changes as they occur." *Employee of the Stock Exchange* defines the class to which *floor reporter* belongs, and *who monitors trades at trading posts and posts price changes as they occur* defines the way in which a floor reporter differs from other employees of the Stock Exchange.

Definitions in a glossary can be brief because the reader has the advantage of seeing the word in context, which will further define it. Avoid using such unnecessary phrases as "a word which means" or "a term which is used to." Mayes's glossary definitions consisted of phrases. Definitions in a glossary can also be complete sentences, but the two structures should not be mixed.

The glossary is usually placed in the back matter but sometimes appears as part of the front matter.

List of References

At the end of your paper, on a separate page, place the list of the sources you have cited. You can label this list Works Cited (used by writers following the author/page system) or References (used by those following either the author/year system or the number system). These lists contain only the works cited in the text of your paper. In an alternate style, the list can be labeled Bibliography and can include background sources as well as sources cited. Some writers even use two lists—Works Cited and Works Consulted.

Your list of references should include all sources: books, articles, chapters of books, pamphlets, unpublished writing, and nonprint sources, such as radio and television programs, paintings, and computer databases. Chapter 11 explains the author/page reference system; Chapter 12, the author/date system; and Chapter 13, the number system.

Proofreading and Duplicating

After your paper has been typed, read it again. Read it aloud, if possible, to force yourself to slow down and recognize typographical and spelling errors. If you have lengthy tables or other groups of figures in your paper, try to find a friend to check your figures as you read them aloud.

Make corrections by using correction tape or white correction fluid. Make brief last-minute insertions by typing or by neatly writing in ink just above the space where you want to add the word or brief phrase. If you have more than two or three corrections on a page, you should retype the page.

Be sure to make a photocopy of your paper for yourself before handing it in. You may be able to submit a good quality photocopy of your paper, but check with your instructor before doing so.

Cover and Binding

Most short student papers need no special cover or binding. A blank sheet of paper before the title page and after the final page helps keep your paper neat. You can secure the pages with a paper clip in the upper left corner. However, if you are writing a formal report or a long paper, you may want to use a cover. Use a lightweight cardboard cover that will lie flat when it's opened. Fasten a label on the cover on which you have typed your name and the title of your paper. Avoid plastic covers with removable spines; they often fall apart when opened.

EXERCISE

As your last entry in your search log, record your final thoughts on this project. What have you learned about your subject that is important to you? What have you learned about the process of writing a paper that you will be able to use when you write future papers? What parts of your process will you repeat? How will you improve your process next time?

Writing a Paper in the Humanities: The Author/Page Style

The suggestions for format and documentation given here and in the sample papers that follow use the guidelines recommended in the *MLA Handbook for Writers of Research Papers* (1984). Parenthetical citations are given in the text of the papers, and a list of works cited is placed at the end.

Parts of the Manuscript

A paper in the humanities usually places its emphasis on the text of the paper itself. Therefore, most papers have only two parts: the text and the list of works cited. However, the following list shows the possible elements of such a paper. Your instructor will help you decide how many of these you need.

Title page (optional)
Outline (optional)
Text of paper
Content notes (if parenthetical documentation is used)
Endnotes (if parenthetical documentation is not used)
Works cited

Format

Title Page

You do not need a title page with your paper unless you include an outline at the beginning of your paper. If you do use a title page, center the following information on the page, using a separate line for each: the title of your paper, your name, instructor, course name, and date. Capitalize the first word, the last word, and all important words in your title. Do not underline or use other punctuation marks unless your title contains a quotation or another title. Use a colon to separate the title from the subtitle.

```
Critics' Changing Views of Troilus and Cressida
```

```
''In the Beginning'':

A Discussion of Metaphors in the Creation Story
```

Use spacing between the lines to make the page attractive.

Margins and Spacing

Leave one-inch margins on all sides of the text, including the top and bottom. Indent paragraphs five spaces, and use double-spacing in the text; in all long quotations, which should be indented ten spaces from the left margin; and in all other parts of your paper including the outline, the works cited section, and notes, if you use them.

Page Numbers

Place page numbers half an inch from the top of the page and one inch from the right on all pages except the title page if you include one. Use arabic numerals without punctuation. If you don't have a title page, number all pages and place your last name before each number beginning with page 2 in order to identify your paper in case pages are separated. If you use a title page and outline, number the pages of the outline with small roman numerals, starting with page ii (the title page is counted as page i but is not numbered).

Headings

Papers in the humanities usually do not have headings within the text. You should have a heading at the beginning of each of these parts of your paper: the outline (if you have one), the text, notes, and works cited. Start each of these on a new page and center the title one inch from the top of the page. Capitalize the first letter of each word; do not underline or use other marks of punctuation.

Outline

If you include an outline, it should come after your title page. Center the heading Outline one inch below the top of the page. Double-space and center the title of your paper. Double-space once more and begin your outline. (See Chapter 7 for the format of outlines.)

First Page

If your paper does not have a title page, place your name, instructor's name, course title, and date (double-spaced) in the upper left corner on the first page half an inch below the page number and one inch from the top. Double-space and center the title of your paper. Then leave four spaces (double-space twice) and begin your text.

If you are using a title page, you need repeat only the title of your paper on the first page of the text. Place it one inch below the top of the page. Double-space twice and begin your text.

Content Notes

Content notes can be used with parenthetical documentation to explain something not important enough to interrupt your text. You may not need to include them, but if you do, avoid lengthy discussions and limit them to brief explanations or bibliographic comments. Use the same format as for endnotes. For further information on these notes and examples, see Chapter 10.

Documentation

Parenthetical Citation

Give the sources of your information in parentheses as close as possible to the material you are documenting—at a natural pause or at the end of a sentence. Your parenthetical citation must give enough information to identify a source in your list of works cited; it must also give the page number on which you found the information. The sample papers in this chapter show how these citations are used.

The following examples illustrate the most common types of parenthetical references.

ENTIRE WORK

You might refer in your text to a whole work along with its author; in that case you wouldn't need a parenthetical citation.

In The Politics of Non-Violent Action, Sharp outlines the long

history of successful nonviolent struggle.

If you do not include the name of the author in the text, include the name in a parenthetical citation.

The Politics of Non-Violent Action outlines the long history of

nonviolent struggle (Sharp).

WORK BY ONE AUTHOR

If you use the author's name as part of your sentence, put only the page number in parentheses.

Wyman mentions that German miners in the sixteenth century used

dowsing to find silver, copper, and lead (47).

If you give neither the name nor the page number in the sentence, then you must give both in parentheses with no punctuation between them.

German miners in the sixteenth century used dowsing to find sil-

ver, copper, and lead (Wyman 47).

Follow the same format for citing the work of an editor, a translator, or compiler. Do not include abbreviations indicating the role of a person: *Smith, ed.* This role will be identified in the list of works cited.

TWO OR MORE WORKS BY THE SAME AUTHOR

If you have included more than one work by an author in your list of works cited, you must include a brief title in your text or in your parenthetical citation.

In fact, Adams admitted that he unwittingly benefited from corrupt

political practices (Education 49).

The complete title of the book cited is *The Education of Henry Adams.* Note that there is no punctuation between the title and the page number.

If you name both the author and the work in your text, you need only the page number in parentheses.

In fact, Adams admitted in his Education that he unwittingly bene-

fited from corrupt political practices (49).

If you name neither the author nor the title in the text, include them both in the parenthetical citation. Note that a comma separates the author from the title.

```
He unwittingly benefited from corrupt political practices (Adams,
Education 49).
```

WORK BY TWO OR THREE AUTHORS

If your source has two or three authors, cite all of them either in your text or in parentheses, as you would a single author.

```
As Friedman and McLaughlin point out, a poem is "a mirror of the
conventions . . . of the period in which it was written" (3).
A poem is "a mirror of the conventions . . . of the period in
which it was written" (Friedman and McLaughlin 3).
```

WORK BY MORE THAN THREE AUTHORS

If your source has more than three authors, give the name of the first author listed in Works Cited, followed by *et al.*, the Latin abbreviation for *et alii*, meaning *and others*. There is no punctuation between the name of the first author and the abbreviation.

```
According to Spiller et al., America was the embodiment of a long-
held European dream (192).
America was the embodiment of a long-held European dream (Spiller
et al. 192).
```

CORPORATE AUTHOR

Give the name of a corporate author (government agency, association, or research organization) in the text or in a parenthetical reference, as you would with a personal author. If the group is known by its abbreviation, give its abbreviation with the first citation and then abbreviate it in subsequent citations. For example, the first citation:

```
In a recent study of freshman writing, the National Council of
Teachers of English (NCTE) found that students think of revising
as nothing more than correcting grammar and punctuation (58).
```

The subsequent reference:

```
The study recommended that . . . (NCTE 92).
```

When the name of a corporate author is long, it is probably best to include it in the text rather than interrupt the text with a long parenthetical reference.

WORK WITHOUT AN AUTHOR

Give in your citation enough of the title to enable your readers to find it in your list of works cited; usually one, two, or three words are enough (including the first word or two of the title as it is listed in Works Cited). For a pamphlet entitled *Marriages of the Dead*:

```
The ceremonial life is not open to everyone (Marriages 71).
```

If you include the title in your sentence, put the page number in the parenthetical reference.

```
In Marriages of the Dead the reader is warned that the ceremonial
life is not open to everyone (71).
```

MULTIVOLUME WORK

In citing one volume of a multivolume work, use the following format. Note that the volume number is followed by a colon and then by the page number.

```
Cardenal tells the group that "in the Old Testament the messianic
era had often been described as an epoch of great abundance of
wine" (1: 154).
```

If you include the author's name in the parenthetical reference, use this format. Do not use a comma between the author and the volume number.

```
"In the Old Testament the messianic era had often been described
as an epoch of great abundance of wine" (Cardenal 1: 154).
```

The next two examples show how to cite the entire volume. A comma separates the author's name from the abbreviation for volume.

```
Volume 1 gradually introduces the Solentiname group through their
interpretations of the stories (Cardenal).
The Solentiname group is gradually introduced through their inter-
pretations of the stories (Cardenal, vol. 1).
```

If you have included only one volume of a multivolume work in your list of works cited, you do not need the volume number in parenthetical citations.

INDIRECT SOURCE

It is best to cite the original source, but if that source is unavailable to you, use the abbreviation *qtd. in* for *quoted in* to indicate that you have used an indirect source for the information.

```
Dodd ascertained that in 1814 "there were 1,733 croppers in Leeds,
all in full employment" (qtd. in Thompson 551).
```

You can include a content note giving the full publication information for the original source, as cited in the indirect source.

TWO OR MORE WORKS BY DIFFERENT AUTHORS IN THE SAME CITATION

When citing two or more authors within the same parentheses, cite each as you normally would but separate the citations with semicolons.

```
It was generally believed that the soldiers acted under a solemn
oath and that disobedience to the general's orders was punished
with death (Carroll 67-70; Lee and Hammonds 261-65).
```

If the citation is long, include it in the text or in a bibliographic content note in order to avoid interrupting the text.

Literary Works.   For literary prose works that might be published in different editions, give the page number first, followed by a semicolon, and then include other identifying information such as book or chapter (328; bk. 3). For classic poems and plays, omit the page number and include the act, scene, or line in the parenthetical reference. This information will enable readers to find the material in different editions.

When you use the title of a literary work several times in your text, write it out the first time and give its abbreviation in parentheses. You can use the abbreviation you find in your source, or create your own from the first letters of the main words: The Winter's Tale (WT).

NOVEL OR OTHER PROSE WORK

```
In Babbitt, Sinclair Lewis portrays a business man who was "no
more conscious of his children than of the buttons on his coat-
sleeves" (227; ch. 18).
```

VERSE PLAY

Omit page numbers; instead, include the act, scene, and line numbers, separating the divisions with periods. Use arabic numerals rather than roman numerals unless your instructor asks you to do otherwise.

```
In Hamlet's famous lines about acting, he says that the purpose of
playing is "to hold, as 'twere, the mirror up to nature" (Hamlet
3.2.23).
```

You can include the title of the play in your text.

According to Shakespeare in <u>Hamlet</u>, the purpose of the theater is
"to hold, as 'twere, the mirror up to nature" (3.2.23).

POETRY

Do not use the abbreviations *l.* or *ll.* for *lines*, because these can be confused with numbers. Include identifying information (book, canto, or part) followed by the line numbers in a parenthetical citation.

Tennyson's <u>In Memoriam</u> reveals his cautious optimism: "I can but
trust that good shall fall / At last . . ." (44.14-15).

If you are citing only lines, use the word *line* or *lines* in your first reference, and from then on cite the numbers only, as in these two examples from Dylan Thomas's ''Fern Hill.'' The first reference:

"In the sun that is young once only / Time let me play and be"
(lines 12-13).

The subsequent reference:

"As I rode to sleep the owls were bearing the farm away" (24).

ONE-PAGE ARTICLES AND
WORKS ARRANGED ALPHABETICALLY

In citing a one-page article from a periodical or an article from a work arranged alphabetically (an encyclopedia or a dictionary, for example), include the author's name in the text or in a parenthetical reference and omit the page number. If an encyclopedia or dictionary article is long, give the page number.

"Although folk belief accepts the skills of dowsers, their successes in finding water are no more frequent than those gained by
other methods" (Middleton).

If the article is not signed, include a brief title in the text or in a parenthetical citation.

He was almost forty years old before his first volume of poetry
was published ("Frost").

List of Works Cited

The Works Cited page follows the content notes, if there are any. Center the heading one inch from the top of the page. Number the page as you would other pages. Arrange the entries alphabetically according to the last name of the author or, if no author is given, by the first word in the title, except for *A*, *An*, or *The*. Arrange the information for each entry in this order (omitting items that do not apply): author's name, title of part of book, title of book, name of editor or translator, edition, number of volumes, series name, place of publication, name of publisher, and date of publication. This information is usually found on the title and copyright pages. If the publisher or publication date is not given, use the abbreviation *n.p.* or *n.d.* in its place.

Begin the first line of each entry at the left margin and indent all other lines five spaces. Double-space throughout—between items and between lines in each item.

Books. Here are examples of the most commonly used entries.

ONE AUTHOR

The last name of the author is first, with periods after the author's name, the title, and the date. The title is underlined. A colon follows the place of publication, and a comma is placed after the publisher.

```
Faulkner, William.  A Fable.  New York: Random House, 1954.
```

TWO OR MORE BOOKS BY THE SAME AUTHOR

Put the titles in alphabetical order. Instead of repeating the author's name, type three hyphens followed by a period.

```
---.  The Reivers: A Reminiscence.  New York: Random House, 1962.
```

Note: If the author of one book is coauthor of another book, do not use three hyphens. Give full name as coauthor.

TWO AUTHORS

The last name of the first author is first; the second author's name is in regular order. Give the names in the order in which they appear on the title page.

```
Kunitz, Stanley J., and Howard Haycraft.  American Authors, 1600-
     1900.  New York: H. W. Wilson, 1938.
```

THREE AUTHORS

```
Parsons, Talcott, Robert F. Bales, and Edward A. Shils.  Working
     Papers in the Theory of Action.  Glencoe, IL: Free Press,
     1953.
```

MORE THAN THREE AUTHORS

Note the comma between the first author and the abbreviation *et al.* because the order of the name has been reversed.

Hubbell, Jay B., et al. Eight American Authors: A Review of
Research and Criticism. New York: Norton, 1963.

CORPORATE AUTHOR

Life Sciences Research Office. Evaluation of the Health Aspects
of Caffeine. Bethesda: Federation of American Societies for
Experimental Biology, 1978.

GOVERNMENT PUBLICATIONS

When the name of the author is not known, give the government
agency as author. Then give title of publication, identifying information such as bill or document numbers, and publication information
(place, publisher, and date).

United States Cong. Senate. Senator Riegle Speaking for Kennedy's
Health Plan. 96th Cong., 1st sess. S. Doc. 1720. Washington: GPO, 1979.

This is a Senate document. Like most government documents, it was
published by the Government Printing Office (GPO). Other types of
congressional publications are House documents (H. Doc. 976), bills
(S 45; HR 52), resolutions (S. Res. 101; H. Res. 45), and reports (S.
Rept. 32; H. Rept. 3).

When the name of the author is known, follow the format for a book
or periodical (see Periodicals, p. 229).

Hile, Joseph P. "Proposed Exemption of Required Label Statements
on Food Containers with Separate Lids." Department of Health
and Human Services. Food and Drug Administration. 21 CFR
Part 101. Federal Register 50 (249): 52937-8.

For references to the *Congressional Record*, you need only the abbreviated title of the publication, date, and page numbers.

Cong. Record. 6 Dec. 1985: S17128.

Note: House and Senate sections are paged separately, so be sure to
give identifying letter.

ANONYMOUS AUTHOR

When the author's name is not given on the title page, the entry begins with the title of the book.

Solid for Mulhooly. New York: G. W. Carleton, 1881.

PSEUDONYMOUS AUTHOR

The author's real name is placed in brackets.

Blot, Thomas [William Simpson]. <u>The Man from Mars</u>. San Francisco: Bacon, 1891.

EDITOR OF AN ANTHOLOGY

Keene, Donald, ed. <u>Anthology of Japanese Literature</u>. New York:
Grove, 1955.

EDITOR

If the focus of your paper is on the work or its author, cite the author
first.

Melville, Herman. <u>Moby-Dick or, the Whale</u>. Ed. Alfred Kazin.
Boston: Houghton Mifflin, 1956.

If the importance to your paper is the editor or the edition used, cite the
editor first.

Kazin, Alfred, ed. <u>Moby-Dick or, the Whale</u>. By Herman Melville.
Boston: Houghton Mifflin, 1956.

TRANSLATOR

If the focus of your paper is on the work or its author, cite the author
first.

Dante. <u>The Inferno</u>. Trans. John Ciardi. New York: New American
Library, 1954.

If the importance to your paper is the translation used, cite the translator first.

Ciardi, John, trans. <u>The Inferno</u>. By Dante. New York: New American Library, 1954.

Note: If two or more works have the same editor, translator, or compiler, put the titles in alphabetical order and type three hyphens instead
of repeating the person's name (as you could do for two or more books
by the same author). The hyphens are followed by a comma and the
appropriate abbreviation—*ed., trans., comp.*

WORK IN A SERIES

After the author and title of the individual work, include the series
name and number, if any, and a period. Do not underline the name of
the series or enclose it in quotation marks.

Meinert, Charles W. Time Shortened Degrees. ERIC/Higher Education Research Report 8. Washington: American Association for
Higher Education, 1974.

WORK IN SEVERAL VOLUMES

Use this format to cite one volume when each volume has a separate title:

Parrington, Vernon L. 1800-1920: The Romantic Revolution in
America. Vol. 2 of Main Currents in American Thought.
3 vols. New York: Harcourt, Brace, 1920.

Use this format if all volumes are listed under one title:

Morrison, Samuel Eliot, and Henry Steele Commager. The Growth of
the American Republic. 2 vols. New York: Oxford UP, 1941.

WORK IN A COLLECTION OF WRITINGS
BY THE SAME AUTHOR

For an essay, short story, or poem, place the title of the work in quotation marks and include page numbers.

Orwell, George. "Shooting an Elephant." A Collection of Essays. Garden City, NY: Anchor-Doubleday, 1954. 154-62.

WORK IN A COLLECTION OF WRITINGS
BY DIFFERENT AUTHORS

Besides the title of the work and page numbers, also identify the collection's editor as given on the title page of the book.

Hearn, Lafcadio. "Mosquitoes." Mentor Book of Modern Asian
Literature. Ed. Dorothy Blair Shimer. New York: New American Library, 1969. 236-38.

For a novel or play, underline the title of the work.

Rizal, Jose. Noli me Tangere. Mentor Book of Modern Asian Literature. Ed. Dorothy Blair Shimer. New York: New American
Library, 1969. 251-74.

In citing a work in a collection of previously published pieces, give the complete information for the original publication if you can, then add *Rpt. in* (for *reprinted in*), and give publication information for the collection.

Oates, Joyce Carol. "Where Are You Going, Where Have You Been?"

The Wheel of Love. New York: Vanguard, 1970. Rpt. in The

Story and Its Writer. Ed. Ann Charters. New York: Bedford

Books-St. Martin's Press, 1983. 1081-94.

Cross-references: If you are citing two or more works from the same collection, you can list the entire collection and then cite individual pieces by referring to the collection. Give the author and title of the piece, followed by the last name of the collection's editor and the page number of the individual piece.

Swansea, Charlene, and Barbara Campbell, eds. Love Stories by New

Women. Charlotte: Red Clay Books, 1978.

Thompson, Jean. "The People of Color." Swansea and Campbell

11-30.

Vreuls, Diane. "The Seller of Watches." Swansea and Campbell

141-49.

INTRODUCTION, PREFACE, FOREWORD, OR AFTERWORD

Use the format in the example if you are citing only the introduction, preface, foreword, or afterword. If the author of the preface is also the author of the book, give only the last name of the author after "By." If you are citing the whole book, use the regular author format and omit the preface citation and page numbers.

Elliott, Osborn. Preface. The Negro Revolution in America. By

William Brink and Louis Harris. New York: Simon and Schus-

ter, 1964. 11-17

REVISED EDITION

Use the designation given in the book on the title page or the copyright page: *Rev. ed., 1st ed., 1985 ed.*

Curti, Merle. The Growth of American Thought. 2nd ed. New York:

Harper, 1951.

REPRINT OF OLDER EDITION

Give the date of the original edition before the publication information of the edition you're using.

Pater, Walter. Marius the Epicurean. 1885. London: Macmillan,

1927.

PUBLISHER'S IMPRINT

Give the name of the imprint followed by a hyphen and the name of the publisher.

```
Hitching, Francis.  Dowsing: The Psi Connection.  Garden City, NY:
    Anchor-Doubleday, 1978.
```

THE BIBLE

No bibliographic listing is necessary if you use the King James version and if your reference is to chapters or verses in the Bible. Give the book, chapter, and verse citation parenthetically in your text: (John 5:3–6). Abbreviate parenthetical references to books of the Bible when they contain five or more letters (Gen. for Genesis, Chron. for Chronicles). Spell them in full in the text. If your reference is to commentary or notes in a particular edition of the King James version or to another translation, give bibliographic information as you would for any book. Use this format for other editions or other translations of the Bible.

```
The New English Bible.  New York: Oxford University Press, 1972.
```

Encyclopedias and Dictionaries.   For encyclopedias, dictionaries, and similar reference works that are regularly updated and reissued, you do not need to supply the editor, publisher, or place of publication. Give the author's name first if the article is signed. If only the author's initials are given, find the full name in the list of authors. Give the title of the article, the name of the reference work, and the edition. Volume and page numbers are unneccessary when the work is arranged alphabetically.

UNSIGNED ARTICLE

```
"Pornography."  Encyclopaedia Britannica: Micropaedia.  1984 ed.
```

Note the British spelling of the title.

SIGNED ARTICLE

```
Bender, Paul.  "Obscenity."  Encyclopedia Americana.  1981 ed.
```

Periodicals.   For all periodicals, you will need to supply the author's name, the title of the article, and the name of the publication. For professional journals you will also need the volume number (and sometimes the issue number), year of publication, and inclusive page numbers. For magazines, which are usually published weekly, biweekly, or monthly, you will need the complete date, instead of volume and issue numbers, as well as the page numbers.

ARTICLE IN JOURNAL WITH CONTINUOUS PAGINATION

Most professional journals use continuous pagination throughout the year. That is, the second and subsequent issues do not begin with page 1 but with the page number that follows the last page number of the previous issue. When bound yearly, the continuous pagination provides easy reference. In your citation, give volume number, year, and inclusive page numbers.

```
Holzman, Michael.  "Writing as Technique."  College English 44
     (1982): 129-34.
```

ARTICLE IN JOURNAL WITH SEPARATE PAGINATION

The issue number (1 in the example) appears after the volume number (30 in the example) so that the article can be located when the issues are bound. An alternative is to add the month or season in parentheses before the year: 30 (Jan. 1982). When a journal uses only an issue number, put the issue number in place of the volume number.

```
Moskey, Stephen T.  "College Instructors as Writing Consultants."
     Technical Communication 30.1 (1983): 12-13.
```

SIGNED ARTICLE IN WEEKLY MAGAZINE

Give the complete date, beginning with the day, and abbreviate all months except May, June, and July.

```
Dyson, Freeman.  "Reflections (Nuclear Weapons--Part IV)."  New
     Yorker 27 Feb. 1984: 54-103.
```

SIGNED ARTICLE IN MONTHLY MAGAZINE

```
Starbird, Ethel A.  "The Bonanza Bean Coffee."  National Geo-
     graphic Mar. 1981: 388-405.
```

UNSIGNED ARTICLE IN MAGAZINE

Alphabetize according to the first word of the title, not including *A*, *An*, or *The*.

```
"Are You a Caffeine Addict?"  Saturday Evening Post May/June
     1982: 50-53.
```

SIGNED, TITLED REVIEW

De Mott, Benjamin. "Tocqueville Meets Narcissus." Rev. of

    American Journey, by Richard Reeves. Psychology

    Today May 1982: 79+.

Use a plus sign (+) instead of an ending page number when pages are not consecutive.

PUBLISHED INTERVIEW

Scarr, Sandra. "What's a Parent to Do?" Interview. Psychology

    Today May 1984: 58-63.

Newspaper Articles. For author and article, use the same format as for other periodicals. In giving the name of the newspaper, omit any introductory article. Then give the date, month, year, and page numbers, including section number if each section starts with 1. If an edition appears on the masthead, show it before the page number.

SIGNED ARTICLE

Brody, Jane. "Weaning the Body from Dependence on Caffeine."

    New York Times 21 Apr. 1982: C6.

UNSIGNED ARTICLE

"Gene's Protein Apparently Aids the Onset of Leukemia." Washing-

    ton Post 20 July 1984: A5.

SIGNED EDITORIAL

Immel, A. Richard. "Ralph Nader's Shoddy Product." Editorial.

    Wall Street Journal 2 Nov. 1971, eastern ed.: 10.

UNSIGNED EDITORIAL

"Lebanon for the Lebanese." Editorial. Times [London] 13 July

    1984: 15.

LETTER TO THE EDITOR

Fallon, James. Letter. Boston Globe 25 July 1985: 23.

Other Written Sources. Here are some examples of citations for other written sources.

UNPUBLISHED DISSERTATION

```
Cox, James Melville.  "Mark Twain: A Study in Nostalgia."  Diss.
     Indiana University, 1955.
```

For a published dissertation, use the same format as you would for a book.

MANUSCRIPT OR TYPESCRIPT

The order should be author, description of material, form of material (*ms.* for manuscript, *ts.* for typescript), identifying number and name of institution, if any, and location. This example cites privately owned and stored papers.

```
Ostby, Vivian.  Journal, ms.  Private papers.  Arlington, VA.
```

MIMEOGRAPHED MATERIAL

```
Task Force on Prison Overcrowding, "A Report of the Task Force on
     Prison Overcrowding to the Honorable Harry R. Hughes, Gover-
     nor of the State of Maryland."  Annapolis, 16 Feb. 1979.
     (Mimeographed.)
```

MONOGRAPH

```
Dale, Richard S., and Richard P. Mattione.  Managing Global Debt:
     A Staff Paper.  Washington: Brookings Institution, 1982.
```

PAMPHLET

Pamphlets are treated like books.

```
Potter, Joseph C., and Edward H. Robinson III.  Parent-Teacher
     Conferencing.  Washington: National Education Association,
     1982.
```

PUBLISHED PROCEEDINGS OF A CONFERENCE

```
Kleimann, Susan, Eric Rice, and Marcy Scheltema, eds.  Proceedings
     of the Third Maryland Composition Conference.  15 Mar. 1985.
     College Park, MD: Maryland U, 1985.
```

LEGAL DOCUMENT

Legal citations are varied. For documents not illustrated here, see *A Uniform System of Citation* published by the Harvard Law Review Association (1986). In referring to the United States Code, give the title number, US Code or USC, section number, and date. Alphabetize under ''US code.''

```
29 US Code.  Sec. 65.  1976.
```

For court cases, give name of case, volume, name and page of report cited, name of court that decided the case, and year. This case, for example, was decided by the U.S. Court of Appeals for the District of Columbia in 1965. It can be found in volume 350 of the *Federal Reporter*, second series, page 445.

```
Williams v. Walker-Thomas Furniture Co.  350 F 2d 445.  DC Cir.
    Ct.  1965.
```

PERSONAL LETTER

```
Earnest, Dorothy.  Letter to the author.  21 July 1982.
```

Nonprint Sources.   In your research some of your sources may not be in printed form. Here are examples of bibliographic entries for nonprint sources.

ART

In a museum:

```
Bernini, Gianlorenzo.  Neptune and Triton.  Victoria and Albert
    Museum, London.
```

Reproduction in a book or periodical:

```
Mondrian, Piet.  Composition.  Albright-Knox Gallery, Buffalo, NY.
    Illus. in Dictionary of Arts and Artists.  By Peter and Linda
    Murray.  New York: Praeger, 1965.
```

INTERVIEW

In person:

```
Van Valkenburgh, Willard.  President, Federal Investment Co.  Per-
    sonal interview.  12 Oct. 1979.
```

By telephone:

```
Ebb, Carmel.  Telephone interview.  2 July 1981.
```

FILM

For a film give the title, director, distributor, and date. Include any other information pertinent to your paper such as writer, performers, producer, and length of film.

> Another Country. Dir. Marek Kanievska. Orion Classics, 1984.

If you are citing a person connected to the film, give that name first.

> Kanievska, Marek, dir. Another Country. Orion Classics, 1984.

LECTURE

In a college class:

> Molin, Eric. Lecture on Samuel Johnson. English 701, George Mason University, 30 Mar. 1984.

At a professional conference:

> Denman, Mary Edel. "Teaching English in China." Panel H-17, Conference on College Composition and Communication. Detroit, 18 Mar. 1983.

DRAMATIC PERFORMANCE

> Pinter, Harold. The Homecoming. Dir. Peter Hall. Music Box Theater, New York. 5 Jan. 1967.

If you wish to cite the performance, give the playwright and title first. If you wish to cite the director, put his or her name first.

> Hall, Peter, dir. The Homecoming. By Harold Pinter. Music Box Theater, New York. 5 Jan. 1967.

MUSICAL PERFORMANCE

> Woodside, Lyndon, dir. War Requiem. By Benjamin Britten. Oratorio Society of New York. Carnegie Hall, New York. 10 May 1984.

If you wish to cite the composer, put his name first.

> Britten, Benjamin. War Requiem. Dir. Lyndon Woodside. Oratorio Society of New York. Carnegie Hall, New York. 10 May 1984.

DANCE PERFORMANCE

> American Ballet Theatre. Swan Lake. By Igor Stravinsky. Metropolitan Opera House, New York. 15 June 1984.

If you are citing the performance of a particular person, begin with that person's name.

RECORDING

Give the name of the person you are citing, the title of the record or tape, artists if you wish, manufacturer, catalog number, and year of issue (if unknown, use *n.d.*). After the name of a cited orchestra conductor, give the name of the orchestra. In the following entry, the date of recording is given in addition to the much later date of issue.

Ellington, Duke, cond. Duke Ellington Orch. Duke Ellington at

Fargo, 1940. Rec. 7 Nov. 1940. Book-of-the-Month Records,

30-5622-F, 1978.

TELEVISION OR RADIO PROGRAM

Give the title of the program, actors' or other pertinent names, network, local station and city, and broadcast date.

Brideshead Revisited, Episode 4. With Anthony Andrews and Jeremy

Irons. PBS. WETA, Washington, DC. 24 July 1984.

VIDEOTAPE

Romeo and Juliet. Videotape. Bolshoi Ballet. MGM, 1976, 109

mins.

MGM is the distributor. Include any other information important to you, such as director, producer, or main performers.

MUSICAL COMPOSITION

Give the composer's name, title (underlined only if identified by name, such as the *Moonlight Sonata*) or form, number, key, and opus number. Here the sonata cited is not identified by name, and it has no number.

Beethoven, Ludwig van. Violin sonata in A major, op. 12.

INFORMATION OBTAINED
THROUGH A COMPUTER DATABASE

Use the same format as you would for a printed reference; then add the name of the vendor and the identifying numbers.

Whitehall, J. "Loopholes for Child Pornography." Medical Jour-

nal of Australia 1980. DIALOG file 12, item 1109-1110.

Documentation Using Footnotes or Endnotes

Although MLA style prefers the use of parenthetical citations in the text and a list of works cited at the end, you may wish to use footnotes or endnotes, either with or without a list of works cited. (Check with your instructor before using notes to cite sources.)

Notes can be placed at the bottom of the page that contains the information to which they refer, or they can be put at the end of your paper. A superscript number is given in the text, like this,[1] to refer readers to the note. To avoid interrupting the text, the number is placed near the cited material where a pause would naturally occur. Notes should be numbered consecutively throughout the paper. If the notes appear at the end, they begin on a separate page following the body of the paper and are labeled Notes or Endnotes.

Number the page the same as for other pages. Place the heading Notes one inch from the top of the page. Then double-space and begin your first note. Indent five spaces, place the superscript number one-half space above the line, leave one space, and type the entry. Type the second line of the entry flush with the left margin.

Footnotes have the same form whether they are at the bottom of the page or at the end of the paper—except for spacing. Notes at the bottom of the page are single-spaced within each entry and double-spaced between entries.

[1] Robert Pattison, On Literacy: The Politics of the Word from Homer to the Age of Rock (New York: Oxford UP, 1982) 42.

[2] Anne Tyler, "Still Just Writing," The Writer on Her Work, ed. Janet Sternburg (New York: Norton, 1980) 5.

Notes at the end of the paper should be double-spaced within the citation and between the citations. In both footnotes and endnotes all the information should be given in the first citation. The order is author, title of book, place of publication, publisher, date of publication, and page number. In subsequent citations of the same source only the last name of the author or authors and the page number are needed.

[1] Susanne K. Langer, Feeling and Form (New York: Scribner's, 1953) 69.

[2] Langer 83.

If you cite more than one work by the same author, however, give a short form of the title also.

   [3] Langer, *Feeling* 97.

Here are some examples of frequently used types of footnotes.

BOOK WITH ONE AUTHOR

   [1] J. Z. Young, *Programs of the Brain* (Oxford: Oxford UP, 1978) 39.

BOOK WITH TWO OR THREE AUTHORS

Use the order of names given on the title page.

   [2] William Brink and Louis Harris, *The Negro Revolution in America* (New York: Simon and Schuster, 1964) 45.

   [3] V. Clyde Arnspiger, W. Ray Rucker, and Mary E. Press, *Personality in Social Process* (Dubuque, IA: W. C. Brown, 1961) 29.

BOOK WITH MORE THAN THREE AUTHORS

   [4] Robert E. Spiller et al., *Literary History of the United States*, 2 vols. (New York: Macmillan, 1948) 2:729.

BOOK WITH A CORPORATE AUTHOR

   [5] Life Sciences Research Office, *Evaluation of the Health Aspects of Caffeine* (Bethesda: Federation of American Societies for Experimental Biology, 1978) 22.

GOVERNMENT PUBLICATIONS

   [6] United States Cong., Senate Select Committee to Study Governmental Operations with Respect to Intelligence Activities, *Alleged Assassination Plots Involving Foreign Leaders*, 94th Cong., 1st sess., S. Rept. 94-465 (Washington: GPO, 1975) 123.

ANONYMOUS AUTHOR

   [7] *Drafting and Design* (New York: Art Press, 1968) 249-55.

WORK IN AN ANTHOLOGY

   [8] Mohan Singh, "Evening," *Mentor Book of Modern Asian Literature*, ed. Dorothy Blair Shimer (New York: New American Library, 1969) 44.

TRANSLATION

   [9] Gustave Flaubert, *Madame Bovary*, trans. Paul De Man (New York: Norton, 1965) 121.

BOOK IN A SERIES

[10] Charles W. Meinert, Time Shortened Degrees, ERIC/Higher Education Research Report 8 (Washington: American Association for Higher Education, 1974) 127.

BOOK IN SEVERAL VOLUMES

See entry 4.

WORK IN A COLLECTION OF WRITINGS
BY THE SAME AUTHOR

[11] George Orwell, "Shooting an Elephant," A Collection of Essays by Orwell (Garden City, NY: Doubleday, 1954) 46.

INTRODUCTION, PREFACE,
FOREWORD, OR AFTERWORD

[12] Osborn Elliott, preface, The Negro Revolution in America, by William Brink and Louis Harris (New York: Simon and Schuster, 1964) 164.

REVISED EDITION

[13] Kenneth Burke, The Philosophy of Literary Form, 3rd ed. (Berkeley: U of California P, 1973) 386.

REPRINT OF AN OLDER EDITION

[14] Walter Pater, Marius the Epicurean (1885; London: Macmillan, 1927) 12.

BOOK WITHOUT
PUBLICATION INFORMATION

Type the entry as you normally would. If the publisher or publication date is not given, use the abbreviation *n.p.* or *n.d.* in its place.

SIGNED ENCYCLOPEDIA ARTICLE

[15] E. Z. Vogt and L. K. Barrett, "Dowsing," Encyclopedia Americana, 1980 ed.

ARTICLE IN JOURNAL WITH
CONTINUOUS PAGINATION

The order is author, title of article, name of journal, volume number, year, and page number.

[16] F. M. Steele, "Extravagance in the Dress of Women," Arena 9 (1894): 656.

ARTICLE IN JOURNAL WITH SEPARATE PAGINATION

The order is author, title of article, name of journal, volume number, issue number, year, and page number.

[17] Kurt Gingold, "The In-house Translator in U.S. Industry," Technical Communication 29.4 (1982): 9.

SIGNED ARTICLE IN WEEKLY MAGAZINE

[18] Arthur M. Schlesinger, Jr., "The Other Henry Adams," The Nation 25 Dec. 1948: 727.

SIGNED ARTICLE IN MONTHLY MAGAZINE

[19] Tony Trabert, "How John McEnroe Launches the Most Lethal Serve in Tennis," Tennis Sept. 1983: 41.

SIGNED, TITLED REVIEW

[20] Benjamin De Mott, "Tocqueville Meets Narcissus," rev. of American Journey, by Richard Reeves, Psychology Today May 1982: 79+.

SIGNED NEWSPAPER ARTICLE

[21] Tom Zito, "Skeletons & Keys: Looking for Capote," Washington Post 13 Mar. 1983: G1.

UNSIGNED NEWSPAPER ARTICLE

[22] "Gene's Protein Apparently Aids the Onset of Leukemia," Washington Post July 1984: A5.

EDITORIAL

[23] A. Richard Immel, "Ralph Nader's Shoddy Product," editorial, Wall Street Journal 2 Nov. 1971, eastern ed.: 10.

LETTER TO THE EDITOR

[24] James Fallon, letter, Boston Globe 25 July 1985: 23.

UNPUBLISHED DISSERTATION

[25] James Melville Cox, "Mark Twain: A Study in Nostalgia," diss., Indiana University, 1955, 107.

PAMPHLET OR BOOKLET

[26] State Education Dept., New York State U, A Guide to Educational Programs in Noncollegiate Organizations (Albany: New York State U, 1974) 15.

INTERVIEW

27 Lois Paul, personal interview, 6 Mar. 1983.

FILM

28 Sydney Pollack, dir., <u>Tootsie</u>, with Dustin Hoffman, Teri Garr, and Jessica Lange, Columbia, 1982.

LECTURE

29 Fred P. Dobson, class lecture, Agronomy 312, U of Maryland, College Park, MD, 28 Oct. 1981.

DRAMATIC PERFORMANCE

30 Bertolt Brecht, <u>Mother Courage</u>, dir. Tim Mayer, Loeb Theater, Cambridge, MA, 5 Jan. 1984.

TELEVISION OR RADIO PROGRAM

31 "Meeting Ground," created by Melisa McCampbell, prod. New England Medical Center, PBS, WGBH, Boston, 12 Feb. 1986.

INFORMATION FROM
A COMPUTER SERVICE

32 J. Whitehall, "Loopholes for Child Pornography," <u>Medical Journal of Australia</u> 1980 (DIALOG file 12, item 1109-1110).

Two Sample Research Papers
Using the Author/Page Style

The author/page system of documentation used in the following two papers is recommended in the *MLA Handbook for Writers of Research Papers* (1984). This system is used by writers in literature and other disciplines in the humanities. In the author/page system, brief parenthetical citations in the text refer to a list of works cited which is placed at the end of the paper. In the first paper, Does Dowsing Work? the writer provides a title page because he includes a formal outline with the paper. In the second paper, a literary research paper on the changing reputation of Robert Frost, the text begins on page one, following a brief heading and the title of the paper.

Does Dowsing Work?

Robert Close

Professor Miller

English 2B

December 12, 198-

If you are handing in an outline with your paper, include a title page. Center the title of your paper (not underlined or enclosed in quotation marks) and type your name, your instructor's name, the course name, and the date below it. If you are not handing in an outline, type identifying information on the first page of the text. (See the sample paper on Robert Frost in this chapter.)

Close ii

Outline

Does Dowsing Work?

Outline follows
title page and
begins p. ii (first
page is counted but
not numbered).
Last name before
the page number
for identification.

Thesis states what
the paper attempts
to prove.

Thesis: Although many dowsers and observers claim that
dowsing works, the scientific community dismisses it as
fakery. More scientific study is needed to establish
whether dowsing works.

Topic outline. You
could also use a
sentence outline.

   I.   Introduction: the decision to write about
      dowsing.

  II.   Background information on dowsing

      A. History

      B. Tools used

          1. Forked stick

          2. Straight wand

          3. Pendulum

          4. Angel rods

 III.   Reported successes with dowsing

      A. On-site dowsing

          1. By utility companies

          2. By engineers

          3. By oil companies

          4. By the Marines

      B. Distance dowsing by Henry Gross

      C. Proportion of successful dowsers

  IV.   Scientific reports on dowsing

      A. Research results supporting dowsing

          1. Research on alpha states and elec-
              tromagnetic forces

Close iii

2. Tromp's research on magnetism and
   biology
3. Presman's research on effects of
   electromagnetic change in animals
4. Harvalik's research on the strength
   of the dowsing signal

B. Scientific arguments against dowsing

V. Evaluation of the evidence

A. Difficulties in finding the truth about
   dowsing

B. Studies of dowsing should be continued

Close 1

Does Dowsing Work?

Center title.
Double-space twice
to text.

Unfamiliar word is
defined when first
used.

I had heard stories about dowsing (locating water
or metal deposits by using a divining rod), but I always
considered them to be just rumors or fairy tales. How-

Writer introduces
paper with an
anecdote and then
states subject. The
order of the paper
is inductive;
conclusions are
drawn after
evidence is
presented.

ever, two years ago when my neighbor had to have his
plumbing system and septic tank approved to obtain a
building permit for an addition, the county sent a
dowser as part of the inspection team. The dowser,
while locating the plumbing system, found an illegal
sewer pipe that my neighbor had laid for washing machine
drainage. In telling me the story, my neighbor, a very
no-nonsense kind of person, said, "If I hadn't been
there myself, I wouldn't have believed it." I decided
to find out, if I could, whether dowsing does work.

Dowsing, sometimes called water witching, has a
long history. Moses, who, the Bible says, struck a rock
and brought forth water, may have been the first dowser.
One of the earliest accounts of the use of dowsing was
De Re Matalia, written by a German scholar, Georgius
Agricola, in 1556. He describes the use of dowsing by
German miners to find ores and minerals. He says they
used "hazel twigs for veins of silver, ash twigs for

Quotation found in
secondary source.
Period placed after
parentheses.

copper; pitch pine for lead" (qtd. in Wyman 47). In
the sixteenth century, Queen Elizabeth I imported diviners from Germany to search for tin in Cornwall.
Scientists such as Leonardo da Vinci, Thomas Edison,
and Albert Einstein are said to have been believers
(Wyman 2).

The most widely used tools in dowsing are the
forked stick, the straight wand, the pendulum, and the
angle rod. The dowser usually walks on the ground hold-

Close 2

ing the device in one or both hands. The instrument
moves up or down or in a circular fashion to indicate
the presence of water or minerals.

    The forked stick, which should be cut from a live
tree, can be hazel, willow, maple, hawthorne, apple, or
rhododendron, depending on the preference of the dowser.
The length of the stick varies from five to twenty
inches. The "Y" or "V" of the fork is about two-
thirds of the length and should have an angle of about
forty-five degrees. The most important characteristic
is flexibility, because the stick has to bend in order
to indicate the presence of water or minerals. The
stick may be held with the fingers or with the whole
hand--with palms up or palms down. Douglas Chadwick, a
skeptic who attended an annual convention for dowsers in
Montana, explained in an article, "Plain and Fancy
Shooting with the Witches," how he was instructed in
the art of dowsing by experienced teachers. One of
them, who himself had been taught by a Mongolian rein-
deer herder in Norway, cautioned Chadwick to hold the
stick firmly because, he said, "if the water happens to
be behind you, the stick could come up and hit you in
the forehead" (54).

    The straight wand, which should also be flexible,
is apparently difficult for the beginner to master.
Usually three to four feet long, the wand can be cut
from plastic tubing, a car radio aerial, or the thinnest
end of a fly rod. In the dowsing reaction, the wand
moves up and down. Because it is "less tiring to
hold," the wand is often preferred by professionals who
are covering large areas of land (Hitching 76).

    The pendulum, which can be as simple as a ring or

Common knowledge; writer does not have to cite source.

Paraphrase, summary, and quotation combined. Author's name is in text, so only page number appears.

Close 3

coin tied to some string, has been used mainly to find
oil. The dowsing reaction is a rotation of the ring.

The use of the metal L-shaped rod (or angle rod)
probably originated in Germany. Its use spread to the
United States after World War II, when returning soldiers brought back this technique from England and Europe. Crews for utility companies use angle rods to
locate pipes and cables buried underground. The device
can be made by cutting two L-shaped wire pieces from
metal coat hangers; one rod is held in each hand. (Angle rods are also sold commercially.) The rods react in
one of three ways: by rotating outward and downward--the
left one to the left, the right one to the right; by

Writer has defined
dowsing and
described the tools
and now gives
examples of their
use.

Superscript
number refers to
content note giving
additional
information at end
of paper.

crossing; or by both moving in the same direction--to
one side or the other (Hitching 73).

Dowsing has been widely used in the everyday operations of those who need to find out what is under the
ground.[1] Many utility companies use rods for locating
utility pipes. W. F. Marklund, a former distribution
supervisor for the Flint, Michigan, Water Supply, said
that dowsing rods were useful in locating "cast iron
water pipe, wrapped galvanized gas pipe, clay-tile
drains, sewer pipes or brick intakes" (Wyman 79). He
said that L-rods were "standard equipment" on their
trucks and were very dependable when maps were inaccu-
rate.

Alan Richard, a surveyor and engineer for the Public Works Department in Arlington County, Virginia, said
in an interview that coat hangers are carried on their
trucks as part of their equipment. They use them to
find underground pipes or culverts in old overgrown
plots of land. Richard explained:

Close 4

> When you have a large field to cover you can't
> spend days digging. We just take a piece of
> coat hanger in each hand and start walking.
> They cross as you walk over the culvert pipe.
> As you back off, they uncross. There's no
> scientific explanation that I know of, but
> when you see it happen you have to believe it.

Richard went on to say that younger engineers were skeptical of dowsing at first, but, like him, when they saw it work they had to accept it. He first used dowsing when he worked with an engineering firm in Manassas, Virginia.

Oil drillers also use dowsers. According to Francis Hitching, a member of the British Society of Dowsers, J. Paul Getty used a dowser in discovering many of his oil wells (24). In 1969 <u>Arco Sparks</u>, the in-house journal of Atlantic Richfield Oil Company, revealed that even "after employing all modern scientific techniques to pinpoint a pool" there are still "oil searchers" who "refuse to start expensive drilling operations until the site has been confirmed by a dowser" (qtd. in Wyman 68).

Dowsing has even been used by the Marines. Louis Matacia, a professional land surveyor who used dowsing to locate underground utilities, was asked in 1966 to demonstrate his skill to the Marines at their base in Quantico, Virginia, to see if dowsing could help to locate mines and other underground hazards in Vietnam. Matacia, it turned out, could locate just about anything, from mines, tunnels, and caves to underground wires, pipes, and even people. The Marines began to cut rods from coat hangers, and those who went to Vietnam

Quotation of more than four lines is indented ten spaces from the left margin and double-spaced. No quotation marks.

Integration of quotations in the sentence.

Close 5

used them there (Bird 206). Hanson Baldwin, military
reporter for the <u>New York Times</u>, wrote from Camp Pendle-
ton in California:

> Coat hanger dowsers, as they are called here,
> are not included in Marine Corps equipment
> manuals. But, according to Marine officers,
> they have been used in Vietnam with marked
> success in the last year, particularly by
> engineer units of the 1st and 3rd Marine Divi-
> sions, which are engaged in mine detection and
> tunnel destruction. (qtd. in Bird 206)

Baldwin called the devices "Matacia's Wire Rudders."
After seeing a demonstration of dowsing by two Marine
officers, Baldwin himself tried using the coat hanger
rods and found a tunnel previously unknown to him.

Reports of successful dowsing are not limited to
on-site performance; the ability to find water by using
only a map, a photograph, or the name of the property
has been documented. The novelist Kenneth Roberts[2]
reported extensively on the distance dowsing (as well as
the on-site) abilities of Henry Gross in <u>Henry Gross and
His Dowsing Rod</u>. Gross's most famous dowsing accom-
plishment was the discovery of fresh water on Bermuda
while looking at a map of the island in his home in
Maine (chs. 13-22). Gross later went to Bermuda to
supervise the drilling of the wells.

Brooks Shepard also wrote an article in <u>Harper's</u>
about Gross's ability to find water from a distance.
During a long period of drought in Vermont, Shepard
corresponded off and on with his friend Kenneth Roberts,
who was in Bermuda with Henry Gross. Roberts referred

No indentation for first line of quotation that does not begin a paragraph in the source.

Citation in parentheses two spaces after end punctuation.

Reference to content note giving biographical information about Roberts.

Reference to chapters of a book.

Close 6

Shepard's problem to Gross, who was able to plot the
precise geographical location of underground water on
Shepard's farm (which Gross had never visited). After
drilling, Shepard found that Gross was correct. Similar
dowsing practices have been documented by Hitching
(227-28).

A few scientists have proposed explanations for the
dowsing phenomenon. In the early twentieth century
Viktor Schumann, a German physicist, discovered a frequency (10 hertz) where the "earth's own magnetic field
pulses most strongly" (Hitching 153). It is also on
this frequency that the brain's dream-like alpha state
(the state in which the brain emits alpha waves) is
found. According to Hitching (163), Professor Michael
Persinger of Laurentian University in Canada has proposed that a connection between the earth's magnetic
field and the brain's alpha state operates in telepathy
and ESP (extrasensory perception). In his book, Dowsing: The Psi Connection, Hitching suggests that successful dowsing is equally a result of this connection. He
also reports on the work of two American scientists, Dr.
Francis Cole, a biologist at the Alton Ochsner Medical
Foundation in New Orleans, and Dr. E. R. Graf of Auburn
University in Alabama, who have theorized that the 10-
hertz frequency may be the "key to the evolution of
life on earth" (163). That is, the earth's protein may
have evolved over millions of years in a 10-hertz field.
If this is true, then it is possible that humans (and
other animals) would be "remarkably sensitive to low-
frequency electromagnetic events" (162).

The strongest scientific evidence that dowsing

After writer explains dowsers' experiences, he gives scientific explanations and results of research.

Writer paraphrases idea to make it clear.

Close 7

works comes from researchers who hypothesize that dowsing is a result of natural magnetic laws that have yet to be thoroughly investigated. Many dowsers themselves favor this explanation. A Dutch geophysicist, Dr. S. W. Tromp, studied dowsing for twenty years. He believes that "geomagnetic forces created by changes in the earth's magnetic fields" cause "a reaction in the nervous system not now understood" and that "the dowser's reactions to underground water and minerals are clearly registered on the electrocardiograph" (Wyman 88).

Writer gives credentials to establish source's authority.

Alexandr Presman, a professor in the Department of Biophysics at Moscow State University, has been doing similar work on biology and magnetism in his experiments to determine the effects of electromagnetic changes on animals. He found that biological changes were produced at extremely low frequencies and that weaker intensities produced more biological changes than stronger intensities (Hitching 143). His results suggest that, if bio-

Writer interprets evidence; he doesn't just report it.

logical changes are produced in animals by changes in the electromagnetic field, dowsers might also sense these changes and react to them.

In an effort to discover exactly how dowsing works, Dr. Zaboj V. Harvalik conducted numerous experiments on the sensitivity of dowsers. A former professor of physics at the University of Arkansas, he was also an advisor to the U.S. Army's Advanced Concepts Materials Agency before he retired. He had the idea that dowsers might be responding to changes above ground in the earth's magnetic field. In one study, he tested two hundred people for their sensitivity to changes in the magnetic field. According to Bird, after several years

Close 8

and hundreds of hours of testing, Dr. Harvalik concluded
that

> . . . 80 percent of his subjects could ini-
> tially obtain a dowsing signal at a current
> strength above 20 milliamperes. The rest
> could continue successfully to record signals
> down to 2 milliamperes, and a select few ob-
> tained reactions when only half a milliampere
> passed through the ground. (261)

Even if Harvalik's experiments and those of others
prove that people can detect changes in the magnetic
field, we still don't know how the body receives this
knowledge. Dr. Harvalik's experiments indicate that the
most sensitive regions may be in the kidney area and the
forehead. After several trials, he designed a belt made
out of a magnetic shielding material. He discovered
that when dowsers wore the shielding material over the
renal glands (in the kidneys) their dowsing ability was
greatly hampered (Bird 261).

Despite all of this evidence for the reliability of
dowsing, there are skeptics and nonbelievers. Evon Z.
Vogt, an anthropologist, and Ray Hyman, a psychologist,
conducted research on dowsing or, as they prefer to call
it, "divining" and concluded that diviners' results
were no better than chance. Despite all of the personal
experiences, there is, they say, no way to scientifically validate dowsing because "we cannot, in most
cases, reproduce the essential conditions and produce an
effect upon which all observers can agree" (66). Vogt
also co-authored an article on dowsing for the Encyclopedia Americana denying that dowsing works: "Controlled

field and laboratory tests have failed to establish the
validity of dowsing, and judged by scientific standards
the practice has little basis in fact" (Vogt and Barrett).

Two months before Shepard's article in Harper's,
Thomas M. Riddick, a water-works engineer and chemist,
published an article in the same magazine ridiculing
dowsing and complaining that Roberts's recently published book on Henry Gross might "do real harm" (68).
He attributes the success of dowsing to the fact that
water is easy to find almost everywhere.

The controversy is likely to continue between nonbelievers and believers. Nonbelievers say that dowsing
cannot be proven scientifically to be reliable; believers say that science ignores the documented experiences
of many successful dowsers and that dowsing skills rely
on forces that science cannot measure or identify. The
problems of measurement do make it difficult to reach a
clear conclusion one way or the other. In the first
place, it's hard to define success. Vogt and Hyman
point out that "often a well that is initially classified as a failure becomes mysteriously productive after
a span of time, whereas one that looked good suddenly
goes bad" (200). And does finding water that is not
potable count as a success? Most dowsers, themselves,
feel that potability and usable quantity are criteria of
a successfully dowsed well. In addition, the skill of
individual dowsers seems to vary. Shepard tried two
other dowsers on his farm before Henry Gross found the
right location. Each of the first two had found water,
but the supply gave out after a short time. The well

Past tense
(*published*)
indicates past
action; present
tense (*attributes*)
used for
information in
print.

Writer summarizes
evidence, explains
problems in
evaluation, and
presents his
conclusions.

Close 10

dowsed by Gross continued to give water through the
drought.

A second problem in evaluating dowsing is the skepticism that exists in regard to a nonscientific activity
like dowsing. People tend to associate it with the
occult; that is, with something mysterious or supernatural. For example, the Encyclopaedia Britannica, in a
brief article, specifically connects it with "occult-
ism" ("Dowsing"). Often the most positive comment made
about dowsing is that it is a folk belief.

For dowsing to be generally accepted, then, two
problems have to be overcome: the difficulties of scientific measurement and dowsing's association with the
supernatural (in some minds dowsers are still water-
witches or diviners). The scientific method has worked
well for us, so we have trouble believing in something
we don't understand or can't prove. But the many positive experiences with dowsing reported by reliable prac-
titioners and observers cannot be dismissed as products
of the imagination or as witchcraft. Dowsing deserves
to be taken seriously and examined further by scientists
and reporters. Studies going on today may eventually
convince the whole scientific community of what many
scientists and laypeople already believe--that dowsing
does work.

Page number not needed because source is alphabetically arranged.

Arguments against dowsing summarized.

Close 11

Place content
endnotes on
separate page.
Center heading
one inch from top
margin, and
number page as
part of text.
Double-space and
type first note.
Indent first line 5
spaces.

Publication data
placed in
parentheses.

Notes

[1] Careful studies of dowsing have been done by
Francis Hitching in Dowsing: The Psi Connection (Garden
City, NY: Anchor-Doubleday, 1978), who admits the problems of proving the validity of dowsing scientifically
but who nevertheless believes that it works; and by Evon
Z. Vogt and Ray Hyman in Water Witching U.S.A. (Chicago: U of Chicago P, 1979), who conclude that dowsing
is a myth--that its successes are due to luck and to
common-sense, "lay of the land" evaluations.

[2] Kenneth Roberts (1885-1957) was a staff corres-
pondent for the Saturday Evening Post and later wrote a
series of historically accurate and widely read historical novels. Among his best known are Rabble in Arms
(1933) and Northwest Passage (1937).

Close 12

Works Cited

Bird, Christopher. The Divining Hand: The Art of
    Searching for Water, Oil, Minerals, and Other
    Natural Resources or Anything Lost, Missing or
    Badly Needed. New York: Dutton, 1979.

Chadwick, Douglas. "Plain and Fancy Shooting with the
    Witches." Blair & Ketchum's Country Journal Aug.
    1981: 54-58.

"Dowsing." Encyclopaedia Britannica: Micropaedia.
    1985 ed.

Hitching, Francis. Dowsing: The Psi Connection. Garden
    City, NY: Anchor-Doubleday, 1978.

Richard, Alan. Personal interview. 12 July 1983.

Riddick, Thomas M. "Dowsing is Nonsense." Harper's
    July 1951: 63-68.

Roberts, Kenneth. Henry Gross and His Dowsing Rod.
    1951. New York: Pyramid, 1969.

Shepard, Brooks. "Firsthand Report on Dowsing."
    Harper's Sept. 1951: 69-75.

Vogt, Evon Z., and L. K. Barrett. "Dowsing."
    Encyclopedia Americana. 1984 ed.

Vogt, Evon Z., and Ray Hyman. Water Witching U.S.A.
    Chicago: U of Chicago P, 1979.

Wyman, Walker D. Witching for Water, Oil, Pipes, and
    Precious Minerals: A Persistent Folk Belief from
    Frontier Days Down to the Present. Park Falls:
    U of Wisconsin-River Falls P, 1977.

Works cited parenthetically in body of paper are listed alphabetically by author's last name.

Book.

Monthly magazine.

Encyclopedia edition given. Page numbers are not necessary.

Anchor is an imprint of Doubleday.

Give date of personal interview.

Reprint of older edition.

Only the first author's name is reversed. Two references by Vogt; references then ordered alphabetically by second authors' names.

1

Format for paper without a title page: heading is typed flush left and double-spaced; title is centered; text begins four spaces below the title.

Chris Schaffer

Professor Marjorie Lyman

English 101

May 10, 198-

The Changing Reputation of Robert Frost

The Complete Poems of Robert Frost opens with "The Pasture," a poem inviting readers to join the speaker as he is "going out to clean the pasture spring" and "going out to fetch the little calf" (3). With its rural setting, simple diction, and clear subject, this poem firmly establishes the image of its author as a poet-farmer. This was the image that Frost himself cultivated and the image that many of his critics and readers praised. As Gerber explains:

Quotation longer than four lines indented ten spaces and double-spaced.

> To his great public Frost was the epitome
> of the benevolent farmer-sage, a type of
> ideal regional figure whose communion with
> nature purified him and raised him to the
> status of a seer, but whose total humility
> rendered him approachable to all. (Robert
> Frost 19)

Short title used because two books by Gerber appear in Works Cited.

The popular image of Frost was challenged by a few critics early on and by others late in the poet's career. These critics focused on a different Frost, one whose sense of the grim and tragic aspects of life pervades his poetry. Another group of critics attacked Frost in the middle of his career as a poet of sentiment and nostalgia--a poet out of touch with the major issues of his time. A study of the critical reception to Frost throughout his career reveals him to be a complex man and poet whose work has provoked a strong and lasting

Thesis states what the paper will demonstrate.

Schaffer 2

Writer's name typed before page number in case pages are misplaced.

critical debate. Frost is a poet whose reputation in American literature is still evolving more than twenty years after his death.

In a career that covered much of this century (he lived from 1874 to 1963), Frost worked hard to be recognized by critics and accepted by readers (Thompson xv-xix). He was almost forty years old before his first volume of poetry, A Boy's Will, was published. Although Frost received mixed reviews in England, where this book first came out, he was championed in America by important literary figures including William Dean Howells and Ezra Pound (Cox 4). Another early supporter, Amy Lowell, gave Frost's second book, North of Boston, a favorable review in the New Republic and then devoted a chapter to Frost in her Tendencies in Modern American Poetry. Lowell was one of the few early critics to focus on what she characterized as Frost's grimly ironic vision: "Mr. Frost's book reveals a disease which is eating into the vitals of our New England life, at least in its rural communities" (81). In discussing the characters in Frost's poems, she called them "the leftovers of the old stock, morbid, pursued by phantoms, slowly sinking to insanity" (81).

Author's name given in text; only page number appears in citation.

Other early critics like Edward Garnett recognized Frost's psychological insight and his ability to respond to both tragic and humorous situations (39-41), but many commentators glossed over the more disturbing images and strains in Frost's poetry. As Gerber explains, Lowell's view of Frost was not echoed by the majority of commentators in the early part of the twentieth century:

Writer introduces long quotation by summarizing the point.

> In writing of Frost's tragic sense (which she felt to be overly obsessive) and the quality

Schaffer 3

of disillusionment that touched so much of his
work, Miss Lowell introduced topics that would
not be dealt with easily by other commentators
for decades to come. (Robert Frost 151)
The more common view was expressed by Sylvester Baxter,
who talked about Frost's "winsome personality" and
about the homesickness the poet felt for his New England
farm while Frost was in England (29). An anonymous
critic in the Philadelphia Public Ledger summed up the
popular image of the poet at this time: "Mr. Frost has
windblown cheeks and clear blue eyes. He's a Yankee of
yankees and glad of it . . ." ("Of Axe-Handles" 48).
Frost himself contributed to this impression. According
to Wayne Tefs, Frost "labored diligently to promote
himself as a kindly, diffident rural sage: as he con-
fided to one of his early correspondents, he wanted to
be perceived as 'Yankier and Yankier' " (224).

    Soon after the publication of his first two books,
Frost became recognized as one of the most important new
poets in America. His works were anthologized in influ-
ential collections of poetry such as Louis Untermeyer's
Modern American Poetry (1919) and Harriet Monroe's The
New Poetry (1917), and he began making reading tours of
college and university campuses across the country (Gerber, Critical Essays 5-6). The next few decades were
filled with such achievement that one of his biogra-
phers, Lawrance Thompson, wrote a book about that period
in Frost's life called The Years of Triumph: 1915-1938.
Literary prizes and honorary degrees became ordinary
events for Frost. By the time he published A Witness
Tree in 1943, he had received four Pulitzer Prizes,

Margin notes:

Single quotation marks used for quotation within a quotation.

Citation for author, short title, and page numbers.

Writer summarizes information found in a chronology of important dates in Frost's life.

Schaffer 4

among other awards; he had been elected to the National
Institute of Arts and Letters; and he had held distin-
guished academic positions at Amherst, Harvard, and the
University of Michigan at Ann Arbor (Cox 199-201).

Yet even after Frost was in his fifties, not everyone was willing to recognize his mastery as a poet.
Certain critics attacked Frost for not writing directly
about the important political and social issues of his
time. In reviewing Collected Poems in 1930, Granville
Hicks claimed that Frost "cannot give us the sense of
belonging in the industrial, scientific, Freudian world
in which we find ourselves. . . . That is why no one
would think of maintaining that he is one of the great
poets of the ages" (78). Ivor Winters complained that
Frost was a "spiritual drifter," and Harold H. Watts
joined Winters in concluding that Frost had not adequately explored the relationship between the individual
and society (Gerber, Robert Frost 160).

For some critics, Frost simply seemed unsophisti-
cated, or worse, politically conservative. Malcolm
Cowley, in "Frost: A Dissenting Opinion," complained
that Frost had become the symbol of those espousing a
narrow nationalism who demanded that "American literature should be affirmative, optimistic, uncritical and
'truly of this nation'" (312). In the second part of
his series, "The Case Against Mr. Frost: II," Cowley
condemned Frost himself for being opposed to "innova-
tions in art, ethics, science, industry or politics"
(345), and for setting limits on the exploration of
himself and "on almost every other human activity"
(346). In his final assessment of Frost, Cowley called

Writer combines
quotation and
paraphrase to
represent other
critical
perspectives.

him "a poet who celebrates the diminished but prosperous and self-respecting New England of the tourist home and the antique shop in the abandoned gristmill" (347).

The attacks on Frost were met with strong defenses of the poet's work. Bernard DeVoto claimed that Frost was a poet with authority: "Frost's poetry is a new assertion of eternal things--that, whether in tragedy or in fulfillment, life counts, is worthy, can be trusted, has dignity. . . . It is the only major affirmation that modern American literature has made" (109). Others agreed with DeVoto, among them George Whicher of Amherst, who praised Frost for maintaining "during a time of general disillusionment" his faith in democracy (Cook 21).

As Gerber recounts in his history of critical response to Robert Frost, the poet survived the attacks of the 1930s and early 40s to find his public reputation secure and growing (Robert Frost 159). Though the negative criticism did not disappear, it was overshadowed by praise and analysis of Frost's later work and by Frost's great popularity with readers and audiences across the country. When Frost turned seventy-five, the United States Senate passed a resolution honoring Frost for writing poems that "have helped to guide American thought with humor and wisdom, setting forth to our minds a reliable representation of ourselves and of all men . . ." (qtd. in Thompson and Winnick 186).

But the prevalent view of Frost as the optimistic voice of American values and hopes was disturbed once again, however, at a public celebration of Frost's eighty-fifth birthday given by his publishers, Henry

Ellipses dots indicate that something was omitted from the original.

Qtd in (*quoted in*) indicates that statement came from secondary source.

Schaffer 6

Holt and Company. Lionel Trilling, who was the speaker
at the dinner, later wrote of the event because his
speech upset many of those present and many who later
heard about the speech. Trilling wanted to know why his
remarks about Frost nearly "approached a scandal"
(151). The provocation in Trilling's speech was his
point that "the manifest America of Mr. Frost's poems
may be pastoral; the actual America is terrifying."
About the characters in Frost's poems, Trilling wondered: "when ever have people been so isolated, so
lightning-blasted, so tried down and calcined by life,
so reduced, each in his own way, to some last irreduc-
ible core of being" (157). Trilling ended by comparing
the poet to Sophocles and by calling Frost a poet "who
could make plain the terrible things" (158). Trilling
did not mean to discredit Frost by focusing on the
darker aspects of his poetry, but to a large group of
his critics and readers, this focus was unacceptable.
J. Donald Adams reprinted parts of the speech and
blasted Trilling for it in the New York Times Book
Review. As Trilling reports in his account of the
event, his speech was taken as an "affront to some
part of American opinion. It was a very deep affront
if I can judge by the letters, published in the Book
Review of April 26th, which applauded Mr. Adams for
his reply to me" (151-52). Trilling's speech polarized
critics to some degree; more importantly, it highlighted again the complexity of Frost's vision of
experience.

Because Frost was such a public figure, up until
his death it was difficult to consider the poetry apart

Trilling is quoted
rather than
paraphrased
because his words
are striking and
evocative.

Writer interprets
Trilling's
intentions and
analyzes the effect
of the event.

Chronological order of paper is useful for illustrating the evolution of Frost's reputation.

from the poet and his public image. And after his death, memoirs of Frost published by friends, collections of his letters, and the three-volume biography of Frost written by Lawrance Thompson provided a great deal of new and controversial material for the debate about this complex man and artist. The question of whether Frost was a benevolent poet-farmer or a terrifying tragic poet was complicated by the new image of Frost that emerged from the letters and from Thompson's biography. Tefs summarizes what was revealed:

> Frost often referred to the "scatteration" of his family and felt profound guilt about his relations with his children. He was a difficult husband and father: as his public stature grew, his household increasingly felt the strain of his intense and stubborn personality. Probably because he was himself so insecure, Frost was often bitingly cruel to colleagues, friends, and family. (227)

It seems that Frost's understanding of isolation and despair, which was noted by Amy Lowell early on and highlighted by Trilling, was rooted in his own personal experience as well as in his observations of life in New England and elsewhere.

Recent critics are now trying to sift through all the evidence to understand Frost, his poetry, and his

Conclusion does not resolve the debate, since studies are ongoing. Instead, writer summarizes agreed-upon strengths of Frost's poetry.

place in American literature. The debate about Frost will not be easily resolved. The poet who expresses the simple values of rural America is the same poet who, acquainted with the night himself, shows us the darkness of night and solitude and reveals to us our own fears.

Schaffer 8

But as Tefs remarks, the poetry itself stands as a triumph over these fears. For many of Frost's critics and
for the great majority of his readers, "the enduring
appeal of his poetry springs from his transcendence of
the fears overshadowing him through formal structures
which testify to the strength and endurance of the human
will" (228-29).

Schaffer 9

                                 Works Cited

Baxter, Sylvester. "New England's New Poet." The
     American Review of Reviews Apr. 1915: 432-34. Rpt.
     in Gerber 26-30.

Cook, Reginald. "The Critics and Robert Frost."
     Frost: Centennial Essays. Comp. Committee on the
     Frost Centennial of the Univ. of Southern Missis-
     sippi. Jackson: U Press of MS, 1974. 15-30.

Cowley, Malcolm. "The Case Against Mr. Frost: II."
     New Republic 18 Sept. 1944: 345-47. Pt. 2 of a
     series begun on 11 Sept. 1944.

---. "Frost: A Dissenting Opinion." New Republic 11
     Sept. 1944: 312-313. Pt. 1 of a series.

Cox, James M., ed. Robert Frost: A Collection of
     Critical Essays. Englewood Cliffs, NJ: Prentice,
     1962.

DeVoto, Bernard. "The Critics and Robert Frost."
     Saturday Review of Literature 1 Jan. 1938. Rpt. in
     Gerber 104-111.

Frost, Robert. Complete Poems of Robert Frost. New
     York: Holt, 1967.

Garnett, Edward. "A New American Poet." Atlantic
     Monthly Aug. 1915. Rpt. in Gerber 35-42.

Gerber, Philip L., ed. Critical Essays on Robert Frost.
     Boston: G.K. Hall, 1982.

---. Robert Frost. Rev. ed. Twayne's United States
     Authors Series. Boston: Twayne, 1982.

Hicks, Granville. "The World of Robert Frost." Rev.
     of Collected Poems by Robert Frost. New Republic 3
     Dec. 1930. 1930: 77-78.

Lowell, Amy. Rev. of North of Boston by Robert Frost.
     New Republic 20 Feb. 1915: 81-82.

List of works cited,
alphabetically
arranged, begins
new page.

Article reprinted
in a collection of
essays.

Serialized article.

Three hyphens
followed by a
period for second
work by an author.

Article from a
weekly magazine.

Schaffer 10

"Of Axe-Handles and Guide-Book Poetry." <u>Philadelphia
Public Ledger</u> 4 Apr. 1916. Rpt. in Gerber 48-50.

Tefs, Wayne. "The Faces of Robert Frost." <u>Canadian
Review of American Studies</u> 13 (1982): 223-29.

Thompson, Lawrance. <u>Robert Frost: The Years of Triumph:
1915-1938</u>. Vol. 2 of <u>Robert Frost</u>. 3 vols. New
York: Holt, 1970.

Thompson, Lawrance, and R.H. Winnick. <u>Robert Frost: The
Later Years: 1938-1963</u>. Vol. 3 of <u>Robert Frost</u>. 3
vols. New York: Holt, 1976.

Trilling, Lionel. "A Speech on Robert Frost: A Cultural Episode." <u>Partisan Review</u> 26 (1959): 445-52.
Rpt. in Cox 151-58.

Anonymous author, no name given.

Journal with continuous pagination.

Each volume in Thompson's three-volume biography has a separate subtitle. The third has a co-author.

CHAPTER 12

Writing a Paper in the Social Sciences: The Author/Date Style

Many writers in anthropology, biology, business, education, economics, psychology, political science, and other social sciences follow the system of documentation known as the author/date style, explained in the *Manual of the American Psychological Association* (1983). These writers prefer to give the author and date in the text because this information is important to readers. Because the APA *Manual* applies primarily to manuscripts that will be submitted for publication, not to college papers or dissertations, many of the suggestions, such as margins and spacing, are designed with the convenience of editors and printers in mind; the authors suggest that students adapt these to their use. Therefore, the following guidelines give priority to the needs of student writers of "final-copy" manuscripts in these disciplines. If you plan to publish your article in a journal, you will find most of these guidelines compatible with your purpose; however, for some formatting details, you should consult the APA *Manual*. Jean Carroll's paper in this chapter uses the APA style.

Parts of the Manuscript

For original research papers	For theoretical papers
title page	title page
abstract	abstract
table of contents	table of contents
list of tables and figure	list of tables and figures
introduction	introduction
method	[content headings]
results	———
discussion	———
content notes	content notes
references	references
appendixes	appendixes

Consult your instructor for the parts that you need for your paper. For example, you many not need a title page, table of contents, or appendixes. Use extra spacing to improve readability, especially before and after headings.

Format

Title Page

On the title page place the title of your paper, your name, and any other information your instructor prefers, such as course number, instructor's name, and date. Center your title on the page, capitalizing the first letter of all important words; don't underline the title or place it in quotation marks. Place each of the other items on a separate line below your title, beginning with your name; double-space between each. You don't need a number on this page, but it should be counted as small roman numeral i. (If you are preparing a manuscript for publication, you should place an arabic numeral 1 in the upper right corner.)

Margins and Spacing

Leave margins of 1 ½ inches on all sides. Double-space throughout the manuscript except for titles of tables and figures, references (double-space between entries), footnotes, and long quotations. Indent the first word of each paragraph five spaces. Indent long quotations five spaces from the left margin. For long quotations of more than one paragraph, indent the first line of subsequent paragraphs five additional spaces.

Page Numbers

In a student paper use small roman numerals for preliminary pages (ii, iii); in papers for publication, use arabic numbers for all pages. Beginning with the introduction, number your pages consecutively throughout the rest of the paper with arabic numerals placed in the upper right corner, two spaces below a shortened title of your paper. Although the APA *Manual* recommends that the title rather than your name be placed at the top of the page for the sake of blind review of your paper for journal publication, your instructor may prefer your last name there for identification.

Abstract

The abstract is a summary of your paper: from 100 to 150 words is appropriate for a primary research paper, from 75 to 100 words for a theoretical paper. It gives the purpose and content of your paper, but does not evaluate or comment on the content. For more information on writing abstracts, see Chapter 10. As part of the front matter of your paper, the abstract should be numbered with small roman numerals; if it appears after your title page, place the number ii in the upper right corner below the short title.

Place the title Abstract at the center of the page two spaces below the page number. Unlike other paragraphs, the text of the abstract begins at the left margin and consists of a single paragraph.

Headings

Headings serve the purpose of an outline. Some papers contain as many as five levels of headings. A student paper, however, is unlikely to contain more than two or three. For clarity, you should make these headings typographically distinct. For two levels, use the following format for a theoretical paper:

```
                    Water Erosion
                  [Level one, centered]


Rainsplash Erosion
[Level two, at left margin and underlined]
```

A two-level heading system for a primary research paper would look like this:

Method
[Level one]

Procedure
[Level two]

If you have three levels of headings, use this system for theoretical papers.

Production
[Level one, centered]

Cost and Efficiency
[Level two, at left margin and underlined]

Larger areas in production.
[Level three, indented five spaces and underlined;
initial capital letter only; text follows on same line]

For a primary source paper, the headings would be *Method* at level one, *Observation* at level two, and *Setting* at level three.

First Page

Type the number 1 under the short title in the upper right corner of the page. Center the title two to four spaces below the page number, capitalizing the first letter of each word. Double-space and begin typing the text.

Introduction

The first paragraphs of the paper introduce readers to the problem being studied, the reasons for the study, and previous work done and literature written on the subject. It may also summarize the research that was done for this particular study. The APA *Manual* recommends that the introduction have no label or heading because its position shows that it is an introduction, but you will see a heading used in some journals. Chapter 8 gives several examples of introductions.

Content Notes

Content notes provide supplementary information not essential to the main text of the paper; they should be used sparingly. They may be placed at the bottom of the page containing the material they refer to or on a separate page following the body of the paper. Superscript numbers should be placed in the text after the material to be footnoted. If you place the notes on a separate page, use the heading Footnotes at the top of the page two spaces below the page number; double-space and begin with the superscript number of the first footnote. Indent the first line of each footnote five spaces and double-space between lines. The same format should be used for footnotes at the bottom of the page, except that the heading is omitted and the first footnote begins two spaces below the last line of the text.

Documentation

Parenthetical Citation

To indicate the source of the information you use, give the author and the year of publication either as part of your text or in parentheses as near as possible to the cited information. Some authors also include the page number: *(Jones, 1984, p. 36)*. Page numbers must be given with quotations.

WORK BY ONE AUTHOR

If you use the author's name as part of your sentence, place only the date of publication in parentheses.

Olson (1984) first reported the results in a recent study.

If you give both date and author in your sentence, you do not need a citation.

In a 1984 study at Stanford, Olson addressed this problem.

If you give neither in your sentence, you must give both in parentheses.

A recent study at Stanford (Olson, 1984) addressed this problem.

WORK BY TWO AUTHORS

Give the names of both authors every time the work is cited.

Barlow and Seidner (1983) contend that . . .

WORK BY THREE, FOUR, OR FIVE AUTHORS

Give the names of all authors the first time the work is cited. When the names are given in parentheses, use an ampersand (&) instead of *and*.

According to Hewitt, Smith, and Larson (1984) . . .

Recent research (Hewitt, Smith, & Larson, 1984) has shown . . .

In later citations, give only the name of the first author, followed by *et al*.

WORK WITH SIX OR MORE AUTHORS

Give only the last name of the first author followed by *et al*. A work written by Wilson, Miles, James, Wylie, Masters, and Flower would be cited as follows:

According to Wilson et al. (1982) . . .

A recent study of phobics (Wilson et al., 1982) showed . . .

CORPORATE AUTHOR

Give the full name of a corporate author (government agency, association, or research organization) each time it occurs in the text. However, if the group is well known by its abbreviation, give its abbreviation with the first citation.

In a recent television series on mental health (National Broad-

casting Company [NBC], 1985) . . .

Abbreviate the name in subsequent citations.

In the first of its series, NBC (1985) . . .

Schizophrenia was shown (NBC, 1985) . . .

WORK WITHOUT AN AUTHOR

In your citation give enough of the title to enable your readers to find it in your reference list; usually two or three words are enough. For example, an article titled ''Power Conflict in Groups'' would be cited: (''Power Conflict,'' 1980).

TWO OR MORE AUTHORS
WITH SAME LAST NAME

If you have used as sources two or more authors with the same last name, you must give their initials each time you refer to their work.

According to C. R. Lewis (1984) and L. M. Lewis (1985) . . .

TWO OR MORE WORKS
BY THE SAME AUTHOR

Give the name followed by the dates of the works.

Research shows (Hallam, 1979, 1984) . . .

If the works were published in the same year, give alphabetical suffixes:

(Marston, 1979a, 1979b)

TWO OR MORE WORKS BY DIFFERENT AUTHORS

When citing two or more authors within the same parentheses, give them in alphabetical order and separate the entries with semicolons.

(Jones, 1983; Mower & Rhodes, 1984)

PART OF A SOURCE

You may want to cite a page, chapter, illustration, or other specific part of a source. When you use a quotation, you must always give the page number.

(Rogers & Martin, 1979, chap. 4)

(see Figure 4 in Lorenzo, 1975, p. 45)

PERSONAL COMMUNICATION

When you refer to letters, interviews, or telephone conversations, give the citation in your text only. Don't include it in your reference list because it cannot be found by anyone else. Give the initials as well as the last name.

According to J. R. Davis (personal communication, March 4,
1985) . . .

LEGAL DOCUMENTS

For court cases mentioned in the text, give the name of the case, underlined, and the date in parentheses.

United States v. Castillo (1975)

If the reference is a parenthetical citation, the entire reference is in parentheses.

(United States v. Castillo, 1975)

For statutes, give the name of the act and year.

Equal Employment Opportunity Act (1972)

or

Equal Employment Opportunity Act of 1972

For other kinds of legal citations, see *A Uniform System of Citation* published by the Harvard Law Review Association (1986).

Reference List

Center the heading References at the top of the page and number the page with the number that continues the numbering of the text. For example, if the text of your paper ends on page 12, the content notes page (if there is one) would be numbered 13, and the list of references would be numbered 14.

Begin each reference at the left margin and indent subsequent lines of the entry three spaces. If you are writing for publication, double-space within and between entries, but if you're writing a final-copy paper (the usual college paper), you can save space by single-spacing within items. Always double-space between items.

Arrange references in alphabetical order according to the last name of the first author. If more than one reference is by the same author, give the author's name each time and arrange the entries in chronological order of publication.

```
Flavell, J. H. (1963).

Flavell, J. H. (1977).
```

If you have entries with the same first author and different second or third authors, the entry with one author precedes multiple-author entries. Then arrange entries alphabetically in order of the subsequent authors.

```
Leakey, R. E. F. (1976).

Leakey, R. E. F., & Lewin, R. (1977).

Leakey, R. E. F., & Walker, A. C. (1976).
```

When two works by the same author are published in the same year, distinguish them by using lowercase letters—a, b, c—after the date.

```
Chomsky, N. (1976a).

Chomsky, N. (1976b).
```

The next sections illustrate formats for references appropriate for most college papers using the author/date system. You'll find an example of a reference list at the end of Jean Carroll's paper (p. 293).

Books. Here are some examples of entries for books in the APA author/date system.

ONE AUTHOR

Give last name of author first, followed by initials only. The date of publication (in parentheses) is followed by a period. Underline the title of the book and capitalize only the first letter in the first word of the title as well as the first letter of the subtitle, if any. Give state or country of publication if needed for clarity. Use short title of publishing company as long as it's intelligible, but give names of university presses in full.

> Goodwin, D. W. (1983). <u>Phobia: The facts</u>. New York: Oxford University Press.

TWO OR MORE AUTHORS

Include all names, no matter how many. (Note that in-text citations use a different format with multiple authors.) Use commas to separate all names; use an ampersand (&) instead of *and* before the last name. Invert all authors' names.

> Blake, R. R., & Mouton, J. S. (1964). <u>The managerial grid</u>. Houston: Gulf Publishing Company.

CORPORATE AUTHOR

Alphabetize corporate authors by the first significant word. When the author and publisher are the same, use *Author* for the name of publisher.

> National Broadcasting Company. <u>Why sales come in curves</u>. New York: Author, 1954.

BOOK WITHOUT AN AUTHOR OR EDITOR

Alphabetize a book with no author by the first significant word in the title; in this case, *uniform*. Use U.S. Postal Service abbreviations for states.

> <u>A uniform system of citation</u>. (1986). Cambridge, MA: Harvard Law Review Association.

REVISED EDITION

> McIlwain, H. (1972). <u>Biochemistry and the central nervous system</u> (rev. ed.). New York: Churchill.

ONE VOLUME IN MULTIVOLUME WORK

> Stouffer, S. A., Suchman, E. A., DeVinney, L. C., Star, S. A., & Williams, R. M., Jr. (1949). <u>Studies in social psychology in World War II: Vol. 1. The American soldier: Adjustment during army life</u>. Manhattan, KS: Military Affairs/Aerospace Historian.

ENGLISH TRANSLATION OF A BOOK

> Bringuier, J. (1980). <u>Conversations with Jean Piaget</u> (B. M. Gu-

lati, Trans.). Chicago: University of Chicago Press. (Original work published 1977)

In your text, use this citation: (Bringuier, 1977/1980).

CHAPTER OR ARTICLE IN EDITED REPRINT OF A BOOK

Place the initials of the editor first when he is not in the author position.

Price, H. H. (1976). The causal theory. In R. J. Swartz (Ed.),
Perceiving, sensing, and knowing (pp. 395-437). Berkeley: University of California Press. (Original work published 1965)

For a reprinted work, use this citation in your text: (Price, 1965/1976).

Periodicals.   Here are some typical entries for periodicals in a reference list.

JOURNAL ARTICLE: ONE AUTHOR

Capitalize the first letter of each main word in the title of the periodical and underline the title; also underline the volume number and follow it with a comma; give beginning and ending page numbers. Use *p.*
or *pp.* before page numbers in references to magazine and newspaper
articles but not in references to journal articles.

Brotsky, S. (1968). Classic conditioning of the galvanic skin
response to verbal concepts. Journal of Experimental Psychology, 70, 244-253.

JOURNAL ARTICLE: TWO AUTHORS

Give last names of both authors first; use an ampersand (&) between
them.

Barlow, D. H., & Seidner, A. L. (1983). Treatment of adolescent
agoraphobics: Effects on parent-adolescent relations. Behavioral Research and Therapy, 21, 519-525.

JOURNAL ARTICLE: THREE OR MORE AUTHORS

Give names of all authors in the list of references regardless of how
many; an ampersand comes before the last name. Underline volume
number and follow it with a comma. In the text, however, when there
are more than five authors, give only the name of the first, followed by
et al. (not underlined).

Telch, M. J., Tearnan, B. H., & Taylor, C. B. (1983). Antidepressant medication in the treatment of agoraphobia: A critical
review. Behavioral Research and Therapy, 21, 505-516.

ARTICLE IN JOURNAL WITH SEPARATE PAGINATION

Place the number of the issue in parentheses after the volume number without a space between them.

Bunney, W. E., Jr. (1976). Acute behavioral effects of lithium carbonate. Neurosciences Research Program Bulletin, 14(2), 124-131.

MAGAZINE ARTICLES

The month follows the year. Use the abbreviation *pp.* for *pages*.

Casson, L. (1985, June). Breakthrough at the first think tank. Smithsonian, pp. 158-168.

SIGNED NEWSPAPER ARTICLE

Give year first, followed by month and day. Give section number, if any, followed by page number. Place a comma between numbers when pages are discontinuous.

Mansfield, S. (1981, October 25). For 30 years she was a prisoner of fear. Washington Post, sec. G, pp. 1, 3.

UNSIGNED NEWSPAPER ARTICLE

When an article has no author, alphabetize the entry by the first significant word of the title.

Grey area of surrogate mother and child. (1985, January 13). Manchester Guardian, p. 1.

LETTER TO THE EDITOR

Hammer, A. (1985, July 26). We have to find domestic fuel solutions [Letter to the editor]. New York Times, sec. A, p. 26.

Other Printed Material. Here are some examples of references for other kinds of printed material.

TECHNICAL OR RESEARCH REPORT

Give identifying information or the report number in parentheses following the title of the report.

Trivett, D. A. (1975). Academic credit for prior off-campus learning (ERIC/Higher Education Research Report No. 2). Washington, DC: American Association for Higher Education.

Congressional Budget Office. (1982). Financing social security: Issues and options for the long run (S/N 052-070-05787-4). Washington, DC: U.S. Government Printing Office.

LEGAL DOCUMENT

This court case was decided by the U.S. Court of Appeals for the District of Columbia in 1965. It can be found in volume 350 of the *Federal Reporter*, second series, page 445.

Williams v. Walker-Thomas Furniture Co., 350 F. 2d 445 (D.C. Cir. 1965).

The following act was codified in title 29 of the *United States Code* in section 65. For legal references, the symbol for *section* (§) if you have it on your typewriter or computer, is preferred to the abbreviation *Sec.* given here.

Occupational Safety and Health Act, 29 U.S.C. Sec. 65 (1976).

PROCEEDINGS OF A MEETING

Austin, J. L. (1956). Ifs and cans. Proceedings of the British Academy, 42, 109–132.

UNPUBLISHED MANUSCRIPT

Meyer, P. (1974). Assessing life/work experience: A rationale for faculty-based models. Unpublished manuscript, Florida International University, Miami.

Nonprint Sources.   The APA *Manual* recommends these formats for nonprint sources.

FILM

Give name and role of the principal contributors or originators first, with their function in parentheses. After date and title, give the medium in brackets. Finally, give the location and name of the distributor or museum (in the case of a work of art). You can use this format for other nonprint media, such as videotapes, slides, and art work.

Turple, J. (Producer). (1981). Acid rain: Requiem or recovery [Film]. New York: National Film Board of Canada.

CASSETTE RECORDING

If you have a number for the recording, give that in parentheses in place of the name of the medium in brackets; for example: (*Cassette Recording No. 192*) instead of [*Cassette recording*].

Kellogg, P. P., & Allen, A. A. (Producers), & Peterson, R. T. (Collaborator). (1982). A field guide to bird songs [Cassette recording]. Boston: Houghton Mifflin.

Sample Research Paper
Using the Author/Date Style

In the following paper Jean Carroll has used the author/date system recommended in the *Manual of the American Psychological Association*. Because the *Manual* is intended to be used primarily by those who are preparing manuscripts for publication in professional journals, the APA advises those who are writing undergraduate or graduate papers to modify the guidelines to conform to their own department's or instructor's requirements. Accordingly, Carroll has adapted the *Manual* suggestions to suit a paper she wrote for an undergraduate audience, her classmates. (Note that she has chosen the option of including page numbers in her citations.) The style used here should be acceptable in most college classes in which the author/date documentation system is recommended.

The Causes and Treatment of Agoraphobia

Jean M. Carroll

Professor Maxfield

May 15, 198-

Title, writer's name, and any other information specified by instructor.

Short title above
page number on
each page. (First
page is counted but
not numbered.)

Abstract is on page
ii, in block form,
and double-spaced.

Abstract

Agoraphobia, or "fear of the marketplace," is a fear of
fear; those who are afflicted are unable to leave their
homes. Recent studies have shown three causes: psychological problems, a single spontaneous attack that is
then repeated, or biological problems. The most common
treatments are psychotherapy, various kinds of behavioral therapy, and drugs. The best results seem to come
from behavior therapy. Clearly, agoraphobics can now
receive help and learn to lead normal lives.

Agoraphobia

1

Text page 1; title is
centered, using
first-level heading.

Introduction is not
labeled.

       The Causes and Treatment of Agoraphobia

     Fear helps us react to danger in order to protect
ourselves. When we recognize danger, our bodies release
extra energy so that we will be ready to do what is
necessary to respond. Our hearts begin to beat more
rapidly; we tense our muscles; we feel hot or cold; we
breathe faster. As a result we are ready to yell, run,
jump, or use force. Some people, though, have these
symptoms even when there is no danger; they may feel
faint or nauseous when they cross a bridge, see a snake,
fly in planes, or ride in elevators. Psychologists call
these victims of irrational, excessive, or uncontrollable fears "phobics."

     Goodwin (1983, p. 25) identifies three classes of
phobias: simple, social, and agoraphobic. A simple
phobia is a fear of objects or situations, such as animals, heights, or illness. A social phobia is a fear of
being seen; common social phobias are the fear of public
speaking, of blushing, or of eating in public. Agoraphobia (literally "fear of the marketplace"), is more
than a fear of a single external object or of an activity; it is a fear of leaving a safe place (a home or a
room) or the companionship of a trusted person. Thus
the fears of agoraphobics make it almost impossible for
them to function outside the home. Because agoraphobia
is a fear, not of the known, but of the unknown, it is
"the most disabling of all the phobias" (Whitehead,
1983, p. 31).

Page number must
be given for direct
quotation.

     Almost two million Americans are afflicted by ago-
raphobia and most of these are believed to be women,
although some researchers think that the statistics may

"reflect in part the willingness of women to be more
open about problems" ("The Fight," 1984, p. 71). But
more women may be agoraphobic because it is easier for
them to stay home without questions from others (Weekes,
1972, p. 12). Agoraphobia in men usually appears as a
reluctance to leave their town.[1] Although most agoraphobics are adults, some children and adolescents
have also sought treatment (Barlow and Seidner, 1983,
p. 519).

The amount of anxiety that accompanies these fears
or the extent of the inconvenience they cause determines
whether the person decides to seek help. A person who
has a panic attack at the sight of a mouse may be able
to avoid mice most of the time. But a person who has
the same symptoms crossing a bridge or riding an elevator to get to work is severely handicapped. As a result
such a person will usually seek help.

Symptoms of Agoraphobia

Sheehan (1983) believes that agoraphobia is not a
single phobia, but is the name given to a group of phobias that are acquired over a period of time: "as far
as acquiring phobias are concerned, the agoraphobia
stage is the end of the line" (p. 68). He explains:

When the condition was named, "agoraphobia" was
chosen from the cluster of phobias as being one of
the most representative or typical of all the many
fears the patient has at this point. Curiously,
the literal symptom of agoraphobia [fear of the
marketplace or fear of crowded places] is not the
most common or even central fear shared by patients

Superscript
number refers to
content note at end
of paper.

First-level heading
format.

Publication date
placed close to
author's name.

Quotation of more
than forty words is
indented five
spaces from the left
margin and
double-spaced.

Brackets enclose
material not in
original.

with the anxiety disease. More common and central
is a fear that might be called "phobiaphobia"--a
fear of having another spontaneous panic attack.
It is usually this fear that is the most intense
and guides their behavior more than any other fear.
(p. 68)

> Page number in
> parentheses after
> the period.

Marjorie Goff, a 64-year-old woman who recovered
from agoraphobia, explained her experience in an interview in the Washington Post (Mansfield, 1981). Her
problem began one Saturday in 1946 when, as a successful
young career woman, she went to the beauty shop where
she regularly had her hair done. She described what
happened:

> Specific case shows
> how symptoms
> develop.

> I was sitting under the dryer, and all of a sudden
> this feeling swept over me. I'm losing my mind, I
> thought. I'm going crazy. My heart started beat-
> ing fast. My legs felt weak. My body trembled.
> It was the most incredible feeling of fear. I
> wanted to scream, to run out of there. I got up
> with all the pins in my hair, slapped a 5-dollar
> bill on the counter and ran all the way home. I
> was white, I felt that everyone was looking at me,
> that everyone knew. I didn't know what was wrong
> with me. (sec. G, p. 1)

Other panic attacks followed--at work, on buses, in the
grocery store, and in elevators. By 1949, Goff's fears
forced her to stay inside her apartment, living on $300
a month sent to her by her father.

> Newspaper section
> number when each
> section begins
> page 1.

Like most other phobics, Goff realized that her
phobia was irrational, but acknowledging the irrational-

Writer makes useful generalization from a specific case.

ity of the fear was not enough to overcome it. For many phobics the stress caused by the bewilderment and fear that accompany their condition so intensifies the problem that they may become depressed. They become caught in a vicious circle in which fear creates fear.

Causes of Agoraphobia

Stress is generally considered the immediate cause of the panic attacks that lead to agoraphobia, but there is little agreement on what causes the stress or on why the stress develops into agoraphobia. In general, theories about the causes of agoraphobia fall into three groups: psychological, behavioral, and biological or genetic causes.

Organization of the section is outlined.

Second-level heading.

Psychological Causes

Theorists who favor the idea that agoraphobia results from psychological causes claim that panic attacks result from unconscious fears that express themselves symbolically. An unconscious conflict over separation from close friend or relative, for example, may cause the initial attack (Lehman, 1985). Whitehead (1983), on the other hand, suggests that agoraphobic anxiety may be a result of clinical depression. According to this theory, agoraphobia can be a way of avoiding a deeper problem. Melville (1977), agreeing with this theory, suggests that agoraphobia is a "subconscious safeguard against a fear of failure" (p. 17) such as a fear of facing marriage, battle, or a job.

Source either in parentheses or as part of text.

Behavioral Causes

Some experts believe that the anxiety attack occurs spontaneously as a result of a single frightening expe-

Agoraphobia

5

rience, which is then reinforced by similar later experiences. According to Wolpe (1981), panic attacks tend
to occur with people "who, because of an early fearful
experience, will be more vulnerable to the later development of severe fears arising from similar experiences" (p. 31).

Although Wolpe (1981) believes that agoraphobics
have an unexpected attack, associate it with the place
where it occurred, and then repeat it, Neuman (1985)
maintains that they learn anxious behavior from "parents who are themselves, one or both of them phobic to
some degree" (p. 15). He believes that parents "communicate a frightened feeling to their children" by constantly warning them about possible dangers. "After a
while the children see the world as a threatening
place" (p. 16).

Writer summarizes contrasting theories.

Biological or Genetic Causes

Many researchers believe that agoraphobia is either
a genetic defect passed on from generation to generation
or a defect in one of the systems of the phobic's body,
such as an "overactivity of certain parts of the brain"
(Lehman, 1985, p. 43). Studies of twins have shown that
identical twins are more likely than nonidentical twins
to develop agoraphobia (Sheehan, 1983, p. 91). Since
the family environment of both kinds of twins would be
the same, the fact that agoraphobia occurs more often in
identical twins suggests to Sheehan that "a genetic
weakness could give rise to biochemical abnormalities"
which in turn would lead to anxiety attacks (p. 91).

Quoted phrases integrated with writer's words.

Other researchers are less certain about the ori-

gins of agoraphobia. Goodwin (1982), for example, is
forced to conclude: "The cause of phobias remains unknown" (p. 89).

Treatment section
organized in
relation to the
causes section.

Treatment

The treatment advocated for agoraphobia is based
primarily on the therapist's or doctor's theory as to
the cause. That is, those who believe in psychological
causes will advocate some type of psychotherapy; those
who believe that it is learned behavior will recommend
behavioral therapy; and those who believe it has a biological or physiological cause will prescribe drugs.
Many therapists and doctors use a combination of these
treatments.

Psychotherapy

Psychotherapy is seen as the most effective treatment by those who believe that the causes of agoraphobia
are largely psychological or emotional. The psychother-
apist or psychologist helps the patient to identify the
cause of the stress or depression that has finally led
to anxiety attacks and agoraphobia. The patient may
have to search the experiences of childhood to find the
cause. One disadvantage of this method is that it is
very time-consuming and consequently very expensive. In
addition, it has a poor success rate (Goodwin, 1983).

Behavioral Therapy

Behavioral techniques are used by those who believe
that, because anxiety attacks are learned behavior,
"treatment is a process of education" (Neuman, p. 27)
or, really, re-education. In behavioral therapy, the
patient is exposed to the situation that brings on the
phobic attack and gradually learns to respond to it

Agoraphobia

7

without fear. Wolpe, in <u>Psychotherapy by Recipro-</u>
<u>cal Inhibition</u> (1958), is generally given the credit for
initiating this type of treatment. He recommends that
therapists abandon the search for underlying causes of
anxiety and attempt to confront their patients' fears
directly. The most common techniques used by therapists
in this relearning process are systematic desensitization, flooding, cognitive therapy, and group therapy.
Relaxation techniques are usually taught along with
these.

Systematic desensitization (or graded exposure).
With systematic desensitization, patients are first
taught to relax, then to imagine the situation or object
that produces the least anxiety for them. Gradually
they are led to imagine fear-producing situations of
greater and greater intensity, until their sense of
control within this special, supportive environment
helps them to face the most terrifying scenes without
anxiety. At this point, they can begin to practice in
real life what they have visualized in the therapist's
office.

Flooding or ungraded exposure. Flooding skips the
slow desensitization process and instead exposes patients immediately to the situation that terrifies them.
The therapist relies on the fact that terror cannot be
sustained indefinitely. Little by little the anxiety
subsides. Flooding can be used either by having patients imagine the feared situation or by putting them
into the real-life setting that they fear. If the patient is afraid of the grocery store, the therapist may
take her to the grocery store and stay with her there

Book title
underlined in text.

Third-level
heading.

Writer has given a
brief but full
description of each
method of
treatment.

Common
knowledge; writer
does not have to
cite specific source
on flooding.

until her anxiety peaks and then wait with her there until it subsides. She would thus learn that the attack has limits and that she can control it. Repeated trips would reinforce the learning.

In imaginary flooding the therapist might ask the patient to visualize herself going into the grocery store during a very busy time when the lines to the check-out counters are long. She would imagine going through the aisles and then waiting in line. As with real-life flooding, the visualization would be repeated until anxiety is reduced.

Flooding can obtain results much faster than other methods. However, it works best with simple phobias, such as fear of bridges, elevators, or animals. For the agoraphobic, it carries the risk of making the anxiety more severe, and attacks often recur (Sheehan, p. 160). Besides, such a technique requires the cooperation of the patient; and some patients do not want to experience again the situation that has caused them so much pain (Goodwin, p. 111). Younger patients, especially, have trouble with this method; Barlow and Seidner (1982) have shown that it does not work with adolescents.

Cognitive therapy. First developed by Aaron Beck and described by him in Cognitive Therapy and the Emotional Disorders (1976), this method relies more on changing behavior through altering thought processes than on changing behavior directly. Many agoraphobics engage in negative thinking ("I won't be able to breathe" or "Everyone will be watching me and will think I am crazy"). The therapist helps the patient identify these thoughts and recognize that they can be

Writer integrates three different sources.

Effective transition made by contrasting cognitive therapy with other methods.

the real cause of an anxiety attack. With this realiza-
tion patients can learn to substitute more positive
thoughts.

Group therapy. Treating agoraphobics in groups has
become widely used among behavioral therapists. Neuman
(1985), has described in Fighting Fear how group therapy, along with exposure therapy, has helped phobics in
the eight-week program at the White Plains Phobia
Clinic, of which he is the associate director. In
groups, he points out, phobics "encourage each other
and learn from each other" (p. 185).

Group therapy allows for the use of such techniques
as behavior rehearsal, role-playing, relaxation training, and social skills and assertiveness training (Lazarus, 1981). Therapists using these methods usually
assemble groups consisting of four to ten members, which
meet for an hour or two once or twice a week. A series
of such meetings commonly lasts from eight to twelve
weeks.

Drug Use. Drugs are used most often by therapists
who believe that the panic attacks of agoraphobics are
caused by chemical imbalances in the body. Sheehan
(1983), an advocate of using drugs, considers the group
of drugs called "MAO inhibitors" (monoamine oxidase
inhibitors) "the single most effective drugs overall"
(p. 131). However, a study by Telch, Tearnan and Taylor
(1983) concludes that "the enthusiasm by advocates of
drug treatments (for example, Sheehan, 1982) seems un-
warranted." They cite the following reasons: (a) "patients' reluctance and in some cases unwillingness to
take the medication"; (b) the undermining of positive

Writer gives credentials to establish source's authority.

Unfamiliar abbreviation spelled out at first use.

Quotations combined with paraphrase.

results of drugs because of side effects; and (c) "re-
lapse following withdrawal of the medication" (516).
Often drugs are used as the first step in treatment with
psychotherapy.

Success Rates

Most therapists use a combination of these techniques and, of course, claim success for their methods.
Precise recovery figures are difficult to find, partly
because recovery can be difficult to measure. However,
the treatment that seems to be reported most often as
effective is one or more of the behavioral techniques in
combination with other treatment. Dr. T. Byram Karasu,
Chair of the American Psychiatric Association's Commission on Treatment of Psychiatric Disorders, claims that
drugs used with behavior therapy succeed for 78% of
patients (Lehman, 1985). Dr. Arthur B. Hardy (1984) in
a workshop at the Fifth Annual National Phobia Conference, discussed his success with psychotherapy plus
group therapy at his treatment center in Menlo Park,
California. He claimed that 40% of his patients recover
in six months and that an additional 40% show improvement in two to three years. The rest drop out early in
the treatment. Hardy speculated that these patients are
not ready and added that some come back later.

In a study by Doctor, Gaer, and Wright (1983), over
94% of patients in their therapy program using a variety
of behavioral techniques reported continuing improvement
one year after treatment. Doctor et al. (1983) also
cite "data from other studies . . . indicating that
three quarters of those who have been in another type of
therapy made no change or actually got worse as a result

Statistics used as
evidence.

Names of all three
authors are given
the first time. After
that, last name of
first author is
given, followed by
et al. and the year.

Agoraphobia

11

of the treatment" (p. 3). In addition they point out
the disadvantages of drug treatment: "inevitable slip-
back or regression" (p. 8) when antidepressant drugs
are withdrawn and, among a large percentage of those
taking drugs, unacceptable side effects.

The case of Marjorie Goff, related earlier, shows
that even a person who has spent thirty years in her
apartment can recover from agoraphobia. Goff was discovered, alone in her apartment, by a volunteer from a
senior citizens' group. She entered a 20-week program
of desensitization and group therapy. Slowly she expanded the length of her trips outside her apartment--
from the mailbox on the corner to a two-block distance
and then to a store. She was able to celebrate Christmas by eating in a restaurant and eventually was able to
return to the beauty shop where her problem began.

Clearly, agoraphobia and other phobias can now be
treated successfully. A good therapist will select the
treatment best suited to the individual patient. The
existence of the Phobia Society of America, which holds
annual conferences, is only one indication of the growth
of knowledge about this affliction.[2] The first and
simplest step agoraphobics can take is to see their
family doctor. Treatment is available, and agoraphobics
can learn to lead normal lives.

Account of
successful
treatment of
agoraphobic
provides satisfying
conclusion.

Ending
summarizes
findings and points
to hopeful future.

Footnotes (content notes) give information not essential to paper but helpful to readers.

Footnotes

[1]Whitehead (1982) has suggested that there may be as many agoraphobic men as women, but they may be "much less willing to reveal their problem to anyone because they fear they will be looked upon as 'sissys'" (p. 31). Most experts, however, still believe that more women than men suffer from the disease. There is little agreement on why this is true.

[2]Information about this organization can be obtained by writing to the Phobia Society of America, 6181 Executive Boulevard, Rockville, MD 20852.

Agoraphobia

13

References

Barlow, D. H., & Seidner, A. L. (1983). Treatment of adolescent agoraphobics: Effects on parent-adolescent relations. Behavioral Research and Therapy, 21, 519-525.

Beck, A. (1976). Cognitive therapy and the emotional disorders. New York: International Universities Press.

Doctor, R. M., Gaer, T., & Wright, M. (1983). Success at one year follow-up for agoraphobia treatment. Paper presented at the fourth annual national phobia conference, White Plains, NY.

The fight to conquer fear. (1984, April 23). Newsweek, pp. 66-72.

Goodwin, D. W. (1983). Phobia: The facts. New York: Oxford University Press.

Hardy, A. B. (1984). Basic evaluation and treatment procedures effective for agoraphobia. Paper presented at the fifth annual national phobia conference, Washington, DC.

Lazarus, A. A. (1981). The practice of multimodal therapy. New York: McGraw-Hill.

Lehman, B. (1985, June 3). Holding fear of fear at bay. Boston Globe, pp. 41, 43.

Mansfield, S. (1981, October 25). For 30 years she was a prisoner of fear. Washington Post, sec. G, pp. 1, 3.

Melville, J. (1977). Phobias and obsessions. New York: Coward, McCann & Geoghegan.

Neuman, F. (1985). Fight fear: An eight-week guide to treating your own phobia. New York: Macmillan.

Sheehan, D. V. (1983). The anxiety disease. New York: Scribner's.

Telch, M. J., Tearnan, B. H., & Taylor, C. B. (1983). Antidepressant medication in the treatment of agoraphobia: A critical review. Behavioral Research and Therapy, 21, 505-516.

Usually, only works cited in text are listed as references. Give last names first, followed by initials.

Journal with continuous pagination.

Book.

Paper presented at a conference.

Magazine article with no author given.

Signed newspaper article; newspaper sections numbered separately.

Journal article by multiple authors.

Weekes, C. (1972). Peace from nervous suffering. New
    York: Hawthorne.

Whitehead, T. (1983). Fears and phobias. New York:
    Arco.

References with
the same author
are ordered by date
of publication,
earliest first.

Wolpe, J. (1958). Psychotherapy by reciprocal
    inhibition. Palo Alto: Stanford University Press.

Wolpe, J. (1981). Our useless fears. Boston: Houghton
    Mifflin.

Writing a Paper in Science or Technology: The Number System

Those who use the number system of citing sources—that is, placing only a number after the information cited in the text—prefer it because its brevity disturbs readers less than other systems. Some form of the number system is usually followed by writers in chemistry, physics, biology, mathematics, engineering, medicine, nursing, and computer science. However, some writers in chemistry and biology follow the author/date (sometimes author/date/page) system. Many writers of technical reports also use the number system. Among writers using the number system, there are several variations in format. Therefore, writers planning to publish should follow the style of the journal they plan to submit their writing to. The number system explained here is one of the most frequently used in science and technology.

Parts of the Manuscript

The elements of a scientific or technical paper vary according to the contents and the purpose for which it is written. Three possible formats appear here. Consult your instructor about the parts you will need in your paper.

For original research papers	For theoretical papers or reviews	For technical reports
title page	title page	title page
abstract	abstract	abstract
introduction	introduction	table of contents
subjects, materials, and method	[headings, as needed]	list of illustrations [optional]
results	[text]	[headings, as needed]
discussion	[text]	[text]
references	references	references
tables	tables	[tables usually included in text]
glossary [optional]	glossary [optional]	glossary [optional]
appendix [optional]	appendix [optional]	appendix [optional]

Format

Title Page

On the title page put the title, your name, and any other identifying information you and your instructor might wish, such as instructor's name, course number, and date. Remember, the title page doesn't usually carry a number but is always counted. If you plan to publish, you may be required to put a running head on the title page as well as on other pages.

Margins and Spacing

Type your manuscript on 8½-by-11-inch paper. Use double-spacing throughout. Leave margins of one inch on all sides of the page. Indent each paragraph five spaces.

Page Numbers

Number all pages consecutively with arabic numerals beginning with the title page, unless there is preliminary material in addition to the abstract. Place the page number in the upper right corner. If you have only a title page and an abstract, count the title page as page 1 and number the abstract page 2; your text would begin on page 3.

When you have front matter and a table of contents, number all pages before the beginning of the text with small roman numerals (ii, iii, etc.). You do not need to place a number on the title page. A running head, a brief form of the title placed before the page number, is sometimes used for papers written for publication so that initial evaluators won't be able to identify the author. Such headings are helpful in any paper because pages may be misplaced. In a college paper, however, you can place your last name instead of the title before the page number.

Abstract

Begin your abstract on a separate page and number it as you would any other page. Abstracts should be concise; usually they are between 125 and 250 words. Give your objectives; the methods, materials, and techniques you have used; and any hypotheses you are testing. If you are not using primary research for your main information source, explain your purpose, the problem studied, or questions being explored. Use abbreviations and symbols sparingly. (See Chapter 8 for more information on writing an abstract.)

Illustrations

You may include a list of illustrations in the front part of a technical report if you have more than three or four. Illustrations for a manuscript submitted for publication should be grouped at the end of the manuscript. They could also be placed in the text near their text reference.

You should identify the source of your information at the bottom of each illustration. If information for a figure comes from several sources, put a superscript lowercase letter (or other footnote symbol, such as an asterisk or a dagger) after the data cited and give the sources in corresponding footnotes at the bottom of the figure. Superscript letters, asterisks, or daggers are used instead of numbers so that the information is not confused with citations in the reference list (which are indicated by numbers in the text).

Headings

To help your readers grasp the structure and the content of your paper, use headings derived from your outline. Avoid using the heading Introduction for your first section. Two or three levels of headings are common. For three levels, the following format is often used in technical writing (for two levels, eliminate the third level).

DISEASES
[First level, centered. For CBE style,
capitalize only the first letter.]

Melioidosis
[Second level, flush with left margin and underlined]

    Skin infections.
    [Third level, run in at the beginning of a paragraph
of text and underlined]

First Page

Place the page number and running head in the upper right corner
at least one-half inch from the top of the page. Double-space twice and
type the title of your paper, centered, in capital letters, as you would
for a first-level heading. Double-space and begin your introduction.

Introduction

The introduction usually doesn't have a heading; its place in the paper is self-explanatory. You should make clear here what your purpose
is or what problem you are studying or trying to solve. However, avoid
writing "My purpose in this paper is. . . ." If you are doing original
research, you should briefly review the relevant writing on the subject
so that your readers know the background of your study.

Footnotes

Use footnotes sparingly to add explanatory material when its inclusion in the text would be disruptive. Place a superscript number after
the material to be explained and place a corresponding superscript
number at the bottom of the page to introduce the footnote. Indent the
first line of each footnote five spaces. Begin with number 1 and number footnotes consecutively.

Documentation

Textual Citation

Although a few scientific writers give references at the bottom of the
page (footnotes) and some use the author/date system, most use a form
of the number system. Writers in the sciences tend to prefer this system
because scientific sources often have multiple authors; the use of num-

bers saves space and disrupts the text less than giving authors' names, especially when several articles are cited for the same information. In the number system, sources in the list of references are assigned numbers that are then used in the text to refer readers to this list. Some writers use superscript numbers, others put the numbers in parentheses, and a few underline the numbers in parentheses. With any of these systems, the number follows the information documented. Superscript numbers, if used, are placed after all marks of punctuation, including periods, without spacing. Parenthetical numbers are placed before all marks of punctuation, with a space before the first parenthesis. Here are some examples.

```
Hayes has proposed several solutions.[1]

Hayes has proposed several solutions (1).

Although Mason has disagreed,[1] Morris maintains . . .

Although Mason has disagreed (1), Morris maintains . . .
```

If you are citing more than one source in the same place, use commas between the numbers.

```
Recent research[2,5] has shown . . .

Recent research (2,5) has shown . . .
```

Reference List

Title your list of sources References, References Cited, Works Cited, or a similar term, and number your entries in one of the following ways:

in the order in which they are mentioned in the text. If you mention a source more than once, use the originally assigned number.

in alphabetical order. Order your list alphabetically and then number the items. If you use this system, the citations in your text won't be in numerical order.

You can punctuate the numbers of the entries in your list of references with parentheses, (1); with a period, 1.; or with the use of a superscript number, [1]. Whichever you choose, be sure to be consistent. If you are writing for publication, use the style of the journal you wish to publish in. For a college paper, any of these is satisfactory.

The following examples, illustrating a list of references using numbers followed by periods, are based on the *CBE Style Manual*, 5th ed. (1983), published by the Council of Biology Editors. Other examples appear in the References section at the end of the sample research paper.

BOOK WITH ONE AUTHOR

Use last name and initials of author. Capitalize only the first word of the title, unless it includes a proper noun. Use a semicolon after publisher's name. Second and subsequent lines of an entry are indented in line with the first letter of the first line. The periods following the numbers should be in line vertically.

1. Restak, R. M.   The brain: the last frontier.   New York: Warner; 1976.

BOOK WITH TWO OR MORE AUTHORS

Give names of all authors, with semicolons between them, regardless of the number.

2. Penfield, W.; Roberts, L.   Speech and brain mechanisms. Princeton, NJ: Princeton University Press; 1959.

CORPORATE AUTHOR

3. Institute of Electrical and Electronics Engineers.   Automating intelligent behavior applications and frontiers.   Silver Spring, MD: IEEE Computer Society Press; 1983.

BOOK WITH EDITOR

4. Bronfenbrenner, U., editor.   Influences on human development. Hinsdale, IL: Dryden; 1972.

CHAPTER OR SELECTION IN EDITED ANTHOLOGY

5. Ransom, C. J.; Hoffee, L. H.   The orbits of Venus.   In: Talbott, S. L., ed.   Velikovsky reconsidered.   New York: Warner Books; 1977:140-147.

ARTICLE IN JOURNAL WITH CONTINUOUS PAGINATION

Capitalize only the first letter of the title of the article (don't capitalize the first letter of the subtitle), and all important words of the journal title. Titles of journals are usually abbreviated following recommendations of the *American National Standard for Abbreviations of Titles of Periodicals*, but some journals don't use such abbreviations in their articles. If you don't know the accepted abbreviation of a journal, it's better to write it out. After the title of the journal, give both the volume number and the page numbers in arabic numerals, followed by a semicolon and the year.

6. Brown, M.; Stewart, J. B.; Garrett, C. J.   Melioidosis: a report on ten cases.   Quarterly Journal of Medicine   153:115-125; 1970.

ARTICLE IN JOURNAL WITH SEPARATE PAGINATION

Place the issue number in arabic numerals in parentheses following the volume number.

7. Keeping up with cholesterol. Harvard Medical School Health
    Letter 10(8):3-5; 1984.

NEWSPAPER ARTICLE

Follow the date with a colon, section and page number, and, in parentheses, column number.

8. Green, H. P. Why E.P.A. supervision is needed. The New York
    Times. 1984 July 15:A2 (col. 3).

MAGAZINE ARTICLE

Put the date in place of the volume number.

9. Bernard, J. Looking at lasers. Radio-Electronics. 1986
    June:39-42.

DISSERTATION

10. Berkman, L. F. Social networks, host resistance and mortal-
     ity: a follow-up study of Alameda county residents. Berke-
     ley: Univ. of California; 1977. Dissertation.

Sample Research Paper
Using the Number System

The number system of documentation used in the following paper is one of the styles suggested in the *CBE Style Manual* (1983), published by the Council of Biology Editors. References are numbered in the order in which they are mentioned in the text, and the list of references at the end of the paper is then arranged in numerical order. When a source is referred to more than once in the text, the original number assigned to it is repeated. Page numbers are given in the text along with the reference number only when the article referred to is lengthy or when a quotation is given.

Although the subject of the paper and many of the articles cited are technical, Margaret Little translated technical terms into language understandable to a general, rather than a primarily professional, audience. She believes that caffeine consumption is of interest to most adults.

CBE style requires title page and abstract.

THE EFFECTS OF CAFFEINE CONSUMPTION

by

Margaret A. Little

The title page, abstract, and table of contents make the paper accessible to a varied audience.

Professor Cline

Nutrition 270

November 13, 198-

ABSTRACT

Studies have shown that the ingestion of caffeine, a widely consumed substance in all age groups, has a harmful effect on the body. It increases heart rate, stimulates gastric secretions, and causes headaches, nervousness, and insomnia in healthy people. Coffee drinkers who consume five or more cups per day can become unknowingly addicted to caffeine. Those with psychological disorders can regress when they consume excessive caffeine. Children are particularly sensitive to the effects of caffeine. Studies also show that pregnant women who drink coffee have a greater risk of problems at delivery, and their children may be born with abnormalities. Whether these effects are permanent has yet to be determined. Even though caffeine has some benefits, people would be well advised to avoid it or use it sparingly.

An informative abstract summarizes the paper's contents. Complete details and statistics are not included.

Table of contents (not required for CBE style) derived from outline is used in technical report. First-level headings are typed flush left; second-level headings are indented five spaces; third-level headings, ten spaces.

Page numbers for third-level headings in paper are optional in table of contents.

Dots connecting heading to page number are optional.

TABLE OF CONTENTS

Page

Abstract ii

List of Illustrations iv

The History of Caffeine 1

Caffeine Consumption 1

Effects of Caffeine on Adults 7

     Effects on normal body processes 7

     Disease states worsened by caffeine 8

          Ulcers

          Heart disease

          Fibrocystic breast disease

          Cancer

     Caffeine addiction 10

     Aggravation of mental and emotional disorders .. 10

Effects of Caffeine on Pregnant Women and Newborns .. 11

Beneficial Effects of Caffeine 12

Conclusion 13

References 15

LIST OF ILLUSTRATIONS

Page

Figure 1 3

Figure 2 6

Table 1 4

Table 2 5

List of illustrations included because there are more than three figures and tables.

Brief title before the page number.

First-level heading.

(1) indicates source of information; it refers to the first item in the reference list.

First part of paper introduces the subject, gives background information, and ends with a summary statement.

Page numbers will help reader locate information. Page numbers are always given for quotations.

THE HISTORY OF CAFFEINE

Since Stone Age people discovered plants containing caffeine and made a beverage from them, caffeine has been used as a stimulant (1). Ethiopians chewed coffee beans before battle, the ancient Chinese drank tea, and the Mayan Indians drank chocolate made from cocoa beans. Other common sources of caffeine are the kola nut, the ilex plant (used for making a Brazilian beverage called maté), tea leaves, and the cassina or Christmas berry tree (2).

Coffee, the most popular source of caffeine, appears in recorded history as early as 1000 A.D., when Arab Muslims included it as part of their daily ritual. Later, when the Islamic faith was accepted by people in Turkey, so was coffee. In 1615, Venetian traders began to fill their boats with coffee in Constantinople; by 1750, most of Western Europe was drinking coffee.

Meanwhile, as the English began to bring back tea from the East, tea drinking became a custom in England and its colonies. England's heavy taxes on colonists' tea, which led to the Boston Tea party, forced Americans to change from tea to coffee (3, pp. 388, 394, 405). Today, according to a report by the Life Sciences Research Office, 62% of Americans drink coffee every day (4, p. 9) and many people who don't drink coffee consume caffeine in other forms. The results afflict people of all ages.

CAFFEINE CONSUMPTION

In the United States 80% of adults are coffee drinkers, with the average consumption 3-1/2 cups a day (5). More people in the 40- and 50-year-old group drink

Effects of Caffeine 2

3 to 5 cups of coffee a day than do those in other
groups (figure 1, p. 3). But much of the caffeine consumed by all groups comes from sources other than
coffee, such as tea, chocolate, soft drinks, and over-
the-counter medications. (Tables 1 and 2, pp. 4-5, show
the caffeine content in these sources.) Many consumers
of these products are children. In fact, children between the ages of 1 and 5 consume more caffeine by body
weight from soft drinks than do people in any other age
group (figure 2, p. 6). Sources of caffeine for children also include iced tea and chocolate products. Even
nursing infants consume caffeine--the equivalent of the
caffeine in 2/3 cup of coffee daily--from breast milk
and from soft drinks, which are sometimes used to treat
colic.

Much of the caffeine taken out of coffee is added
to soft drinks, the largest-selling beverage in the
United States. Although people expect to find caffeine
in their cola drinks, it may be surprising that three
drinks without "cola" in their names (Mountain Dew,
Mellow Yello, and Sunkist Orange) contain more caffeine
than many so-called colas. On the other hand, two
"colas"--RC-100 and Cragmont--do not have any caffeine
(6). In those cola drinks that contain caffeine, manu-
facturers claim that over 95% is added in order to enhance flavor. However, a Consumers Union triangle test[1]

[1] Panelists were given samples of three beverages
and were asked to identify the one that was supposed to
taste different.

References to figures and tables for sources of data. Statistics are interpreted and related to the discussion.

Detailed information establishes Little's point about caffeine consumption.

Superscript number refers to footnote adding explanatory material.

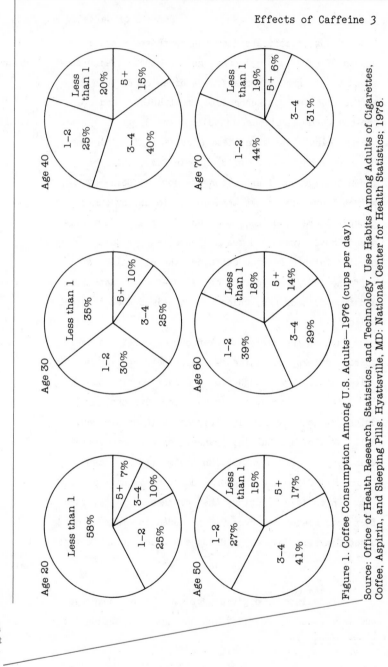

Figure 1. Coffee Consumption Among U.S. Adults—1976 (cups per day).

Source: Office of Health Research, Statistics, and Technology. Use Habits Among Adults of Cigarettes, Coffee, Aspirin, and Sleeping Pills. Hyattsville, MD: National Center for Health Statistics; 1978.

Source of information identified at bottom of illustration.

Effects of Caffeine 4

Table 1. Common sources of caffeine.

NONPRESCRIPTION DRUGS, one tablet	Milligrams of Caffeine
Anacin	32
Aspirin	0
Dexatrim	200
Dristan	16
Empirin	32
Excedrin	65
Midol	32
No Doz	100
Vanquish	33

SOFT DRINKS, 12 oz	
Coca-Cola	39
Diet Pepsi	34
Diet Sunkist Orange	0
Dr. Pepper	61
Fanta Orange	0
Fresca	0
Ginger Ale	0
Hires Rootbeer	0
Mountain Dew	54
Mr. Pibb	57
Nehi Orange	0
Pepsi Cola	38
Pepsi Free	0
RC Cola	36
7 Up	0
Sunkist Orange	42

In scientific papers, measurements are abbreviated without a period.

COFFEE, 5 oz	
Automatic drip	110–150
Percolated	64–124
Instant	40–108
Decaffeinated brewed	2–5
Instant decaffeinated	2

CHOCOLATE	
Cocoa beverage (6 oz)	10
Milk chocolate (1 oz)	6
Baking chocolate (1 oz)	35

Source: Consumer Reports 1981 October:598.

Table 2.   Caffeine in teas (in milligrams)

HOT TEA--Domestic

Brand Name	Type	Strength*		
		Weak	Medium	Strong
Red Rose	bag	45	62	90
Salada	bag	25	60	78
Lipton	bag	25	53	70
Tetley	bag	18	48	70

HOT TEA--Imported

Brand Name	Type	Strength*		
		Weak	Medium	Strong
English Breakfast	bag	26	78	107
(Twinings)	loose	39	84	90
Darjeeling	bag	39	74	91
(Twinings)				
Formosa Oolong	loose	42	65	78
(Jacksons)				

INSTANT TEA (prepared according to package directions)

Lipton	62
Nestea	48
Lipton with sugar and lemon	76
Nestea with sugar and lemon	67

*Determined by color intensity in 6 oz hot water.

Source: Daniel S. Groisser.   A study of caffeine in tea.
American Journal of Clinical Nutrition 31:1729.

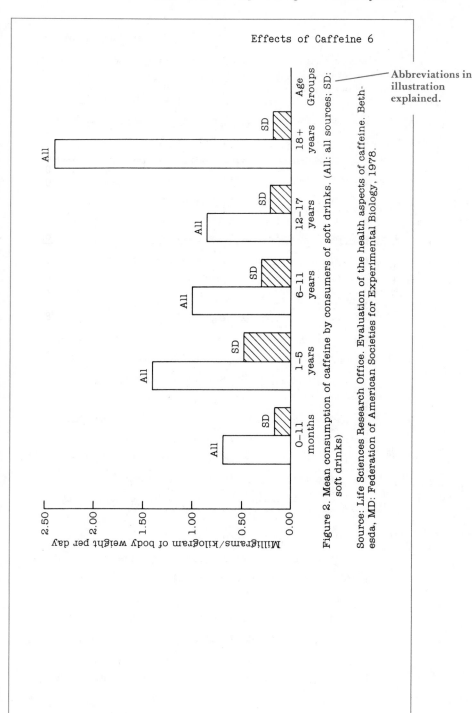

Effects of Caffeine 6

Figure 2. Mean consumption of caffeine by consumers of soft drinks. (All: all sources; SD: soft drinks)

Source: Life Sciences Research Office. Evaluation of the health aspects of caffeine. Bethesda, MD: Federation of American Societies for Experimental Biology, 1978.

Abbreviations in illustration explained.

showed that women could not detect a taste difference
between noncaffeinated and caffeinated orange drinks
(6). Many consumers believe that soft drink manufactur-
ers add caffeine to their products to cause children to
become addicted to the caffeine in them (7).

Although people consume less tea than either coffee
or soft drinks, tea is still an important source of
caffeine. The amount of caffeine in tea depends greatly
on the length of time it is brewed as well as on the
brand used. (Table 2, p. 5, lists the caffeine content
of teas according to brand and brewing time.)

EFFECTS OF CAFFEINE ON ADULTS

Effects on normal body processes

Caffeine, a white, needle-shaped methylxanthine
compound, is a drug that stimulates the central nervous
system (CNS). According to the Food and Drug Administration (FDA) (8, p. 68929), it is the only ingredient
added to food at levels that will achieve its pharmaco-
logical effect, that is, the stimulation of the CNS. As
a result, the FDA has proposed that caffeine be removed
from the Generally Recognized As Safe (GRAS) List to an
interim category until it has been further tested (9).

One of the major effects of caffeine on the body is
the dilation the heart's blood vessels. Caffeine re-
laxes smooth muscles in vessel walls so that the heart
rate increases. At the same time, caffeine stimulates a
section of the brain to decrease heart rate. These
antithetical effects result in an overall increase in
heart rate. If the brain did not slow the heart, the
increase in heart rate would be greater.

Caffeine also decreases the blood flow in the brain
by constricting its blood vessels, decreases blood glu-

Second-level
heading.
Descriptive
headings aid the
reader in finding
particular sections
of the paper.

At first use,
technical term is
spelled out and
followed by its
abbreviation; the
abbreviation is
used from then on.

Effects of Caffeine 8

cose and pancreatic insulin output, increases urine output, stimulates gastric secretion, and increases basal metabolic rate (10).

"Restless legs syndrome" can afflict some coffee drinkers. In his study of this condition, Lutz (11) describes the symptoms as "unpleasant, creeping sensations in the lower legs between the knee and ankle" (p. 693), as well as restlessness in the arms and shoulders. Those who spend much of their time in sedentary occupations or pastimes are most often afflicted, and their discomfort usually occurs in the evening and at night. Once the sensations start, those who suffer from the syndrome find it impossible to keep their legs still and feel the need to get up and walk. All of Lutz's 62 patients with "restless legs syndrome" had consumed methylxanthine stimulants equivalent to at least 1 cup of coffee daily.

Disease states worsened by caffeine

Ulcers. Scientists have known for many years that caffeine and other methylxanthines stimulate secretion of two digestive juices, hydrochloric acid and pepsin, increasing the chances of developing ulcers. A University of California study of 25 000 college students found that those who drank 2 or more cups of coffee per day had a 70% greater chance of developing ulcers later in life than their classmates who consumed no coffee (12). Other studies of humans and animals have shown that caffeine significantly stimulates secretion of gastric juices (4, p. 64).

Heart disease. Although a 200 mg dose of caffeine causes the heart to pump faster, correlations between caffeine and heart disease are difficult to make. Kan-

Lutz, an authority, is quoted because his words provide the most accurate description of symptoms. Source is given after author, page reference is given after quotation.

Third-level heading. Section discusses general effects first, then disease-related effects.

In scientific papers, a space instead of a comma separates numbers of five or more digits.

nel and Dawber (4) found "no relation between coffee consumption and myocardial infarction [damaged heart muscle or heart attack]" (p. 63). But they did find that the heart rate and blood pressure of fasting, non-coffee drinkers increased 1 hour after ingestion of 250 mg caffeine--a result suggesting that persons prone to dysrhythmias (abnormal heart beats) should restrict their caffeine consumption (p. 31). Dobmeyer et al. (13) concluded that patients who show arrhythmic symptoms (irregular heart beats) after caffeine administration "should avoid caffeine" (p. 815). A study by the Boston Drug Surveillance Program (12) found that persons drinking 5 cups of coffee daily had a 50% greater risk of heart attack than coffee nondrinkers. Those drinking 6 or more cups increased their chances of heart attack by 100%.

Fibrocystic breast disease. A surgeon at Ohio State University, John Minton, studied 88 women with fibrocystic breast disease (benign breast lumps). After their condition was diagnosed, 45 of these women gave up caffeine entirely. Minton reported that, of the 45, "37 experienced total disappearance of breast lumps, and 7 reported some disappearance" (7, p. 20). Of the 88 women, 15 continued consuming their usual amount of caffeine. Only 2 of those women reported that their breast lumps disappeared spontaneously. Boyle et al. corroborated some of Minton's findings (14). However, Heyden and Muhlbaier (15) were unable to report similar dramatic results in their study of the same disease. They concluded that it is difficult to relate the amount of methylxanthine consumption to fibrocystic breast disease because the condition itself is so variable (it

---

Place additions that aren't part of the quotation in brackets.

In scientific or technical papers, use numerals, not words, for numbers over ten or for statistics. Use %, not *percent*.

When a source has more than two authors, give the first author followed by *et al.*

Little reports differing results. Researchers, especially in science, should include conflicting data.

Effects of Caffeine 10

has such a high degree of waxing and waning with or
without treatment). They recommend greater experimental
controls in future testing.

Cancer. Studies have not demonstrated a cause-
and-effect relationship between coffee drinking and
cancer, though James and Stirling found "a relatively
strong relationship" between cancer of the pancreas and
coffee drinking (16). The FDA has claimed that bladder
cancer is more prevalent among coffee drinkers than
noncoffee drinkers, and a correlation between deaths
from renal cancer and coffee consumption has been observed (8, p. 69828).

Caffeine addiction

Most people who consume 5 or more cups of coffee
per day (about 500 mg) have caffeinism, an addiction to
caffeine (17). As figure 1 (p. 3) shows, 17% of U.S.
adults, age 50, qualify as addicts.

Coffee drinkers can detect caffeinism by curbing
caffeine intake for 1 to 2 days and checking for the
following symptoms: sensations of fullness in the head,
drowsiness, euphoria, nausea, excessive yawning, constant runny nose, and throbbing headache made worse by
bending over and exercising. Withdrawal symptoms can
last up to two weeks. A person can alleviate the pain
of withdrawal by gradually decreasing caffeine consumption. For example, a coffee drinker can blend decaffeinated coffee with regular coffee, gradually
increasing the ratio of decaffeinated to regular over a
2- to 3-week period (18).

Aggravation of mental and emotional disorders

Mentally retarded and emotionally disturbed persons
are particularly susceptible to the effects of caffeine.

Smooth transition
made by repeating
caffeinism and by
moving from a
generalization
about the number
of addicts to
specific symptoms.

Heading signals
shift in focus.

Podboy and Mallory (19) observed fifteen severely retarded women accustomed to drinking 4 to 15 cups of coffee per day (mean consumption was 7.1 cups). These women often kicked other patients and, waking at night, yelled and walked about. When decaffeinated coffee was given to them, the average number of aggressive outbursts per week decreased from 14.78 to 6.35 during the last 2 weeks of the 6-week treatment period. The women also drank their decaffeinated coffee more slowly and asked for fewer refills.

Clear, effective
summary of
procedures and
results of two
studies.

In another study, Bezchlebnyk and Jeffries (20) observed the coffee-drinking habits of psychiatric patients in a Canadian institution. The patients were offered coffee or tea 6 times a day, and they consumed as many as 1000 mg of caffeine daily. Doctors at the institution noticed that patients consuming over 250 mg per day were more anxious, depressed, and likely to be diagnosed psychotic; caffeine also worsened schizophrenic symptoms among these patients. When 14 inpatients were covertly switched to decaffeinated coffee for 3 weeks, their hostility, suspiciousness, anxiety, and irritability diminished. Only the originally diagnosed levels of psychiatric disorders remained.

Little moves from
effects of caffeine
on adults to a
special case.
Heading is worded
as it was in the
table of contents.

EFFECTS OF CAFFEINE ON PREGNANT WOMEN AND NEWBORNS

In a 1977 study (21), P. S. Weathersbee found evidence of abnormal deliveries among pregnant women who drank coffee. "Of 16 women who drank 8 or more cups of coffee per day (600+ mg) during pregnancy," he reported, "only one had an uncomplicated delivery of a normal term infant" (p. 160). On the other hand, 72% of 104 women who drank no more than 45 mg of caffeine daily had normal deliveries. Evidence of birth defects

Direct quotation
and paraphrase are
combined.

Effects of Caffeine 12

from caffeine was found by the FDA in a 1980 study (17) in which rats were fed the equivalent of 2 cups of coffee per day. The result was a delay in the skeletal development of the offspring.

Still, the links between pregnancy and caffeine are not completely proven. Weathersbee was unable to establish a firm cause-and-effect relationship between caffeine ingestion and abnormal deliveries, and researchers at Boston University and Howard University (18) could not duplicate the correlation between coffee and birth defects in their similar studies. They also found it difficult to interpret results of studies with rats because of the differences in the way rats and humans metabolize caffeine. Nevertheless, the FDA recommends that women avoid caffeine during pregnancy because any drug crossing the placenta, especially during the first 3 months, can be dangerous to the fetus (17).

> The word *still* makes a smooth transition to a paragraph that qualifies Weathersbee's findings.

Infants may be exposed to caffeine immediately after birth. Horning et al. (4, p. 13) analyzed human breast milk and found it to contain 1.3 to 6.9 mg caffeine per liter. An infant consuming 150 ml breast milk per kg (of infant weight) has a daily caffeine intake of 1.2 mg per kg, the equivalent of the consumption of 1 cup of perked coffee per day by a 154 lb adult. Horning also confirmed that infants are exposed to caffeine before birth; urine samples of 100 newborn infants whose mothers consumed caffeine all contained caffeine.

> Writer uses an analogy to clarify her point.

BENEFICIAL EFFECTS OF CAFFEINE

Although most of the evidence suggests that caffeine consumption is harmful to human health, there are some beneficial effects of the drug. According to Stephenson (10), caffeine consumption relieves respira-

> Little incorporates contradictory evidence showing that caffeine can be beneficial.

Effects of Caffeine 13

tory failure caused by morphine and codeine overdoses, energizes elderly persons who have brain damage and atherosclerosis, and improves interest and lessens irritability in severely regressed psychiatric patients. In addition, caffeine has been found to enhance the speed and accuracy of those performing physical tasks such as typing (4); it also increases endurance during exercise by reducing carbohydrate oxidation and increasing fat metabolism (22).

CONCLUSION

Little summarizes her findings and makes a recommendation.

Research into the effects of caffeine on human health has increased greatly in the last 5 years. Because many studies have found caffeine to be harmful and because caffeine consumers themselves have observed harmful effects of the drug, the public has become more wary of ingesting products with caffeine in them. Industries have responded to these worries by developing caffeine-free, cola-flavored soft drinks and decaffeinated coffees and teas.

Little strikes a balance between contradictory evidence.

Still, scientists have been unable to prove that these harmful effects cause permanent health damage among healthy adults. Insomnia, nervousness, and rapid heart rate disappear soon after caffeine is removed from the body. The effects on infants, young children, and people prone to heart disease may be less benign, but the evidence, though strongly suggestive of permanent damage, is not yet conclusive. The FDA has encouraged further research on this subject.

Despite the lack of conclusive evidence, adults, children, and especially pregnant women would do well to decrease their consumption of caffeine. Within the next

Effects of Caffeine 14

few years, scientists should be able to state with more certainty correlations between caffeine and various health disorders. Already, as James and Stirling point out, "growing numbers of authorities are voicing their alarm and recommending moderation in the use of this drug" (16, p. 255).

Paper ends with quotation from two authorities to support the point about the dangers of caffeine.

REFERENCES

Begin new page, center heading, and double-space throughout.

1. Caffeine: what it does. Consumer Reports 1981 Oct.:595-596.

Author's initials follow last name. Abbreviate periodical title if you wish.

2. Graham, D. M. Caffeine--its identity, dietary sources, intake and biological effects. Nutrition Reviews 36:97-102; 1978.

3. Starbird, E. Z. The bonanza bean coffee. National Geographic 1981 Mar.:388-405.

Corporate author given first as for an individual author.

4. Life Sciences Research Office. Evaluation of the health aspects of caffeine. Bethesda, MD: Federation of American Societies for Experimental Biology; 1978.

For a weekly magazine, give date instead of volume and issue number.

5. Is caffeine bad for you? Newsweek 1982 July 19:62-64.

6. Caffeine: how to consume less. Consumer Reports. 1981 Oct.:597-599.

7. The caffeine catch. Family Health. 1981 Apr.: 20-21.

8. Department of Health and Human Services. Soda water: amendment to standard. Federal Register 45:69816-69838; 1980.

For personal communications, give source, affiliation, type of communication, and date.

9. Lin, L., Consumer Safety Officer, Division of Toxicology, Food and Drug Administration, interview, 1982 Feb. 9.

10. Stephenson, P. E. Psychologic and psychotropic effects of caffeine on man. Journal of the American Dietetic Association 71:242-245; 1977.

11. Lutz, E. G. Restless legs, anxiety, and caffeinism. Journal of Clinical Psychology 39:693-696; 1978.

For a magazine, give date of issue instead of volume number.

12. Are you a caffeine addict? Saturday Evening Post. 1982 May/June:50-53.

13. Dobmeyer, D. J.; Stine, R. A.; Leier, C. V.; Green-
berg, R.; Schaal, S. F. The arrhythmogenic effects
of caffeine in human beings. New England Journal
of Medicine 308:814-816; 1983.

14. Boyle, C. A.; Berkowitz, G. S.; LiVolsi, V. A.;
Ort, S.; Merino, M. J.; White, C.; Kelsey, J. L.
Caffeine consumption and fibrocystic breast disease: a case-control epidemiologic study. Journal
of the National Cancer Institute 72:1015-1019; 1984.

15. Heyden, S.; Mulhbaier, L. H. Prospective study of
"fibrocystic breast disease" and caffeine consumption. Surgery 96:479-483; 1984.

16. James, J. E.; Stirling, K. P. Caffeine: a survey
of some of the known suspected deleterious effects
of habitual use. British Journal of Addiction
78:251-258; 1983.

17. Burros, M. Caffeine controversy. The New York
Times. 1982 April 21:C1 (col. 5), C6 (col. 1).

18. Brody, J. Weaning the body from dependence on
caffeine. The New York Times. 1982 April 21:C6.

19. Podboy, J. W.; Mallory, W. A. Caffeine reduction
and behavior change in the severely retarded.
Mental Retardation 15:40; 1977.

20. Bezchlebnyk, K.; Jeffries, J. Should psychiatric
patients drink coffee? Canadian Medical Association Journal 124:357-358; 1981.

21. Caffeine, cigarette smoke: effects on the unborn
child. Hospital Practice 15 (Oct.):160, 164; 1980.

22. Costell, D. L.; Dalsky, G. P.; Fink, W. J. Effects
of caffeine ingestion on metabolism and exercise
performance. Medicine and Science in Sports
10:155-158; 1978.

Newspaper article with separate pagination. When page numbers are discontinuous, use a comma between them.

APPENDIX 1

Annotated List
of References

This guide to reference sources provides you with a shortcut in your search for information by listing many of the books and journals that contain titles of specific books and articles about your subject. In your card catalog search you will be able to go directly to these specific works. The list is arranged from the most general levels of sources to the most specific; you can start your search at the level that suits your situation best. In general, the less you know about a subject, the more you will benefit from a wider initial view. However, some of the general sources, such as *Ulrich's International Periodicals Directory* or the *Vertical File Index*, can be helpful whatever your level of knowledge. The annotations accompanying each entry will help you decide whether a source will be useful.

The first group of books, General Sources, provides the names of bibliographies or general books as well as indexes on a range of subjects, directories of periodicals, sources of biographies, and books containing specific data or facts. At the next level, you will find sources in three primary disciplinary groups; the humanities, the social sciences, and science and technology. Many students find that using the books in one of these groups is a good way to start.

Finally, you will find specific reference books for over twenty-five subjects arranged alphabetically within each subject. The standard encyclopedia or dictionary references can help you focus a topic by providing brief definitions, giving background information, and suggesting a few related citations with which you can begin your search. For most subjects, you will also find a guide to the literature describing research methodology in the subject area and providing relevant reference sources. For each subject, indexes, collections of abstracts, computer databases (when they exist), and at least three primary journals are provided. Notice that the title is listed first for sources better known by their titles than by their authors or editors (for example, the *Readers' Guide to Periodical Literature*).

When you consult any of these reference sources, be sure to read the explanatory material at the beginning of the book to find out how it is organized, what information is provided, and what the abbreviations and symbols mean.

Brief Contents

I. General Sources
   A. Guides to Reference Works
   B. Bibliographies and Book Catalogs
   C. Indexes
   D. Directories of Periodicals
   E. Biographical Reference Sources
   F. Yearbooks and Almanacs
II. Sources in Primary Disciplinary Groups
   A. Humanities
   B. Social Sciences
   C. Science and Technology
III. Sources in Specific Academic Disciplines
   A. Accounting
   B. Agriculture
   C. Anthropology and Archaeology
   D. Art
   E. Biology and Agriculture
   F. Business, Accounting, and Economics
   G. Chemistry and Physics
   H. Communications (Radio, Television, Speech, Journalism)
   I. Computer Science
   J. Drama
   K. Education
   L. Engineering and Electronics
   M. Environmental and Earth Sciences
   N. Film
   O. Folklore
   P. Geography
   Q. History
   R. Literature
   S. Medicine and Nursing
   T. Music
   U. Philosophy and Religion
   V. Physical Education and Sports
   W. Political Science and Government
   X. Psychology
   Y. Sociology

I. General Sources

A. Guides to Reference Works

Borgman, Christine L., Dineh Moghdam, and Patti K. Corbett. *Effective On-line Searching*. New York: Marcel Dekker, 1984.

Discusses search-strategy development, databases, vocabulary control, and evaluation of searches; also includes step-by-step instruction in searching techniques. The chapter on databases refers students to useful directories, such as Williams's *Computer-Readable Data Bases: A Directory and Data Sourcebook*.

Katz, William. *Introduction to Reference Work*. 4th ed. 2 vols. New York: McGraw-Hill, 1982.

A more comprehensive and sophisticated guide than *Your Library: A Reference Guide*. The second volume of this work covers on-line searching and computer databases.

————. *Your Library: A Reference Guide*. 2d ed. New York: Holt, Rinehart and Winston, 1984.

A handbook on the use of libraries for the beginning researcher. Discusses ways to familiarize yourself with library facilities and collections. A chapter is included on finding sources for a research paper. Following chapters on general reference books, a final section describes the best reference books to use in different subject disciplines according to the type of information you are looking for.

Sheehy, Eugene P. *Guide to Reference Books*. 9th ed., with supplements. Chicago: American Library Assn., 1976.

Identifies reference books in all subjects. Annotated entries are arranged by subject; includes an index arranged by title.

Walford, A. J. *Walford's Guide to Reference Material*. 4th ed. London: The Library Assn., 1980–.

An international guide to bibliographies and reference books. Volume 1 covers science and technology; Volume 2 covers social sciences, history, religion, and philosophy; a third volume on general sources, literature and language, and the arts is planned. The reference works are grouped by subject. Each entry gives a complete citation and critical description of the work. Although Walford is more current than Sheehy, its focus is on British reference works. Walford's *Concise Guide to Reference Material* (1 vol., 1981) covers all subjects.

B. Bibliographies and Book Catalogs

Besterman, Theodore. *A World Bibliography of Bibliographies*. 4th ed. 5 vols. Lausanne: Societas Bibliographica, 1965–1966.

A classified listing of bibliographies published through 1963. The fifth volume provides access by author, by title for serial and anonymous works, and by library or archive.

Bibliographic Index: A Cumulative Bibliography of Bibliographies. New York: Wilson, 1938–. Published 3 times a year; 3d issue is cumulative.

Useful to bring Besterman up to date. Arranged alphabetically by subject, this listing includes bibliographies published in books and periodicals as well as bibliographies that have been separately published.

Books in Print. New York: Bowker, 1948–. Annual, with midyear supplements since 1975.

A guide to books of all types, including textbooks, paperbacks, and children's books, that are currently in print. Books are listed by author and title, and information is given for purchasing the books. A list of publishers and their addresses is given at the end of the final Title volume. The *Subject Guide to Books in Print* (New York: Bowker) identifies books currently in print by subject, using the Library of Congress subject headings. It also provides ordering information.

C. Indexes

American Statistics Index. Washington, DC: Congressional Information Service, 1972–. Monthly, with annual cumulations.

Indexes all U.S. government statistical publications by subject, place or agency name, program name, and personal name. Summaries are given in the Abstract volume and the actual documents are available on microfiche.

Biography Index. See entry under E., Biographical Reference Sources.

Book Review Digest. New York: Wilson, 1905–. Monthly, except February and July, with quarterly and annual cumulations.

Useful because it includes excerpts from selected book reviews. Nonfiction works are included if they have been reviewed at least twice and fiction works if there have been at least four reviews. Reviews indexed are from general and scholarly journals.

Book Review Index. Detroit: Gale, 1965–.

Indexes reviews from 450 publications, including popular magazines like the *Atlantic Monthly* as well as scholarly journals. Entries are listed alphabetically according to the name of the author reviewed. The listings do not include excerpts of reviews, but they do include the reviewer's name and the data and place of publication of the review.

Congressional Information Service, *CIS Annual.* Washington, DC: Congressional Information Service, 1970–. Monthly, with annual cumulations.

Indexes all congressional publications, including hearings, committee reports, and publications of congressional offices, such as the Congressional Budget Office. Publications are indexed by subject and name as well as by bill number, document number, Senate hearing number, and committee chairmen. Summaries of the publications (which also include SuDoc numbers) can be found in the companion volumes. *CIS Annual* is also available as a computer database that can be searched from 1970 to the present.

Dissertation Abstracts International. Ann Arbor, MI: University Microfilms International, 1938–. Monthly.

Includes abstracts of doctoral dissertations from universities in the U.S. and Canada. Since 1966, the abstracts have been divided into two sections: humanities and social sciences, and sciences and engineering. The abstracts are divided by subject categories outlined in the table of contents. The author and Keyword indexes at the end of each listing cumulate annually in the *Comprehensive Dissertation Index* (same publisher). Copies of dissertations included in *Dissertation Abstracts International* are available from the publisher in hard copy or on microfilm. *DAI* is also available as a computer database that can be searched online through DIALOG.

Essay and General Literature Index. New York: Wilson, 1900–. Annual, with five-year cumulations.

An aid to locating essays, primarily in the humanities and social sciences, that are part of collections not otherwise easily located. Access is by author and by subject; essays written by C. S. Lewis, for example, can be found as well as essays about him and his individual works.

Magazine Index. Belmont, CA: Information Access 1959–.

A microfilm index to over 400 general interest magazines. Information is listed for the preceding four years by subject, author, and product name; book, movie, play, and restaurant reviews are included. Microfilm is updated monthly. Indexes for the previous years are available on microfiche. This index is also available as a computer database through DIALOG.

The National Newspaper Index. Belmont, CA: Information Access, 1979–. Monthly.

This guide (on microfilm and microfiche) indexes articles from five newspapers: the *Christian Science Monitor, Los Angeles Times, New York Times, Wall Street Journal,* and *Washington Post.*

New York Times Index. New York: New York Times, 1913–. Semimonthly, with annual cumulations.

Because a short summary is given for each entry instead of a title, this index can be used to answer questions about dates and sequences of events as well as to identify specifications. Abbreviations (S, M, L) indicate the length of the original article. The *Personal Name Index to the New York Times Index* (25 vol.), by Byron J. Falk, Jr., and Valerie R. Falk (Verdi, NV: Roxbury Data Interface) indexes names appearing in the *New York Times* for 1851 to 1979.

Readers' Guide to Periodical Literature. New York: Wilson, 1900–. Semimonthly, with quarterly and annual cumulations.

An index arranged by author and subject to articles in over 150 general, nontechnical magazines; includes reviews of books, motion pictures, television shows, and plays.

United States Department of Commerce, Bureau of the Census. *Statistical Abstract of the United States 1985.* 105th ed. Washington, DC: GPO, 1984. Annual.

Summarizes statistical information on economic, social, and political subjects for the U.S. Some international statistics are included. Statistics are grouped by general subject, such as foreign commerce and aid or agriculture, with a detailed index providing access to specific data. Each graph or table has a citation to the government document from which it was taken.

United States Superintendent of Documents. *Monthly Catalog of United States*

Government Publications. Washington, DC: 1895–. Monthly, with quarterly cumulations and semiannual index cumulations.

Lists government publications published each month. Entries are arranged alphabetically by issuing agency and are indexed by author, title, subject (using Library of Congress subject headings), report, contract number, and title keyword. Entries marked with a black dot are available at federal depository libraries. The *Monthly Catalog* can be searched through the GPO Monthly Catalog database.

Vertical File Index. New York: Wilson, 1935–. Monthly, except August, with annual cumulations.

A subject and title index to pamphlets. Complete bibliographic and ordering information is given for each pamphlet. Brief summaries or descriptions are included for most entries. Arrangement is by subject; title index.

D. Directories of Periodicals

Katz, Bill. *Magazines for Libraries*. 4th ed. New York: Bowker, 1982.

A selective, annotated listing of over 6,000 periodicals grouped by subject. Bibliographic information and subscription rate and frequency are given. Annotations describe the contents and specific features of the periodical and give a recommendation of the value of the periodical for different types of libraries.

Ulrich's International Periodicals Directory. New York: Bowker, 1932–. Annual, with quarterly updates.

Describes over 66,000 periodicals currently published on a regular basis. Periodicals are arranged by subject with cross-references to related subjects. Complete bibliographic information for each title, including address, subscription price, frequency of publication, date of original publication, and a list of indexes and abstracting services that include the journal (if it is indexed). Periodicals that appear on an irregular basis are covered by the companion volume, *Irregular Serials and Annuals* (New York: Bowker, 1967–).

Union List of Serials in Libraries of the United States and Canada. 3d ed. 5 vols. New York: Bowker, 1965.

Useful in locating a particular periodical, the *Union List* is an alphabetical listing of over 155,000 serial titles held by 956 libraries in the U.S. and Canada. Entries give the beginning and ending dates of publication (or indicate if the serial is still currently published), selected locations, and any name changes of the serial. Entries indicate which issues of a serial a particular library has. The *Union List* is supplemented by *New Serial Titles*, which lists serials published after 1949. There is a subject guide to *New Serial Titles*.

E. Biographical Reference Sources

Biography and Genealogy Master Index. Ed. Miranda C. Herbert and Barbara McNeil. 2d ed. Detroit, MI: Gale, 1980. Annual supplements.

A master index to over 350 biographical dictionaries and subject encyclopedias, such as *Who's Who in America*, the *Dictionary of American Biography*, and the *Oxford Companion to English Literature*. Entries in the alphabetical listing of names give birth and death dates and indicate by title abbreviation which reference books include further biographical information.

Biography Index: a Cumulative Index to Biographical Material in Books and Magazines. New York: Wilson, 1946–. Quarterly, with annual and three-year cumulations.

An important index to biographical information published in English-language books and periodicals. Works cited include memoirs, journals, obituaries, and collective biographies as well as works that are strictly biographical. Each issue includes an index by profession.

Current Biography. New York: Wilson, 1940–. Monthly, with annual cumulations.

Contains lengthy biographic sketches of men and women currently in the news. Entries include references to additional sources of information. Each issue has an index classified by profession and obituaries.

Dictionary of American Biography. 11 vols., with index and supplements. New York: Scribner's 1928–1937.

Consists of long scholarly articles about American men and women who were not living at the time the *Dictionary* was published. Bibliographies are included at the end of each entry. Indexes are arranged by place of birth, college, and profession.

McGraw-Hill Encyclopedia of World Biography. 12 vols. New York: McGraw-Hill, 1973.

Contains short biographies of approximately 5,000 world figures. Entries include suggestions for further reading. The illustrations are a valuable feature. The index volume provides access by name and by subject.

Notable American Women, 1607–1950: A Biographical Dictionary. 3 vols. Cambridge, MA: Belknap Press of Harvard Univ. Press, 1971.

Presents scholarly articles (patterned after the *Dictionary of American Biography*) of American women living between 1607 and 1950 who made contributions to American society. Articles include bibliographies. Vol. III lists names by profession. *Notable American Women: The Modern Period* (Cambridge, MA: Belknap Press of Harvard Univ. Press, 1980) gives biographical sketches for American women who died between 1951 and 1975.

Who's Who in America. Chicago: Marquis Who's Who, 1899–. Biennial.

The standard biographical dictionary on living Americans. Biographical information is given in concise form. Besides *Who's Who in America*, a number of more specific biographical dictionaries, such as *Who's Who in the Midwest, Who's Who in American Politics, Who's Who Among Black Americans*, and *Who's Who in France* focus on a particular geographic area or group.

F. *Yearbooks and Almanacs*

Facts on File. New York: Facts on File, 1941–. Weekly, with annual cumulations.

A weekly summary in looseleaf format of U.S. and world news events as covered in over 50 U.S. and international documents, government publications, and news releases. Every two weeks a new index gives access to specific news items. At the end of the year a cumulated *Facts on File Yearbook* replaces the looseleaf binder. *Facts on File* is particularly useful for verifying dates and tracing the sequence of events.

World Almanac and Book of Facts. New York: Newspaper Enterprise Assn., 1868–. Annual.

A comprehensive source of statistics, geographical and historical data, and current events information. The *World Alamanac* includes information ranging from color illustrations of the flags of the world to a chronology of the events of the previous year. Sources are given for each set of facts. A general subject index is located in the front of the volume.

II. Sources in Primary Disciplinary Groups

A. *Humanities*

Arts and Humanities Citation Index (AHCI). Philadelphia: Institute for Scientific Information, 1978–. Bimonthly, with annual cumulations.

A multidisciplinary index composed of three separate indexes to over 1,000 periodicals in the arts and humanities. *AHCI* allows the researcher three different methods of identifying information. If you want to find new articles by an author whom you already know, use the *Source Index*. To search for a corporate author, use the corporate index section of the *Source Index*. The *Citation Index* is used to determine who has cited (footnoted) an important author. By using the *Permuterm Subject Index*, you are no longer restricted to standard subject headings. This index allows you to combine any two terms that have appeared together in the title of a journal article. If a title is cryptic, additional terms are added in brackets to clarify the meaning.

Current Contents: Arts and Humanities. Philadelphia: Institute for Scientific Information, 1979–. Weekly.

A weekly compilation of the tables of contents of over 1,300 humanities periodicals arranged in eight general subject categories. This publication provides the most current access to the content of these journals through a title keyword (subject) index and an author index.

Humanities Index. New York: Wilson, 1974–. Quarterly, with annual cumulations. Supersedes *Social Sciences and Humanities Index*, 1965–1974 and *International Index to Periodicals*, 1907–1965.

Provides access by subject and author to over 250 core periodicals in the classics, archaeology, language, literature and literary criticism, folklore, religion and philosophy, area studies, history, theater, and film. Book reviews are included alphabetically by author in a separate listing at the end of the volume.

Index to Book Reviews in the Humanities. Williamston, MI: Phillip Thomson, 1960–.

A comprehensive index to book reviews included in several hundred general and scholarly humanities periodicals. Through 1970 the subject coverage included history and some social sciences; since 1971 coverage has been confined to the arts and humanities. Access is by author's name.

Rogers, A. Robert. *The Humanities: A Selective Guide to Information Sources*. 2d ed. Littleton, CO: Libraries Unlimited, 1979.

A guide to the literature of the humanities covering information sources in philosophy and religion, visual arts, performing arts, and language and literature. For each subject, there is a chapter on how to obtain information in that field and a chapter on the major reference works and periodicals. Evaluative annotations that explain coverage, arrangement, and most appropriate use accompany each citation.

B. Social Sciences

Book Review Index to Social Science Periodicals. Ed. Arnold M. Rzepecki. Ann Arbor, MI: Pierian Press, 1964–1974.

Indexes book reviews by the name of the author in approximately 300 social science periodicals published from 1964 to 1974. Since 1970, history journals have been included in this coverage. Book reviews published after 1974 can be found in the *Social Sciences Index*.

Current Contents: Social and Behavioral Sciences. Philadelphia: Institute for Scientific Information, 1974–. Weekly.

A compilation of the tables of contents of over 1,300 social and behavioral science periodicals arranged by thirteen subject disciplines. Provides the most current access to the contents of these journals through a title keyword (subject) index and an author index.

International Encyclopedia of the Social Sciences. Ed. David L. Sills. 17 vols. New York: Macmillan, 1968.

Contains signed scholarly articles on the concepts, methods, major persons, and theories in anthropology, economics, geography, history, law, political science, psychology and psychiatry, sociology, and statistics. Articles are arranged alphabetically by topic with additional access provided by a detailed index (Volume 17) and cross-references. Each article has a bibliography of references. Volume 18 (1980) provides a biographical supplement. This encyclopedia updates but does not replace the classic *Encyclopedia of the Social Sciences* (New York: Macmillan, 1930–1935).

Public Affairs Information Service Bulletin (PAIS). New York: Public Affairs Information Service, 1915–. Published semimonthly, with quarterly and annual cumulations.

Provides access by subject and author to periodical articles, government documents, books, and reports in the area of public policy. Subject areas covered include economics, public administration, international relations, demographics, law, journalism, and politics. *PAIS* is also available online as PAIS International, which includes citations from *PAIS Foreign Language Index* as well as *PAIS Bulletin*.

Social Science Citation Index (SSCI). Philadelphia: Institute for Scientific Information, 1969–. Bimonthly, with annual cumulations.

Indexes over 1,000 periodicals in the behavioral and social sciences. Following the same plan as ISI's other citation indexes, *Social Sciences Citation Index* has three separate ways of finding information in the indexed periodicals. The *Citation Index* includes authors who have been cited and the citing references. The *Source Index* lists journal articles by author's name and the *Permuterm Subject Index* allows the combination of any two terms that have appeared together in the title of an article. To search for a corporate author, search the corporate index section of the *Source Index*. *SSCI* can be searched online or through the database SOCIAL SCISEARCH (1972-).

Social Sciences Index. New York: Wilson, 1974-. Quarterly, with annual cumulations. Supersedes *Social Sciences and Humanities Index*, 1965-1974, and *International Index to Periodicals*, 1907-1965.

Provides access by subject and author to the major English-language periodicals in political science, sociology, economics, anthropology, psychology, planning and public affairs, environmental sciences, law, criminology, and behavioral sciences. Book reviews are listed alphabetically by author at the end of each volume.

White, Carl M., and associates. *Sources of Information in the Social Sciences: A Guide to the Literature*. 2d ed. Chicago: American Library Assn., 1973.

The standard guide to the social sciences with sections on social science literature in general, history, geography, economics, business administration, sociology, anthropology, psychology, education, and political science. For each discipline there is an essay reviewing the basic works and methodologies in that field and an annotated guide to abstracts, periodicals, current and retrospective bibliographies, dictionaries, handbooks, and other reference works.

C. Science and Technology

American Men and Women of Science: Physical and Behavioral Sciences. Ed. Jaques Cattell Press. 15th ed. 7 vols. New York: Bowker, 1982.

A biographical directory of over 130,000 living American scientists. Arranged alphabetically, the entries include data on age, educational background, professional experience and memberships, mailing address, and area of research. Behavioral and social scientists were included in the first 13 editions. This directory may be searched online.

Chen, Ching-Chih. *Scientific and Technical Information*. Cambridge, MA: MIT Press, 1977.

An annotated guide to reference books in all areas of science and technology except medicine. The book is arranged by type of reference book (dictionaries, handbooks, abstracts) and by subject within each category.

Current Contents: Life Sciences. Philadelphia: Institute for Scientific Information, 1958-. Weekly.

A weekly compilation of the tables of contents of over 1,100 life science periodicals arranged in eleven subject groups. This publication provides current access to the contents of these journals by subject (through a title keyword index) and by author. ISI publishes similar publications in other areas of science: *Current Contents: Agriculture, Biology and Environmental Sci-*

ences; *Current Contents: Physical, Chemical and Earth Sciences; Current Contents: Engineering, Technology and Applied Sciences;* and *Current Contents: Clinical Practice.*

General Science Index. New York: Wilson, 1978–. Quarterly, with annual cumulations.

Provides subject access to approximately 85 core science periodicals in the fields of biology, medicine, environmental science, mathematics, chemistry, geology, astronomy, meteorology, physics, and general science. A separate listing of book reviews arranged alphabetically by author is included.

McGraw-Hill Dictionary of Scientific and Technical Terms. 3d ed. New York: McGraw-Hill, 1984.

Designed to supplement general dictionaries by providing brief and up-to-date definitions of specialized scientific and technical words. Line drawings illustrate some of the definitions.

McGraw-Hill Encyclopedia of Science and Technology. 5th ed. 15 vols. New York: McGraw-Hill, 1982.

Covers all areas of science and technology, including medicine. With emphasis on recent advances, the articles include both broad surveys as well as discussions of more specific, technical concepts. Articles are arranged alphabetically by topic with cross-references to the text and bibliographies included for most articles. Vol. 15, the *Index*, includes both an analytical index (every concept, person, and term) and a topical index (grouping all articles under 75 general subject headings). The encyclopedia is updated by the *McGraw-Hill Yearbook of Science and Technology*.

Primack, Alice Lifler. *Finding Answers in Science and Technology.* New York: Van Nostrand Reinhold, 1984.

A guide to sources of scientific information for beginning researchers. Two initial chapters explain search strategy and give information on libraries and computer searching; the arrangement of the rest of the book is arranged by subject discipline. Each chapter discusses the reference works used in a specific discipline from general introductory works to specialized indexes.

Science Citation Index (SCI). Philadelphia: Institute for Scientific Information, 1955–. Bimonthly, with annual cumulations.

Indexes over 1,000 periodicals and monographic serials in science, technology, medicine, agriculture, and the behavioral sciences. *SCI* does not include book reviews except those published in *Science* and *Nature*. Following the same plan as ISI's other indexes, *SCI* has three separate indexes for accessing information. The *Citation Index* includes authors who have been cited and the citing references. The *Source Index* lists journal articles by authors' names and the *Permuterm Subject Index* allows the combination of any two terms that have appeared together in the title of an article. To search for a corporate author, use the corporate index section of the *Source Index*. *Science Citation Index* can be searched online through the SCISEARCH database (1970–).

Technical Book Review Index. Pittsburgh: JAAD Publishing, 1935–. Monthly, with annual cumulations.

Identifies book reviews in English-language journals in all areas of science, medicine, and technology. The reviews are arranged alphabetically by author within broad subject groups. An author index is located at the end of each annual cumulation. Short excerpts from the reviews are included.

III. Sources in Specific Academic Disciplines

A. Accounting.   See F., Business, Accounting, and Economics.

B. Agriculture.   See E., Biology and Agriculture.

C. *Anthropology and Archaeology*

Abstracts in Anthropology. Farmingdale, NY: Baywood Publishing, 1970-. Quarterly.
  Consists of abstracts in the fields of archaeology, cultural and physical anthropology, and linguistics; the abstracts are grouped in a classified arrangement, with author and subject indexes.

The Cambridge Encyclopedia of Archaeology. Ed. Andrew Sherratt. New York: Cambridge Univ. Press, 1980.
  Instead of being arranged alphabetically by subject, the chapters are arranged in three groups. Chapters 1–7 deal with the development of modern archaeology. Chapters 8–61 cover different archaeological periods and regions. The final chapters discuss methodology and provide a chronological atlas. A bibliography, organized by the chapter divisions, and a detailed subject index conclude the volume.

Encyclopedia of Anthropology. Ed. David E. Hunter and Phillip Whitten. New York: Harper and Row, 1976.
  Short, signed articles arranged alphabetically on concepts, methodology, and major anthropologists; some articles include bibliographies.

Frantz, Charles. *The Student Anthropologist's Handbook: A Guide to Research, Training and Careers.* Cambridge, MA: Schenkman, 1972.
  A guide to the history and nature of anthropology and to research in the field and in the library; the final chapter discusses the profession.

Heizer, Robert F., et al. *Archaeology: A Bibliographical Guide to the Basic Literature.* New York: Garland, 1980.
  A guide to the literature on the history and methodology of archaeology. The final chapter lists bibliographies, dictionaries, and atlases. The detailed table of contents provides access by subject and an author index is included.

JOURNALS

American Anthropologist. Washington, DC: American Anthropology Assn., 1888-. Quarterly.
  Scholarly articles and research reports covering all areas of anthropol-

ogy. A section of Commentaries provides a forum for discussion of previous research and there is an extensive bibliography of book and film reviews arranged by subject.

American Journal of Archaeology. Bryn Mawr, PA: Archaeological Institute of America, 1885–. Quarterly.

Publishes research articles on the archaeology and art history of the Mediterranean region with some articles on neighboring areas. Also includes notes, grant information, and book reviews.

Anthropological Quarterly. Washington, DC: Catholic Univ. of America Press, 1928–. Quarterly.

Contains 3–4 scholarly articles per issue as well as lengthy book reviews.

Archaeology. Boston, MA: Archaeological Institute of America, 1948–. Bimonthly.

Intended for lay readers as well as scholars, articles report results of archaeological research in all regions of the world. Book reviews and information on exhibitions, new books, tours, and excavations are included.

Current Anthropology: World Journal of the Sciences of Man. Chicago: Univ. of Chicago Press, 1960–. 5 issues per year.

Prints lengthy articles covering international research in anthropology as well as articles in English with abstracts in other languages. Each issue also includes a section of shorter articles, reports of research conclusions, a section of discussion and criticism, an annotated list of recent publications, and information on research grants.

D. Art

Artbibliographies Modern. Santa Barbara, CA: ABC-Clio, 1974–.

This online database provides access to the literature on modern art and design found in books, periodicals, dissertations, and exhibition catalogs.

Art Index. New York: Wilson, 1929–. Quarterly, with annual cumulations.

An index by author and subject to approximately 200 international periodicals, yearbooks, and museum bulletins on art and related subjects, such as aesthetics, design, film, and photography. *Art Index* can be searched by computer on the Wilsonline database.

Ehresmann, Donald. *Fine Arts: A Bibliographic Guide to Basic Reference Works, Histories and Handbooks.* 2d ed. Littleton, CO: Libraries Unlimited, 1979.

An annotated guide to the literature of painting, sculpture, and architecture. The first part covers bibliographies, library catalogs, indexes, and dictionaries as well as references on iconography. The second part provides references to histories and handbooks on historic periods in a chronological arrangement. An author/title/subject index is included for the whole volume.

Encyclopedia of World Art. 16 vols. New York: McGraw-Hill, 1968.

Presents lengthy articles arranged alphabetically on concepts, artists, periods, and geographic regions. Each article is signed and gives a bibliography of further references; Vol. 15 is an index to the rest of the volumes.

Oxford Companion to Art. Ed. Harold Osborne. Oxford: Clarendon Press, 1970.

Contains brief nontechnical articles, definitions, and biographical information on the visual arts and artists. The articles cover all time periods and geographic regions; entries for artists list their major works and place them in the appropriate school or movement. An extensive bibliography is given.

JOURNALS

Art Bulletin. New York: College Art Assn. of America, 1912–. Quarterly.

Prints scholarly articles on art and art history, often grouped by related subjects, with each issue covering several topics; research notes; and lengthy book reviews.

Art in America. New York: Art in America, 1913–. Monthly.

Consists of review articles and commentary on American art and artists covering all historical periods as well as contemporary art. It also publishes book reviews and reviews of exhibitions.

Art Journal. New York: College Art Assn. of America, 1941–. Quarterly.

Includes scholarly articles on American art and artists. Recent issues have focused on topics such as the poster and art and science. Book reviews and museum news.

Burlington Magazine. London: Burlington Magazine Publications, 1903–. Monthly.

Publishes 2–3 scholarly articles per issue on individual artists, works of art, schools, and periods of art history; shorter research articles; extended book reviews; and exhibition reviews.

E. Biology and Agriculture

Bibliography of Agriculture. Phoenix, AZ: Oryx Press, 1942–. Monthly, with annual cumulations.

Provides access by subject and author to the world literature on agriculture and related fields, such as food and nutrition. The *Bibliography* includes periodicals, books, government documents, and conference proceedings and is available online through the AGRICOLA database.

Bibliography of Bioethics. Detroit: Gale, 1975–. Annual.

A subject index to magazine and newspaper articles, audiovisual materials, books, and government documents in bioethics. The subject headings used are listed in the thesaurus in Vol. I; each volume also contains an author and title index.

Biological Abstracts. Philadelphia: BioSciences Information Service, 1926–. Semimonthly, with semiannual cumulations.

Covers international research literature in all the life sciences except clinical medicine. Five indexes provide access to the abstracts: author, subject, generic (organism name), biosystematic, and concept. The subject index lists keywords from the titles of the articles. The concept index indexes the articles by one of 500 major concepts. *Biological Abstracts* can be searched online through BIOSIS, a database that provides coverage from 1969 to the present.

Biological and Agricultural Index. New York: Wilson, 1916–. Monthly, with annual cumulations. Formerly *Agricultural Index*, 1916–August 1964.

Provides subject indexing to approximately 200 periodicals in the life sciences and agriculture. Book reviews arranged alphabetically by author are included in each annual volume. This index can be searched online on the Wilsonline database.

Encylcopedia of Bioethics. Ed. Warren T. Reich. 4 vols. New York: Macmillan/ Free Press, 1978.

Contains lengthy scholarly articles on moral and ethical aspects of the life sciences, such as euthanasia, drug use, ethical use of technology, and behavior control. Extensive cross-references and bibliographies are included.

Gray, Peter, ed. *The Encyclopedia of the Biological Sciences.* 2d ed. New York: Van Nostrand Reinhold, 1970.

Consists of signed articles on major biologists and concepts that cover all areas of the life sciences. The arrangement is alphabetical and most articles contain bibliographies.

Guide to Sources on Agricultural and Biological Research. Ed. J. Richard Blanchard and Lois Farrell. Berkeley: Univ. of California Press, 1980.

An annotated guide to research tools in agriculture and the life sciences. The introduction explains the communication process used in science. Following a chapter on general life sciences information sources, chapters describe reference works in the plant sciences, animal sciences, physical sciences, food sciences and nutrition, environmental sciences, and the relevant social sciences; the final chapter discusses computerized databases.

Smith, Roger C., et al. *Smith's Guide to the Literature of the Life Sciences.* 9th ed. Minneapolis: Burgess, 1980.

A guide to research in the life sciences. After an introductory section on research and libraries, the book is arranged by class of research tool, such as indexes, primary research journals, ready reference works, and taxonomic literature. Smith also includes chapters on research methods and scientific writing.

Tootill, Elizabeth. *The Facts on File Dictionary of Biology.* New York: Facts on File, 1981.

Gives brief definitions of biological terms, concepts, processes, and descriptions of organisms. Diagrams and charts illustrate such concepts as the carbon cycle or the geological time scale.

JOURNALS

American Journal of Botany. Columbus, OH: Botanical Society of America, 1914–. 10 issues per year.

Presents original research articles in all areas of botany, including economic botany and paleobotany.

American Zoologist. Thousand Oaks, CA: American Society of Zoologists, 1961–. Quarterly.

Includes original research and review articles as well as symposium papers on specific zoological topics; also includes information on the society and occasional book reviews.

Crop Science. Madison, WI: Crop Science Society of America, 1961–. Bimonthly.

Publishes articles on crop genetics, physiology, production, and ecology; also provides news about the society and notes. Sections report the registration of crop cultivars, germplasms, and parental lines. Each issue has an author index.

Ecology. See entry under M., Environmental and Earth Sciences.

Journal of Animal Science. Champaign, IL: American Society of Animal Science, 1942–. Monthly.

Prints research and review articles on animal science and livestock production arranged by subject: applied animal science, breeding and genetics, developmental biology, nutrition, pharmacology, and physiology and endocrinology. News, notes, and job placement information are included.

F. Business, Accounting, and Economics

Business Periodicals Index. New York: Wilson, 1958–. Monthly, with annual cumulations.

Provides subject access to over 200 English-language periodicals and trade journals on management, accounting, economics, labor relations, data management, advertising, and other business-related fields; individual companies can be searched by name. Since 1972, book review citations have been included in a separate listing. *BPI* can be searched online on the Wilsonline database.

Daniells, Lorna M. *Business Information Sources.* Berkeley: Univ. of California Press, 1976.

The first nine chapters cover information sources, such as libraries and general reference books including indexes, directories, statistical sources, and investment sources. The remainder of the book discusses management resources on accounting, information systems, banking, insurance, marketing, personnel management, and related fields. Entries are annotated and a subject, author, and title index is included.

The Encyclopedia of Management. Ed. Carl Heyel. New York: VanNostrand Reinhold, 1982.

Contains signed articles on management concepts and techniques, accounting, labor relations, and related subjects. Most articles give additional sources of information; an outline of core subject readings can be used to guide a reading program.

Wall Street Journal Index. New York: Dow Jones, 1958–. Monthly, with annual cumulations.

Indexes the final eastern edition of the *Wall Street Journal* and *Barron's* (since 1981). The index to *Barron's* (the green pages at the end of the volume) include entries by subject and corporate name; the rest of the index is divided into two sections: general and corporate. Entries give a citation and brief summary of the contents of the article.

COMPUTER DATABASES

A number of databases cover business-related topics. ABI/INFORM (DataCourier, 1971–) covers the literature on business management and PTS F&S INDEXES (Predicasts, 1972–) can be searched for information on specific industries and companies. Others are *Standard and Poor's Corporation Descriptions* (Standard and Poor's, current); *Disclosure* (Disclosure, Inc., current); and *D & B—Dun's Market Identifiers* (Dun's Marketing Services, current).

JOURNALS

American Economic Review. Nashville, TN: American Economic Assn., 1911–. Quarterly.
   Includes both lengthy articles and short papers on economic topics as well as commentary and notes.

Harvard Business Review. Boston: Harvard Univ., 1922. Bimonthly.
   Articles discuss issues, problems, and theories in the field of management; Ideas for Action has brief articles reporting developments and trends. Occasional book reviews are included.

Journal of Accountancy. New York: American Institute of Certified Public Accountants, 1905–. Monthly.
   Provides 3–4 major articles per issue discussing issues, developments, and practical applications in accounting; brief news reports; professional news; book reports; and brief notes on articles of interest in other periodicals.

Journal of Business. Chicago: Univ. of Chicago Press, 1928–. Quarterly.
   Contains empirical and theoretical studies of business and economics topics; lists of books received; and news on appointments, grants, retirements, and dissertations.

Journal of Economic Literature. Nashville, TN: American Economic Assn., 1963–. Quarterly.
   In addition to scholarly articles in economics, over half of each issue contains a bibliography of current books and periodical articles. There is a classified subject index and an author index to the periodicals as well as a listing of selected abstracts; annotations for the books are also arranged according to a classified system.

G. Chemistry and Physics

Applied Science and Technology Index. See entry under L., Engineering and Electronics.

Besancon, Robert M. *The Encyclopedia of Physics*. 3d ed. New York: Van Nostrand Reinhold, 1985.
   A one-volume encyclopedia with signed, scholarly articles. Articles on major topics are less technical for general readers, while specific articles are more advanced.

Chemical Abstracts. Columbus, OH: American Chemical Society, 1907–. Weekly, with semiannual cumulations.

Provides access to the world's chemical and chemical engineering research literature. Besides a general subject index that uses a controlled vocabulary, there are also a chemical substance index, a formula index, an index of ring systems, a patent index, and an author index; all of these indexes provide access to the weekly abstracts that are arranged by subject classifications. CA SEARCH is the online equivalent of *Chemical Abstracts*.

CRC Handbook of Chemistry and Physics. 65th ed. Boca Raton, FL: Chemical Rubber Co., 1984.

A compilation of formulas, tables, and charts presenting data of use to chemists, researchers in the physical sciences, and mathematicians. Information is grouped in six broad categories with a subject index included at the end of the volume.

Kirk-Othmer Encyclopedia of Chemical Technology. 3d ed. 24 vols., with supplement and index. New York: Wiley, 1978.

Consists of background articles on chemical technology and related issues, such as energy and toxicology. Approximately half of the articles discuss chemical substances and describe chemical properties and the manufacturing process; a separate index provides subject access to the entire set.

Malinowksy, H. Robert, and Jeanne M. Richardson. *Science and Engineering Literature*. See entry under L., Engineering and Electronics.

Physics Abstracts. Surrey, Eng.: Institution of Electrical Engineers, 1898–. Published twice monthly, with cumulative subject and author indexes published every six months.

Publishes abstracts for English-language journals, books, reports, dissertations, and conference proceedings on physics. Abstracts are grouped in ten major subject classifications with subdivisions; a detailed summary of the classification system as well as a subject index are given at the beginning of each issue. Each set of six months' cumulated index volumes contains the following indexes: subject, author, bibliography, conference, and corporate author.

JOURNALS

American Chemical Society Journal. Washington, DC: American Chemical Society, 1879–. Biweekly.

Publishes research articles; brief articles discussing, correcting, or amending earlier research; and book reviews.

American Journal of Physics. New York: American Institute of Physics, 1933–. Monthly. Formerly *American Physics Teacher*, 1933–1940.

Contains technical research and review articles on physical science, particularly the instructional and social aspects; short reports on new apparatus or new techniques; and book reviews.

Chemical Reviews. Washington, DC: American Chemical Society, 1924–. Bimonthly. Reports research in chemistry and allied fields.

Physics Today. New York: American Institute of Physics, 1948–. Monthly. Provides research and review articles; occasional articles on special topics such as neutron scattering; book reviews and reports on new products; and institute news.

H. Communications (Radio, Television, Speech, Journalism)

Blum, Eleanor. *Basic Books in the Mass Media*. 2d ed. Urbana, IL: Univ. of Illinois Press, 1980.

An annotated bibliography of reference books and other sources of information on mass communications, book publishing, broadcasting, film, magazines, and advertising. Titles are arranged by broad subject categories with access by subject and author-title indexes.

Communications Abstracts. Beverly Hills, CA: Sage Publications, 1978–. Quarterly.

Abstracts articles from more than 60 journals as well as research reports and books in the areas of communication theory, mass communications, journalism, broadcasting, advertising, speech, and radio and television. Subject and author indexes appear in each issue and cumulate in each year's final issue.

Longman's Dictionary of Mass Media and Communication. Ed. Tracy Daniel Connors. New York: Longman, 1982.

Gives brief definitions of terms and acronyms used in broadcasting, advertising, journalism, marketing, publishing, and other communications-related fields.

JOURNALS

Columbia Journalism Review. New York: Columbia Univ., 1962–. Bimonthly.

Publishes articles intended for lay readers and professionals analyzing issues in journalism. A section, Briefings, gives short reviews of symposia, books, and media productions. Book reviews are included.

Communication Quarterly. University Park, PA: Eastern Communication Assn., 1953–. Quarterly. Continues *Today's Speech*.

Contains scholarly articles on all aspects of communication, including public speaking, nonverbal communication, and interpersonal communication; lengthy book reviews.

Journal of Broadcasting. Washington, DC: Broadcast Education Assn., 1956–. Quarterly.

Publishes research articles on issues in broadcasting (a recent issue discussed the fairness doctrine and religious broadcasting); some shorter research reports and industry commentary; and lengthy book reviews.

Journal of Communication. Philadelphia: Annenberg Press, 1951–. Quarterly.

Covers communication theory and practice. In addition to research articles, each issue focuses on a specific review topic, such as the international flow of information. A section, Intercom, provides professional news, book reviews, and commentary.

Journalism Quarterly (JQ). Columbia, SC: Assn. for Education in Journalism and Mass Communications, 1924–. Quarterly.

Presents scholarly articles reporting research in mass communications and journalism; brief research reports; book reviews; and annotated bibliographies of articles on mass communications.

I. Computer Science

Computer Literature Index. Phoenix, AZ: Applied Computer Research, 1980–. Continues *Quarterly Bibliography of Computers and Data Processing*, 1968–1979. Quarterly.

A comprehensive index to the professional literature, covering periodicals, books, conference proceedings, trade journals, and technical reports. Entries are arranged by subject classifications and cover computer hardware, software, and applications; brief abstracts are given for most entries.

Data Base Directory, 1984–1985. White Plains, NY: Knowledge Industries, 1984.

A directory of machine-readable databases in all subjects. Types of databases included are bibliographic, full text, numeric, and referral. Arranged alphabetically, the entries describe subjects covered, time coverage, means of subject access, producer, vendor, and price information. A subject index is included.

Dictionary of Computing. Oxford: Oxford Univ. Press, 1983.

Briefly defines technical terms, concepts, and acronyms related to computer science.

Encyclopedia of Computer Science and Engineering. Ed. Anthony Ralston. 2d ed. New York: VanNostrand Reinhold, 1983.

Contains signed articles on computer hardware and software, information systems management, theory and methodology of computing, and computer applications. Articles are arranged alphabetically, with a general classification system described in the front of the volume to guide reading on general subject areas; some articles have bibliographies. Appendixes provide helpful information in the form of acronym lists, lists of journals and of universities offering Ph.D. programs in computer science as well as a glossary of major terms in five languages.

Myers, Darlene, ed. *Computer Science Resources: A Guide to Professional Literature.* White Plains, NY: Knowledge Industries, 1981.

A guide to reference books in all areas of computer science and data processing. In addition to a bibliography of important computer books published during the 1970s, the text covers journals, technical reports, indexes and abstracts, dictionaries, directories, newsletters, software resources, and programming languages. An appendix includes information on acronyms, trade fairs, and computer center libraries.

JOURNALS

Association for Computing Machinery Journal. New York: Assn. for Computing Machinery, 1954–. Quarterly.

Includes technical articles on programming languages, system analysis, computing theory, and artificial intelligence.

Byte: The Small Systems Journal. Peterborough, NH: McGraw-Hill, 1975–. Monthly.

Contains 12–18 feature articles per issue as well as reviews of books, software, hardware, and computer languages. Selected programs, computer news, and an international calendar of events are presented.

Communications of the ACM. New York: Assn. for Computing Machinery, 1958–. Monthly.

Presents research and review articles on the design and applications of computers. Occasional issues focus on topics such as computer science education and professional news.

Computers and People. Newtonville, MA: Berkeley Enterprises, 1951–. Bimonthly. Continues *Computers and Automation*, 1952–1974.

Publishes review articles on computers, computer applications, artificial intelligence, social implications of computers, and computer games.

Datamation. New York: Technical Publishing Co., 1957–. Twice monthly.

Contains news and review articles on developments in computer hardware and software. Descriptive reviews of hardware and software.

J. Drama

Breed, Paul F., and Florence M. Sniderman, eds. *Dramatic Criticism Index.* Detroit: Gale Research, 1972.

A bibliography of books and articles on modern American and foreign playwrights. Citations are arranged alphabetically by playwright and then by name of play; indexes of play titles and critics are included.

McGraw-Hill Encyclopedia of World Drama. 2d ed. 5 vols. New York: McGraw-Hill, 1984.

Provides articles on dramatists, directors, national, regional, and ethnic dramas as well as on aspects of performance, such as make-up and costume. Articles on major dramatists give biographical and critical information, bibliographies, and plot summaries for the plays. Vol. 5 includes a glossary with definitions of concepts and terms, a play title list giving authors' names, and an author/title/subject index.

The New York Times Theater Reviews. 10 vols. New York: New York Times, 1971.

A chronological reproduction of theater reviews appearing in the *New York Times* from 1920 to 1970. Vols. IX and X have indexes by title, by production company, and by personal name; Vol. IX also has an appendix listing theater awards and prizes and summaries of productions and runs by season.

Whalon, Marion K. *Performing Arts Research: A Guide to Information Sources.* Detroit: Gale Research, 1976.

Annotated bibliography of sources on theater, dance, musical theater, and motion pictures. The reference sources, arranged by type, include guides, dictionaries and handbooks, directories, play indexes, review sources, bibliographies and indexes, and picture and audiovisual sources. An author/title/subject index is provided.

JOURNALS

Drama: The Quarterly Theatre Review. London: British Theatre Assn., 1919–. Quarterly.

Prints reviews of British drama; interviews with directors and actors; and book reviews.

The Drama Review. Cambridge, MA: MIT Press, 1955–. Continues the *Tulane Drama Review.* Quarterly.

Covers the international avant-garde in performance art and theater. Each issue contains 6–10 articles focusing on a single topic, for example, French theater. *TDR* also includes short descriptive reports on contemporary works, short plays, and book reviews. Well-illustrated with photos.

Theatre Journal (TJ). Washington, DC: University and College Theatre Assn., 1949–. Quarterly. Continues *Educational Theatre Journal.*

Contains 5–6 scholarly articles per issue; theater review and book review sections; and a list of books received arranged by subject.

Theatre Research International. Oxford: Oxford Univ. Press, 1958–. 3 issues per year. Continues *Theatre Research.*

Provides scholarly historical and critical articles on drama along with lengthy book reviews.

K. Education

Berry, Dorothea M. *A Bibliographic Guide to Educational Research.* 2d ed. Metuchen, NJ: Scarecrow Press, 1980.

A guide to research sources in education. The book is an annotated bibliography arranged by type of information source, such as bibliographies, indexes, research studies, government documents, nonprint materials, and reference books. These categories are subdivided by area of education, such as special education, curriculum, international education, and educational technology. The final chapter focuses on guides to research; the *Guide* also includes an author/editor index, a title index, and a subject index.

Education Index. New York: Wilson, 1929–. 10 times a year, with annual cumulations.

A subject and author index to English-language periodicals, monographs, and yearbooks in educational administration; teaching from preschool through adult; and curriculum and teaching methods in all subject fields. From 1961–1969, author indexing and book reviews were omitted; since 1969, book reviews have been included. This index can be searched online on the Wilsonline database.

The Encyclopedia of Education. Ed. Lee C. Deighton. 10 vols. New York: Macmillan, 1971.

Contains 1,000 articles on educational history, philosophy, theory, and practice. Concerned mainly with education in America. Entries are signed and have bibliographies. Volume 10 has a directory of contributors, a guide to articles (grouped by subject area and giving cross-references), and a subject index.

ERIC (Educational Resources Information Center). *Current Index to Journals in Education (CIJE).* Phoenix, AZ: Oryx Press, 1969–. Monthly, with semiannual cumulations.

A subject index to almost 800 educational journals; access is through a controlled vocabulary, the *Thesaurus of ERIC Descriptors*. Each citation includes a list of assigned descriptors and an abstract. An author index and a journal contents index are also included. May be searched online through the ERIC database (1966–).

ERIC (Educational Resources Information Center). *Resources in Education (RIE)*. Phoenix, AZ: Oryx Press, 1969–. Monthly, with semiannual cumulations.

A companion to *CIJE, Resources in Education* provides indexing for educational research reports, books, government publications, conference papers, and unpublished manuscripts. Documents are available on microfiche or in hard copy through the ERIC Document Reproduction Service. An abstract is given for each document. May be searched online through the ERIC database (1966–).

Good, Carter V., ed. *Dictionary of Education*. 3d ed. New York: McGraw-Hill, 1973.

Gives brief definitions for specialized terms and concepts in all areas of education; personal and institution names are not included.

JOURNALS

American Educational Research Journal. Washington, DC: American Educational Research Assn., 1964–. Quarterly.

Contains empirical research articles on issues in education.

American Journal of Education. Chicago: Univ. of Chicago Press, 1893–. Quarterly. Continues *School Review*, 1893–1979.

Presents research and review articles and book reviews. Some issues focus on a specific topic such as the development of literacy in American schools.

Harvard Educational Review. Cambridge, MA: Harvard Univ., 1931–. Quarterly. Continues *Harvard Teachers Record*.

Publishes scholarly articles reporting research and opinion on educational topics as well as both extended and brief book reviews. Special issues treat topics such as education and the threat of nuclear war.

Journal of Educational Psychology. Washington, DC: American Psychological Assn., 1910–. Bimonthly.

Presents original research on psychological aspects of learning.

L. Engineering and Electronics

Applied Science and Technology Index. New York: Wilson, 1958–. Continues *Industrial Arts Index*. Quarterly, with annual cumulations.

Subject index to over 300 English-language journals in engineering, earth sciences, food technology, textile production, energy, computer science, petroleum, metallurgy, physics, electronics, and other related fields; book reviews are listed by author in a separate section. *ASTI* can be searched online on the Wilsonline database.

Engineering Index. New York: Engineering Information, 1884–. Monthly, with annual cumulations.

Provides abstracts for the world's literature in engineering sciences taken from journals, technical reports, books, and conference proceedings; the abstracts are arranged by subject with additional access through an author index and an author affiliation index. *Engineering Index* can be searched online through the COMPENDEX databases.

IEEE Standard Dictionary of Electrical and Electronics Terms. New York: Institute of Electrical and Electronics Engineers, 1984.

Each entry in this alphabetical list has a number that keys it to a source in the back of the book. There is also a separate list of abbreviations, symbols, code names, project names, and acronyms.

McGraw-Hill Dictionary of Engineering. Ed. Sybil P. Parker. New York: McGraw-Hill, 1984.

Presents the specialized vocabularies of thirteen different engineering disciplines, including civil, mechanical, aerospace, and systems engineering. Does not include chemical, electrical, or food engineering terms.

Malinowsky, H. Robert, and Jeanne M. Richardson. *Science and Engineering Literature.* 3d ed. Littleton, CO: Libraries Unlimited, 1980.

Contains introductory chapters on scientific literature and the methods of locating this literature, followed by a section on multidisciplinary reference tools and sections on each scientific discipline. The physical sciences covered are mathematics, astronomy, physics, chemistry, geoscience, energy, and engineering; each of these chapters is divided by type of reference tool. A bibliography on science librarianship and an author/title/subject index are also provided.

JOURNALS

Electronics Week. New York: McGraw-Hill, 1930–. Weekly. Continues *Electronics.*

Contains articles on new developments in technology and news of the electronics industry; one section covers previews of new products.

IEEE Spectrum. New York: Institute of Electrical and Electronics Engineers, 1964–. Monthly.

Prints technical articles on new technological developments and their applications; articles on systems and analysis of specific problems; and book reviews.

Mechanical Engineering. New York: American Society of Mechanical Engineers, 1906–. Monthly.

Reviews developments in mechanical engineering; contains sections on computer applications, information on new products, society news, and book reviews.

M. Environmental and Earth Sciences

Ecology Abstracts. Bethesda, MD: Cambridge Scientific Abstracts, 1975–. Monthly.

Abstracts of articles from approximately 5,000 journals on topics related to ecology. Abstracts are grouped into 56 subject categories with more specific access through a subject index that can be searched through the Life Sciences Collection database (Cambridge Scientific Abstracts, 1978–).

Environmental Periodicals Bibliography. Santa Barbara, CA: Environmental Studies Institute, 1972–. 6 issues per year, with annual cumulative index.

Contains the tables of contents of journals dealing with environmental topics; journals are grouped by general subject with access to specific subjects through a keyword index. The *Bibliography* can be searched as a computer database through DIALOG (Environmental Studies Institute, 1973–).

Geological Society of America. *Bibliography and Index of Geology.* Alexandria, VA: American Geological Institute, 1933–. Monthly, with annual cumulations.

Indexes the world's literature (books, periodicals, reports, maps, and North American theses and dissertations) on geology. Each month the Fields of Interest section gives bibliographic citations for all documents covered, grouping the citations by subject category and then by document type; each issue also contains subject and author indexes. In the annual cumulation, citations in the Fields of Interest section are in alphabetical order.

Grzimek's Encyclopedia of Ecology. Ed. Bernhard Grzimek. New York: Van Nostrand Reinhold, 1976.

Publishes background articles on ecology grouped in two categories: environment of animals and environment of human beings. A detailed table of contents and an index identify specific topics.

McGraw-Hill Dictionary of the Geological Sciences. Ed. Daniel N. Lapedes. New York: McGraw-Hill, 1978.

Contains signed background articles on geology, the earth sciences, and related subjects in oceanography and meteorology. Except for brief entries, most articles have bibliographies.

McGraw-Hill Encyclopedia of Environmental Science. 2d ed. New York: McGraw-Hill, 1980.

Consists of signed scholarly articles of some length on subjects related to the environment, including meteorology, public health, agriculture, and geology; articles include bibliographies. Besides the general articles arranged alphabetically, major essays in the beginning of the volume discuss topics such as urban planning and environmental analysis.

Smith's Guide to the Literature of the Life Sciences. See entry under E., Biology and Agriculture.

Ward, Dederick C., Marjorie W. Wheeler, and Robert A. Bier. *Geologic Reference Sources.* 2d ed. Metuchen, NJ: Scarecrow, 1981.

Annotated entries are divided into general reference sources (indexes, directories, encyclopedias); a subject section that describes sources for earth science, meteorology, oceanography, geology, mineralogy, soil science, petrology, paleontology, environmental geology, and other related subjects; and a regional section. There are subject and geographic indexes.

JOURNALS

Earth Science Reviews. Amsterdam, Netherlands, 1966–. Quarterly.

Articles in English from many countries on current developments and research. Each issue contains two long articles with extensive bibliographies. An especially valuable news supplement to each issue, *Atlas*, lists the contents of selected other geological journals and contains 8–10 book reviews.

Ecology. Tempe, AZ: Ecological Society of America, 1920–. Bimonthly.

Concerned with the study of organisms in relation to the environment, *Ecology* contains research articles (about 25 per issue), a notes and comments section and lengthy book reviews. *Ecological Monographs* (same publisher) is a quarterly journal for longer articles (more than 20 pages).

Environment. Washington, DC: Helen Dwight Reid Educational Foundation and the Scientists' Institute for Public Information, 1958. 10 issues per year.

Contains technical articles (about three per issue) on environmental problems and solutions as well as abstracts for these articles in the table of contents. Also included are short book reviews and an overview on current environmental topics.

Environmental Geology. New York: Springer-Verlag, 1975–. Bimonthly.

Prints international research articles on natural and manmade pollution in the geological environment; also includes environmental impact studies.

Journal of Geology. Chicago, IL: Univ. of Chicago Press, 1893–. Bimonthly.

Contains 4–6 research articles, with abstracts, on all aspects of theoretical and applied geology; a section titled Geological Notes; and book reviews of varying lengths. Occasional issues are devoted to particular subjects.

N. Film

Film Literature Index. Albany, NY: Film and Television Documentation Center, 1973–. Quarterly, with annual cumulations.

A subject and author index to the world's periodical literature on film covering over 200 magazines and newspapers. Citations indicate whether the articles include screen credits, biographical information, interviews, or illustrations.

New York Times Film Reviews. New York: Times Books, 1970–.

A collection of film reviews from the *New York Times* arranged chronologically and including films made from 1913 to 1982. Entries are reproductions of the actual signed reviews and include the credits and photographs (if any accompanied the original review); indexes by title, personal name, and corporate name are included.

The Oxford Companion to Film. Ed. Liz-Anne Bawden. New York: Oxford Univ. Press, 1976.

Publishes short unsigned articles on all aspects of cinema, including film production, actors, directors, and movies. Lists of films by specific actors or directors are not necessarily comprehensive; cross-references to related articles are included.

Whalon, Marion K. *Performing Arts Research: A Guide to Information Sources*. See entry under J., Drama.

JOURNALS

Film Comment. New York: Film Society of Lincoln Center, 1962–. Bimonthly.
Each issue has 3–4 extended articles and several brief articles on films, directors, and actors.

Film Quarterly. Berkeley: Univ. of California Press, 1945–. Quarterly.
Contains articles for nonspecialists and specialists on film, film production, and specific movies; articles and interviews with directors and actors, book reviews and film reviews on foreign and domestic films, documentaries, and experimental films.

Sight and Sound: The International Film Quarterly. London: British Film Institute, 1932–. Quarterly.
Presents articles about film and film production worldwide with emphasis on Great Britain; has film and book reviews.

O. Folklore

Abstracts of Folklore Studies. Austin, TX: American Folklore Society, 1963–1975. Quarterly.
Contains abstracts from approximately 40 international folklore periodicals arranged alphabetically by the name of the periodical; no index.

Brunvand, Jan Harold. *Folklore: A Study and Research Guide*. New York: St. Martin's, 1976.
A research guide consisting of essays that place the study of folklore in context, discuss reference tools for folklore study, and explain the methodology for writing research papers; glossary and author index are included.

Jobes, Gertrude. *Dictionary of Mythology, Folklore, and Symbols*. 3 vols. New York: Scarecrow, 1961.
Vols. 1 and 2 contain alphabetically arranged explanations of mythological and folklore characters and symbols. Vol. 3 is an index to the first two volumes with entries grouped in two tables: deities, heroes, and personalities, and mythological affiliations.

Mythology of All Races. Ed. Louis H. Gray. 13 vols. New York: Cooper Square, 1964.
Publishes scholarly descriptions of the mythology of the world. Each volume covers one area's mythology, including Roman and Greek, Teutonic, Celtic and Slavic, Finno-Ugric and Siberian, Semitic, Indian and Persian, Armenian and African, Chinese and Japanese, Malayo-Polynesian and Australian, Egyptian, and North and South American Indian. Each volume has its own bibliography, and Vol. 13 is an index to the whole set.

JOURNALS

Folklore. London: Folklore Society, 1878–. Semiannual. Continues *Folklore Record* and *Folklore Journal*.
Publishes scholarly articles on folk culture, folk music, and the oral tradition of literature; society news and book reviews.

Journal of American Culture. Bowling Green, OH: Bowling Green State Univ., 1978–. Quarterly.

Prints scholarly articles on American culture with an emphasis on popular culture; special issues are devoted to specific topics, such as Chicano culture or television and society.

Journal of American Folklore. Washington, DC: American Folklore Society, 1888–. Quarterly.

Publishes 3–4 articles per issue on folk culture, folklore, and folk music; Notes section includes shorter discussion and review articles; lengthy book, record, and film reviews are included.

Southern Folklore Quarterly. Gainesville, FL: Univ. of Florida, 1937–. Quarterly.

Presents scholarly historical and comparative studies of American and international folk cultures; book reviews are included.

P. Geography

Geo Abstracts, A–G. Norwich, Eng.: Geo Abstracts Ltd., 1972–. Bimonthly.

The major abstracting source in geography, *Geo Abstracts* consists of seven parts covering landforms, climatology and hydrology, economic geography, social and historical geography, sedimentology, regional and community planning, and remote sensing and cartography. Each part is published separately and has a classified arrangement described in a table of contents; the final issue each year has author and regional indexes.

Lock, C. B. Muriel. *Geography and Cartography: A Reference Handbook*. 3d ed. London: Clive Bingley, 1976.

Presents annotated sources of information in geography and cartography; includes biographical information and information on societies and institutions but does not define terms and concepts.

Longman's Dictionary of Geography. Ed. Laurence Dudley Stamp. London: Longman, 1970.

Consists of short entries arranged alphabetically defining geographic terms, describing geographic locations, and giving biographical information on explorers. Also includes various lists; for example, a ranking of countries by size and chronologies of explorers and earthquakes. An appendix gives a selective bibliography.

The New York Times Atlas of the World. Rev. ed. New York: Times Books in collaboration with the Times of London, 1980.

In addition to maps of the world, this atlas also includes an introduction on the origin and geology of the earth, its resources, and its physical nature. Human settlement and population patterns, trade, and industry are also considered.

JOURNALS

Association of American Geographers Annals. Washington, DC: Assn. of American Geographers, 1911–. Quarterly.

Publishes scholarly research reports in all aspects of geography; includes papers from the association's meetings, commentary, and book reviews.

Geographical Review. New York: American Geographical Society, 1916–. Quarterly.

Contains scholarly research and review articles, brief reports in Geographical Record, and book reviews.

Journal of Historical Geography. London: Academic Press, 1975–. Quarterly.

Prints research and review articles on historical geography and related subjects, such as agriculture, archaeology, and anthropology; includes an extensive book review section.

Q. History

America: History and Life. Santa Barbara, CA: ABC-Clio, 1955–.

A bibliography with abstracts of the historical literature of North America (Canada and the U.S.); abstracts are arranged chronologically within geographic groups. Also includes an index to book reviews (Part B), a section on American history bibliography containing books and dissertations (Part C), and an annual subject and author index (Part D). This bibliography can be searched online for literature published since 1964.

American Historical Association. *Guide to Historical Literature*. New York: Macmillan, 1963.

Assists in historical research for all areas of the world. Following section on general works and references, the book is divided geographically and then chronologically. Within each section, sources are arranged by form: bibliographies, reference works, geographies, anthropological and demographic studies, histories, biographies, government publications, and periodicals. Evaluative annotations are particularly helpful.

Brooks, Philip C. *Research in Archives: The Use of Unpublished Primary Sources*. Chicago: Univ. of Chicago Press, 1969.

Because much historical research involves collections of unpublished materials, this work is helpful in explaining research methods and ways of identifying archival collections.

C.R.I.S.: The Combined Retrospective Index Set to Journals in History, 1838–1974. 11 vols. Washington, DC: Carrollton Press, 1977.

A comprehensive keyword index for 243 periodicals covering all historical periods and geographic areas. The first nine volumes are subject indexes grouped geographically (with four volumes for world history and five for American history); Vols. 10 and 11 are author indexes.

Dictionary of American History. Rev. ed. 7 vols. New York: Scribner's, 1976.

A collection of articles arranged alphabetically on all aspects of American history and life; articles are signed and each has at least one bibliographical reference.

Freidel, Frank, ed. *Harvard Guide to American History*. Cambridge, MA: Belknap/Harvard Univ. Press, 1974.

Vol. 1 contains background articles and bibliographies on research methods and materials, biographies, comprehensive and regional histories, and histories of special subjects, such as economics, immigration, education. The bibliographies in Vol. 2 are arranged chronologically; Vol. 2 also contains a subject index and an index of names to both volumes.

Historical Abstracts. Santa Barbara, CA: ABC-Clio, 1955–.

A bibliography with abstracts of the research literature on world history except the history of the U.S. and Canada. *Historical Abstracts* consists of two parts: *Modern History Abstracts, 1450–1914* and *Twentieth Century Abstracts, 1914–*; subject and author indexes are included. This bibliography can be searched online for literature published since 1973.

Langer, William L., ed. *The New Illustrated Encyclopedia of World History*. 2 vols. New York: Abrams, 1975.

A comprehensive encyclopedia covering history from prehistory to space exploration. Arranged chronologically, the articles are supplemented by approximately 2,000 illustrations, maps, and chronological tables; Vol. 2 has an index to both volumes.

The New Cambridge Modern History. Ed. G. R. Potter. 14 vols. Cambridge, Eng.: Cambridge Univ. Press, 1957.

The classic scholarly history of the Western world from the Renaissance through World War II. Each volume has its own subject index; Vol. XIV is a historical atlas. The *Cambridge Ancient History* and the *Cambridge Medieval History* cover prehistoric time through the 15th century.

JOURNALS

American Historical Review. Washington: American Historical Assn., 1895–. 5 issues a year.

Contains 4–5 scholarly articles per issue; also research notes, an extensive book review section subdivided by geographic region and historic period, and a section listing documents and bibliographies.

English Historical Review. Harlow, Eng.: Longman, 1886–. Quarterly.

Publishes scholarly articles covering all fields of history; issues also include research notes, book reviews, and an extensive section of short notices.

Journal of American History. Bloomington, IN: Organization of American Historians, 1914–. Quarterly. Continues *Mississippi Valley Historical Review*.

Prints research articles on American history; also extensive book reviews, a bibliography of articles and dissertations and lists of bibliographies and archive acquisitions.

Journal of Modern History. Chicago: Univ. of Chicago Press, 1929–. Quarterly.

Publishes research and review articles on modern European history since the Renaissance and lengthy book reviews. Special issues focus on topics such as political practice in the French Revolution.

R. Literature

Abstracts of English Studies. Calgary, Alberta, Can.: Univ. of Calgary Press, 1958–. Quarterly.

Abstracts of articles from over 700 journals concerned with English language, English and American literature, and world literature published in English; these abstracts are grouped in four broad classes and are then arranged either chronologically or geographically. Each issue has its own index; the fourth issue of the year has an annual cumulative index.

American Women Writers: A Critical Reference Guide from Colonial Times to the Present. Ed. Lina Mainiero. 4 vols. New York: Ungar, 1979–82.

Biographical data, critical assessments, and bibliographical lists for 1,000 women writers. Vol. 4 contains an index to names and subjects.

Black American Writers: Bibliographical Essays. Ed. M. Thomas Inge, Maurice Duke, and Jackson R. Bryer. 2 vols. New York: St. Martin's, 1978.

A good preliminary source for the study of black writers, these volumes evaluate biographical and critical writings about selected black authors and offer suggestions for further study. Essays are organized by topic, such as slave narratives and Harlem Renaissance, as well as by individual author.

Contemporary Authors. Detroit: Gale, 1972–.

Records biographic information on living international authors writing in all subject areas. Each entry includes biographic information, a list of works published, and works in progress. Because entries are often updated and revised, the most recent cumulative index should be checked to find complete listings.

Encyclopedia of World Literature in the 20th Century. Rev. ed. 4 vols. New York: Ungar, 1981–1985.

Contains short articles (1–2 pages) on authors who have produced their major works in the 20th century, and on national literatures, genres, and movements. Articles on authors give brief biographical information, discuss and list their major works, and supply further references.

Hart, James D. *The Oxford Companion to American Literature.* 5th ed. New York: Oxford Univ. Press, 1983.

A one-volume encyclopedia that serves as a companion to American literature and American studies. Brief articles on American authors (with biographical information and bibliographies), literary works, and allusions as well as persons and events important in social and cultural history. Articles on individual literary works give summaries of the works and include verse form for poems. A chronological index lists a parallel chronology of American literary history and social history.

Harvey Paul. *Oxford Companion to Classical Literature.* Oxford: Clarendon Press, 1940.

Provides articles and descriptions of classical Greek and Roman authors, works of literature, mythology, genres, and social and historical events relevant to the literature.

Humanities Index. See entry under II. A., Humanities.

Literary History of the United States. Ed. Robert E. Spiller et al. 4th ed. 2 vols. New York: Macmillan, 1974.

Vol. 1 contains scholarly essays tracing the social and cultural history of American literature from colonial times through the 1960s; at the end of the volume is a bibliography for further reading. Vol. 2 is a guide to literary resources and bibliographies on American literature and culture; these bibliographies include listings on literary periods (arranged by genre), American cultural background, language, folklore, popular culture, literary movements and influences, and individual authors. Bibliographies on individual authors provide evaluative comments on editions of their works and on biography and criticism of the authors.

The MLA International Bibliography of Books and Articles on the Modern Languages and Literature. New York: Modern Language Assn., 1921–. Annual.

A classified list of international periodical articles, festschriften, books, and dissertations on modern languages, literature, and folklore. Citations are grouped by national literature and then chronologically. To find references for an author, first locate the appropriate national literature and time period and then follow the alphabetical sequence of authors' names. Since 1981, the *MLA Bibliography* has been published in two volumes, one volume in the traditional format and the other as a subject index; the subject index can be used to search by names, genres, themes, approaches, influences, language, and other subjects. The *MLA Bibliography* can be searched online through DIALOG for material published since 1970.

New Cambridge Bibliography of English Literature. Ed. George Watson. 5 vols. Cambridge, Eng.: Cambridge Univ. Press, 1974.

A comprehensive bibliography of English literature from A.D. 600 through 1950. Arranged chronologically, each section lists general works and genre studies and then individual authors. For each author, bibliographies and information on special collections or location of manuscripts are given; collections are listed chronologically. Also included is a comprehensive international bibliography of criticism. Besides the index in each volume, Vol. 5 contains an index to the whole set.

The Oxford Companion to English Literature. Ed. Margaret Drabble. 5th ed. Oxford: Clarendon Press, 1985.

A one-volume encyclopedia with brief articles on English authors (some American authors are included), literary works, literary societies, characters, and allusions. Facts about each author's life and a list of major works with dates are given.

Oxford English Dictionary. Ed. James A. H. Murray. 12 vols., with supplements. Oxford: Clarendon Press, 1933.

Presents the definition, history, and usage of English-language words. Besides tracing the changes and developments in meaning, the dictionary gives examples to illustrate these changes. Supplements give additional examples and update changes in meaning.

Patterson, Margaret. *Literary Research Guide.* 2d ed. New York: Modern Language Assn., 1983.

Annotated bibliography of reference books in the field of literature. The *Guide* first discusses general research tools, such as national and annual bibliographies, indexes and abstracts, sources on specific genres, and periodicals. The main section is divided by national literature and arranged chronologically with general sources discussed first; most major national literatures and classical literature are included. A final section covers literature-related subjects, such as autobiographies, book collecting, film, folklore, linguistics, textual criticism, and women's studies. Glossary of bibliography terms; a particularly helpful feature is the Short-Title Table of Contents.

American Literature: A Journal of Literary History, Criticism, and Bibliography. Durham, NC: Duke Univ. Press, 1929–. Quarterly.

Publishes scholarly historical and critical articles on American authors; includes 20–25 lengthy books reviews per issue with an additional section (Brief Mention) of short book reviews. Each issue also contains a selected annotated bibliography on American literature.

ELH (English Literary History). Baltimore: Johns Hopkins Univ. Press, 1931–. Quarterly.

Provides lengthy critical articles on British literature, about 10 per issue.

Modern Fiction Studies. West Lafayette, IN: Purdue Univ., 1955–. Quarterly.

Publishes literary criticism and bibliographic articles on modern (post–1880) fiction together with lengthy book reviews; two issues each year focus on one writer or on a special topic, such as modern war fiction.

Modern Poetry Studies. Buffalo, NY: Media Study/Buffalo, 1970–. 3 issues per year.

Prints critical studies of modern poets and poetry and original poetry.

PMLA (Publication of the Modern Language Association). New York: Modern Language Assn. of America, 1884–. 6 issues per year.

Contains scholarly articles on themes, critical approaches, and other aspects of modern languages and literature along with association news and commentary.

S. Medicine and Nursing

Cumulative Index to Nursing and Allied Health Literature. Glendale, CA: Glendale Adventist Medical Center, 1977–. Continues *Cumulative Index to Nursing Literature*, 1956–1976. Bimonthly, with annual cumulations.

Indexes approximately 300 English-language journals in nursing, health, and health-care-related fields; pamphlets, audiovisual materials, and book reviews are included. A list of subject headings (organized in a hierarchical structure) is used to assign terms for a subject index. This index can be searched through the Nursing and Allied Health database (1983–).

Harrison's Principles of Internal Medicine. Ed. Robert G. Petersdorf et al. 10th ed. 2 vols. New York: McGraw-Hill, 1983.

This textbook on internal medicine is used in most libraries as a major source of background information on health concerns. After an introductory section on clinical medicine, two volumes are divided into sections on disease: the clinical manifestations, biological aspects, biological and environmental causes, and organ systems. The section on each disorder includes a definition and background information, description of symptoms, complications, diagnosis and treatment, and additional references. An index at the end of each volume provides access by specific disease or disorder.

Index Medicus. Bethesda, MD: National Library of Medicine, 1960–. Monthly, with annual cumulations. Continues *Quarterly Cumulative Index Medicus*, 1928–1959, and *Index Medicus*, 1879–1927.

Indexes the world periodical literature in medicine; subject access is through headings assigned from *Medical Subject Headings* (MeSH), which arranges terms from general concepts to specific terms. There is also an Author section (all authors are cross-referenced) and a Medical Reviews section. *Index Medicus* can be searched online through the MEDLINE database.

Roper, Fred W., and Jo Anne Boorkman. *Introduction to Reference Sources in the Health Sciences*. Chicago: Medical Library Assn., 1980.

A guide to research in the health sciences divided into two main sections: bibliographic sources and information sources. Bibliographic sources discuss reference books used to locate books, periodical articles, government documents, conference proceedings, and reviews. Information sources describe sources for medical terminology, handbooks, statistics, biographical and historical information, audiovisual resources, and drug information. Descriptive annotations are given for each resource in each category.

JOURNALS

American Journal of Human Genetics. Chicago: American Society for Human Genetics, 1949–. Bimonthly.

Publishes research and review articles on heredity and genetic applications in sociology, anthropology, and medicine; book reviews and society news.

American Journal of Nursing. New York: American Journal of Nursing, 1900–. Monthly.

Publishes articles reporting developments in techniques and treatment in clinical medicine; brief clinical news reports and professional news.

JAMA: The Journal of the American Medical Association. Chicago: American Medical Assn., 1848–. Weekly.

Contains brief reports on medical news, original research articles and case studies in clinical medicine and related areas, association news, and book reviews.

Journal of Nutrition. Rockville, MD: American Institute of Nutrition, 1928–. Monthly.

Contains scholarly articles reporting original research on the physiology of nutrition.

New England Journal of Medicine. Boston: Massachusetts Medical Society, 1812–. Weekly.

Prints articles reporting original research and case studies; editorials, commentary, correspondence, and occasional book reviews.

T. Music

Duckles, Vincent. *Music Reference and Research Materials: An Annotated Bibliography*. 3d ed. New York: Free Press/Macmillan, 1974.

An annotated guide to references for music and musicology divided by type of reference book, such as dictionaries, histories, bibliographies, and discographies; indexes provide access by subject, title, and author/editor/reviewer.

The Music Index. Detroit, MI: Information Coordinators, 1949–. Monthly, with annual cumulations.

An index by subject, author, and title of work to periodicals on music and dance. Book reviews are listed alphabetically by author; reviews of performers and music are listed under the performer's or composer's name, and record reviews are listed under Recordings.

The New Grove Dictionary of Music and Musicians. Ed. Stanley Sadie. 20 vols. London: Macmillan, 1980.

A scholarly encyclopedia on all aspects of music. Entries cover terminology, performers, theory, instruments, composers, history, music of all regions of the world, and folk music; many articles include bibliographies and lists of works; a glossary of terms used in non-Western music is included in Vol. 20.

JOURNALS

Acta Musicologica. Basel: International Musicological Society, 1928–. 2 issues per year.

Publishes articles by international scholars on musicology, the history of music.

American Musicological Society Journal. Philadelphia: American Musicological Society, 1948–. 3 issues per year.

Prints scholarly articles on musicology; issues contain lengthy book reviews and lists of publications received.

Journal of Music Theory. New Haven, CT: Yale School of Music, 1957–. 2 issues per year.

Contains scholarly articles on music theory, lengthy book reviews and bibliographies of books and articles on music theory.

U. Philosophy and Religion

Adams, Charles J. *A Reader's Guide to the Great Religions.* 2d ed. New York: Macmillan/Free Press, 1977.

Contains bibliographic essays describing resources for research on primitive religions; religions of the ancient world, Mexico, and China; Hinduism; Buddhism; Sikhism; Jainism; religions of Japan; early, classical, medieval, and modern Judaism; Christianity; and Islam. Author and subject indexes are given.

Brandon, S. G. F., ed. *A Dictionary of Comparative Religion.* New York: Scribner's, 1970.

Provides brief descriptive entries on all aspects of world religions, including deities, religious leaders, concepts, sects, geographic locations, rites, and rituals. Many articles have bibliographies.

DeGeorge, Richard T. *The Philosopher's Guide to Sources, Research Tools, Professional Life, and Related Fields.* Lawrence: Regents Press of Kansas, 1980.

An annotated guide to the literature of philosophy that includes a guide to research tools and a bibliography of sources on the history of philosophy and the various branches, schools, and national philosophies. The bibliography also includes a section on philosophical periodicals and professional issues, such as publishing, associations, and research centers; an index by author, title, and subject is provided.

Encyclopedia Judaica. 16 vols. New York: Macmillan, 1972.

Contains signed scholarly articles as well as brief descriptions of topics in all areas of Jewish history, religion, and culture; most articles have short bibliographies. Vol. I indexes the entire set.

The Encyclopedia of Philosophy. Ed. Paul Edwards. 8 vols. New York: Macmillan, 1967.

Publishes scholarly articles on Eastern and Western philosophy and on philosophers, concepts, and theories from ancient to modern times; bibliographies are given at the end of each article. Vol. 8 includes a subject index.

Encyclopedia of Religion and Ethics. Ed. James Hastings. 13 vols. New York: Scribner's, 1908–1926.

The classic, authoritative encyclopedia covering world religions and ethical systems as well as related subjects, such as psychology, anthropology, and folklore; articles are signed and most have extensive bibliographies. Vol. 13 is a detailed subject index.

Nelson's Complete Concordance to the Revised Standard Version Bible. Ed. John Ellison. 2d ed. New York: Thomas Nelson, 1984.

Arranged alphabetically, this reference gives the context and location of nearly every word in the RSV Bible. Nelson also publishes *Young's Analytical Concordance to the King James Version of the Bible* (rev. ed., 1982), which gives the context, location, and Hebrew and Greek words from which the English was translated. *Young's* contains a Universal Subject Guide to the Bible.

The Philosopher's Index. Bowling Green, OH: Philosophy Documentation Center, 1967–. Quarterly, with annual cumulations.

Indexes all English-language books and English, French, German, Spanish, and Italian philosophy journals as well as some journals in related fields; abstracts are provided for many of the citations in the author index; also included are a subject index and a book review index. This index can be searched online through the Philosopher's Index database (1940–).

Religion Index One: Periodicals. Chicago: American Theological Assn., 1977–. Continues *Index to Religious Periodical Literature,* 1949–1976.

Indexes over 300 journals in religion and theology. Abstracts are included for many of the citations in the author index; a subject index and an index of book reviews are also provided. This index can be searched using the Religion Index database (1975–).

JOURNALS

Ethics: An International Journal of Social, Political and Legal Philosophy. Chicago: Univ. of Chicago Press, 1890–. Quarterly.

Publishes scholarly articles on the social, ethical, and legal aspects of philosophy; book reviews and book notes; short discussions, survey articles, and reviews.

Journal of Biblical Literature. Chico, CA: Society of Biblical Literature, 1882–. Quarterly.

> Contains scholarly papers on the Old and New Testaments, lengthy book reviews, a section on essay collections, and a list of books received.

Journal of Philosophy. New York: Journal of Philosophy, Inc.: 1904–. Monthly.

> Presents scholarly papers in all areas of philosophy; some issues include papers from various symposia; comments and criticism.

Journal of Religion. Chicago: Univ. of Chicago Press, 1882–. Quarterly.

> Publishes critical, scholarly articles on theology and related religious studies, review articles, and book reviews.

Journal of Symbolic Logic. Providence, RI: Assn. for Symbolic Logic, 1936–. Quarterly.

> Publishes technical articles on symbolic logic and related fields, such as mathematics and philosophy; book reviews and association news.

V. Physical Education and Sports

Encyclopedia of Physical Education, Fitness and Sports. Ed. Thomas K. Cureton, Jr. 3 vols. Salt Lake City, UT: Brighton, 1980.

> Each volume covers one area of physical education in detail and has its own table of contents, index, and biographical directory. Vol. 1 covers the philosophy and history of physical education and programs for schools, the armed forces, and the handicapped. Vol. 2 has sections on training and conditioning, nutrition, and fitness for children and adults. The third volume contains articles on types of sports, dance, and related physical activities.

Physical Education Index. Cape Girardeau, MO: Ben Oak, 1978–. Quarterly.

> Indexes to English-language periodicals covering physical education, physical therapy, health, dance, recreation, sports, and sports medicine. Entries include research reports, legislation, biographies, and reports from associations; a book review listing is given.

JOURNALS

American Journal of Sports Medicine. Baltimore, MD: American Orthopaedic Society for Sports Medicine, 1972–. Bimonthly.

> Publishes review and research articles on the medical aspects of sports and sports injuries, society news, book reviews, and an annual bibliography on sports medicine.

Journal of Physical Education, Recreation and Dance. Reston, VA: American Alliance for Health, Physical Education, Recreation and Dance, 1896–. Monthly, except July.

> Contains brief news and research reports, review articles on issues and techniques in sports and physical education, and book reviews. Issues occasionally focus on one topic, such as gymnastics.

The Physical Educator. Indianapolis, IN: Phi Epsilon Kappa Fraternity, 1940–. Quarterly.

> Publishes articles on the history, theory, and philosophy of sports and

physical education. Each issue focuses on one of four themes: special populations, program development, foundations, or human performance.

Research Quarterly for Exercise and Sport. Reston, VA: American Alliance for Health, Physical Education, Recreation and Dance, 1930–. Quarterly.

Presents lengthy, scholarly articles reporting the results of empirical research and short articles reporting research in progress.

W. Political Science and Government

ABC Pol Sci: Advanced Bibliography of Contents: Political Science and Government. Santa Barbara, CA: ABC-Clio Press, 1969–. Bimonthly.

A subject index and an author index provide access to the tables of contents of over 300 U.S. and international journals in political science and related subjects, such as area studies and sociology.

Holler, Frederick L. *Information Sources of Political Sciences*. 3d ed. Santa Barbara, CA: ABC-Clio, 1981.

A detailed annotated guide to research resources. Holler begins with a general section on political science research and then discusses specific tools classified as general reference sources, social sciences, American government and politics, international relations, political theory, and public administration; there are indexes by subject, author, and title.

International Encyclopedia of the Social Sciences. See entry under II. B., Social Sciences.

Laqueur, Walter, *A Dictionary of Politics*. Rev. ed. New York: Macmillan, 1974.

Contains brief entries arranged alphabetically that explain terms and give biographical, geographical, and historical information about contemporary politics; events included date mainly from 1933 to the publication date.

Public Affairs Information Service Bulletin. See entry under II. B., Social Sciences.

JOURNALS

American Journal of Political Science. Austin, TX: Univ. of Texas Press, 1957–. Quarterly.

Published for the Midwest Political Science Assn.; contains scholarly articles mainly concerned with American politics but also covering international politics.

American Political Science Review. Washington, DC: American Political Science Assn., 1906–. Quarterly.

Presents scholarly papers on American government, political science, and related fields, such as area studies, law, and economics; also extensive book reviews and review essays grouped by subject.

Foreign Affairs. New York: Council on Foreign Relations. 1922–. 5 issues per year.

Publishes articles expressing opinions and discussing issues in international relations, occasionally written by national and international political leaders; brief book reviews and bibliographies of relevant government documents and other related publications.

Journal of Politics. Gainesville, FL: Southern Political Science Assn., 1939–. Quarterly.

Publishes scholarly articles on political science, research notes, book reviews (including review essays), and association news.

X. Psychology

Bell, James Edward. *A Guide to Library Research in Psychology*. Dubuque, IA: Wm. C. Brown, 1971.

Besides chapters on using the library and writing research papers, Bell gives an overview of the research tools used in psychology. The remainder of the book is a detailed bibliography of psychology reference books, journals, government documents, textbooks, and anthologies.

Encyclopedia of Psychology. Ed. Raymond J. Corsini. 4 vols. New York: John Wiley, 1984.

Signed background articles on all aspects of psychology and biographical articles on important psychologists. Some articles have bibliographies and all references mentioned in the articles are listed in complete form in a single bibliography in Volume 4. Volume 4 also includes a name index (persons and titles) and a subject index.

Psychological Abstracts. Arlington, VA: American Psychological Assn., 1927–. Monthly, with semiannual cumulations.

A bibliography with abstracts of the world's literature in psychology and related fields. Entries include journal articles, books, technical reports, and dissertations. Abstracts are grouped in sixteen subject classifications with more specific access through subject and author indexes. *Psychological Abstracts* can be searched online through the PSYCHINFO database (1967–).

JOURNALS

American Psychologist. Washington, DC: American Psychology Assn., 1946–. Monthly.

Issues contain review articles and articles reporting empirical research, a section titled Psychology in the Public Forum, association news, and a commentary section.

Journal of Counseling Psychology. Washington, DC: American Psychological Assn., 1954–. Quarterly.

Publishes research articles on counseling arranged by subject: counseling process and outcomes, counseling assessment, career development, group intervention, special populations and setting, professional issues and training, and research methodology; brief research reports; comments section.

Journal of Personality and Social Psychology. Washington, DC: American Psychological Assn., 1965–. Monthly.

Publishes scholarly articles covering empirical and theoretical studies grouped in three sections: attitudes and social cognition, interpersonal relations and group processes, and personality processes and individual differences.

Psychological Bulletin. Washington, DC: American Psychological Assn., 1904–. Bimonthly.

Presents review articles evaluating and synthesizing research and methodological studies in psychology as well as articles on quantitative methods in psychology.

Y. Sociology

Book Review Index to Social Science Periodicals. See entry under II. B., Social Sciences.

C.R.I.S.: The Combined Retrospective Index Set to Journals in Sociology, 1895–1974. 6 vols. Washington, DC: Carrollton Press, 1978.

A comprehensive index to journals in sociology and related fields, such as anthropology, covering the literature since 1895. Articles are arranged in the first five volumes by subject keyword within 86 subject categories. The sixth volume is an author index.

International Encyclopedia of the Social Sciences. See entry under II. B., Social Sciences.

Social Sciences Index. See entry under II. B., Social Sciences.

Sociological Abstracts. San Diego, CA: Sociological Abstracts, 1952–. 5 issues per year.

A bibliography with abstracts of the periodicals in sociology and related fields, such as education and anthropology; the abstracts are grouped in thirteen subject classifications.

Women Studies Abstracts. Rush, NY: Rush Publishing, 1972–. Quarterly.

Indexes general magazines and scholarly journals concerned with all phases of women's studies, from literature to sports to women in developing countries. Citations are grouped by broad subject with abstracts provided for some of the entries. A subject index is included in each issue; a cumulative index is included at the end of the year.

JOURNALS

American Journal of Sociology. Chicago: Univ. of Chicago Press, 1895–. Bimonthly.

Publishes articles reporting empirical and theoretical research in sociology and related fields, such as social psychology; includes research notes, review essays, discussion, and lengthy book reviews.

American Sociological Review. Washington, DC: American Sociological Assn., 1936–. Bimonthly.

Contains scholarly papers on research and theoretical and methodological developments in sociology; also includes research notes, comments, and articles on professional issues.

Sociology and Social Research: An International Journal. Los Angeles: Univ. of Southern California, 1916–. Quarterly.

Presents research and review articles on sociology and related fields, such as urban sociology, sociology of education, and family studies; also contains book reviews.

APPENDIX 2

Style Manuals
and Handbooks
in Various Disciplines

Any one of the three documentation styles explained in this book and illustrated in the sample papers in Chapters 11, 12, and 13 can be used in most of the papers written by college students. The style manuals and handbooks presented in this appendix are useful especially for those wishing to publish in a specific discipline. They contain detailed information about bibliographic format and about such matters as punctuating and spelling scientific terminology. Some of them contain suggestions on the process of research and writing in particular subject areas.

Agronomy

American Society of Agronomy. *Handbook and Style Manual for ASA, CSSA and SSSA Publications*. 6th ed. Madison, WI: American Society of Agronomy, 1984.

Biochemistry

Handbook of Biochemistry and Molecular Biology. Ed. Gerald D. Fasman. 3rd ed. Cleveland: CRC Press, 1976. Series of multivolume handbooks in four areas.

Business. See also Economics.

Dawe, Jessamon. *Writing Business and Economics Papers, Theses, and Dissertations*. Totawa, NJ: Littlefield, 1975.

Smith, Charles B. *A Guide to Business Research: Developing, Conducting, and Writing Research Projects*. Chicago: Nelson-Hall, 1981.

Chemistry

American Chemical Society. *Handbook for Authors of Papers in American Chemistry Society Publications*. Washington, DC: American Chemical Society, 1978.

Handbook for AOAC Members. 5th ed. Washington, DC: Association of Official Analytical Chemists, 1982.

Earth Science, Geology

Cochran, Wendell, Peter Fenner, and Mary Hill, eds. *Geowriting: A Guide to Writing, Editing, and Printing in Earth Science*. 4th ed. Alexandria, VA: American Geological Institute, 1979.

Economics. See also Business.

Officer, Lawrence H., Daniel H. Sachs, and Judith A. Saks. *So You Have to Write an Economics Term Paper*. East Lansing, MI: Michigan State University Press, 1981.

Education

Katz, Sidney B., Jerome T. Kapes, and Percy A. Zirkel. *Resources for Writing for Publication in Education*. New York: Teachers College Press, Columbia University, 1980.

Engineering

Michaelson, Herbert B. *How To Write and Publish Engineering Papers and Reports*. Philadelphia: Institute for Scientific Information, 1986.

Geography

Haring, L. Lloyd, and John F. Lounsbury. *Introduction to Scientific Geographic Research*. 3rd ed. Dubuque, IA: William C. Brown, 1982.

History

McCoy, Florence N. *Researching and Writing in History: A Practical Handbook for Students*. Berkeley: University of California Press, 1974.

Steiner, Dale R. *Historical Journals: A Handbook for Writers and Reviewers*. Santa Barbara, CA: ABC-Clio, 1981.

Stoffle, Carla, and Simon Karter. *Materials and Methods for History Research*. New York: Neal-Schuman, 1979.

Law

The Columbia Law Review et al. *A Uniform System of Citation.* 13th ed. Cambridge, MA: The Harvard Law Review Association, 1981.

Library Science

Manheimer, Martha L. *Style Manual: A Guide for the Preparation of Reports and Dissertations.* Vol. 5 of *Books in Library and Information Science.* New York: Marcel Dekker, 1973.

Linguistics

Linguistic Society of America. "LSA Style Sheet." *LSA Bulletin.* December 1986. Annually.

Literature

Gibaldi, Joseph, and Walter Achtert. *The MLA Handbook for Writers of Research Papers.* 2nd ed. New York: Modern Language Association of America, 1984.

Mathematics

American Mathematical Society. *A Manual for Authors of Mathematical Papers.* 8th ed. Providence, RI: American Mathematical Society, 1980.

Swanson, Ellen. *Mathematics into Type.* Providence, RI: American Mathematical Society, 1982.

Medicine

Huth, Edward. J. *How to Write and Publish Papers in the Medical Sciences.* Philadelphia: Institute for Scientific Information, 1982.

Manual for Authors and Editors: Editorial Style and Manuscript Preparation. Ed., William R. Barclay, M. Therese Southgate, and Robert W. Mayo. 7th ed. Los Altos, CA: Lange Medical, 1981.

Modern Languages. See Literature.

Music

Helm, Ernest Eugene, and Albert T. Luper. *Words and Music: Form and Procedure in Theses, Dissertations, Research Papers, Book Reports, Programs, and Theses in Composition.* Valley Forge, PA: European American Music, 1982.

Nonprint Sources

Fleisher, Eugene B. *A Style Manual for Citing Microform and Nonprint Media.* Chicago: American Library Association, 1978.

Physical Therapy

American Physical Therapy Association. *Style Manual: Physical Therapy*. 5th ed. Washington, DC: Journal of the American Physical Therapy Association, 1985.

Physics

American Institute of Physics. *Style Manual*. 3rd ed. New York: American Institute of Physics, 1978.

Political Science

Goehlert, Robert U. *Political Science Research Guide*. Monticello, IL: Vance Bibliographies, 1982.

Stoffle, Carla J., Simon Karter, and Samuel Pernacciaro. *Materials and Methods for Political Science Research*. New York: Neal-Schuman, 1979.

Psychology

American Psychological Association. *Publication Manual of the American Psychological Association*. 3rd ed. Washington, DC: American Psychological Association, 1983.

Sternberg, Robert J. *Writing the Psychology Paper*. Woodbury, NJ: Barron, 1977.

Religion

Sayre, John L. *A Manual of Forms for Research Papers and D. Min. [Doctor of Ministry] Field Project Reports*. Enid, OK: Seminary Press, 1984.

Science—General

American National Standard for the Preparation of Scientific Papers for Written or Oral Presentation. New York: American National Standards Institute, 1979.

Barrass, Robert. *Scientists Must Write: A Guide to Better Writing for Scientists, Engineers and Students*. New York: Methuen, 1978.

CBE Committee on Graduate Training in Scientific Writing. *Scientific Writing for Graduate Students: A Manual on the Teaching of Scientific Writing*. Bethesda, MD: Council of Biology Editors, 1968.

Day, Robert A. *How To Write and Publish a Scientific Paper*. 2nd ed. Philadelphia: ISI, 1983.

Social Work

National Association of Social Workers. *Information for Authors About NASW Publications*. Silver Spring, MD: NASW, 1985.

Sociology

Gruber, James, and Judith Pryor. *Materials and Methods for Sociology Research.* New York: Neal-Schuman, 1980.

Mullins, Carolyn J. *A Guide to Writing and Publishing in the Social and Behavioral Sciences.* 1977. New York: Krieger, 1983.

The Research Experience. Ed. M. Patricia Golden. Itasca, IL: Peacock, 1976.

Sociology Writing Group. *A Guide to Writing Sociology Papers.* New York: St. Martin's, 1986.

Acknowledgments *(continued from page iv)*

Congressional Information Service Annual 1972, from Part One—*Abstracts of Congressional Publications and Legislative Histories* 3:1-12. Reprinted with permission from the *1972 CIS/Annual*. Copyright 1973 by Congressional Information Service, Inc. (Washington, DC). All rights reserved.

Consumer Reports, from "Caffeine: How to Consume Less." Copyright 1981 by Consumers Union of United States, Inc., Mt. Vernon, New York 10553. Reprinted from CONSUMER REPORTS, October 1981.

Encyclopedia Britannica, from the *Propaedia* and the *Index*, Vol. 2. Reprinted with permission from *Encyclopaedia Britannica*, 15th edition, © 1985 by Encyclopaedia Britannica.

Encyclopedia Americana, from Vol. 22, entry under *Pirandello, Luigi*. Reprinted with permission of the *Encyclopedia Americana*, © 1985 by Grolier, Inc.

Essay and General Literature Index. 1980–1984, from entries under *Thoreau, Henry David*. *Essay and General Literature Index* Copyright © 1980, 1981, 1982, 1983, 1984, and 1985 by The H. W. Wilson Company. Material reproduced by permission of the publisher.

William Gass, from *Writers at Work*, George Plimpton, editor. New York: Penguin, 1981.

Daniel S. Grossier, from "A Study of Caffeine in Tea" in *American Journal of Clinical Nutrition* 31. © *American Journal of Clinical Nutrition* by the American Society of Clinical Nutrition.

Humanities Index, April 1983 to March 1984, from Vol. 10, entry under *Melville, Herman*. *Humanities Index* Copyright © 1983, 1984 by The H. W. Wilson Company. Material reproduced by permission of the publisher.

Bill Katz and Berry G. Richards, from *Magazines for Libraries*, 3rd ed. Published by R. R. Bowker, Division of Reed Publishing, USA. Copyright © 1978 by Reed Publishing USA, a division of Reed Holdings, Inc. All rights reserved. Reprinted by permission of R. R. Bowker.

Library of Congress Subject Headings, 8th ed., from Vol. II, entry under *Solar energy*.

The Literary Essays of Thomas Merton, edited by Brother Patrick Hart, from copyright page. Copyright © 1981 by the Trustees of the Merton Legacy Trust and Our Lady of Gethsemani Monastery. Reprinted by permission of New Directions Publishing Corp.

1983 MLA International Bibliography of Books and Articles on the Modern Languages and Literatures, from *Subject Index* and *Classified Listings with Author Index*. Copyright © 1984 by the Modern Language Association. Reprinted by permission of the Modern Language Association.

Ogden Nash, "Song of the Open Road" from *Verses from 1929 On* by Ogden Nash. Copyright 1932 by Ogden Nash. First appeared in *The New Yorker*. Reprinted by permission of Little, Brown and Company (Inc.).

Elizabeth A. Nist, from "Tattle's Well's Faire: English Women Authors of the Sixteenth Century" by Elizabeth A. Nist in *College English* 46:7 (November 1984). Reprinted by permission of the National Council of Teachers of English.

Online search printout, from "Social Sciences Citation Index, 77–85/Jul." Reprinted by permission of the Institute for Scientific Information.

The Oxford English Dictionary, definition of *educate*. Copyright 1933. Reprinted by permission of Oxford University Press.

Miriam Polster and Erving Polster, *International Encyclopedia of Psychiatry, Psychology, Psychoanalysis, and Neurology*, from Vol. 5, entry under *Gestalt Therapy*, edited by Benjamin B. Wolman. Copyright © 1977 by Aesculapius Publishers, Inc., New York. Reprinted by permission of Aesculapius Publishers, Inc.

Readers' Guide to Periodical Literature, March 1984–February 1985, from Vol. 44, entries under *Paleontology* and *Wattenberg, Ben J*. *Readers' Guide to Periodical Literature* Copyright © 1984, 1985 by The H. W. Wilson Company. Material reproduced by permission of the publisher.

Carl Sagan, from *The Dragons of Eden: Speculations of the Evolution of Human Intelligence* by Carl Sagan. Copyright © 1977 by Carl Sagan. Reprinted by permission of Random House, Inc.

Social Sciences Citation Index: 1984 Annual, from Part 2, *Citation Index*; Part 4, *Source Index*; Part 6, *Permuterm Subject Index*. Copyright © 1985 by the Institute for Scientific Information, Inc. Reprinted by permission of the Institute for Scientific Information, Inc.

Henry David Thoreau, from *H. D. Thoreau: A Writer's Journal*, Laurence Stapleton, editor. New York: Dover, 1960.

Ulrich's International Periodicals Directory, 23rd ed., from Vol. 1. Published by R. R. Bowker, Division of Reed Publishing, USA. Copyright © 1984 by Reed Publishing USA, a division of Reed Holdings, Inc. All rights reserved. Reprinted by permission of R. R. Bowker.

Vertical File Index: A Subject and Title Index to Selected Pamphlet Materials, December 1984, from Vol. 53, No. 11, entries under *Joyce, James*, and *Investment trusts*. *Vertical File Index* Copyright © 1984 by The H. W. Wilson Company. Material reproduced by permission of the publisher.

Gore Vidal, from *Writers at Work*, George Plimpton, editor. New York: Penguin, 1981.

Walford's Guide to Reference Material, 4th ed., edited by A. J. Walford, from Vol. 2, *Social and Historical Sciences, Philosophy, and Religion*. © A. J. Walford 1982. Reprinted by permission of Library Association Publishing Ltd.

Index

Abbreviations, 200, 205–206, 300
Abstract(s), research paper, 161–162, 210
  descriptive, 94–95, 161–162
  informative, 161, 162
  of paper in sciences, 297
  of paper in social sciences, 268
  writing, 161–162
Abstracts (printed), 58, 70, 325, 333–361
Abundance, in research process, 11, 69, 88
Accounting, reference sources in, 337–338
Adjectives, coordinate, 201
Agreement
  pronoun, 193
  subject/verb, 192
Agriculture, reference sources in, 335–337
Almanacs, 329
American National Standard for Abbreviations of Titles of Periodicals, 300
American Statistics Index, 325
Anecdote, beginning introduction with, 138
Annual Statistics Index (ASI), 56
Anthropology, reference sources in, 333–334
APA Manual. See Manual of the American Psychological Association
Apostrophe, 203
Appendixes, 211–212
Archaeology, reference sources in, 333–334
Art, reference sources in, 334–335
Articles, newspaper
  citing, 239, 276, 301
  indexes to, 52, 326

Articles, periodical
  citing, 34–35, 223, 229–231, 238–239, 275–276, 300–301
  indexes to, 37, 46–52, 326
  scanning, 83–85
  scientific, 75–76
  See also Periodical(s)
Audience
  focusing on, 132–143
  promise to, 183
Author(s)
  biographical facts about, 72, 83
  credentials of, 70, 72, 77–78
Author/date (or year) documentation style, 153, 155–156, 213, 266–294, 295
  parenthetical citations in, 270–272
  reference list in, 273–277
  student example, 278–294
Author/page documentation style, 153–155, 212, 216–265
  list of works cited in, 223–235
  parenthetical citation in, 218–223
  student examples, 240–265
Authority, quoting an, 93

Background, beginning introduction with, 138–139
Back matter, 208, 211–214
Basic Research Methods (Saslow), 106
Bias, in sources, 70, 73, 78–79
Bible, citing, 229
Bibliographic Index: A Cumulative Bibliography of Bibliographies, 43–44, 324–325
Bibliographic information, 43–46
  computerized, 28–29, 56–58
  general sources of, 43–44
  recording, 34–36

Bibliographic search, 32–68
  computerized, 28–29, 56–58
  student examples, 65–67
Bibliography(ies), printed, 18, 44–
  46, 83, 324–325
  of bibliographies, 43–44, 324–325
  of books, 44–46, 324–325
  computerized, 28–29, 33, 47, 48,
   50, 56–58
  in evaluating a source, 74
  international, 44
Bibliography, research paper, 22, 34,
  214
  working, 32–68, 70
  See also Documentation
Bibliography cards, 34–36, 62, 70
  for encyclopedia articles, 41–42
  for interview, 103, 105
Bibliography of bibliographies, 43–
  44, 324–325
Biographical indexes, 46, 72, 325,
  327–328
Biography Index, 46, 325, 328
Biology, reference sources in, 335–
  337
Body of paper, 140–151
  coherence and unity in, 141
  headings in, 140–141
  integrating sources into, 141–142
  quotations in, 143–151
Book(s)
  bibliographies of, 44–46, 324–
   325
  citing. *See* Books, citing
  content of, 75–79
  evaluating, 70–72, 73–79
  locating, 69–70
  reading, 82–86
  recording bibliographic information on, 34, 35
  reviews of, 74–75
  scanning, 82–83
Book Review Digest, 74, 325
Book Review Index, 74, 325
Book reviews
  in evaluating a source, 74–75
  indexes to, 74, 325, 329–330, 332
  in *Readers' Guide*, 47

Books, citing, 219–223, 224–229,
  237, 238
  on bibliography cards, 34–36
  in footnotes, 237–238
  in list of works cited, 224–229
  in parenthetical citation, 219–223,
   270–272
  in reference list, 273–275, 300
Books in Print, 44, 45, 325
Brackets, 148–149, 202–203
British Books in Print, 45
Business, reference sources in, 337–
  338

Call numbers, library, 59, 60, 69
Capitalization, 205
Card catalog, library, 37, 58–62
  author-title cards, 62
  bibliographic information in, 34,
   62, 72
  subject headings in, 61–62
Catalog of National Archives Microfilm
  Publications, 114
CBE (Council of Biology Editors)
  Style Manual, 137, 153, 236, 299,
   301
Chambers of commerce, as informa-
  tion source, 100
Change, recommending, 160
Charts. *See* Graphs
Chemistry, reference sources in, 338–
  339
Choice, 75
CIS (Congressional Information
  Service) *Annual*, 325
Classification systems, library, 59–62
  Dewey Decimal, 59
  for government documents, 55
  Library of Congress, 60–62, 70
Clauses
  coordinate, 188–189
  independent, 201
  main and subordinate, 187–188,
   202
  nonrestrictive, 201
Coherence, 136, 141
  checking for, 178, 181
  in paragraphs, 185

Colon, 146, 147, 201–202
Comma, 146, 147, 199, 201
Communications, reference sources in, 340
Completeness, checking for, 178, 181
Computer(s)
  home, 29, 34–35
  revising on, 175–176, 198–199
  as a search tool, 28–29, 56–58
  See also Computer programs; Computer services; Databases, online; Word processor
Computer-assisted instruction (CAI), 176
Computer databases, 28–29, 56–58
Computer magazines, 47
Computer networks, 58
Computer programs, 29
  for developing a topic, 20
  for revising, 175–176, 198–199
Computer science, reference sources in, 341–342
Computer searching, 28–29, 56–58
Computer services, library, 28–29, 33, 56–58
Concise Guide to Reference Material (Walford), 44, 324
Conclusion
  of a book or an article, 83, 84–85
  research paper, 123, 127, 159–160
Congressional Information Service (CIS) Index, 55–56
Congressional Record, 56
Conjunctions, coordinating, 201
Consistency, maintaining, 194–195
Consumer Reports, 76, 77
Content notes, 135, 155, 208, 212–213, 218, 269–270
Contractions, forming, 203
Controlling idea, 16–17. *See also* Thesis statement
Coordinate adjectives, 201, 204
Coordinating conjunctions, 201
Coordination, 188–189
Copyright date, 70, 71–72
Copyright page, 34, 71
Corrections, making, 214. *See also* Revising

Cover, of research paper, 215
Cross-references, 228
Cumulative Subject Index to the Monthly Catalog, 1900–1971 (Buchanan and Kanely), 55

Darwin, Charles, 5, 6, 7
Dashes, 203
Databases, online, 28–29, 56–58
  journal indexes, 48, 50
  magazine index, 47
Decennial Cumulative Personal Author Index (Przebienda), 55
Definition(s), 134–135
  beginning introduction with, 139
  in content notes, 135
  in glossary, 213–214
Descriptive abstracts, 94–95
Descriptors, in computer search, 57
Dewey Decimal classification system, 59
Diagrams, 170
DIALOG database, 48
Diaries, as information sources, 112–113
Dictionaries, 34, 52–54
  citing, 223, 229
  special, 54
Dictionaries, Encyclopedias, and Other Word-Related Books (Brewer), 54
Dictionary of Symbols, 54
Dissertation Abstracts International, 325–326
Documentation, 152–156, 208
  at end of paper, 152, 236–240, 273–277, 299–301
  within text, 152, 218–223, 270–272
Documentation systems/styles, 34, 152–156, 196, 208, 216–321
  APA, 137, 153, 163, 236, 266, 268, 278. *See also* author/date style, *below*
  author/date style, 153, 155–156, 213, 266–294, 295
  author/page style, 153–155, 212, 216–265
  CBE, 137, 153, 236, 299, 301. *See also* number style, *below*

Documentation systems/styles [*cont.*]
  footnotes and endnotes, 236–240
  in humanities, 153, 216–265
  list of works cited, 214, 223–235
  MLA, 35, 130, 153, 163, 216, 236,
    240. *See also* author/page style,
    above
  number style, 153, 156, 196, 213,
    295–321
  parenthetical citation, 218–223,
    270–272
  reference list, 273–277, 299–301
  in sciences, 153, 155, 156, 196,
    213, 295–321
  in social sciences, 153, 155, 266–
    294
  student examples, 240–265, 278–
    294, 301–321
Draft(s)
  final, 10, 25, 198–215
  first, 10–11, 24–25, 132–172
  revising, 173–197
  second, 11, 179, 182–196
Drama, reference sources in, 342–
  343
Drawings, 163, 169
Duplicating (photocopying), 31, 70,
  90–91, 96, 214

Earth sciences, reference sources in,
  345–347
Economics, reference sources in,
  337–338
Editions, 71
Education, reference sources in,
  343–344
Electronics, reference sources in,
  344–345
Ellipsis points, 96, 147–148, 149–
  150, 202
Encylopedia(s), 17, 18, 34, 39–43
  bibliography card for, 41–42
  citing, 41–43, 223, 229, 238
  exploratory reading in, 34, 36, 39
  general, 17, 39–43
  note card for, 41, 43
  specialized, 43

Encyclopedia Americana, 41, 42, 43
Encyclopedia Britannica, New, 39–41,
  43, 63
Encyclopedia of Associations, 101
Encyclopedia of Religion and Ethics, 43
Endnotes, 135, 151, 153, 213, 218,
  236–240
Engineering, reference sources in,
  344–345
Environmental sciences, reference
  sources in, 345–347
Essay and General Literature Index, 46,
  326
Evaluating, in conclusion, 160
Experimentation, as information
  source, 116–117
Explanatory notes, 155, 212–213. *See
  also* Content notes
Explanatory sentences, 16, 26
Exploration, as information source,
  116–117
Exploratory categories, 19–20
Exploring. *See* Searching

Faulty connections, correcting, 192–
  194
Field log, for recording interview
  information, 103. *See also* Search
  log
Figures, 163
Film(s)
  reference sources in, 347–348
  reviews of, 47
Final draft, 10, 25, 198–215
  elements of, 208
  format of, 209–210
  typing, 25, 208–214
Final revision, 198–208
First draft, 10–11, 24–25, 132–172
  preparing to write, 132–137
  revising, 173–197
  writing from note cards, 141–142
First page
  of paper in humanities, 218
  of paper in sciences, 298
  of paper in social sciences, 269
Flow charts, 170–171

Focus, shift in, 181
Focusing
  on documentation, 196
  on parts of the paper, 182–196
  student example, 179–182
  on the whole paper, 176–182
Folklore, reference sources in, 348–349
Folklore research, 112
Footnotes, 98, 135, 151, 153, 213, 236–240, 298
Footnote symbols, 163
Format, 209–210
  of paper in humanities, 217–218
  of paper in sciences, 296–298
  of paper in social sciences, 267–271
Freedom of Information Act, 115
Front matter, 208, 209–211

Geography, reference sources in, 349–350
Glossary, 134, 213–214
Government, reference sources in, 359–360
Government documents, 55–56, 326–327
Government Printing Office, 114
Government publications, citing, 225, 237
Government records
  federal, 113–116
  state and county, 113
  student example of search, 115–116
Grammar, 199
Grammatik (software), 198
Graphics, designing, 162–171
Graphs, 163, 165–169
Guide to Reference Books (Sheehy), 324
Guide to Reference Material (Walford), 33, 324

Handbook for Authors of Papers in American Chemical Society Publications, 137, 299
Heading(s), 140–141
  "Introduction" as, 127, 137, 297, 298

in papers in humanities, 140, 141, 217–218
in papers in sciences, 297–298
in papers in social sciences, 268–269
His/her, to avoid sexism, 193
History, reference sources in, 350–351
Home computer
  database searching on, 29
  storing bibliographic information on, 29, 34–35
  See also Computer(s); Word processor
Homophones, 199
Humanities, 71, 207
  documentation style in (author/page), 153, 216–265
  elements of papers in, 216
  format of papers in, 140, 141, 217–218
  journal indexes in, 48–49, 329–330
  reference sources in, 329–330
Humanities Index (formerly *Social Sciences and Humanities Index; International Index*), 48, 49
Humor, 136
Hyphen, 204

"I," in research paper, 136, 194–195
Idea(s)
  controlling, 16–17
  main, reading for, 86
Illustrations, 162–163, 211, 297
Incubation period, 25, 133, 174
Index(es), 325–327
  of bibliographies, 44–46, 325
  biographical, 46, 72, 325, 327–328
  book, scanning, 82–84
  to government documents, 55–56
  to newspapers, 52, 326
  to periodicals, 37, 46–52, 326, 329–333
  for specific disciplines, 51, 329–361
Information, 8, 10–11, 32–33
  bibliographic, 34–36, 43–44

Information [*cont.*]
    recording, 9, 34–36, 88–96, 102
    researching, 10
    reviewing, 121–122
    sources of. *See* Source(s)
    storing in computer, 29, 34–35
Interlibrary loan services, 58, 114
Interview(s), 99–112
    conducting, 102–103
    following up on, 103
    by mail, 106
    open ended, 112
    personal, 100–105
    preparing for, 101–102
    recording information on, 102,
        103, 105
    student examples of, 103–105,
        109–110
    tape-recorded, 102, 103, 111–112
    by telephone, 105–106, 109–110
Interviewing, 99–112
Introduction, 123, 127, 137–140
    of a book, 83
    as a heading, 127, 137, 297, 298
    to paper in sciences, 298
    to paper in social sciences, 269
    ways to begin, 138–140, 298
Introduction to Reference Work (Katz),
    56, 324

Jargon, avoiding, 191
Journal, keeping a, 7, 9
Journals (periodicals), 37, 46, 48
    evaluating, 72–73
    indexes to, 48–52, 329–332
    in specific disciplines, 333–361
    See also Periodical(s)

Key words
    in computer search, 29
    in transitions, 178

Latin terms, 206
Legal documents, citing, 232–233,
    272, 277
Letters, personal
    citing, 233, 272
    as information sources, 112–113

Librarians, 17, 37, 57–58, 74
Library(ies), 33, 37–38
    academic and research, 33
    card catalog in, 34, 37, 58–62, 72
    computer services in, 28–29, 33,
        56–58
    interlibrary loan services, 58, 114
    locating materials in, 69–70
    reference area of, 37–58
    sources in, 7–8, 27–28, 37–58,
        69–96
Library Literature, 75
Library of Congress classification
    system, 60–62, 70
Library of Congress Subject Headings, 61
Linking verbs, 186, 191
List of references, 214, 273–277,
    299–301
List of works cited, 214, 223–235
Literary works, citing, 222–223
Literature, reference sources in,
    351–354
Literature review, in introduction,
    139–140, 298

Magazine Index, 47–48, 326
Magazines, 37, 46–47
    evaluating, 73
    indexes to, 47–48, 326
    See also Periodical(s)
Magazines for Libraries (Katz), 73
*Manual for Authors of Mathematical Pa-
    pers, A* (American Mathematical
    Society), 299
*Manual of the American Psychological
    Association* (*APA Manual*), 137,
    153, 163, 236, 266, 268, 278
Manuscript, parts of
    in humanities, 216
    in sciences, 295–296
    in social sciences, 267
Maps, 163
Margins, 209, 217, 267, 296
Materials, assembling, 30–31, 132,
    209
    for graphics, 164–165, 167
Medicine, reference sources in, 354–
    355

Microforms (microfiche and micro-
film), 33, 37, 70, 114
*MLA Handbook for Writers of Research
Papers*, 130, 153, 163, 216, 236,
240
*MLA International Bibliography of Books
and Articles on the Modern Lan-
guages and Literature*, 48–49, 72
MLA (Modern Language Associa-
tion) style, 35, 130, 153. *See also*
Author/page documentation
style; *MLA Handbook*
*Monthly Catalog of United States Govern-
ment Publications*, 55, 326–327
Movie reviews. *See* Film(s)
Music, reference sources in, 355–356

National Archives, 113–114
National Newspaper Index, The, 52, 326
New Columbia Encyclopedia, 42, 43
New Encyclopedia Britannica, 39–41,
43, 63
Newspaper indexes, 52, 326
Newspapers, 52
citing, 237, 239, 276, 301
indexes to, 52, 326
New York Times Index, 326
Nonprint sources, 28, 99–117, 233–
235, 240, 277
Note cards, 9, 30, 31, 87–88, 89, 90
arranging for outline, 124–125,
131
for encyclopedia article, 41, 43
interview notes on, 102, 103, 105
paraphrasing on, 89–90, 159
personal comments on, 94–95
quoting on, 93
summarizing on, 91–92
writing first draft from, 141–142
Notes, taking, 86–87, 88. *See also* Note
cards
Nouns
with participles, 192–193
plural, 193
from verb and preposition, 204
Numbers, 203, 206–208
in earth and applied sciences, 207–
208

in humanities and social sciences,
207
in a list, 200
in parenthetical citation, 154, 200
in reference lists, 273, 299
superscript, 155, 163, 212, 299
Number style of documentation,
153, 156, 196, 213, 295–321
reference list in, 299–301
student example, 301–321
textual citation in, 298–299
Numerals, using, 207–208. *See also*
Numbers
Nursing, reference sources in, 354–
355

Observation, as information source,
116–117
OCLC (Online Computer Library
Center), 58
On-line bibliographic databases, 28–
29, 47–48, 50, 56–58
Oral history, 111–112
Organization, research paper, 177–
178, 181
Outline(s), 10–11, 123–131, 141
balance in, 126
at first revision stage, 176–178,
179, 180
formal, 124
form of, 128–129
introductory, 211
logic of, 125–128
for paper in humanities, 218
preliminary, 26
punctuating, 200
purpose of, 124–125
types of, 129–131
working, 124–125
Oxford English Dictionary (OED), 53–54

Page headings, 210. *See also* Headings
Page numbers, 209–210, 217, 268,
296–297
Pamphlet file, 54
Paperbound Books in Print, 46
Paragraph(s)
checking, 182–185

Paragraph(s) [*cont.*]
  coherence in, 185
  integrating sources in, 182–183
  unified, 183–184
Parallelism, 189–190
Paraphrasing, 88–90, 159
  plagiarism and, 97
  quotations and, 143, 144
  while reading, 86
Parentheses, 203
  in documentation, 218–223
  with numbers, 200
Parenthetical citation, 153–154
  for paper in humanities, 218–223
  for paper in social sciences, 270–272
  punctuating, 218, 219
Participles, "dangling," 192–193
Passive voice, 136, 186, 191
Periodical(s), 37, 70
  citing, 223, 229–231, 238–239, 275–276, 300–301
  directories of, 45, 327
  evaluating, 72–73
  indexes to, 37, 46–52, 326, 329–333
  library's holdings, 52
  recording information on, 34, 35
  scanning, 83–85
Periodical file, 52, 53
Periodical indexes, 37, 46–52, 326, 329–333
  for journals, 48–52
  for magazines, 47–48
  for newspapers, 52
  for specific disciplines, 51, 329–361
Periods, 200
  with ellipsis marks, 96
  in quotations, 147, 200
  spaced, to indicate omission, 150
Personal comments, 94–96
Personal Name Index to the New York Times Index (Falk), 52, 326
Personal papers, as information sources, 112–113
Philosophy, reference sources in, 356–358

Phone book, as information source, 100
Photocopying, 31, 36, 70, 90–91, 96, 215
Photographs, 163
Physical education, reference sources in, 358–359
Physics, reference sources in, 338–339
Plagiarism, 86, 151, 157
  avoiding, 96–98, 157–159
  forms of, 97
Poetry
  citing, 223
  quoting from, 147, 150–151, 204
Point of view, 194–195
Political science, reference sources in, 359–360
Polling, 106–107
Possessive, forming, 203
Predicting, in conclusion, 160
Preface
  of book, 83
  research paper, 208
Prepositions, 199
Procrastination, 133
Product information, 48
Promise to reader, 183–184. *See also* Audience
Pronoun reference, 194
Pronouns
  agreement in, 193
  consistency in, 192, 194
  plural, 193
Proofreading, 211, 214
Psychology, reference sources in, 360–361
Public Affairs Information Service Bulletin (PAIS), 50, 300
Publication date, 70, 71–72
Publication Manual of the American Psychological Association. See Manual of . . .
Public library, 33. *See also* Library
Punctuation, 199–205
  correcting, 195–196
  in documentation, 154, 155, 218, 219, 299

in quotations, 96, 146–151, 155, 200, 205

Question marks, 147, 200
Questionnaires, 106, 107–109
Questions, 107–109
Quotation(s), 92–94, 143–151, 202
    brackets in, 148–149, 202
    clarifying, 148
    direct, 103, 144, 152, 155
    ellipsis points in, 96, 147–148, 149–150, 202
    integrating, 144–145, 201, 202
    introducing, 146–147
    long, 146, 148, 154, 156, 268
    omitting/adding words in, 96, 145, 202
    overuse of, 86
    and plagiarism, 97–98
    from poetry, 147, 150–151, 204
    punctuating, 96, 146–151, 155, 200, 205
    sic in, 149, 203
    unfinished, 147
Quotation marks, 97, 98, 143, 144, 147–148, 202

Random sample, 107
RASSL/Learning Services, 20
Reader. *See* Audience
Readers' Guide to Periodical Literature, 28, 47, 48, 326
Reading, 82–86
    close, 85–86, 88
    for main ideas, 86
    with a purpose, 85–86
    scanning, 82–85
Recommendations, in evaluating a source, 73–74
Records, government, 113–116. *See also* Government documents
Records, keeping, 8–9, 33–36
Records search, 113–116
Reference area, library, 37–58
Reference librarians, 17, 37
References, list of, 214, 223–235
    for paper in sciences, 299–301

for paper in social sciences, 273–277
    punctuating, 299
Reference sources, 37–58, 322–361
    biographical, 46, 72, 325, 327–328
    general, 17, 324–329
    in primary discipline groups, 329–333
    in specific academic disciplines, 333–361
    See also Source(s)
Reliability of sources, evaluating, 70–81
Religion, reference sources in, 356–357
Re-Search, 3–11, 121–122
Research
    abundance in, 11, 69, 88
    original, 76–77, 116–117, 140–141, 267, 296
    See also Searching
Research paper
    audience for, 134–135, 142–143, 183
    body of, 140–151
    final copy, 198–215
    good, characteristics of, 177–178, 180–182
    graphics in, 162–171
    organization of, 177–178, 181
    preparing to write, 132–137
    revising, 173–197
    shaping, 179–182
    writing, 3–4, 10–11, 132–172
Research projects, student examples, 116–117
Reviews
    book, 47, 74–75, 325
    citing, 231
    in evaluating a source, 74–75
    movie, 47
Revising, 25, 132, 173–197
    computer programs for, 175–176, 198–199
    final, 198–208
    first stage, 176–182
    of paragraphs, 182–185
    plan for, 175–176

Revising [*cont.*]
  preparing for, 174–175
  second stage, 182–196
  of sentences, 185–191
  with a word processor, 175–176
  of words, 185–191
Revision
  first stage, 176–182
  second stage, 182–196
RightWriter (software), 199
RLIN (Research Libraries Information Network), 58
Running heads, 298. *See also* Headings

Samples, in polling, 106–107
Scanning, 82–85
Schedule, 11, 57. *See also* Timetable
Sciences, 71, 207
  documentation style in (number style), 153, 155, 156, 196, 213, 295–321
  elements of papers in, 216
  format of articles in, 75–76
  format of papers in, 140–141, 296–298
  journal indexes in, 50, 331–333
  original research in, 116–117, 140–141, 296
  reference sources in, 331–333
Scope, adjusting, 26–27, 278–279
Searching, 6–9
  bibliographic, 32–68
  computer database, 28–29, 56–58
  strategy of, 23–31, 37–38
Search log, 9, 23, 159
  interview notes in, 102
  listing sources in, 27–28, 35, 36
  listing subjects in, 14–15
  reviewing in, 58, 121, 137–138
  student examples, 19, 36, 65–67
  and topic selection, 16, 18, 19
Search strategy, 23–31
Semicolons, 147, 199–200, 201
Sentence(s)
  checking, 185–191
  combining, 188–189
  exploratory, 15–16, 26

faulty connections in, 192–194
  improving, 186
  length of, 187–188
  summary (thesis), 122–123, 125, 160, 178
  topic, 183
  transitional, 181–182
Serials, 37. *See also* Periodical(s)
Serials list, 37, 52
Sexism, avoiding, 193
Sic, in quotations, 149, 203
Slash (virgule), 150, 204
Social sciences, 71, 207
  documentation style in (author/date), 153, 155, 266–294
  elements of papers in, 267
  format of papers in, 140–141, 217–218
  journal indexes in, 50, 330–331
  reference sources in, 330–331
Social Sciences and Humanities Index. See Humanities Index; Social Sciences Index
Social Sciences Citation Index, 50–52, 57–58, 72
Social Sciences Index (formerly *Social Sciences and Humanities Index; International Index*), 50
Sociology, reference sources in, 361
Source(s)
  acknowledging, 151–156. *See also* Documentation
  bias in, 70, 73, 78–79
  evaluating, 70–81
  indirect, 221–222
  integrating into text, 141–142, 182–183
  library, 7–8, 27–28, 37–58, 69–96
  list of, 27–29, 33–36, 214
  nonlibrary, 28, 99–117
  nonprint, citing, 233–235, 240, 277
  primary/secondary, 75, 77, 140, 141
  putting in order, 29–30, 62
  reading, 82–87
  recording information from, 88–98

reference. *See* Reference sources
reliability of, 70
Source evaluation, 70–81
Spacing, 209, 217, 267–268, 296
Specialized terms, 191. *See also* Technical terms
Spelling, 199
Sports, reference sources in, 358–359
Stacks, library, 37, 69–70
Statistical Abstract of the United States, 326
Statistics, 78–79, 106
Style, establishing, 135–137
Subject(s)
adjusting scope of, 26–27
categorizing, 18–20
controversial, 70, 78
listing in search log, 14–15
sources of, 14–15
See also Topic(s)
Subject Guide to Books in Print, 325
Subject-verb agreement, 192
Subordination, 188
Subtitles, 82, 202. *See also* Titles/subtitles
Summarizing, 90–92, 159
Summary, 139, 159. *See also* Abstract
Summary sentence, 122–123, 125, 160, 178
SuperFile (software), 29
Superscript letters, 163, 297
Superscript numbers, 155, 163, 212, 299
Surveying, 106, 109–110
Symbols, footnote, 163
Syntax, 136

Table of contents
of book, 82
research paper, 210–211
Tables, 163, 164–165
Tape-recording, in interview, 102, 103, 111–112
Technical terms, 86
glossary for, 134
in journals, 48
paraphrasing, 89–90
in research paper, 134, 135, 301

Technical writing, 48
abbreviations in, 206
decimal outline in, 130
format of, 75–76, 141
glossary in, 213
Technology, reference sources in, 331–333
Telephone
interview by, 105–106, 109–110
survey by, 109–110, 111
Terkel, Studs, 111–112
Textual citation, 298–299
Thesis statement, 16–17, 122–123, 160–161
Thoreau, Henry David, 4–5, 7, 69
Timetable, 24–25, 133. *See also* Schedule
Title(s)
of college courses, 205
personal and professional, 205, 206
Title page
of book, 34, 71
of research paper, 209, 217, 218, 267, 296
Titles/subtitles
of books, 82, 205
of research papers, 160–161, 202, 204–205
Tone, establishing, 135–137, 203
Topic(s)
back-up, 21
choosing, 7, 12–22
converting to outline form, 124
developing, with a computer program, 20
focusing, 63–65
See also Subject(s)
Topic sentence, 183
TOPOI (software), 20
Transitions, 178, 181–182
Typing
of final copy, 25, 208–214
of first draft, 132
of notes, 30

Ulrich's International Periodicals Directory, 45, 322, 327
Underlining, 90–91, 204–205

United States Government Manual, 115
Unity, 136, 141, 177, 180–181
UTLAS (University of Toronto Library Automation System), 58

Verbs
  agreement with subject, 192
  linking, 186, 191
  strong, 186–188, 190
Verb tense, 136–137, 195
Vertical file, 54
Vertical File Index: A Subject and Title Index to Selected Pamphlet Materials, 54, 322, 327
Virgule (slash), 150, 204
Vocabulary, 134–135. *See also* Technical terms
Voice, 136, 144

Walford's Guide to Reference Material, 44, 324
Webster's Third New International Dictionary of the English Language, 52
Who's Who in America, 72, 327
Who's Who series, 72, 380
WLN (Washington Library Network), 58
Word Plus, The (software), 198–199

Word processor, 132, 209
  revising with, 175–176
  See also Computer(s)
Words, 205
  adding/omitting in quotes, 145
  checking, 185–191
  compound, 204
  dividing, 204
  foreign, 205
  geographical, 206
  hyphenated, 204
  joining, 204
  key, 29, 178
  quoting significant, 145–146
  repetition of, 188, 189, 190–191
  transitional, 178, 182
  unnecessary, 190
Word usage, 199
Working (Terkel), 111–112
Works cited list, 214, 223–235. *See also* References, list of
World Bibliography of Bibliographies, A (Besterman), 324
Writing materials, 30–31, 132, 209

Yearbooks, 328–329
Yellow pages, as information source, 100
"You," in research paper, 136